简明实用汉字教程

天津市普通高校"十三五"综合投资规划项目成果
（项目编号：60100110SSW1640403）

崔蓬克 编著

SPM
南方出版传媒
广东人民出版社
·广州·

图书在版编目（CIP）数据

简明实用汉字教程 / 崔蓬克编著. —广州：广东人民出版社，2020.8
ISBN 978-7-218-14035-3

Ⅰ. ①简… Ⅱ. ①崔… Ⅲ. ①汉字—对外汉语教学—教材 Ⅳ. ①H195.4

中国版本图书馆CIP数据核字（2019）第258656号

JIANMING SHIYONG HANZI JIAOCHENG
简 明 实 用 汉 字 教 程
崔蓬克 编著　　　　　　　　　　　　　　　　版权所有 翻印必究

出 版 人：肖风华

责任编辑：林小玲　曾白云
责任技编：吴彦斌　周星奎

出版发行：广东人民出版社
地　　址：广东省广州市海珠区新港西路204号2号楼（邮政编码：510300）
电　　话：（020）85716809（总编室）
传　　真：（020）85716872
网　　址：http://www.gdpph.com
印　　刷：广州市浩诚印刷有限公司
开　　本：787mm×1092mm　1/16
印　　张：20.75　　字　数：489千
版　　次：2020年8月第1版
印　　次：2020年8月第1次印刷
定　　价：60.00元

如发现印装质量问题，影响阅读，请与出版社（020-85716849）联系调换。
售书热线：（020）85716826

前 言
Foreword

本教程特点 Features of this book

1. 作为一本指导汉字学习的教材，本教程重视汉字的层级结构和使用频率，部件和汉字的编排遵循的是使用频率由高到低的顺序，使用频率越高的部件和汉字越早讲解。此外，本教程还注重对部件和汉字的扩展讲解：对于部件，介绍与之相关的若干汉字的含义；对于汉字，则给出相关词语的含义。

As a book instructing the learning of Chinese characters, this book values the structure and the utility frequency of the characters. The arrangement of radicals and characters in this book is based upon their utility frequency, and the more frequently used, the earlier a radical or a character is explained. What's more, by explaining meanings of characters concerning a radicaland those of words or phrases concerning a character, this book expands the explanations of radicals and characters.

2. 全书内容分为两个部分。第一部分包括100个高频汉字部件，这些部件的特点是构字能力极强。这一部分内容对这100个汉字部件的含义结合相关例字作了解释，为学习者学习汉字打下基础。第二部分为500个高频汉字，这些都是中国人日常使用最频繁的字。这一部分内容介绍了这500个汉字的读音、部件、结构、笔画数等，并提供与这些汉字相关的词语和例句，让学习者在实际运用场景中学习汉字。

Two parts constitute the main content. The first part consists of 100 high-frequency radicals, which are characterized by their extremely strong abilities to form characters. In this part, their meanings are explained with reference to relevant characters to lay the foundation for learning Chinese characters. The second part introduces 500 characters which are most commonly and frequently used in the daily life of Chinese people. This part provides the pronunciation, the radicals, the structure and the stroke number of each of these 500 characters, as well as examples of their relevant words, phrases and sentences, so that the learner can learn these characters in the actual application scenes.

3. 每个部件和汉字都提供了记忆贴士，通过意义溯源和形体拆分，加深学习者的理解，从而帮助记忆。

There are memory tips for each radical and Chinese character, in which their original meanings are traced and their structures deconstructed, so as to help learners understand and remember them effectively.

4. 书中内容采用中英双语对照的形式来呈现，方便母语非汉语的学习者使用。需要指出的是，英文内容与中文内容大多数情况下是对应的，然而前者有时并不是对后者逐字逐句的翻译。

The text is presented both in Chinese and in English to facilitate foreign learners. It should be pointed out that although the English content is in accordance with its Chinese counterpart for the most part, it is occasionally not the result of word-to-word translation of the latter.

适用对象 Target readers

本教程的适用对象主要为在中国留学的外国学生、母语非汉语的汉语学习者。

This book is appropriate for foreign students who are studying in China and non-native speakers who want to learn Chinese.

如何使用本教程 How to use this book

学习者可以从部件学起，首先掌握高频部件的名称、形体和意义。部件是构成汉字的材料，掌握了部件的知识，对于学习汉字会有很大帮助。有些部件可以独立构成一个汉字，学习了这个部件就等于学会了一个汉字。还有许多部件不能单独构成汉字，必须和其他的部件一起组成汉字。对于所有部件，本书都给出了一些例字来帮助学习者了解它们的用法，通过揭示汉字的构成规律帮助学习者提高学习效率。

The learner may begin the learning process with the radicals. As the first step, try to grasp the names, the shapes and the meanings of these radicals. The learning of characters will be benefited notably by the knowledge of radicals, which are the component materials for characters. Some radicals can be used independently as characters, which means that the grasp of such radicals is tantamount to that of certain characters. Other radicals, however, can only serve as a part of a character. This book provides each radical with several characters so as to help the learner better understand its usage and tries to promote the learner's learning efficiency by revealing the forming patterns of the characters.

学习完100个高频部件之后，就可以进行500个高频汉字的学习了。学习者首先要知道一个汉字的读音以及组成这个字的部件有哪些，同时还要知道这个字的结构类型。本教程力求从文字的源流上对汉字的本义进行讲解，从而加深学习者的理解，方便记忆。学习汉字不仅要掌握汉字知识，更重要的还有书写练习。在练习书写汉字的时候，学习者须注意用正确的笔顺来书写。无论是部件还是汉字，教程都给出了分笔画的书写演示。

After learning these radicals, the learner may continue to learn the following 500 characters. In this section, the learner, first of all, should know the pronunciation, the radicals and the structural type of the character to be learned. This book strives to show the original meanings of the characters, so as to deepen the learner's comprehension about them and make them easy to memorize. It is not enough just to know the characters by heart. Practicing writing them is even more important. When practicing, the learner should make sure that the strokes are written in the right order. This book demonstrates the right order of writing for every radical and character.

体例 Content layout

部件部分 Radical part

1. 形体展示 radical
2. 名称 name
3. 本义 original meaning
4. 相关汉字举例 Related characters
5. 记忆贴士 memory tips
6. 分笔顺展示 order of strokes

汉字部分 Character part

1. 形体展示和字形演变 character and its evolution
2. 读音 pronunciation
3. 部件 radicals
4. 部首 indexing component
5. 结构 structure
6. 六书 Six Categories of Chinese Characters
7. 笔画数 stroke number
8. 本义 original meaning
9. 相关词语举例 related words and phrases[*]
10. 相关句子举例 related sentences
11. 记忆贴士 memory tips
12. 分笔顺展示 order of strokes

名词解释 Glossary

六书：指汉字的六种构成或使用方式，包括象形、会意、指事、形声、转注、假借。前四种是构字法，后两种是用字法。

Six Categories of Chinese Characters: according to the differences of the ways of making or using characters, Chinese characters are generally divided into six categories, including pictographic characters, associative compound characters, self-explanatory characters,

---

[*] 个别汉字由于仅作为助词在句子中出现，故无法提供相关词语举例。
Owing to the fact that some characters can only appear in the sentences as auxiliary words, their related words and phrases will be omitted.

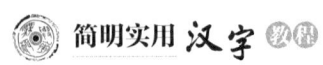

pictophonetic characters, mutually explanatory characters and phonetic loan characters. The first four categories are based upon character-making methods and the last two upon character-using ones.

指事符号：指事字的构字部件，一般是抽象的符号，无法单独使用，需要和象形的部件相结合，用于体现难以具体画出来的意思。

Indicative symbol: radical of the self-explanatory character. Usually the meaning is abstract and the symbol should be used together with pictographic radicals instead of being used independently, so as to express meanings that are difficult to illustrate with the pictographic method.

结构：指汉字的结构类型，包括独体、左右、左中右、上下、上中下、半包围、全包围等。

Structure: the structural types of Chinese characters, including single, left-right, left-middle-right, upper-lower, upper-middle-lower, encircle and half-encircle, etc.

甲骨文：主要指中国商朝晚期王室用于占卜记事而在龟甲或兽骨上契刻的文字，是目前已知的最古老的汉字。

Oracle bone script: the form of Chinese characters used on oracle bones—animal bones or turtle plastrons used in divination—in Shang dynasty, and is the earliest known form of Chinese writing.

金文大篆：中国古代的一种书体名称，指的是铸造在殷周青铜器上的铭文，在周代成为书体的主流。

Bronze inscription: the form of ancient Chinese characters inscribed on the bronze objects mainly in Zhou dynasty.

小篆：是秦统一后通行的一种书体，一直流行到西汉末年。这种书体字呈竖势，笔画复杂，线条圆匀。

Xiaozhuan script: also known as the small seal script. It is the form of ancient Chinese characters formulated by the ruler of Qin dynasty and remains the mainstream till the end of Western Han dynasty. This form of characters assumes a slender shape; the strokes are thin and curly, as well as complex, and their layouts are even.

隶书：一种常见的汉字字体，字形略微宽扁，横画长而直画短。它起源于秦代，在东汉时期达到顶峰。隶书的出现是汉字演变史上的一个转折点，奠定了楷书的基础。

Clerical script: a common style of calligraphy of Chinese characters. Usually the horizontal strokes are long and the vertical ones are short, thus making the shape of the character wide and flat. It originates in Qin dynasty, and arrives at the peak of its development during Eastern Han dynasty. Its appearance is the turning point in the history of the evolution of Chinese characters, laying the foundation for the regular script.

楷体：由隶书逐渐演变而来的一种字体。这种汉字字体端正，笔画更简，横平竖直，是现代通行的汉字手写正体字。

Regular script: a style of calligraphy of Chinese characters evolved from the clerical script.

The strokes of this character type are generally fewer than those of the older ones. Both the vertical and horizontal strokes are straight, so the shape of the character appears to be upright. It is extensively used as the standard handwriting character form in modern times.

繁体字：针对已有简化字替代的字而言，指笔画未经简化的汉字。

Traditional character: the term is used only for characters that have simplified forms. If a character has simplified form to replace it, then it is called a traditional character.

简体字：与繁体字相对，现在通行的简体字是中国中央人民政府自20世纪50年代起开始在中国推行的，是现代汉字的标准字形。

Simplified character: the term is used in comparison with the traditional character. The simplified characters that are now commonly used are stipulated by the Central People's Government of China since the 1950s. They are the standardized form of Chinese characters in modern times.

目 录
CONTENTS

第一部分
Part One

100个
常用汉字部件
100 Radicals

第 一 节	口　日	/ 3
	木(木)　扌	/ 4
	氵　艹	/ 5
	一　亻	/ 6
	土　人	/ 7
第 二 节	宀　月	/ 9
	又	/ 10
	十　亠	/ 11
	女(女)　八	/ 12
	大　讠	/ 13
	贝	/ 14
第 三 节	纟　辶	/ 15
	冖　虫	/ 16
	阝	/ 17
	钅　心	/ 18
	刂	/ 19
	禾(禾)　田	/ 20
第 四 节	寸　厶	/ 22
	力	/ 23
	又　忄	/ 24
	火　月	/ 25
	攵	/ 26
	勹　攵	/ 27
第 五 节	尸　丶	/ 29
	广	/ 30
	目　石	/ 31

	刀　巾	/ 32
	山(山)　屮	/ 33
	𥫗	/ 34
第 六 节	子(子)　隹	/ 35
	疒	/ 36
	白　车(车)	/ 37
	米(米)　立(立)	/ 38
	夕	/ 39
	疒　几	/ 40
第 七 节	止　工(工)	/ 41
	儿	/ 42
	口　足(足)	/ 43
	厂	/ 44
	方(方)　马(马)	/ 45
	王(王)　羊	/ 46
第 八 节	匕　冫	/ 48
	示	/ 49
	覀　斤	/ 50
	欠　犭	/ 51
	灬	/ 52
	门　彡	/ 53
第 九 节	耳(耳)　皿	/ 54
	罒	/ 55
	卜　小(小)	/ 56
	匚　彳	/ 57
	穴(穴)　雨(雨)	/ 58
	戈	/ 59
第 十 节	酉　艮	/ 60
	户	/ 61
	衤　干	/ 62
	鸟	/ 63
	矢(矢)　饣	/ 64
	见	/ 65
	弓	/ 66

1

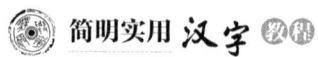

第二部分 Part Two

500个常用汉字
500 Characters

第一节	的 一	/69
	是 不	/70
	了 在	/71
	有 人	/72
	这 上	/73
第二节	大 来	/74
	和 我	/75
	个 中	/76
	地 为	/77
	他 生	/78
第三节	要 们	/79
	以 到	/80
	国 时	/81
	就 出	/82
	说 会	/83
第四节	也 子	/84
	学 发	/85
	着 对	/86
	作 能	/87
	可 于	/88
第五节	成 用	/89
	过 动	/90
	主 下	/91
	而 年	/92
	分 得	/93
第六节	家 种	/94
	里 多	/95
	经 自	/96
	现 同	/97
	后 产	/98
第七节	方 工	/99
	行 面	/100
	那 小	/101
	所 起	/102
	去 之	/103
第八节	然	/104
	进	/105
	都 还 体	/106
	理 实	/107
	定 么	/108
第九节	如 法	/109
	物 好	/110
	你 民	/111
	性 天	/112
	从 等	/113
	化 本	/114
第十节	力 心	/115
	长 部	/116
	把 样	/117
	义 看	/118
第十一节	事 当	/119
	因 高	/120
	十 开	/121
	些 社	/122
	前 又	/123
第十二节	其 水	/124
	想 没	/125
	意	/126
	三 点	/127
	重 只	/128
第十三节	与 使	/129
	但 度	/130
	由 道	/131
	全 制	/132
	明 相	/133
第十四节	两 情	/134
	外 间	/135
	二 关	/136
	活 正	/137
	合 者	/138
第十五节	形 应	/139
	头 无	/140
	量 气	/141
	象 文	/142
	系 展	/143
第十六节	加 各	/144
	很 教	/145
		/146

目　录

	向　/147
第十七节	新　她　/148
	机　此　/149
	内　变　/150
	老　结　/151
	原　手　/152
	问　利　/153
第十八节	质　已　/154
	最　政　/155
	儿　见　/156
	并　平　/157
	资　比　/158
第十九节	特　果　/159
	什　建　/160
	反　常　/161
	知　第　/162
	电　思　/163
第二十节	立　提　/164
	或　通　/165
	解　身　/166
	四　品　/167
	几　位　/168
第二十一节	别　论　/169
	公　给　/170
	少　条　/171
	观　回　/172
	海　基　/173
第二十二节	次　被　/174
	山　才　/175
	己　期　/176
	西　术　/177
	济　认　/178
第二十三节	先　命　/179
	走　真　/180
	员　及　/181
	数　话　/182
	门　级　/183
第二十四节	军　统　/184
	光　声　/185
	题　入　/186
	美　口　/187
	感　战　/188
第二十五节	科　程　/189
	式　指　/190
	世　必　/191
	放　打　/192
	接　总　/193
第二十六节	做　东　/194
	区　农　/195
	强　造　/196
	类　受　/197
	场　五　/198
第二十七节	直　月　/199
	流　决　/200
	干　　　/201
	则　更　/202
	色　处　/203
	路　　　/204
第二十八节	运　任　/205
	具　目　/206
	再　治　/207
	神　求　/208
	件　管　/209
第二十九节	组　根　/210
	阶　将　/211
	改　导　/212
	眼　规　/213
	识　革　/214
第三十节	计　白　/215
	马　金　/216
	界　取　/217
	市　设　/218
	语　完　/219
第三十一节	究　党　/220
	女　传　/221
	风　信　/222
	名　便　/223
	保　育　/224
第三十二节	队　带　/225
	叫　研　/226
	领　北　/227
	较　张　/228
	即　至　/229
第三十三节	许　步　/230
	往　听　/231
	调　务　/232

第三十四节	花线每难共确据	争呢边太交劳达	/233 /234 /235 /236 /237 /238 /239
第三十五节	住候转南格	收需百清影	/240 /241 /242 /243 /244
第三十六节	书且志联极	切却热安今	/245 /246 /247 /248 /249
第三十七节	单料深增近	商技验记言	/250 /251 /252 /253 /254
第三十八节	整集连觉价	精空报车音	/255 /256 /257 /258 /259
第三十九节	响存病图例	办怎快况消	/260 /261 /262 /263 /264
第 四十 节	容非万构	史离亲八族	/265 /266 /267 /268 /269
第四十一节	石何律林王	满广青克历	/270 /271 /272 /273 /274
第四十二节	权	素断	/275 /276

第四十三节	九积态证创望群	际吃艺众红须师	/277 /278 /279 /280 /281 /282 /283
第四十四节	该细土服德	复包持笑般爱远	/284 /285 /286 /287 /288 /289
第四十五节	准算死布	写火半随元	/290 /291 /292 /293 /294
第四十六节	六低引失视段	称照养习字	/295 /296 /297 /298 /299
第四十七节	织团兴效斯	斗器乐显千	/300 /301 /302 /303 /304
第四十八节	落仅似除标	企备支早周	/305 /306 /307 /308 /309
第四十九节	吧速七状约	跟采吗城专	/310 /311 /312 /313 /314
第 五十 节	层划拉适告值	轻英讲	/315 /316 /317 /318 /319 /320

Part One

100个常用汉字部件
100 Radicals

第一节

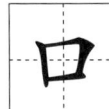	名　称：口字旁
	本　义：嘴
	例　字：吸、叫、曰

记忆贴士

"口"的甲骨文字形像嘴,本义是嘴。"吸"由"口"和"及"(得到)组成,意思是通过口鼻吸入空气。"叫"由"口"和"丩"(声旁)组成,意思是呼喊。"曰"由"口"和"一"(表示说出的话)组成,意思是说话,用于文言文。

Name: kǒu zì páng
Original meaning: mouth
Related characters: 吸 (inhale), 叫 (shout), 曰 (speak)

Memory tips

口(oracle bone script is ) is like a mouth, meaning mouth. 吸 consists of 口(mouth) and 及(get). It means to inhale fresh air through the nose and mouth. 叫 consists of 口(mouth) and 丩 (indicates pronunciation). It means to shout. 曰 consists of 口(mouth) and 一(words). It means to speak and is used in classical Chinese.

日	名　称：日字旁
	本　义：太阳
	例　字：星、明、昏

记忆贴士

"日"的甲骨文字形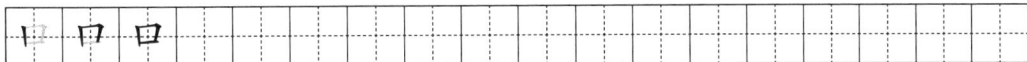像太阳,本义是太阳。"星"由"日"和"生"(夜空中生出来的)组成,意思是星星。"明"由"日"和"月"组成,意思是日光或月光把空间照亮。"昏"由"氏"(低)和"日"组成,意思是太阳西下的时候。

Name: rì zì páng
Original meaning: sun
Related characters: 星 (star), 明 (bright), 昏 (dusk)

Memory tips

日(oracle bone script is 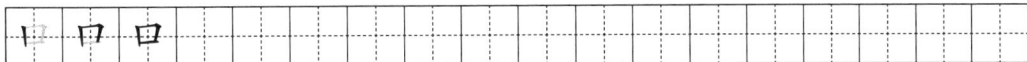) is like the sun, meaning sun. 星 consists of 日(star) and 生 (appears like growing), meaning star. 明 consists of 日(sun) and 月(moon), meaning that sunlight or moonlight illuminates the space. 昏 consists of 氏(low) and 日(sun), meaning the time of dusk.

木	木	**名　称**：木字旁
		本　义：树
		例　字：末、本、梢

记忆贴士

"木"的金文字形 ✱ 像一棵树，本义是树。"末"（金文字形为 ✱）由"木"（树）和"一"（指事符号）组成，意思是树梢。"本"（金文字形为 ✱）由"木"（树）和"一"（指事符号）组成，意思是树根。"梢"由"木"（树）和"肖"（小）组成，意思是树枝尾部新生的嫩枝条。

Name: mù zì páng
Original meaning: tree
Related characters: 末 (treetop, end), 本 (root), 梢 (end of a branch)

Memory tips

木(bronze inscription is ✱) is like a tree, meaning tree. 末(bronze inscription is ✱) consists of 木(tree) and 一(indicative symbol), meaning treetop. 本(bronze inscription is ✱) consists of 木(tree) and 一(indicative symbol), meaning root. 梢 consists of 木(tree) and 肖(young), meaning new shoots at the end of the branches.

扌		**名　称**：提手旁
		本　义：手
		例　字：把、技、扶、抱

记忆贴士

"把"由"扌"（手）和"巴"（一动不动，也作声旁）组成，表示一动不动地握住，本义是持握。"技"由"扌"（手）和"支"（竹竿，小篆字形为 ）组成，表示使用竹竿，本义是巧妙使用工具的方法。"扶"（小篆字形为 ）由"扌"（手）和"夫"（人）组成，意思是搀扶。"抱"由"扌"（手）和"包"（包住，小篆字形为 ）组成，意思是用双臂包住。

Name: tí shǒu páng
Original meaning: hand
Related characters: 把 (hold), 技 (skill), 扶 (support), 抱 (hug)

Memory tips

把 consists of 扌(hand) and 巴(still, also indicates pronunciation). It means to hold motionlessly. The original meaning is to hold. 技 consists of 扌(hand) and 支(xiaozhuan script is , meaning bamboo). It means to use a bamboo pole. The original meaning is the skill for using tools. 扶(xiaozhuan script is) consists of 扌(hand) and 夫(man), meaning to support. 抱 consists of 扌(hand) and 包 (xiaozhuan script is , meaning to encircle). It means to hold with arms.

第一部分 100个常用汉字部件

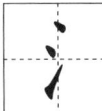

名　称：	三点水
本　义：	水
例　字：	沙、河、汁、波

记忆贴士

"氵"是水（甲骨文字形为 ）的简写，本义是水。"沙"由"氵"和"少"（小沙粒）组成，意思是水边的沙粒。"河"由"氵"和"可"（声旁）组成，意思是水道。"汁"由"氵"和"十"（很多）组成，意思是很多液体。"波"由"氵"和"皮"（起伏，"坡"的省写）组成，意思是水面因风吹过而起伏的样子，像地上的坡。

Name: sān diǎn shuǐ
Original meaning: water
Related characters: 沙 (sand), 河 (river), 汁 (juice), 波 (wave)

Memory tips

氵 (oracle bone script is ) is like a river, meaning water. 沙 consists of 氵(water) and 少(tiny grain of sand), meaning sand. 河 consists of 氵(water) and 可(indicates pronunciation), meaning river. 汁 consists of 氵(water) and 十(too much), meaning juice. 波 consists of 氵(water) and 皮 (omitted form of 坡, means slope). It means that the undulations of the water surface caused by the wind are like hill slopes.

名　称：	草字头
本　义：	草
例　字：	草、英、芳、花

记忆贴士

带"艹"的字意思往往和植物有关。"草"由"艹"（植物）和"早"（声旁）组成，意思是野草。"英"由"艹"（植物）和"央"（声旁）组成，意思是花。"芳"由"艹"（植物）和"方"（声旁）组成，本义是花草的香味。"花"由"艹"（植物）和"化"（声旁）组成，本义是种子植物的繁殖器官。

Name: cǎo zì tóu
Original meaning: grass
Related characters: 草 (grass), 英 (flower), 芳 (fragrance of flowers and grasses), 花 (flower)

Memory tips

The meanings of characters containing 艹 are related to plant. 草 consists of 艹(plant) and 早(indicates pronunciation), meaning grass. 英 consists of 艹(plant) and 央(indicates pronunciation), meaning flower. 芳 consists of 艹(plant) and 方(indicates pronunciation), meaning fragrance of flowers and grasses. 花 consists of 艹(plant) and 化(indicates pronunciation), meaning flower.

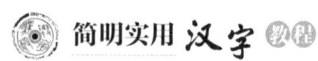

一	**名 称**：一字头、一字底
	本 义：象形符号
	例 字：旦、从、灭、夫

记忆贴士

"一"可以做各种象形符号，比如："旦"和"从"里的"一"表示地面，"灭"上面的"一"表示盖在火上使火熄灭的东西，"夫"上面的"一"表示成年男子头上戴的帽子。

Name: yī zì tóu, yī zì dǐ
Original meaning: pictogram symbol
Related characters: 旦 (morning), 从 (clump), 灭 (extinguish), 夫 (man)

Memory tips

The shape of 一 looks like the ground or an extended thing. 旦 consists of 日(sun) and 一(horizon). You can picture the sun rising from the horizon. 从 consists of 从(two people) and 一(ground). You can imagine many people gathering together on the ground. 灭 consists of 一(something) and 火(fire). You can imagine that the fire is covered and put out by something. 夫 consists of 一(hat) and 人(man). You can imagine a man wearing a hat.

亻	**名 称**：单人旁
	本 义：人
	例 字：你、们、休、住

记忆贴士

带"亻"的字意思往往和人有关。"你"由"亻"和"尔"（古汉语中第二人称代词，汉代以后口语中第二人称代词被"你"替代，文言中仍然使用"尔"）组成，表示第二人称代词。"们"由"亻"和"门"组成，表示人的复数后缀。"休"由"亻"和"木"组成，表示人倚靠着树休息。"住"由"亻"和"主"（声旁）组成，意思是人们在某处定居。

Name: dān rén páng
Original meaning: person
Related characters: 你 (you), 们 (plural suffix), 休 (have a rest), 住 (live)

Memory tips

The meanings of characters containing 亻 are usually related to person. 你 consists of 亻(person) and 尔(you). It is used as the second person pronoun. 们 consists of 亻(person) and 门 (indicates pronunciation). It is used as a plural suffix for people. 休 consists of 亻(person) and 木(tree). It means a person resting against the tree. 住 consists of 亻(person) and 主(indicates pronunciation). It means that people are settled somewhere.

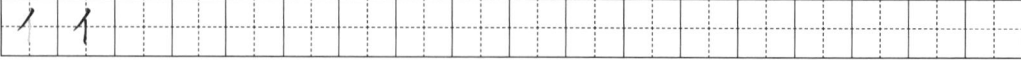

第一部分 100个常用汉字部件

名 称：提土旁
本 义：泥土
例 字：地、堤、城、址

记忆贴士

"土"的甲骨文字形 像地上放着一些土块，"土"的本义是泥土。带"扌"的字意思往往和泥土有关。"地"由"扌"和"也"（蛇，小篆字形为 ）组成，表示蛇在地上爬，意思是土地。"堤"由"扌"和"是"组成，表示由土石筑成的防洪堤坝。"城"由"扌"和"成"（武装守城）组成，表示有武装保护的城墙。"址"由"扌"和"止"（脚趾）组成，表示墙脚。

Name: tí tǔ páng
Original meaning: soil
Related characters: 地 (ground), 堤 (dam), 城 (city), 址 (foundation)

Memory tips

土(oracle bone script is) is like clays on the ground, meaning soil. The meanings of characters containing 扌 are usually related to soil. 地 consists of 扌 and 也(xiaozhuan script is , meaning snake). You can picture a snake crawling on the ground and it means ground. 堤 consists of 扌 and 是(raise), meaning dam with earth and stones. 城 consists of 扌 and 成(guard city), meaning armed city wall. 址 consists of 扌 and 止(foot), meaning the foot of a wall.

名 称：人字旁
本 义：人
例 字：从、坐、介、囚

记忆贴士

"人"的甲骨文字形 像一个侧面的人，本义是人。带"人"的字意思往往和人有关。"从"（甲骨文字形为 ）由两个"人"组成，表示跟从。"坐"（小篆字形为 ）由两个"人"和"土"组成，表示坐下休息。"介"（甲骨文字形为 ）由"人"（人）和"川"（铠甲）组成，表示士兵的铠甲。如今意为"在……之间"。"囚"（小篆字形为 ）由"人"和"口"（监狱）组成，表示囚犯。

Name: rén zì páng
Original meaning: person
Related characters: 从 (follow), 坐 (sit), 介 (between), 囚 (prisoner)

Memory tips

人(oracle bone script is) is like a person, meaning person. The meanings of characters containing 人 are usually related to person. 从(oracle bone script is) consists of two 人(person), meaning a person following another person. 坐(xiaozhuan script is 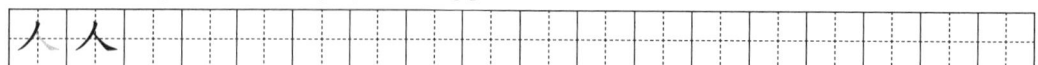) consists of two 人(person) and 土(ground), indicating people sitting on the ground. 介(oracle bone script is) consists of 人(person) and 丿l(armor), meaning soldier's armor. Now it means between. 囚(xiaozhuan script is) consists of 人(person) and 囗(jail), meaning prisoner.

第二节

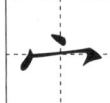

名　称：宝盖头
本　义：房子
例　字：家、安、宝、室

记忆贴士

"宀"最初的形体是房子的形状，带"宀"的字意思往往和房子有关。"家"由"宀"和"豕"（猪）组成，表示有房子和猪的地方就是家。"安"由"宀"和"女"组成，表示有房子和妻子就是安定。"宝"由"宀"和"玉"组成，表示藏在家中的珍宝。"室"由"宀"和"至"（躺下）组成，意思是卧室。

Name: bǎo gài tóu
Original meaning: house
Related characters: 家 (home), 安 (stability), 宝 (treasure), 室 (bedroom)

Memory tips

The shape of 宀 looks like a house, the meanings of characters containing 宀 are usually related to house. 家 consists of 宀 and 豕(pig). It means that the place with a house and a pig is home. 安 consists of 宀 and 女(wife). It means having a house and a wife is stability. 宝 consists of 宀 and 玉(jade), meaning treasure at home. 室 consists of 宀 and 至(lie down), meaning bedroom.

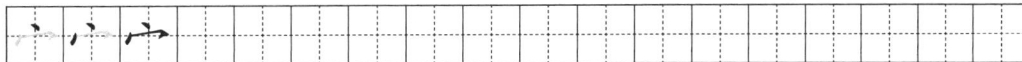

名　称：月字旁
本　义：肉或月亮
例　字：脸、胖、期、朗

记忆贴士

带"月"的字意思往往和肉或者月亮有关。"脸"由"月"（肉）和"佥（声旁）"组成，表示面部。"胖"由"月"（肉）和"半"（把牛从中间劈开，小篆字形为半）组成，本义是祭祀中用的半边牲肉，如今意为身上脂肪多。"期"由"其"（声旁）和"月"（月亮）组成，表示一段时间。"朗"由"良"（好）和"月"（月亮）组成，表示月光很明亮。

Name: yuè zì páng
Original meaning: flesh or moon
Related characters: 脸 (face), 胖 (fat), 期 (a period of time), 朗 (bright)

Memory tips

The meanings of characters containing 月 are usually related to flesh or moon. 脸 consists of

月(flesh) and 佥(indicates pronunciation), meaning face. 胖 consists of 月(flesh) and 半(xiaozhuan script is 半, meaning to dismember a cow). It originally means half a cow used for sacrifice. Now it means fat. 期 consists of 其(indicates pronunciation) and 月(moon), meaning a period of time. 朗 consists of 良(good) and 月(moon), meaning bright like the full moon.

名　称：	又字旁
本　义：	手
例　字：	受、支、对、邓

记忆贴士

带"又"的字意思往往和手的动作有关，但是在简体字中很多"又"并不是手的意思，而是代替繁体字中复杂部件的符号，比如：邓（鄧）、对（對）、双（雙）。"受"由"爫"（手）、"冖"（物品）和"又"（手）组成，表示接受的意思。"支"由"十"（棍子）和"又"（手）组成，表示用手拿棍子支撑自己的身体。"对"（繁体字为"對"）由"又"（武器）和"寸"（手）组成，本义是两支军队对峙，引申出向着、正确等含义。"又"用来代替繁体字中的复杂部件。"邓"（繁体字为"鄧"）由"又"和"阝"（城邑）组成，表示地名，简体字"邓"用"又"代替了"登"。

Name: yòu zì páng
Original meaning: hand
Related characters: 受 (accept with hand), 支 (support oneself with stick), 对 (right), 邓 (a place name)

Memory tips

The meanings of some characters containing 又 are usually related to hand, but for some other characters, 又 is used to replace a complex radical of the traditional character to reduce the strokes. 受 consists of 爫(hand), 冖(something) and 又(hand). It means to accept something from another hand. 支 consists of 十(stick) and 又(hand). It means to support oneself with a stick. 对（traditional character is 對） consists of 又(weapon) and 寸(hand). The original meaning is military confrontation and extended to mean to face and right etc. 又 is used as the substitution for the complex radical in simplified character. 邓(traditional character is 鄧) consists of 又 and 阝(city). It's a place name. 又 is used as the substitution for the complex radical(登) in simplified character.

第一部分　100个常用汉字部件

名　称：	十字旁
本　义：	数字10或象形符号
例　字：	什、古、早、土

记忆贴士

带"十"的字意思往往和数字10有关，"十"也可作为象形符号来使用。"什"由"亻"（人）和"十"组成，表示十个人为一组。"古"由"十"（言极多）和"口"组成，表示无数代口口相传的久远时代。"早"由"日"（太阳）和"十"（草）组成，表示太阳在草上升起来。"土"由"十"（土块）和"一"（地面）组成，表示泥土。

Name: shí zì páng
Original meaning: number 10 or something shaped like 十
Related characters: 什 (ten people), 古 (ancient), 早 (morning), 土 (soil)

Memory tips

十 can be used as the number 10 or to indicate something shaped like 十. 什 consists of 亻 (person) and 十(ten), meaning ten people organized as a group. 古 consists of 十(many) and 口. It means the time before many generations. 早 consists of 日(sun) and 十(grass), indicating that the sun rising above the grass. It means morning. 土 consists of 十(clays) and 一(ground). It is like clays on the ground and means soil.

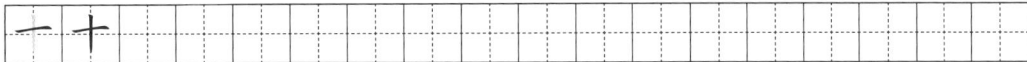

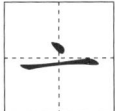

名　称：	六字头
本　义：	象形符号
例　字：	六、文、立、亦

记忆贴士

"亠"可以表示屋顶，如"六"的甲骨文字形像一栋房子。"亠"也可以表示人的头和臂膀，如"文"的甲骨文字形像一个有文身的人，"立"的甲骨文字形像一个站立的人，"亦"的甲骨文字形在人的腋下加上两点，表示人的腋下，"亦"的本义已经消失。

Name: liù zì tóu
Original meaning: pictogram symbol
Related characters: 六 (six), 文 (culture) , 立 (stand) , 亦 (also)

Memory tips

亠 looks like a roof, such as 六. The oracle bone script of 六 is 𠔋. It looks like a house and now means number six. 亠can also indicate head and two arms, such as 文. The oracle bone script of 文 is 𠁁. It looks like a person with tattoo on the chest. The oracle bone script of 立 is 𡗗. It looks like a standing person. The oracle bone script of 亦 is 𠃛. It looks like a person with two dots under the arms and the original meaning is armpit. Now the original meaning is out of use.

名　称：	女字旁
本　义：	女性
例　字：	妈、奶、好、她

记忆贴士

带"女"的字意思往往和女性有关。"女"的甲骨文字形 像一个坐着的女子。"妈"由"女"和"马（声旁）"组成，意思是母亲。"奶"由"女"和"乃"（声旁）组成，意思是乳汁。"好"由"女"和"子"（孩子）组成，表示美好。"她"由"女"和"也"（蛇）组成，表示指称女性的第三人称代词。

Name:	nǔ zì páng
Original meaning:	female
Related characters:	妈 (mother), 奶 (milk), 好 (good), 她 (she or her)

Memory tips

The oracle bone script of 女 is . It looks like a sitting woman. The meanings of characters containing 女 are usually related to female. 妈 consists of 女 and 马(indicates pronunciation), meaning mother. 奶 consists of 女 and 乃(indicates pronunciation), meaning milk. 好 consists of 女 and 子(kid), meaning good. 她 consists of 女 and 也(snake), meaning she.

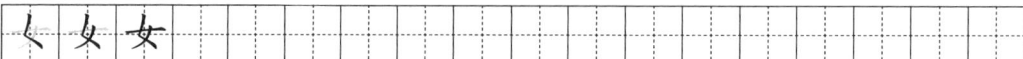

名　称：	八字旁
本　义：	相背分开
例　字：	分、公

记忆贴士

带"八"的字意思往往和分割或者相背有关。"分"由"八（分开）"和"刀"组成，意思是用刀分割某物。"公"由"八（相背）"和"厶（私）"组成，表示"私"的反义词。

Name:	bā zì páng
Original meaning:	separate
Related characters:	分 (divide), 公 (public)

Memory tips

The meanings of characters containing 八 are usually related to cut or opposite. 分 consists of 八(separate) and 刀(knife). It means to divide something with a knife. 公 consists of 八(opposite) and 厶(private), meaning public.

第一部分　100个常用汉字部件

名　称：	大字旁
本　义：	成年人
例　字：	太、奇、奔、天

记忆贴士

"大"的甲骨文字形 像一个人，本义是成年人，带"大"的字意思往往和人有关。"太"由"大"和"丶"组成，意思是过于大。"奇"由"大"（人）和"可"（吆喝催马）组成，本义是骑马，现在意为奇怪。"奔"的甲骨文字形 表示很多人一起奔跑的意思。"天"由"一"（指事符号）和"大"组成，意思是人头顶的空间。

Name: dà zì páng
Original meaning: adult
Related characters: 太 (too), 奇 (strange), 奔 (run), 天 (sky)

Memory tips

The oracle bone script of 大 is . It originally means the adult. The meanings of characters containing 大 are usually related to person. 太 consists of 大 and 丶, meaning too big. 奇 consists of 大 and 可(harness a horse orally). It originally means a person riding a horse and now means strange. The oracle bone script of 奔 is . It looks like many people running together. 天 consists of 一(indicative symbol) and 大, indicating the space above a person's head. It means sky.

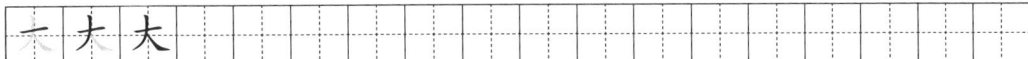

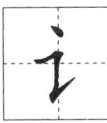

名　称：	言字旁
本　义：	说话
例　字：	说、让、话、谁

记忆贴士

带"讠"的字意思往往和说话有关。"说"由"讠"和"兑"（祷告）组成，表示说话。"让"由"讠"和"上"（辅佐，繁体字部件为"襄"）组成，表示许诺给予别人方便，自己退让。"话"由"讠"和"舌"组成，表示说出来的话。"谁"由"讠"和"隹"（鸟）组成，表示通过模仿鸟叫来问来人是何人。

Name: yán zì páng
Original meaning: speak
Related characters: 说 (speak), 让 (promise to make concession), 话 (words), 谁 (who)

Memory tips

The meanings of characters containing 讠 are usually related to speaking. 说 consists of 讠 and 兑 (pray). It means to speak. 让 consists of 讠 and 上(the radical of the traditional character is 襄, meaning to assist). It means to promise to make concession. 话 consists of 讠 and 舌(tongue), meaning words. 谁 consists of 讠 and 隹(bird). It means to ask the visitor's name by imitating the singing of the birds.

名　称：	贝字旁
本　义：	可以作为货币的贝壳
例　字：	赚、财、货、败

记忆贴士

带"贝"的字意思往往和钱财有关。"赚"由"贝"（钱）和"兼"（同时）组成，表示通贱买贵卖来挣钱。"财"由"贝"（钱）和"才"（有用的东西）组成，表示钱和有用之物。"货"由"化"（转化）和"贝"（钱）组成，表示能换成钱的东西。"败"由"贝"（宝物）和"攵"（敲打）组成，表示把宝物打碎。

Name: bèi zì páng
Original meaning: shell used as money
Related characters: 赚 (make money), 财 (fortune), 货 (good), 败 (ruin)

Memory tips

The meanings of characters containing 贝 are usually related to money. 赚 consists of 贝(money) and 兼(at the same time). It means to make money. 财 consists of 贝(money) and 才(useful thing), meaning money and useful thing. 货 consists of 化(convert) and 贝(money). It means the item that can be exchanged with money. 败 consists of 贝(treasure) and 攵(hit). It means to damage the treasure.

第三节

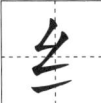

名 称：	绞丝旁
本 义：	丝线
例 字：	线、经、结、绝

记忆贴士

带"纟"的字意思往往和丝线、绳子以及纺织等有关。"线"由"纟"和"戋"（细小）组成，表示用丝、金属、棉或麻等制成的细长东西。"经"由"纟"和"圣"（织布机，繁体字部件为"巠"）组成，表示织物的竖线。"结"由"纟"和"吉"（声旁）组成，表示线缠绕在一起。"绝"由"纟"和"色"（⺈表示刀）组成，表示切断丝线。

Name: jiǎo sī páng
Original meaning: silk thread
Related characters: 线 (thread), 经 (vertical line), 结 (knot), 绝 (cut the thread)

Memory tips

The meanings of characters containing 纟 are usually related to thread, silk, rope, weaving, etc. 线 consists of 纟 and 戋(small), meaning thread. 经 consists of 纟 and 圣(the radical of the traditional character is 巠, meaning loom), meaning vertical line of fabric. 结 consists of 纟 and 吉(indicates pronunciation), meaning lines are entangled. 绝 consists of 纟 and 色(⺈ means knife). It means to cut the thread.

名 称：	走之旁
本 义：	走路
例 字：	过、进、逐、达

记忆贴士

带"辶"的字意思往往和走路有关。"过"由"辶"和"寸"（繁体字部件为"咼"，意思是旋涡）组成，表示经过旋涡。"进"由"辶"和"井"（繁体字部件为"隹"，意思是鸟）组成，表示打猎时跟在鸟后面往前走。"逐"由"辶"和"豕"（甲骨文字形为犭，意思是猪）组成，表示捕捉猪。"达"由"辶"和"大"（甲骨文字形为𠂉，意思是人）组成，表示道路通畅，人可以通过。

Name: zǒu zhī páng
Original meaning: walk
Related characters: 过 (pass by), 进 (go forward), 逐 (chase), 达 (walk unimpededly)

Memory tips

The meanings of characters containing 辶 are usually related to walking. 过 consists of

辶 and 寸(the radical of the traditional character is 咼, meaning vortex). It means to pass by the vortex. 进 consists of 辶 and 井 (the radical of the traditional character is 隹, meaning bird). It means to chase birds and go forward. 逐 consists of 辶 and 豕(oracle bone script is 豕, meaning pig). It means to chase a pig. 达 consists of 辶 and 大(oracle bone script is 大, meaning person). It means that the road is unblocked and a person can walk freely.

名　称：	秃宝盖
本　义：	房子
例　字：	冗、写、劳、冤

记忆贴士

带"冖"的字意思往往和房子或某个区隔空间有关。"冗"由"冖"（房子）和"几"（人）组成，意思是待在家里的剩余劳动力。"写"（小篆字形为 鳥，繁体字为"寫"）由"冖"（鸟巢）和"与"（鸟，繁体字部件为"舄"）组成，意思是书写，一笔一画写汉字就像小鸟筑巢。"劳"由"艹"（繁体字部件为"炏"）"冖"（房子）和"力"（劳力）组成，表示在家里热火朝天地干活。"冤"由"冖"（网）和"兔"组成，表示兔子落入网中，无力反抗，引申出无处申诉的意思。

Name: tū bǎo gài
Original meaning: house
Related characters: 冗 (redundant), 写 (write), 劳 (work), 冤 (grievance)

Memory tips

The meanings of characters containing radical 冖 are usually related to house or separated space. 冗 consists of 冖(house) and 几(person). It means redundant workforce staying in the house. 写(xiaozhuan script is 鳥) consists of 冖 (nest) and 与(the radical of the traditional character is 舄, meaning bird). It means to write. Writing Chinese character stroke by stroke is like the bird building a nest. 劳 consists of 艹(the radical of the traditional character is 炏), 冖 (house) and 力 (labor). It means to work hard in the house. 冤 consists of 冖(net) and 兔(rabbit), indicating that a rabbit falls into the net and could not escape. It means grievance.

名　称：	虫字旁
本　义：	虫
例　字：	蛇、虹、蚕、蚊

记忆贴士

带"虫"的字意思往往和昆虫或其他动物有关。"蛇"由"虫"（甲骨文字形为 ）

和"它"(甲骨文字形为 ）组成，意思是蛇。"虹"由"虫"和"工"（巨大）组成，意思是像大虫一样的彩虹。"蚕"由"天"和"虫"组成，意思是上天赐予人类的会吐丝的虫子。"蚊"由"虫"和"文"（声旁）组成，意思是一种"文文"（嗡嗡）叫的虫子。

Name: chóng zì páng
Original meaning: insect
Related characters: 蛇 (snake), 虹 (rainbow), 蚕 (silkworm), 蚊 (mosquito)

Memory tips

The meanings of characters containing 虫 are usually related to insect or other animals. 蛇 consists of 虫(oracle bone script is ）and 它(oracle bone script is , meaning snake). It means snake. 虹 consists of 虫(snake) and 工(giant). It means rainbow which looks like a giant snake in the sky. 蚕 consists of 天(heaven) and 虫(worm). It means a magic worm given by heaven to produce silk. 蚊 consists of 虫(insect) and 文(indicates pronunciation), meaning mosquito.

名　称：	1. 左耳旁　2. 右耳旁
本　义：	1. 土山　2. 邑
例　字：	坠、阳、郑、邦

记忆贴士

"阝"如果出现在左边，表示这个字和地势有关，如果出现在右边，表示这个字和城邑、邦郡有关。"坠"由"队"（本义是从高处坠落，甲骨文字形 像一个人从墙上坠落）和"土"组成，意思是从高处坠落。"阳"由"阝"（山坡）和"日"组成，意思是阳光直射的山坡，即山的南面。"郑"由"关"和"阝"（城邑）组成，是古地名。"邦"由"丰"（草木茂盛）和"阝"（邦郡）组成，意思是国家。

Name: 1. zuǒ ěr páng　2. yòu ěr páng
Original meaning: 1. dirt hill　2. city
Related characters: 坠 (drop), 阳 (hillside on the southern side of the mountain), 郑 (name of an ancient place), 邦 (state)

Memory tips

The meanings of characters containing 阝 (appears on the left side of the character) are usually related to terrain; the meanings of characters containing 阝 (appears on the right side of the character) are usually related to city or state. 坠 consists of 队(oracle bone script is , looking like a person falling down from a wall) and 土(soil). It means to fall from a high place. 阳 consists of 阝(hillside) and 日(direct sunlight). It means hillside on the southern side of the mountain. 郑 consists of 关 and 阝(city). It is the name of an ancient place. 邦 consists of 丰 (lush vegetation) and 阝(state), meaning state.

阝	阝														

钅	**名 称**：金字旁
	本 义：金属
	例 字：钱、银、钞、铁

记忆贴士

　　带"钅"的字意思往往和金属有关。"钱"由"钅"和"戋"（繁体字部件为"戔"，由两个"戈"组成，表示使用兵器来保护）组成，意思是货币。"银"由"钅"和"艮"（跟随）组成，表示银跟随着金，都是贵金属。"钞"由"钅"和"少"（不足）组成，意思是用来代替贵金属的纸质凭证，即纸钞。"铁"由"钅"和"失"（繁体字部件为"戴"，意思是匠人打造兵器）组成，意思是用来打造兵器的金属。

Name: jīn zì páng
Original meaning: metal
Related characters: 钱 (money), 银 (silver), 钞 (paper money), 铁 (iron)

Memory tips

　　The meanings of characters containing 钅 are usually related to metal. 钱 consists of 钅 (precious metal) and 戋(the radical of the traditional character is 戔, meaning to protect with weapons), meaning money. 银 consists of 钅 (precious metal) and 艮(follow). It means precious metal besides gold, namely silver. 钞 consists of 钅 (precious metal) and 少(few, not enough). It means paper money used to replace precious metals. 铁 consists of 钅 (metal) and 失(the radical of the traditional character is 戴, meaning that a smith forges the weapon). It means the metal used to make the weapon.

心	**名 称**：心字底
	本 义：心脏
	例 字：您、念、思、想

记忆贴士

　　带"心"的字意思往往和心理活动有关。"您"由"你"和"心"组成，是对说话对象的尊称，表示从心底里尊敬对方。"念"由"今"（吟诵，"吟"的省写）和"心"组成，表示吟诵并且记住。"思"由"田"（大脑）和"心"组成，表示用脑子和心来思考。"想"由"相"（观察）和"心"组成，表示看到某物后想得到它。

Name: xīn zì dǐ

Original meaning: heart

Related characters: 您 (honorific form of you), 念 (read; miss), 思 (think; miss), 想 (want; think; miss)

Memory tips

The meanings of characters containing 心 are usually related to mental activities. In ancient Chinese concept, 想(want), 念(read and memorize) and 思(miss) are related to the heart. 您 consists of 你(you) and 心. It is the honorific of the second person pronoun. It means that the respect comes from the bottom of the heart. 念 consists of 今(omitted form of 吟, means to chant) and 心. It means to chant and memorize. 思(xiaozhuan script is ) consists of 田(brain) and 心. It means to think with brain and heart. 想 consists of 相(observe) and 心. It means to want to get something after seeing it.

名　称：立刀旁
本　义：刀
例　字：利、则、别、到

记忆贴士

带"刂"的字意思往往和刀有关，或者这个字以"刀"（dāo）为声旁。"利"由"禾"（庄稼）和"刂"（刀）组成，表示用快刀割庄稼。"则"由"贝"（鼎）和"刂"组成，表示在鼎上铸法律条文。"别"由"另"（骨）和"刂"组成，意思是用刀剔骨头上的肉，把肉和骨头分离，意思是分解。"到"由"至"（到达）和"刂"（声旁）组成，表示到达。

Name: lì dāo páng

Original meaning: knife

Related characters: 利 (sharp), 则 (rule), 别 (don't), 到 (arrive)

Memory tips

The radical 刂 indicates that the meanings of the character are related to knife or the pronunciation of the character is similar to that of 刀(dāo). 利 consists of 禾(crop) and 刂 (knife). It means to harvest crops with a sharp knife. 则 consists of 贝(a kind of ancient cooking vessel) and 刂 (knife). It means to cast legal provisions on an ancient cooking vessel which is the symbol of dynasty. 别 consists of 另(bone) and 刂 (knife). It means to remove the meat from the bone with a knife. Now it is commonly used as a negative adverb. 到 consists of 至(arrive) and 刂 (indicates pronunciation). It means to arrive.

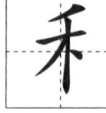		名　称：禾字旁
		本　义：禾苗
		例　字：季、香、秀、和

记忆贴士

　　带"禾"（甲骨文字形为 ）的字意思往往和禾苗有关，或者这个字以"禾"（hé）作为声旁。"季"由"禾"（禾苗）和"子"（籽）组成，指禾苗产籽的季节，是最后的阶段。"香"由"禾"（禾苗，泛指粮食）和"曰"（像舌头加一点，表示味觉）组成，指粮食的香味。"秀"由"禾"（禾苗）和"乃"（抽穗）组成，指禾苗抽穗。"和"由"禾"（禾苗）和"口"（吹）组成，指吹禾管乐器，引申出协调等含义，另外，"和"也用作连词。

Name: hé zì páng
Original meaning: grain seedling
Related characters: 季 (season), 香 (fragrant; savory), 秀 (put forth flowers or ears; excellent), 和 (and; harmonious)

Memory tips

　　The radical 禾(oracle bone script is) indicates that the meanings of the character are usually related to grain seedling or the pronunciation of the character is similar to that of 禾(hé). 季 consists of 禾(grain seedling) and 子(seed). It means the season of seed production. 香 consists of 禾(grain seedling) and 曰(tongue). It means the scent of grain. 秀 consists of 禾(grain seedling) and 乃(ear sprouts). It means grain earing. 和 consists of 禾(grain seedling) and 口(blow). It originally means to blow an instrument which is made of grain pipe and is extended to mean harmonious and so on. Besides, it is also used as a conjunction which means "and."

	名　称：田字旁
	本　义：田野
	例　字：奋、男、亩、界

记忆贴士

　　带"田"的字意思往往和田地有关。"奋"（金文字形为 ，繁体字为"奮"）由"大"（"奞"的省略形式，表示一只鸟往空中飞）和"田"（田野）组成，指鸟在田野里向上飞。"男"由"田"和"力"组成,指在田地里用"力"劳动。"亩"由"亠"和"田"组成,是田地的面积单位。"界"由"田"(领土)和"介"(处于两者之间)组成,指的是两个地方的分界。

Name: tián zì páng
Original meaning: field
Related characters: 奋 (strive), 男 (male), 亩 (an area unit), 界 (boundary)

Memory tips

The meanings of characters containing 田 are usually related to field or territory. 奋(bronze inscription is 𡙻, and the traditional character is 奮) consists of 大(omitted form of 奞, means a bird flying to the sky) and 田(field). It means a bird flying to sky in the open field. 男 consists of 田(field) and 力(strength). It means a man working in the field. 亩 consists of 亠 and 田(field). It is an area unit of the field. 界 consists of 田(territory) and 介(between), meaning the boundary of two places.

丨	冂	日	田	田															

第四节

名　称：	寸字旁
本　义：	手腕
例　字：	寻、付、过、村

记忆贴士

"寸"（小篆字形为ヨ）的本义是手腕，"、"作为指事符号表示这个字的意思是手腕。带"寸"的字意思往往和手有关，或者这个字以"寸"（cùn）作为声旁。"寻"由"ヨ"（手）和"寸"（手）组成，意思是张开两手臂丈量物品长度。"寻"现在的意思是寻找，可以将"寻"想象成使用两只手找东西。"付"由"亻"（人）和"寸"（手）组成，指的是用手把东西给别人。"寸"可以是简体字中的替代符号，比如："过"用"寸"取代繁体字"過"中的"咼"。"寸"也可以作为声旁，比如："村"中的"寸"表示读音。

Name: cùn zì páng
Original meaning: wrist
Related characters: 寻 (look for), 付 (give, pay), 过 (pass), 村 (village)

Memory tips

The original meaning of 寸 is wrist. The xiaozhuan script of 寸 consists of ヨ(hand) and 一(indicative symbol), meaning wrist. The meanings of characters containing 寸 are related to hand or their pronunciations are similar to the pronunciation of 寸(cùn). 寻 consists of ヨ(hand) and 寸(hand). It means to measure thing with both arms. Now 寻 commonly means to look for. You can picture it as looking for something with both hands. 付 consists of 亻(person) and 寸(hand). It means to give something to somebody. 寸 can be used to replace a complex radical to simplify a traditional character, such as 过(traditional character is 過). 寸 can also be used to indicate the pronunciation of the character, such as 村.

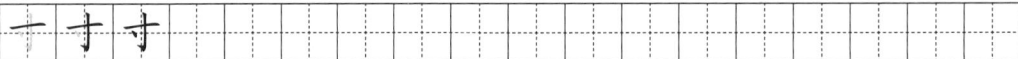

名　称：	厶字旁
本　义：	自己的
例　字：	私、公、云、允

记忆贴士

带"厶"的字意思往往和"自己"有关。"私"由"禾"（庄稼）和"厶"（自己的）组成，合起来可以理解为自己的财产。"公"由"八"（相背）和"厶"（自己的）组成，合起来表示属于大家的，即公共的。"厶"也可以是不同的象形符号，比如气流和人的头部。"云"中的"厶"就是气流的样子。"允"由"厶"（人的头部的样子）和"儿"（人的身体和腿）组成，合在一起表示点头（应允）。

Name: sī zì páng
Original meaning: personal
Related characters: 私 (private), 公 (public), 云 (cloud), 允 (permit)

Memory tips

The meanings of characters containing 厶 are usually related to self. 私 consists of 禾(crop) and 厶(self). It means that the crop is private property. The meaning of 私 is private. 公 consists of 八(opposite) and 厶(self). It means the opposite of private. 厶 is also a pictogram symbol. In 云 it is the image of air flow. 允 consists of 厶(human head) and 儿(human body and legs). It means to nod and permit.

名　称：	力字旁
本　义：	力气
例　字：	加、男、动、功

记忆贴士

带"力"的字意思往往和力气有关。"加"由"力（力气）"和"口（说话）"组成，表示用力说话，造成夸张的效果，引申出增加的意思。"男"由"田（田地）"和"力（力气）"组成，表示用力在田中劳动，意思是男性。"动"（繁体字为"動"）由"云"（繁体字部件为"重"，声旁）和"力"组成，表示行动。"功"由"工"（工具）和"力"（力气）组成，表示用工具劳动。

Name: lì zì páng
Original meaning: strength
Related characters: 加 (increase), 男 (female), 动 (act), 功 (work)

Memory tips

The meanings of characters containing 力 are usually related to strength. 加 consists of 力(strength) and 口(speak). It means to speak hard and cause exaggeration. It is extended to mean to increase. 男 consists of 田(field) and 力(strength). It means to work hard in the field and refers to male. 动(traditional character is 動) consists of 云(the radical of the traditional character is 重, indicating pronunciation) and 力(strength). It means to act. 功 consists of 工(tool) and 力(strength). It means to work with tools.

	名　称:	乂字旁
	本　义:	割（草）或收割（谷物）
	例　字:	爻、文、义、区

记忆贴士

带"乂"的字意思往往和割有关，"乂"或作为其他象形符号（比如：算筹、花纹），或者在简体字中作为代替其他部件的符号。"爻"是古代占卜的工具，是算筹交叉的形象。"文"是一个胸口有文身的人的形象。"义"用"、"表示"收割"的正确性，即"正义"。"区"的繁体字写作"區"，"品"表示很多物品，用"匚"作区分，"区"是区分的意思。简体字"区"使用"乂"代替"品"。

Name: yì zì páng

Original meaning: mow(the grass) or harvest(the grain)

Related characters: 爻 (trigram), 文 (culture), 义 (justice), 区 (distinguish)

Memory tips

The meanings of characters containing 乂 are usually related to cut. 乂 is also used as a pictogram symbol or the substitution for a complex radical. 爻 looks like two couples of counting rods crossing each other. It is a fortune-telling tool. 文(oracle bone script is 𠆢) looks like a person with a tattoo on the chest. The original meaning is tattoo. Now it means culture. 义 consists of 乂 (harvest) and 、. It means justice. 、 is used to indicate the correctness of harvest. 区(traditional character is 區) consists of 匚(distinguish) and 乂(the radical of the traditional character is 品, meaning many materials). It means to distinguish.

	名　称:	竖心旁
	本　义:	心脏
	例　字:	快、怕、悦、恨

记忆贴士

带"忄"的字意思往往和心理活动有关。"快"由"忄"和"夬"（开口表达）组成，表示因心情舒畅而感到高兴。"怕"由"忄"和"白"（空白）组成，表示因恐惧而心里一片空白的状态。"悦"由"忄"和"兑"（说话）组成，表示因谈话投机而开心。"恨"由"忄"和"艮"（瞪眼）组成，表示怨恨。

Name: shù xīn páng

Original meaning: heart

Related characters: 快 (happy), 怕 (fear), 悦 (pleased), 恨 (hate)

Memory tips

The meanings of characters containing 忄 are related to mental activity. 快 consists of 忄

(heart) and 夬(express). It means to feel comfortable and happy. 怕 consists of 忄(heart) and 白 (blank). Fear makes the mind blank, so 怕 means to fear. 悦 consists of 忄(heart) and 兑(speak). It means to feel very pleased because of the pleasant conversation. 恨 consists of 忄(heart) and 艮 (glower), meaning to hate.

| 名　称：火字旁 |
| 本　义：火 |
| 例　字：炊、烂、烘、灰 |

记忆贴士

带"火"的字意思往往和火有关。"炊"由"火"和"欠"（人吹气，小篆字形为 ）组成，表示吹火做饭。"烂"由"火"和"兰"（声旁）组成，表示煮烂。"烘"由"火"和"共"（双手捧着，小篆字形为 ）组成，表示用手捧着东西在火上烘干。"灰"由"𠂇"（手）和"火"组成，表示用手拿棍拨火使柴火充分燃烧，最终成为灰。

Name: huǒ zì páng
Original meaning: fire
Related characters: 炊 (cook), 烂 (well-cooked), 烘 (dry), 灰 (ash)

Memory tips

The meanings of characters containing 火 are usually related to fire. 炊 consists of 火 and 欠(xiaozhuan script is , meaning to blow). It means to blow the firewood and cook on fire. 烂 consists of 火 and 兰(indicates pronunciation). It means that food is well cooked. 烘 consists of 火 and 共(xiaozhuan script is , meaning to hold with both hands). It means to dry something over a fire. 灰 consists of 𠂇(hand) and 火. It means to hold a stick to make the firewood fully burned and eventually turned into ash.

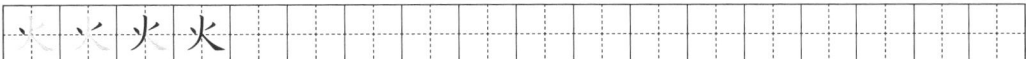

| 名　称：肖字底 |
| 本　义：肉或舟 |
| 例　字：肖、肩、前、育 |

记忆贴士

带"月"的字意思往往和肉（小篆字形为 ）或舟（小篆字形为 ）有关。"肖"（小篆字形为 ）由"⺌"（形体小）和"月（肉体）"组成，合起来指婴儿，表示孩子像父母。"肩"（小篆字形为 ）由"户"（骨骼）和"月"（肌肉）组成，表示身体骨骼和肌肉强健的位置，即肩膀。"前"（小篆字形为𦎧）中的"月"表示"舟"，"刂"本是纤夫的形象，"前"的上半部分是"脚"的变形，合起来表示纤夫拉着船往前走。"育"（小篆字形为𣫻）的上半部分"云"表示婴儿，下半部分"月"表示肉，合起来表示让婴儿长肉，是养育的意思。

Name: xiāo zì dǐ
Original meaning: flesh or boat
Related characters: 肖 (similar), 肩 (shoulder), 前 (forward), 育 (raise)

Memory tips

The meanings of characters containing 月 are usually related to flesh(xiaozhuan script is 𦙶) or boat(xiaozhuan script is 舟). 肖(xiaozhuan script is 𦙾) consists of 小(small) and 月 (flesh). It means that the baby is similar to parents. 肩(xiaozhuan script is 𦘠) consists of 户(bone) and 月 (muscle). It means the strong and muscular part of the body, namely shoulder. 前(xiaozhuan script is 𦎧) consists of 止(foot), 月 (boat) and 刂 (boat tracker). It means that a boat tracker pulls the boat forward. 育(xiaozhuan script is 𣫻) consists of 云 (baby) and 月 (flesh). It means to raise a baby.

名　称	冬字头
本　义	终结或手持武器或脚
例　字	冬、务、各

记忆贴士

"夂"的来源有 🔗（绳子两端打结，如"冬"）、⼅（手持武器，如"务"）和 👣（脚，如"各"）。"冬"是绳子两端打结的形象，表示一年的终结。"务"是用"力"手持"武器"执行打仗的任务。"各"是"脚步"到达"城邑"，现在表示每个的意思。

Name: dōng zì tóu
Original meaning: end or hold weapon or foot
Related characters: 冬 (winter), 务 (task), 各 (each)

Memory tips

The oracle bone script of 冬 is 🔗. It looks like a rope knotted at both ends. 冬 means the end of a year. 务 consists of 夂 (original form is ⼅, meaning to hold a weapon) and 力(oracle bone script is ⼒, meaning strength). It means to carry out combat missions with the weapon in hand. 各 consist of 夂 (oracle bone script is 👣, meaning foot) and 口(city). Its original meaning is to arrive a city. Now it means each.

第一部分　100个常用汉字部件

勹	**名　称**：句字框 **本　义**：连接或子宫或食器或手 **例　字**：句、包、勺、旬

记忆贴士

"句"（金文字形为 🔾）由"勹"（连接）和"口"（词语）组成，表示词语连接起来形成一句话。"包"（小篆字形为 🔾）由"勹"（子宫）和"巳"（胎儿）组成，表示子宫包裹住胎儿。"勺"（小篆字形为 🔾）由"勹"（拥有长把手的器具）和"、"（食物）组成，表示有长把手的盛食物器具。"旬"（金文字形为 🔾）由"勹"（手）和"日"（天）组成，表示用十根手指数十天就是一旬。

Name: jù zì kuàng

Original meaning: connect or womb or spoon or hands

Related characters: 句 (sentence), 包 (wrap), 勺 (spoon), 旬 (a period of ten days)

Memory tips

句(bronze inscription is 🔾) consists of 勹(connect) and 口(words), meaning connected words. 包(xiaozhuan script is 🔾) consists of 勹(womb) and 巳 (fetus). It means that the womb encases the fetus. 勺(xiaozhuan script is 🔾) consists of 勹(a food utensil with a long handle) and 、(food), meaning spoon. 旬(bronze inscription is 🔾) consists of 勹(hand) and 日 (day), meaning ten days.

攵	**名　称**：反文旁 **本　义**：拿着棍子敲打 **例　字**：牧、教、改、放

记忆贴士

"攵"和"攴"同源，"攵"的甲骨文字形 🔾 像手拿着棍子作敲打状。带"攵"或"攴"的字意思往往和敲打有关。"牧"由"牜"（甲骨文字形为 🔾）和"攵"组成，合起来表示放牧。"教"（金文字形为 🔾）由"爻"（文字，金文字形为 🔾）"子"（孩子，金文字形为 🔾）和"攵"组成，表示拿教鞭教孩子学习。改（甲骨文字形为 🔾）由"己"（孩子，甲骨文字形为 🔾）和"攵"组成，表示用棍棒教育孩子改错。"放"由"方"（远方）和"攵"组成，表示驱逐和流放的意思，引申出放置等含义。

Name: fǎn wén páng

Original meaning: beat with stick

Related characters: 牧 (herd), 教 (teach), 改 (change), 放 (put)

27

Memory tips

攵 has the same root as 支. Its oracle bone script is 攴, which looks like a hand holding a stick. It means to beat with stick. The meanings of characters containing 攵 or 支 are usually related to beating. 牧(bronze inscription is 牧) consists of 牛(oracle bone script is 牛) and 攵. It means to herd. 教(bronze inscription is 教) consists of 爻(bronze inscription is 爻, meaning character), 子(bronze inscription is 子, meaning kid) and 攵. It means to teach kids. 改 (oracle bone script is 改) consists of 己(oracle bone script is 己, meaning kid) and 攵. It means to teach the kid to correct mistakes. 放 consists of 方(distant place) and 攵. It means to exile and is extended to mean to put and so on.

第五节

名　称：	尸字旁
本　义：	身体
例　字：	居、展、尾、屋

记忆贴士

带"尸"的字意思往往和身体有关。"居"（金文字形为 ）由"尸"（女子）和"古"（婴儿）组成，意思是女人生完孩子在房子里坐月子。"展"（小篆字形为 ）由"尸"（身体）和"衺"（衣服）组成，意思是展开衣服穿上。"尾"（小篆字形为 ）由"尸"（身体）和"毛"组成，意思是身体后面的装饰物。"屋"（小篆字形为 ）由"尸"（身体）和"至"（躺下）组成，表示供人坐卧的屋子。

Name: shī zì páng
Original meaning: human body
Related characters: 居 (live), 展 (unfold), 尾 (tail), 屋 (room)

Memory tips

The meanings of characters containing 尸 are usually related to human body. 居(bronze inscription is) consists of 尸(woman) and 古(infant). It means that a woman rests indoors after giving birth to a child. 展(xiaozhuan script is) consists of 尸(body) and 衺(clothes). It means to unfold the clothes and put them on. 尾(xiaozhuan script is) consists of 尸(body) and 毛(hair). It means the decoration behind the body. 屋(xiaozhuan script is) consists of 尸(body) and 至(rest on the floor). It means a room where people can sit and lie down.

尸	尸	尸														

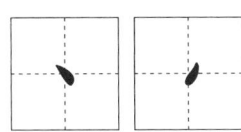

名　称：	点字旁
本　义：	指事符号或象形符号
例　字：	太、刃、亦、火

记忆贴士

"丶"在汉字中可以作为指事符号用来构成指事字。除了指事符号之外，"丶"还广泛地用于其他类型的汉字。"太"由"大"和"丶"（指事符号）组成，意思是太大。"刃"由"刀"和"丶"（指事符号）组成，意思是刀剑等锋利的部分。"亦"的小篆字形为 ，由"大"（人）和"丶"（指事符号）组成，意思是腋下，现在的意思是"也"。"火"的小篆字形 像火焰，"丶"是火焰的一部分。

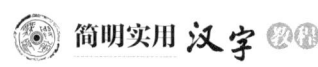

Name: diǎn zì páng
Original meaning: indicative symbol or pictogram symbol
Related characters: 太 (too), 刃 (blade), 亦 (also), 火 (fire)

Memory tips

、 can be used as a symbol to form a self-explanatory character. In addition, it can be widely used in other types of characters. 太 consists of 大(big) and 、(indicative symbol), meaning too big. 刃(xiaozhuan script is 刃) consists of 刀(knife) and 、(indicative symbol), meaning blade. 亦 (xiaozhuan script is 亦) consists of 大(person) and two 、(indicative symbol). It originally means the armpit. Now it means "also." 火(xiaozhuan script is 火) looks like fire. 、 is part of fire.

名　称：广字旁
本　义：房子
例　字：府、库、庞、庭

记忆贴士

带"广"的字意思往往和房子有关。"府"由"广"（房子）和"付"（交付）组成，表示国家存放文书和财宝的房子。"库"由"广"（房子）和"车"（兵车）组成，表示国家存放武器的房子。"庞"由"广"和"龙"组成，表示能装下龙的大屋子。"庭"由"广"和"廷（金文字形为 廷，表示群臣在台阶下站立）"组成，意为宫中的大殿。

Name: guǎng zì páng
Original meaning: house
Related characters: 府 (mansion), 库 (storeroom), 庞 (huge), 庭 (main hall)

Memory tips

The meanings of characters containing 广 are usually related to house. 府 consists of 广 (house) and 付(give), meaning the big house where documents and treasures are stored. 库 consists of 广(house) and 车(military vehicle), meaning the big house where weapons are stored. 庞 consists of 广(house) and 龙(Chinese dragon), meaning the big house that can hold a Chinese dragon. 庭 consists of 广(house) and 廷(bronze inscription is 廷, meaning that the ministers stand under the stairs). It means the main hall in the palace.

第一部分 100个常用汉字部件

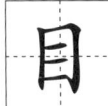

名 称：	目字旁
本 义：	眼睛
例 字：	眼、相、看、眉

记忆贴士

带"目"的字意思往往和眼睛有关。"眼"由"目"和"艮"（看）组成，合起来表示眼睛。"相"由"木"（树）和"目"（看）组成，合起来表示站在树上向远方眺望。"看"由"手"（手）和"目"（眼睛）组成，合起来表示用手遮住阳光向远处看。"眉"由"尸"（眉毛的样子）和"目"（眼睛）组成，合起来表示眉毛。

Name: mù zì páng
Original meaning: eye
Related characters: 眼 (eye), 相 (observe), 看 (look), 眉 (eyebrow)

Memory tips

The meanings of characters containing 目 are usually related to eye. 眼 consists of 目(eye) and 艮(look), meaning eye. 相 consists of 木(tree) and 目(look). It means to stand in the tree to look into the distance. 看 consists of 手(hand) and 目(eye). It means to block out the sunlight with hand and look into the distance. 眉 consists of 尸(eyebrow) and 目(eye), meaning eyebrow.

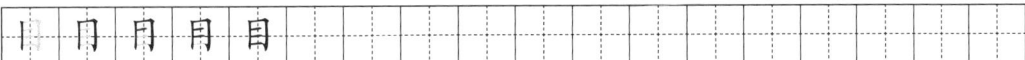

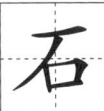

名 称：	石字旁
本 义：	石头
例 字：	岩、磊、破、硕

记忆贴士

带"石"（金文字形为 ）的字意思往往和石头有关。"岩"由"山"和"石"组成，表示山上的石头。"磊"由三个"石"组成，表示一堆石头。"破"由"石"和"皮"（剥动物皮）组成，表示切开石块。"硕"由"石"和"页"（头）组成，表示大头。

Name: shí zì páng
Original meaning: rock
Related characters: 岩 (rock), 磊 (a pile of stones), 破 (cut), 硕 (giant)

Memory tips

The meanings of characters containing 石 are usually related to rock. 岩 consists of 山 (mountain) and 石(stone), meaning stones on the mountain. 磊 consists of three 石, meaning many stones stacked together. 破 consists of 石(stone) and 皮(bronze inscription is 皮, meaning to peel the skin of an animal). It means to cut open a rock. 硕 consists of 石(stone) and 页(head), meaning big head.

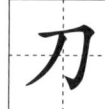	**名 称**: 刀字旁
	本 义: 刀
	例 字: 刃、分、切、解

记忆贴士

带"刀"的字意思往往和刀有关。"刃"由"刀"和"丶"组成,"丶"是指事符号,表示刀剑等锋利的部位。"分"由"八"(分开)和"刀"组成,表示切分。"切"由"七"(分割)和"刀"组成,表示切分。"解"由"角"(牛角,甲骨文字形为 )、"刀""牛"组成,表示肢解牛。

Name: dāo zì páng
Original meaning: knife
Related characters: 刃 (blade), 分 (cut), 切 (cut), 解 (dismember)

Memory tips

The meanings of characters containing 刀 are usually related to knife. 刃 consists of 刀(knife) and 丶 (indicative symbol), meaning blade. 分 consists of 八(original meaning is to seperate and now means eight) and 刀(knife). It means to split something. 切 consists of 七(original meaning is to cut and now means seven) and 刀(knife). It means to cut something. 解 consists of 角 (oracle bone script is , meaning horn), 刀(knife) and 牛(cow). It means to dismember a cow.

	**名 称**: 巾字旁
	本 义: 织物
	例 字: 帛、帘、帐、帖

记忆贴士

带"巾"的字意思往往和织物相关。"帛"由"白"(白色)和"巾"(织物)组成,表示白色的绸布。"帘"由"穴"(窗或门)和"巾"(织物)组成,表示窗帘或门帘。"帐"由"巾"(织物)和"长"组成,表示长而宽大的用于遮蔽的布。"帖"由"巾"(织物)和"占"(占卜)组成,表示将占卜结果写在布帛上。

Name: jīn zì páng
Original meaning: cloth
Related characters: 帛 (white silk), 帘 (curtain), 帐 (tent), 帖 (silk with the word)

Memory tips

The meanings of characters containing 巾 are usually related to cloth. 帛 consists of 白(white) and 巾(cloth), meaning white silk. 帘 consists of 穴(window or door) and 巾(cloth), meaning curtain. 帐 consists of 巾(cloth) and 长(long and wide), meaning tent. 帖 consists of 巾(cloth) and 占(divine), meaning to write words of divination results on the cloth.

第一部分　100个常用汉字部件

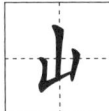 

名　称：	山字旁
本　义：	地面上由土石构成的隆起
例　字：	岭、峰、崛、岩

记忆贴士

带"山"的字意思往往和山峰有关。"岭"由"山"和"令"（带领，"领"的省写，也作声旁）组成，意为山的领袖，指山系中最高的山脉。"峰"由"山"和"夆"（刀锋，"锋"的省写，也作声旁）组成，把山顶喻为刀锋，指山顶。"崛"由"山"和"屈"（弯腰或者蹲下撅起屁股，金文字形 由"尾"和"脚"构成）组成，意思是从地面陡然升起的山势。"岩"由"山"和"石"组成，本义是山崖，也指岩石。

Name: shān zì páng
Original meaning: mountain
Related characters: 岭 (ridge of mountain), 峰 (top of mountain), 崛 (mountain rising abruptly), 岩 (rock)

Memory tips

The meanings of characters containing 山 are usually related to mountain. 岭 consists of 山 and 令(omitted form of 领, means to lead). It means the ridge of mountain. 峰 consists of 山 and 夆(omitted form of 锋, means blade). It means the top of mountain. 崛 consists of 山 and 屈(bend down and raise ass). It means mountain rising abruptly. 岩 consists of 山 and 石(stone), meaning cliff and rock.

名　称：	尚字头
本　义：	火把或小
例　字：	尚、光、肖、堂

记忆贴士

"⺌"这个部件表示很多意思。"尚"（金文字形为 ）由"八"（分开）和"向"（向北的窗户）组成，表示在屋顶开窗户，让气流往上走，引申出高尚的意思。"光"由"⺌"（火把）和"兀"（人，金文字形为 ）组成，意思是火把的光亮。"肖"由"⺌"（小）和"月"（肉，小篆字形为 ）组成，表示婴儿和父母长得像。"堂"由"龸"（高）和"土"组成，表示高大的房屋。

Name: shàng zì tóu
Original meaning: torch or small
Related characters: 尚 (lofty), 光 (light), 肖 (baby looks like its parents), 堂 (lofty hall)

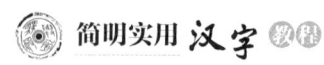

Memory tips

尚(bronze inscription is 尚) consists of 八(seperate) and 向(north-facing window). It means to open the roof window and keep the airflow up. 尚 is extended to mean lofty. 光 consists of ⺌ (torch) and 兀(bronze inscription is 𠆢, meaning person). It means the light of torch. 肖 consists of ⺌ (small) and 月(xiaozhuan script is 𠕋, meaning flesh). It means that a baby looks like its parents. 堂 consists of 尚 (high) and 土(soil), meaning lofty hall.

名 称:	竹字头
本 义:	竹子
例 字:	笔、笑、笛、竿

记忆贴士

带"⺮"的字意思往往和竹子有关。"笔"由"⺮"（由竹子做成的毛笔笔杆）和"毛"（动物毛发）组成，意思是书写工具。"笑"（小篆字形为𥬇）由"⺮"（人笑的时候眼睛像竹子的叶子）和"夭"（手舞足蹈的样子，小篆字形为𠚖）组成，意思是手舞足蹈地大笑。"笛"由"⺮"（竹子）和"由"（引导气流经过）组成，意思是中国传统竹质八孔管乐器。"竿"由"⺮"（竹子）和"干"（主干）组成，意思是竹子的主干。

Name: zhú zì tóu
Original meaning: bamboo
Related characters: 笔 (pen), 笑 (laugh), 笛 (flute), 竿 (bamboo trunk)

Memory tips

The meanings of characters containing ⺮ are usually related to bamboo. 笔 consists of ⺮ (Chinese traditional pen uses bamboo as the pen tube) and 毛(hair), meaning pen. 笑(xiaozhuan script is 𥬇) consists of ⺮ (a smiling person's eyes are like bamboo leaves) and 夭(xiaozhuan script is 𠚖, looking like a person with hands swinging and feet stomping). It means to laugh and dance. 笛 consists of ⺮(bamboo, the material of Chinese traditional flute) and 由(conduct airflow through), meaning flute. 竿 consists of ⺮(bamboo) and 干(trunk), meaning bamboo trunk.

第六节

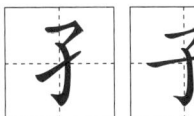

名 称:	子字旁
本 义:	孩子
例 字:	孙、孔、孤、孝

记忆贴士

带"孑"或"子"的字意思往往和孩子有关。"孙"由"子"（儿子）和"小"（比儿子小一辈）组成，表示儿子的下一代。"孔"（金文字形为 ）由"子"（小孩）和"乚"（指事符号）组成，本义是小孩的囟门，现在指小洞。"孤"由"子"（孩子）和"瓜"（小篆字形 是藤上结了一个瓜的样子，有孤单的含义）组成，表示没有父母的孩子。"孝"（金文字形为 ）由" "（老人，金文字形 像一个长发拄拐的老人）和"子"组成，表示孝顺。

Name: zǐ zì páng
Original meaning: kid
Related characters: 孙 (grandchild), 孔 (hole), 孤 (lonely), 孝 (filial piety)

Memory tips

The meanings of characters containing 孑 or 子 are usually related to kid. 孙 consists of 子(son) and 小(the next generation of the son), meaning grandchildren. 孔(bronze inscription is) consists of 子(kid) and 乚(indicative symbol). Its original meaning is fonticulus. Now it means small hole. 孤 consists of 子(kid) and 瓜(xiaozhuan script is , meaning any kind of melon or gourd). It means that an orphan is like a lonely melon on a vine. 孝(bronze inscription is like a kid helping an old person) consists of (old person) and 子(kid). It means that a kid shows filial piety by helping the elderly.

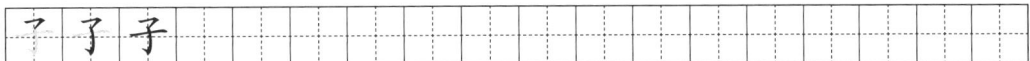

名 称:	隹字旁
本 义:	短尾鸟
例 字:	唯、集、雀、雄

记忆贴士

带"隹"的字意思往往和鸟有关。"唯"由"口"（说话）和"隹"（鸟）组成，意思是允诺，允诺就像鸟儿的叫声一样好听。"集"（甲骨文字形为 ）由"隹"（鸟）和"木"（树）组成，意思是许多鸟儿落在树上休息。"雀"（甲骨文字形为 ）由"少"和"隹"组成，意思是一种小型鸟类。"雄"由"厷"（有力的胳膊，男性的象征）和"隹"（鸟）组成，意思是雄性的鸟。

Name: zhuī zì páng
Original meaning: short-tailed bird
Related characters: 唯 (promise), 集 (gather), 雀 (small bird), 雄 (male bird)

Memory tips

The meanings of characters containing 隹 are usually related to bird. 唯 consists of 口(speak) and 隹(bird). It means that a promise is like a nice bird song. 集(oracle bone script is 🐦) consists of 隹(bird) and 木(tree), meaning that birds gather to rest in the tree. 雀(oracle bone script is 🐦) consists of 少(small) and 隹(bird), meaning a kind of small bird. 雄 consists of 厷(strong arm, represents male) and 隹(bird), meaning male bird.

ノ	亻	亻	亻	亻	亻	隹	隹												

名 称:	左字框
本 义:	手
例 字:	左、右、有、友

记忆贴士

带"𠂇"的字意思往往和手有关。"左"（小篆字形为🖐）由"𠂇"（手，小篆字形为🖐）和"工"（使用工具，指被统治者）组成，表示左手。"右"由"𠂇"（手）和"口"（发号施令，指统治者）组成，表示右手。"有"（小篆字形为🖐）由"𠂇"（手）和"月"（肉，小篆字形为🖐）组成，表示手里拿着肉。"友"（小篆字形为🖐）由"𠂇"（手）和"又"（手）组成，表示彼此紧握着手的一对朋友。

Name: zuǒ zì kuàng
Original meaning: hand
Related characters: 左 (left), 右 (right), 有 (have), 友 (friend)

Memory tips

The meanings of characters containing 𠂇 are usually related to hand. 左(xiaozhuan script is 🖐) consists of 𠂇(xiaozhuan script is 🖐, meaning hand) and 工(tool, represents the ruled), meaning left. 右(xiaozhuan script is 🖐) consists of 𠂇(hand) and 口(order, represents the ruler), meaning right. 有(xiaozhuan script is 🖐) consists of 𠂇(hand) and 月(xiaozhuan script is 🖐, meaning meat). It means to hold a hunk of meat. 友(xiaozhuan script is 🖐) consists of 𠂇(hand) and 又(hand). It means two friends clenching each other's hands.

一	𠂇																		

名　称:	白字旁
本　义:	白色
例　字:	伯、柏、泉、帛

记忆贴士

带"白"的字意思往往和白色有关。"伯"（小篆字形为 伯）由"亻"（人）和"白"（白头发）组成，意思是部落里的白发长者，长者作为部落首领。"柏"（小篆字形为 柏）由"木"（树）和"白"（"伯"的省写，意思是第一）组成，意思是树中之王（柏树是一种生命力很强的树种）。"泉"由"白"（白色，泉水的颜色）和"水"组成，意思是水流源头。"帛"由"白"（白色）和"巾"（绸布）组成，意思是白色的、空白的绸布。

Name: bái zì páng
Original meaning: white color
Related characters: 伯 (elder), 柏 (cypress), 泉 (fountain), 帛 (white silk)

Memory tips

The meanings of characters containing 白 are usually related to white. 伯(xiaozhuan script is 伯) consists of 亻(person) and 白(gray hair), meaning elder. The elders are the tribal leaders. 柏 (xiaozhuan script is 柏) consists of 木(tree) and 白(omitted form of 伯, means foremost), meaning king of tree. 柏 refers to cypress. 泉 consists of 白(white, the color of fountain) and 水(water), meaning fountain. 帛 consists of 白(white) and 巾(cloth), meaning white silk.

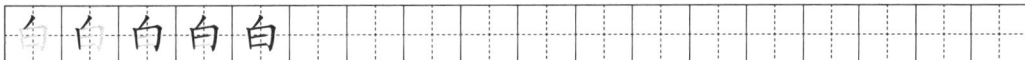

名　称:	车
本　义:	车辆
例　字:	轩、较、轮、轧

记忆贴士

带"车"的字意思往往和车辆有关。"轩"由"车"和"干"（篷子的竖杆）组成，意思是有篷子的车。"较"由"车"和"交"（声旁）组成，本义是古代车厢两旁木板上的横木，引申出比较等含义。"轮"由"车"和"仑"（多而有序，金文字形 仑 像多管笛子）组成，意思是有辐条的轮子。"轧"由"车"和"乚"（人的身体）组成，意思是车辆轧人。

Name: chē zì páng
Original meaning: vehicle
Related characters: 轩 (carriage with canopy), 较 (compare), 轮 (wheel with spokes), 轧 (roll)

Memory tips

The meanings of characters containing 车 are usually related to vehicle. 轩 consists of 车(carriage) and 干(veticle pole used to hold the canopy), meaning carriage with canopy. 较 consists of 车(carriage) and 交(indicates pronunciation), meaning the beam of wooden boards on both sides of the ancient carrige. Now 较 commonly means to compare. 轮 consists of 车(carriage) and 仑(bronze inscription ⾁ is like a multi-barrelled flute，meaning numerous and orderly), meaning wheel with spokes. 轧 consists of 车(carriage) and ⺄(human body). It means to roll.

名　称：	米字旁
本　义：	粟的籽粒
例　字：	粮、粉、精、粒

记忆贴士

带"米"的字意思往往和谷物、粮食有关。"粮"由"米"和"良"（好）组成，意思是粮食。"粉"由"米"和"分"（分解）组成，意思是磨碎的粉状物。"精"由"米"和"青"（漂亮，"倩"的省写）组成，意思是精心挑选的小米。"粒"由"米"和"立"（声旁）组成，本义是小米粒，现在的意思是小而圆的东西。

Name: mǐ zì páng
Original meaning: millet grain
Related characters: 粮 (grain), 粉 (powder), 精 (refined millet grain), 粒 (particle)

Memory tips

The meanings of characters containing 米 are usually related to grain. 粮 consists of 米(millet grain) and 良(good), meaning grain. 粉 consists of 米(millet grain) and 分(grind), meaning powder. 精 consists of 米(millet grain) and 青(omitted form of 倩, means beautiful), meaning refined millet grain. 粒 consists of 米(millet grain) and 立(indicates pronunciation). Its original meaning is millet grain. Now the meaning is particle.

名　称：	立字旁
本　义：	站立
例　字：	靖、竣、端、站

记忆贴士

带"⽴"的字意思往往和站立有关。"靖"（小篆字形为 ⿰立青 ）由"⽴"和"青"（漂亮，"倩"的省写）组成，意思是漂亮的站姿，本义是站立不动，引申出"使……安定"的意思。"竣"（小篆字形为 ⿰立夋 ）由"⽴"（站立）和"夋"（后退）组成，表示退下的意思，引申出完成的含义。"端"（小篆字形为 ⿰立耑 ）由"⽴"（站立）和"耑"（老人）组成，意思是老人端正地站立。"站"由"⽴"（站立）和"占"（声旁）组成，意思是直立。

Name: lì zì páng

Original meaning: stand

Related characters: 靖 (stabilize), 竣 (complete), 端 (upright), 站 (stand)

Memory tips

The meanings of characters containing 立 are usually related to standing. 靖(xiaozhuan script is ) consists of 立 and 青(omitted form of 情, means beautiful). The original meaning is to stand still. It is extended to mean to stabilize. 竣(xiaozhuan script is 峻) consists of 立 (stand) and 夋 (retreat). The original meaning is to retreat. It is extended to mean to complete. 端(xiaozhuan script is 端) consists of 立 (stand) and 耑 (old person). It means upright standing posture of the old person. 站 consists of 立 (stand) and 占 (indicates pronunciation). It means to stand.

名 称:	夕字旁
本 义:	月亮或肉
例 字:	外、名、多、歹

记忆贴士

带"夕"的字意思往往和月亮或肉有关。"外"（金文字形为 𣥌）由"夕"（月亮，甲骨文字形为 𖤍）和"卜"（占卜）组成，表示夜晚在月下占卜，引申出在外面的意思。"名"由"夕"（月亮，甲骨文字形为 𖤍）和"口"（说话）组成，意思是在月夜下遇到人报上自己的名字。"多"（小篆字形为 多）由两个"夕"（肉）组成，表示肉多。"歹"（甲骨文字形为 𣥌）由"一"（骨头）和"夕"（剩余的肉）组成，表示剔除了肉的骨架。现在的意思和"好"相对，是坏、恶的意思。

Name: xī zì páng

Original meaning: moon or meat

Related characters: 外 (outside), 名 (name), 多 (much), 歹 (bad)

Memory tips

The meanings of characters containing 夕 are usually related to moon or meat. 外(bronze inscription is 𣥌) consists of 夕(oracle bone script is 𖤍, meaning moon) and 卜 (divine). The original meaning is to divine under the moonlight. Now it means outside. 名 consists of 夕(oracle bone script is 𖤍, meaning moon) and 口(speak). It means that a person tells his or her own name to someone he or she meets in the evening. 多(xiaozhuan script is 多) consists of two 夕(meat), meaning too much meat. 歹(oracle bone script is 𣥌) consists of 一(bone) and 夕(residual meat), meaning skeleton with meat removed and now its meaning is bad or evil.

	名　称：病字框
	本　义：疾病
	例　字：病、疾、疲、疫

记忆贴士

带"疒"的字意思往往和疾病有关。"病"（小篆字形为𤵸）由"疒"（卧床休息）和"丙"（声旁）组成，表示因健康原因卧床休息。"疾"（小篆字形为𤕫）由"疒"（卧床休息）和"矢"（箭）组成，表示由于受箭伤而卧床休息。"疲"（小篆字形为𤸁）由"疒"（卧床休息）和"皮"（声旁）组成，意思是身体疲劳。"疫"（小篆字形为𤶦）由"疒"（卧床休息）和"殳"（声旁，"役"的省写）组成，意思是传染性疾病。

Name: bìng zì kuàng
Original meaning: disease
Related characters: 病 (disease), 疾 (disease), 疲 (fatigue), 疫 (infectious disease)

Memory tips

病(xiaozhuan script is 𤵸) consists of 疒(rest on bed, implying disease) and 丙(indicates pronunciation), meaning poor health. 疾(xiaozhuan script is 𤕫) consists of 疒 and 矢(arrow), meaning arrow injury. 疲(xiaozhuan script is 𤸁) consists of 疒 and 皮(indicates pronunciation), meaning physical fatigue. 疫(xiaozhuan script is 𤶦) consists of 疒 and 殳(omitted form of 役, indicates pronunciation), meaning infectious disease.

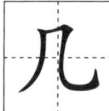	名　称：几字旁
	本　义：凳子或人
	例　字：机、冗、虎

记忆贴士

带"几"的字意思往往和凳子或人有关。"几"（小篆字形为𠘧）本义是凳子。"机"由"木"（树）和"几"（凳子）组成，本义是一种树的名字，这种树可以用来做凳子，现在通常指机器。"冗"由"宀"（房子）和"几"（人）组成，意思是待在房子里的多余人。"虎"由"虍"（老虎）和"几"（人）组成，意思是一种会袭击人类的大型猫科动物。

Name: jǐ zì páng
Original meaning: stool or person
Related characters: 机 (machine), 冗 (redundant), 虎 (tiger)

Memory tips

几(xiaozhuan script is 𠘧) is like a stool, meaning stool. 机 consists of 木(tree) and 几(stool). It means a kind of tree that can be used to make stools. 机 now commonly means machine. 冗 consists of 宀(house) and 几(person). It means redundant people staying in the house. 虎 consists of 虍(tiger) and 几(person). It means tiger that may attack humans.

第七节

名　称：止
本　义：脚
例　字：企、正、步

记忆贴士

带"止"的字意思往往和脚有关。"止"的甲骨文字形像脚，本义是脚，现在的意思是停止。"企"（甲骨文字形为）由"人"和"止"（脚）组成，意思是踮起脚。"正"（甲骨文字形为）由"一"（国家）和"止"（脚）组成，表示征讨不义之国，有匡扶正义的意思，现在的意思是不偏斜。"步"（甲骨文字形为）由"止"（脚）和"少"（脚）组成，意思是两脚交替前进。

Name: zhǐ zì páng

Original meaning: foot

Related characters: 企 (stand on tiptoe), 正 (upright), 步 (step)

Memory tips

止(oracle bone script is) is like a foot. Its original meaning is foot. Now it commonly means to stop. 企(oracle bone script is) consists of 人(person) and 止(foot). It means to stand on tiptoe. 正(oracle bone script is) consists of 一(country) and 止(foot). It means to crusade against unjust countries. 步(oracle bone script is) consists of 止(foot) and 少(foot). It means two feet alternately moving forward.

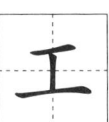

名　称：工字旁
本　义：工具
例　字：攻、江、贡

记忆贴士

"工"（甲骨文字形为）的本义是工具，它还有"巨大"的意思。带"工"的字意思往往和工具有关，或者和"巨大"的意思有关。"攻"由"工"（工具）和"攵"（敲打）组成，表示用攻城工具攻打城池的意思。"江"由"氵"（水）和"工"（巨大）组成，意思是大河。"贡"由"工"（巨大）和"贝"（珍宝）组成，意思是用来作为贡品的大珍宝。

Name: gōng zì páng

Original meaning: tool

Related characters: 攻 (attack), 江 (river), 贡 (tribute)

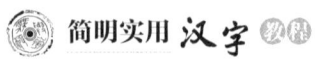

Memory tips

工(oracle bone script is 舌) is like a tool, meaning tool. It also means huge. 攻 consists of 工 (tool) and 攵(hit). It means to use tools to attack a city. 江 consists of 氵(water) and 工(huge), meaning huge river. 贡 consists of 工(huge) and 贝(treasure). It means that huge treasure used as tribute.

名 称:	儿字旁
本 义:	孩子
例 字:	兄、先、元

记忆贴士

儿（金文字形为 ，繁体字为"兒"）像一个头大身小的儿童，本义是孩子。带"儿"的字意思往往和人有关。"兄"（甲骨文字形为 ）由"口"（祈祷）和"儿"（人）组成，表示一个人对天祈祷，本义是兄长。"先"（甲骨文字形为 ）由"止"（脚）和"儿"（人）组成，表示走在人前面。"元"由"二"（上）和"儿"（人）组成，表示人身体上面的部位，本义是头。

Name: ér zì páng

Original meaning: child

Related characters: 兄 (elder brother), 先 (before), 元 (head)

Memory tips

儿(bronze inscription is and traditional character is 兒) is like a child, meaning child. The meanings of characters containing 儿 are usually related to people. 兄(oracle bone script is) consists of 口(speak) and 儿(person). It means a person praying to heaven. The original meaning is elder brother. 先(oracle bone script is) consists of 止(foot) and 儿(person). It means to walk in front of other people. 元 consists of 二(upper) and 儿(person). It indicates that the head is located at the upper part of the body. The original meaning is head.

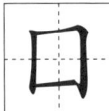

| 名　称：囗字框 |
| 本　义：边界和范围 |
| 例　字：围、圈、囿、园 |

记忆贴士

带"囗"（不是"口"）的字意思往往和边界、范围有关。"围"（金文字形为 ▨）由"囗"和"韦"（金文字形为 ▨，繁体字为"韋"，像两只脚在绕城巡逻）组成，本义是包围，现在的意思是围绕。"圈"（小篆字形为 ▨）由"囗"和"卷"（小篆字形 ▨ 里面有"人""手""米"，意思是人用谷物喂养牲畜）组成，意思是圈养牲畜。"囿"（小篆字形为 ▨）由"囗"和"有"（小篆字形 ▨ 像手里拿着猎物）组成，意思是供打猎的围场，也表示限制的意思。"园"由"囗"和"元"（声旁）组成，意思是种植蔬菜瓜果的地方或供人们游览娱乐的地方。

Name: wéi zì kuàng
Original meaning: borders and territories
Related characters: 围 (surround), 圈 (keep livestock in a fence), 囿 (animal farm for hunting), 园 (a place for growing plants or public recreation)

Memory tips

The meanings of characters containing 囗 are usually related to border or territory. 围(bronze inscription is ▨) consists of 囗(closed area) and 韦(the radical of the traditional character is 韋, and bronze inscription is ▨ , looking like two feet walking around the city). It means to besiege. Now its common meaning is surround. 圈(xiaozhuan script is ▨) consists of 囗(closed area) and 卷(xiaozhuan script is ▨ , meaning that people feed livestock with grain). It means to rear livestock in pens. 囿 (xiaozhuan script is ▨) consists of 囗(closed area) and 有 (xiaozhuan script is ▨ , meaning to hold prey in hand), meaning animal farm for hunting. 园 consists of 囗(closed area) and 元(indicates pronunciation). It means a place for growing plants or for public recreation.

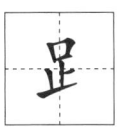

| 名　称：足字旁 |
| 本　义：脚 |
| 例　字：跟、路、践、跌 |

记忆贴士

带"𧾷"的字意思往往和脚有关。"跟"由"𧾷"（脚）和"艮"（回头看）组成，意思是脚后跟，引申为跟随。"路"由"𧾷"（脚）和"各"（到来，甲骨文字形为 ▨ ）组成，意思是道路。"践"由"𧾷"（脚）和 "戋"（武器，繁体字部件为"戔"）组成，本义是踩踏。"跌"由"𧾷"（脚）和"失"（因失手而使东西掉落）组成，意思是跌倒。

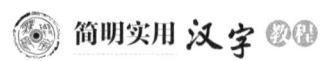

Name: zú zì páng
Original meaning: foot
Related characters: 跟 (follow), 路 (road), 践 (tread), 跌 (fall down)

Memory tips

The meanings of characters containing 足 are usually related to foot. 跟 consists of 足 (foot) and 艮(look back). It means heel and is extended to mean to follow. 路 consists of 足 (foot) and 各(oracle bone script is 𠙵, meaning to arrive), meaning road. 践 consists of 足 (foot) and 戋(the radical of the traditional character is 戔, meaning weapon). The original meaning is to tread. 跌 consists of 足 (foot) and 失(something drops from the hand). It means to fall down.

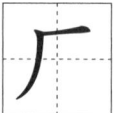

名　称：	厂字旁
本　义：	山崖
例　字：	仄、厄、厉

记忆贴士

"厂"（金文字形为 ）本义是可供居住的石崖，现在的意思是工厂。带"厂"的字意思往往和山崖有关。"仄"（小篆字形为 ）由"厂"（山崖）和"人"（低着头的人）组成，表示人低着头经过山崖狭窄的地方，本义是倾斜，引申为狭窄。"厄"（小篆字形为 ）由"厂"（山崖）和"㔾"（屈服的人）组成，表示人在山崖下面无路可走，有困厄的意思。"厉"（小篆字形为 ）由"厂"（山崖）和"万"（有毒的蝎子，繁体字为"萬"，金文字形为 ）组成，本义是磨刀石，引申为厉害。

Name: chǎng zì páng
Original meaning: cliff
Related characters: 仄 (narrow), 厄 (stranded), 厉 (severe)

Memory tips

The original meaning of 厂(bronze inscription is) is a cliff with caves for living. Now it commonly means factory. The meanings of characters containing 厂 are usually related to cliff. 仄(xiaozhuan script is) consists of 厂(cliff) and 人(person). It indicates that people bow their heads under the narrow cliffs, meaning narrow. 厄(xiaozhuan script is) consists of 厂(cliff) and 㔾(obedient person), meaning that people have no way to go under the cliff. 厉(xiaozhuan script is) consists of 厂(cliff) and 万(traditional character is 萬, and bronze inscription is , meaning poisonous scorpion). The original meaning is rubstone. Now it means severe.

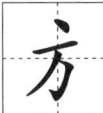 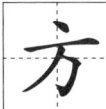

名　称：方字旁
本　义：刀锋
例　字：放、旁、纺

记忆贴士

"方"的甲骨文字形由"刀"和"一"组成,本义是刀锋利的边缘。现在的意思是方形或方向。"放"由"方"(边缘地区)和"攵"(驱逐)组成,本义是驱逐流放,现在的意思是放置和放开。"旁"(甲骨文字形为)由"宀"(区域)和"方"(边缘地区)组成,表示边缘地区,现在的意思是旁边。"纺"由"纟"(丝)和"方"(声旁)组成,意思是纺织。

Name: fāng zì páng
Original meaning: sharp edge of knife
Related characters: 放 (put), 旁 (side), 纺 (spin)

Memory tips

方(oracle bone script is) consists of 刀 and 一. Its original meaning is the sharp edge of knife. It now commonly means square or direction. 放 consists of 方(edge area) and 攵(banish). Its original meaning is to exile. It now commonly means to put or let go. 旁 consists of 宀 (area) and 方(edge area). It means edge area. It now commonly means side. 纺 consists of 纟(silk) and 方(indicates pronunciation). It means to make textiles.

 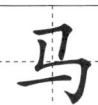

名　称：马字旁
本　义：马
例　字：验、驾、驹

记忆贴士

"马"(小篆字形为)的本义是头小脸长颈上有鬃毛的家畜,能供人骑或拉东西。带"马"的字意思往往和马有关。"验"由"马"和"佥"(检验,"检"的省写)组成,本义是马名,现在的意思是检验。"驾"由"加"("力"是有力的手臂,"口"是命令)和"马"组成,意思是以人的意志操控马匹,也表示驾驶车辆。"驹"由"马"和"句"(毛弯曲)组成,意思是少壮的马。

Name: mǎ zì páng
Original meaning: horse
Related characters: 验 (examine), 驾 (drive), 驹 (foal)

Memory tips

The meaning of 马(xiaozhuan script is , looking like a horse) is horse. The meanings of characters containing 马 are usually related to horse. 验 consists of 马 and 佥(omitted form of 检, means to examine). Its original meaning is horse's name and borrowed to mean to examine. 驾 consists of 加(力 means strong arm and 口 means to order) and 马. It means to harness horses and drive. 驹 consists of 马 and 句(curly horse hair), meaning foal.

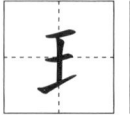 

名　称:	王字旁
本　义:	玉
例　字:	玉、现、理、弄

记忆贴士

带"王"的字意思往往和玉有关。"玉"的甲骨文字形 丰 像一串玉。"现"由"王"（玉）和"见"（看见）组成，意思是出现，如今的意思是现在。"理"由"王"（玉）和"里"（声旁）组成，意思是切割和加工玉石。"弄"由"王"（玉）和"廾"（双手，小篆字形为 𠬞）组成，意思是把玩玉器。

Name: wáng zì páng
Original meaning: jade
Related characters: 玉 (jade), 现 (now), 理 (carve and polish jade), 弄 (play with hands)

Memory tips

The meanings of characters containing 王 are usually related to jade. 玉(oracle bone script is 丰) is like a string of jade, meaning jade. 现 consists of 王(jade) and 见(see). It means to appear and now commonly means now. 理 consists of 王(jade) and 里(indicates pronunciation). It means to carve and polish jade. 弄 consists of 王(jade) and 廾(xiaozhuan script is 𠬞, meaning two hands). It means to play with jade with both hands.

名　称:	羊字旁
本　义:	羊
例　字:	群、善、养

记忆贴士

"羊"的甲骨文字形 ᲾY 像羊，本义是羊。带"羊"的字往往和羊有关，有的字以"羊"为声旁。"群"由"君"（手拿羊鞭并吆喝，金文字形为 ）和"羊"组成，意思是羊群聚集在一起，现在它既可以指一群人也可以指一群动物。"善"由"羊""言"（表示和善的目光，部件形体像眼睛）和"口"（和善的言辞）组成，意思是和善。"养"（繁体字为"養"），由"羊"（也作声旁）和"介"（繁体字部件为"食"）组成，意思是饲养。

Name: yáng zì páng
Original meaning: sheep
Related characters: 群 (crowd), 善 (kindness), 养 (feed)

Memory tips

羊(oracle bone script is 𐃼) is like sheep, meaning sheep. The meanings of characters containing 羊 are usually related to sheep. 羊 can also be used to indicate pronunciation. 群 consists of 君(bronze inscription is 𠂤, meaning to hold a whip and issue commands) and 羊. Its original meaning is flock of sheep. Now it can refer to a group of people or animals. 善 consists of 羊(sheep), 䒑(looks like eyes, meaning amicable eyes) and 口(amicable words), meaning kindness. 养(traditional character is 養) consists of 羊(sheep, also indicates pronunciation) and 介 (the radical of the traditional character is 食, meaning food). It means to feed.

第八节

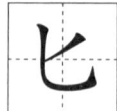

名 称:	匕字旁
本 义:	人
例 字:	比、此、北

记忆贴士

"匕"（甲骨文字形为 ）像一个人形，最初指人，现指一种刀具。带"匕"的字意思往往和人有关。"比"（甲骨文字形为 ）由两个"匕"（人）组成，意思是两个人挨着，引申出"比较"的意思。"此"（金文字形为 ）由"止"（脚，金文字形为 ）和"匕"（人）组成，意思是一只脚踏在人的身上，也指称自己所站立的地方。"北"（甲骨文字形为 ）由"亻"（人）和"匕"（人）组成，表示两个人背对背，本义是违背或后背，现在由"背"表示其本义。"北"现在的意思是北方。

Name:	bǐ zì páng
Original meaning:	person
Related characters:	比 (compare), 此 (this), 北 (north)

Memory tips

匕 (oracle bone script is) looks like a person. Its original meaning is person. Now it refers to a kind of knife. The meanings of characters containing 匕 are usually related to person. 比(oracle bone script is) consists of two 匕(person). It means two people standing next to each other. It is extended to mean to compare. 此(bronze inscription is) consists of 止(bronze inscription is , meaning foot) and 匕(person). It means a foot stepping on a person's body and is used to point out where a person himself or herself stands. 北(oracle bone script is) consists of 亻(person) and 匕(person), indicating two people standing back to back and the original meaning is back or to violate. Now 背 takes the original meaning of 北 and 北 means north.

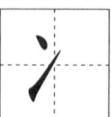

名 称:	两点水
本 义:	冰
例 字:	冰、冷、冯、次

记忆贴士

带"冫"的字意思往往和冰有关。"冰"由"冫"（冰）和"水"组成，意思是由水凝结成的固态物。"冷"由"冫"（冰）和"令"（金文字形为 ，作声旁）组成，意思是温度低。"冯"由"冫"（冰）和"马"组成，表示马凭借冰在河面上行走，"冯"有凭借的意思。"次"由"冫"（冷）和"欠"（打哈欠，小篆字形为 ）组成，意思是因为天气寒冷和困乏停滞不前，驻扎休息，引申出质量欠佳和次序等含义。

Name: liǎng diǎn shuǐ
Original meaning: ice
Related characters: 冰 (ice), 冷 (cold), 冯 (by means of), 次 (inferior; measure word)

Memory tips

The meanings of characters containing 冫 are usually related to ice. 冰 consists of 冫(ice) and 水(water)，meaning ice. 冷 consists of 冫(ice) and 令(bronze inscription is , indicating pronunciation). It means cold. 冯 consists of 冫(ice) and 马(horse). It means horse crossing the river that has iced up. One of meanings of 冯 is by means of. 次 consists of 冫(cold) and 欠 (xiaozhuan script is , meaning to yawn). It means stagnation due to cold weather and the lack of sleep. It is extended to mean poor quality and order, etc.

名 称：	示字旁
本 义：	启示
例 字：	宗、禁、祭

记忆贴士

"示"的甲骨文字形 由"二"和"丨"组成，意思是上天的启示。"宗"由"宀"（房子）和"示"（启示）组成，意思是祭祀祖宗的地方，通过祭祀得到祖先的启示。"禁"由"林"（树林）和"示"（启示）组成，意思是受上天启示不许砍伐和狩猎。"祭"由"夕"（牺牲，祭祀用的肉）"又"（手）和"示"（启示）组成，意思是为得到上天的启示而祭祀。

Name: shì zì páng
Original meaning: revelation
Related characters: 宗 (ancestor), 禁 (prohibit), 祭 (sacrifice)

Memory tips

示(oracle bone script is) consists of 二(heaven) and 小(revelation), meaning heaven's revelation. 宗 consists of 宀(house) and 示(revelation). It means to worship the ancestors and get the revelation at a specific location. 禁 consists of 林(forest) and 示(revelation). It means to forbid tree-cutting and hunting in the light of heaven's revelation. 祭 consists of 夕(meat), 又(hand) and 示 (revelation). It means to worship heaven to get the revelation.

名 称:	爪字头
本 义:	手
例 字:	采、受、觅、乳

记忆贴士

"采"（金文字形为 ）由"爫"（手）和"木"（树）组成，意思是采摘树上的树叶或果实。"受"（金文字形为 ）由"爫"（手）"一"（东西）和"又"（手）组成，表示一只手给另一只手递东西，意思是接受。"觅"（金文字形为 ）由"爫"（手）和"见"（观察）组成，表示仔细观察并探索，有寻找的意思。"乳"（小篆字形为 ）由"爫"（手）、"子"（婴儿）和"乚"（乳房）组成，表示用手抱着孩子喂奶。

Name: zhǎo zì tóu
Original meaning: hand
Related characters: 采 (pick), 受 (accept), 觅 (look for), 乳 (breastfeed)

Memory tips

采(bronze inscription is) consists of 爫(hand) and 木(tree). It means to pick leaf or fruit from the tree. 受(bronze inscription is) consists of 爫(hand), 一(object) and 又(hand). It indicates that one hand gives something to the other and means to accept. 觅(bronze inscription is) consists of 爫(hand) and 见(observe). It indicates to observe carefully and explore. It also means to look for. 乳(xiaozhuan script is) consists of 爫(hand), 子(infant) and 乚(breast). It means to hold a baby to breastfeed.

名 称:	斤字旁
本 义:	斧子
例 字:	斧、析、折

记忆贴士

"斤"的甲骨文字形 像一把斧子，它的本义是斧子，现在是重量单位。带"斤"的字意思往往和斧子有关。"斧"由"父"（声旁）和"斤"（斧子）组成，本义是斧子。"析"（甲骨文字形为 ）由"木"（木头）和"斤"（斧子）组成，本义是用斧子劈木头，引申出分析的意思。"折"（甲骨文字形为 ）由"扌"（甲骨文字形是两截木头）和"斤"（斧子）组成，本义是从中间砍断，引申为物体在外力作用下折断。

Name: jīn zì páng
Original meaning: axe
Related characters: 斧 (axe), 析 (analysis), 折 (break)

Memory tips

斤(oracle bone script is) is like a axe. Its original meaning is axe. Now it is used as a weight unit. The meanings of characters containing 斤 are usually related to axe. 斧 consists of 父 (indicates pronunciation) and 斤(axe), meaning axe. 析(oracle bone script is 𣂞) consists of 木(tree) and 斤(axe). It means to chop the wood with an axe and is extended to mean to analyze. 折(oracle bone script is 𣂚) consists of 扌 (original form is two pieces of wood) and 斤(axe). It indicates to cut off from the middle and now it means to break.

名　称：欠字旁
本　义：呼气
例　字：吹、欣、坎

记忆贴士

"欠"小篆字形𣍘像一个人口中吹气，表示呼气的意思，现在的意思是亏欠和缺乏。"吹"（小篆字形𠿒）由"口"（嘴）和"欠"（呼气）组成，意思是合拢嘴唇用力出气。"欣"（小篆字形𣢜）由"斤"（斧子）和"欠"（呼气）组成，意思是工作时愉快地歌唱。"坎"由"土"和"欠"（缺乏）组成，合起来是欠缺土，意思是地面的坑。

Name: qiàn zì páng
Original meaning: exhale
Related characters: 吹 (blow), 欣 (joyful), 坎 (pit)

Memory tips

欠(xiaozhuan script is 𣍘) is like a person with a big mouth exhaling. Now it means to owe and lack. 吹(xiaozhuan script is 𠿒) consists of 口(mouth) and 欠(exhale). It means to blow hard. 欣(xiaozhuan script is 𣢜) consists of 斤(axe) and 欠(exhale). It means to sing joyfully while working. 坎(xiaozhuan script is 𡎚) consists of 土(soil) and 欠(lack). It means pit in the ground because of the lack of soil.

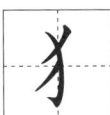

名　称：反犬旁
本　义：狗
例　字：狗、狐、犯、狠

记忆贴士

带"犭"的字意思往往和动物有关。"狗"（小篆字形为𤜂）由"犭"和"句"（弯曲）组成，意思是一种嗅觉灵敏能帮人看门、打猎的家畜（狗的特征是尾巴卷起来）。"狐"（小篆字形为𤞞）由"犭"和"瓜"（独来独往，"孤"的省写）组成，意思是狐

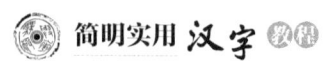

狸。"犯"（小篆字形为 ）由"犭"和"巳"（人）组成，意思是动物攻击人。"狠"（小篆字形为 ）由"犭"和"艮"（瞪眼）组成，意思是捕食者狠狠地盯着猎物。

Name: fǎn quǎn páng
Original meaning: dog
Related characters: 狗 (dog), 狐 (fox), 犯 (violate), 狠 (ferocious)

Memory tips

The meanings of characters containing 犭 are usually related to animal. 狗(xiaozhuan script is) consists of 犭 and 句(curl), meaning dog. 狐 (xiaozhuan script is) consists of 犭 and 瓜 (omitted form of 孤, means alone). It means fox. 犯(xiaozhuan script is) consists of 犭 and 巳 (person). It means animal attacking human. 狠(xiaozhuan script is) consists of 犭 and 艮(stare), meaning that the predator fixes the eyes on the prey ferociously.

名 称：	横四点
本 义：	火
例 字：	热、烈、然、焦

记忆贴士

带"灬"（火，小篆字形为 ）的字意思往往和火有关。"热"（小篆字形为 ）由"执"（手持，小篆字形为 ）和"灬"（火）组成，意思是温度高。"烈"（小篆字形为 ）由"列"（剔骨头上的肉，小篆字形为 ）和"灬"（火）组成，意思是火势猛。"然"（小篆字形为 ）由"夕"（肉，小篆字形为 ）、"犬"（狗，小篆字形为 ）和"灬"（火）组成，本义是燃烧，后用"燃"代替"然"表示燃烧。"焦"（小篆字形为 ）由"隹"（鸟，小篆字形为 ）和"灬"（火）组成，意思是烧焦。

Name: héng sì diǎn
Original meaning: fire
Related characters: 热 (hot), 烈 (fierce), 然 (burning; right), 焦 (scorched)

Memory tips

The meanings of characters containing 灬(xiaozhuan script is , meaning fire) are usually related to fire. 热(xiaozhuan script is) consists of 执(xiaozhuan script is , meaning to hold) and 灬(fire), meaning that the temperature is high. 烈(xiaozhuan script is) consists of 列(xiaozhuan script is , meaning to remove meat from bones) and 灬(fire), meaning that the fire is fierce. 然(xiaozhuan script is) consists of 夕(xiaozhuan script is , meaning meat), 犬(xiaozhuan script is , meaning dog) and 灬(fire). Its original meaning is burning and now this meaning is taken by 燃. 焦(xiaozhuan script is) consists of 隹(xiaozhuan script is , meaning bird) and 灬(fire), meaning scorched.

第一部分　100个常用汉字部件

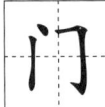

名　称：	门字框
本　义：	房屋的出入口
例　字：	闭、闪、闷

记忆贴士

"门"的甲骨文字形  像门,是房屋的出入口。带"门"的字意思往往和门有关。"闭"(金文字形为) 由"门"和"才"(棍子)组成,意思是关上门后用棍子顶住,是彻底的关门。"闪"(小篆字形为) 由"门"和"人"组成,意思是一个人往门里窥探后迅速离开。"闷"(小篆字形为) 由"门"和"心"组成,意思是郁结于胸,无处倾诉。

Name: mén zì kuàng
Original meaning: door
Related characters: 闭 (locked), 闪 (flash), 闷 (low-spirited)

Memory tips

The meanings of characters containing 门 are usually related to door. 门(oracle bone script is) is like a door, meaning door. 闭(bronze inscription is) consists of 门(door) and 才(stick). It means to close the door and keep it from opening with a stick. 闪(xiaozhuan script is) consists of 门(door) and 人(person). It means a person peeps through the door and leaves quickly. 闷(xiaozhuan script is) consists of 门(door) and 心(heart). It means the emotions are pent up in the chest and there is no one to talk to.

名　称：	彡字旁
本　义：	少量的布或装饰物或胡须等
例　字：	衫、彩、须、参

记忆贴士

"衫"由"衤"(衣服)和"彡"(少量的布)组成,意思是轻薄的衣服。"彩"由"采"(采集)和"彡"(装饰物)组成,意思是多种颜色。"须"由"彡"(胡须)和"页"(头)组成,意思是胡须。"参"由"厶"(星座)"人""彡"(胡子)组成,意思是长胡须的老者观察星象,引申出参考的意思。

Name: sān zì páng
Original meaning: a small amount of cloth or decorations or beard, etc
Related characters: 衫 (shirt), 彩 (colorful), 须 (beard), 参 (consult)

Memory tips

衫 consists of 衤(clothes) and 彡(a small amount of cloth), meaning thirt. 彩 consists of 采(collect) and 彡(decorations), meaning multiple colors. 须 consists of 彡(beard) and 页(head), meaning beard. 参 consists of 厶(constellation), 大(person) and 彡(beard). It means an old person observing astrology and is extended to mean to consult.

第九节

名　称：	耳字旁
本　义：	耳朵
例　字：	耻、聆、闻

记忆贴士

"耳"的甲骨文字形为♪，本义是耳朵。带"耳"的字意思往往和耳朵有关。"耻"由"耳"（耳朵）和"止"（本应是"心"，因"心"的小篆字形和"止"的小篆字形相似而产生讹误）组成，意思是听到批评心里感到羞耻。"聆"由"耳"（耳朵）和"令"（命令，金文字形）组成，意思是恭敬地听上级传达命令。"闻"由"门"和"耳"（耳朵）组成，意思是在门外探听。

Name: ěr zì páng

Original meaning: ear

Related characters: 耻 (shame), 聆 (listen respectfully), 闻 (hear)

Memory tips

耳(oracle bone script is ♪) is like an ear, meaning ear. The meanings of characters containing 耳 are related to ear. 耻 (xiaozhuan script is) consists of 耳(ear) and 止(replaces 心 which is the original radical, because the xiaozhuan scripts of the two characters look similar). It means to feel ashamed to hear reprimands. 聆 consists of 耳(ear) and 令(bronze inscription is , meaning order). It means to listen respectfully to the superior who is making a command. 闻 consists of 门 (door) and 耳(ear). It means to listen outside the door.

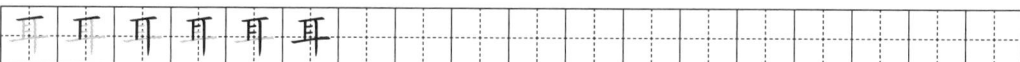

名　称：	皿字底
本　义：	器皿
例　字：	盘、盆、盏

记忆贴士

"皿"的甲骨文字形像一个敞口高脚容器，意思是器皿。带"皿"的字意思往往和器皿有关。"盘"（繁体字为"盤"）由"舟"（搬运，"般"的省写）和"皿"组成，意思是盛放菜肴的容器。"盆"由"分"（宽）和"皿"组成，意思是宽底敞口容器。"盏"由"戈"（浅）和"皿"组成，意思是浅底容器。

Name: mǐn zì dǐ

Original meaning: vessel

Related characters: 盘 (dish), 盆 (basin), 盏 (shallow-bottomed container)

> **Memory tips**

皿(oracle bone script is 𝕐) is like an open and uncovered high-foot container, meaning utensil. The meanings of characters containing 皿 are usually related to utensil. 盘(traditional character is 盤) consists of 舟(omitted form of 般, means to move) and 皿. It means dish. 盆 consists of 分(wide) and 皿, meaning basin. 盏 consists of 戋(shallow) and 皿, meaning a kind of shallow-bottomed container.

名 称:	罒字头
本 义:	网
例 字:	罗、罪、罹、罚

> **记忆贴士**

"罒"的甲骨文字形是 𐠧，本义是网。"罗"（繁体字为"羅"）由"罒"（网）和"夕"（繁体字部件为"維"，"纟"是网上的线，"隹"是鸟）组成，本义是用网捕鸟。"罪"由"罒"（网）和"非"（错误，甲骨文字形为 𐠲，表示认为对方头脑中的观点是错误的）组成，表示抓捕犯罪嫌疑人。"罹"由"罒"（网）"忄"（心）和"隹"（鸟）组成，本义是遭遇不幸。"罚"由"罒"（网）"讠"（拷问）和"刂"（刑罚）组成，意思是犯罪嫌疑人被捕后受到的拷问和刑罚。

Name: wǎng zì tóu
Original meaning: net
Related characters: 罗 (catch birds with a net), 罪 (crime), 罹 (suffer from), 罚 (punish)

> **Memory tips**

The oracle bone script of 罒 is 𐠧, meaning net. The meanings of characters containing 罒 are usually related to net. 罗(traditional character is 羅) consists of 罒(net) and 夕(the radical of the traditional character is 維, in which 纟 means thread of the net and 隹 means bird). It means to catch bird with net. 罪 consists of 罒(net) and 非(oracle bone script is 𐠲, meaning to think that other's opinion is wrong). It means to capture criminal suspects. 罹 consists of 罒(net), 忄(heart) and 隹(bird). It means to suffer misfortune. 罚 consists of 罒 (net), 讠 (interrogate) and 刂 (penalize). It means the interrogation and punishment following the arrest of a criminal suspect.

⺊	**名 称**: 贞字头	
	本 义: 占卜	
	例 字: 贞、占	

记忆贴士

"贞"（小篆字形为 ）由 "⺊"（卜）和 "贝"（鼎）组成，意思是用神鼎占卜并观察神迹，引申出有信仰、忠诚等意思。"占"由 "⺊"（卜）和 "口"（问）组成，意思是通过占卜获得上天的旨意。现在的"占"合并了"佔"（占领）的含义。

Name: zhēn zì tóu

Original meaning: divine

Related characters: 贞 (observe, faithful), 占 (divine, occupy)

Memory tips

贞(xiaozhuan script is ) consists of 卜 (divine) and 贝(sacrificial vessel). It means to observe heaven's revelation after divination using sacrificial vessels. It is extended to mean faithful and loyal. 占(xiaozhuan script is ) consists of 卜 (divine) and 口(ask). It means to ask heaven's will through divination. Now 占 merges the meaning of 佔(occupy).

小	**名 称**: 小字头	
	本 义: 细小	
	例 字: 雀、尖、尘	

记忆贴士

"小"的甲骨文字形 ，像小沙粒，本义是小。带"小"的字意思往往和小有关。"雀"由"小"和"隹"（鸟，金文字形为 ）组成，意思是一种小型的鸟。"尖"由"小"（细小）和"大"组成，意思是物体锐利的末端。"尘"由"小"（微小）和"土"（泥土）组成，意思是微小的泥土。

Name: xiǎo zì tóu

Original meaning: small

Related characters: 雀 (small bird), 尖 (sharp tip), 尘 (dust)

Memory tips

小(oracle bone script is ) is like tiny grains of sand, meaning small. The meanings of characters containing 小 are usually related to small. 雀 consists of 小(small) and 隹(bronze inscription is , meaning bird). It means a kind of small bird. 尖 consists of 小(small) and 大(big), meaning sharp tip. 尘 consists of 小(small) and 土(soil), meaning dust.

第一部分　100个常用汉字部件

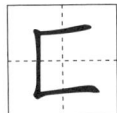

名　　称：	区字框
本　　义：	区分
例　　字：	区、匡、匠、医

记忆贴士

带"匚"的字意思往往和区分有关。"区"由"匚"和"乂"（东西）组成，意思是确定边界以示区分。"匡"由"匚"和"王"（器具）组成，本义是放器具的筐子，引申出纠正的意思。"匠"由"匚"和"斤"（斧子）组成，表示装斧子的筐子，指代木匠。"医"由"匚"和"矢"（箭）组成，意思是装箭的筐子。现在"医"取代了"醫"（本义是用药酒治疗箭伤），指医疗。

Name: qū zì kuàng
Original meaning: distinguish
Related characters: 区 (distinguish), 匡 (correct), 匠 (craftsman), 医 (cure)

Memory tips

The meanings of characters containing 匚 are usually related to distinguishing. 区 consists of 匚 and 乂(things). It means to set the boundaries to show the difference. 匡 consists of 匚 and 王(utensil). Its original meaning is basket for holding utensil and extended to mean to correct. 匠 consists of 匚 and 斤(axe). It is like a basket for holding axe and means carpenter. Now it is used to refer to craftsman. 医 consists of 匚 and 矢(arrow). Its original meaning is basket for holding arrows. Now it's the substitution of 醫(medical treatment) which means to treat arrow injury with medical liquor.

名　　称：	双人旁
本　　义：	走路
例　　字：	往、征、径、徒

记忆贴士

带"彳"的字意思往往和走路有关。"往"由"彳"（走路）和"主"（声旁）组成，意思是"到……"。"征"由"彳"（走路）和"正"（征讨）组成，意思是派兵征伐。"径"由"彳"（走路）和"圣"（织布机上的经线，"经"的省写）组成，意思是直着往前走，现在指小路。"徒"由"彳"（走路）、"土"（尘土）和"龰"（脚）组成，意思是步行。

Name: shuāng rén páng
Original meaning: walk
Related characters: 往 (go), 征 (expedition), 径 (path), 徒 (walk)

57

Memory tips

The meanings of characters containing 彳 are usually related to walk. 往 consists of 彳(walk) and 主(indicates pronunciation). It means to go somewhere. 征 consists of 彳(walk) and 正(oracle bone script is 𠣞, meaning to go on a punitive expedition). It means to send troops to fight evil and uphold justice. 径 consists of 彳(walk) and 圣(omitted form of 经, means straight line of fabric). It means to go straight ahead. Now 径 means path. 徒(bronze inscription is 𡲰) consists of 彳(walk), 土(dust) and 止(bronze inscription is 屮, meaning foot), meaning to walk.

名 称：	穴字头
本 义：	洞穴
例 字：	空、究、窒

记忆贴士

"穴"的小篆字形 像山洞，本义为山洞。"空"（金文字形为 ）由"穴"和"工"（大，金文字形为 ，也作声旁）组成，意思是孔穴，引申为空旷。"究"由"穴"和"九"（手，金文字形为 ，也作声旁）组成，意思是用手在洞穴里探索。"窒"由"穴"和"至"（箭落地，金文字形为 ，也作声旁）组成，意思是堵塞不通。

Name: xué zì tóu
Original meaning: cave
Related characters: 空 (empty), 究 (explore), 窒 (block)

Memory tips

穴(xiaozhuan script is) is like a cave, meaning cave. The meanings of characters containing 穴 are usually related to cave. 空(bronze inscription is) consists of 穴(cave) and 工(bronze inscription is , meaning big and also indicating pronunciation). It means big cave and is extended to mean empty. 究 consists of 穴(cave) and 九(bronze inscription is , meaning hand and also indicating pronunciation). It means to explore with hands in the cave. 窒 consists of 穴(cave) and 至(bronze inscription is , meaning arrow falling onto the ground and also indicating pronunciation). It means to block.

名 称：	雨字头
本 义：	天上的水汽
例 字：	雪、霜、雷

记忆贴士

"雨"的甲骨文字形 像下雨，本义是雨。带"雨"的字意思往往和空气中的水汽有关。

"雪"由"⻗"（天上的水汽）和"彐"（扫帚，"帚"的省写）组成，意思是天气寒冷时天空中降下的由水汽凝结成的白色晶体，落在地上可以用扫帚打扫。"霜"由"⻗"（天上的水汽）"木"（树）和"目"（果实的形状）组成，意思是一种能使树木和果子衰败的天气。"雷"由"⻗"（天上的水汽）和"田"（雷声回响的形象）组成，意思是天空发出巨响的自然现象。

Name: yǔ zì tóu
Original meaning: water vapor from the sky
Related characters: 雪 (snow), 霜 (frost), 雷 (thunder)

Memory tips

雨(oracle bone script is ) is like raining. It means rain. The meanings of characters containing ⻗ are usually related to water vapor in the air. 雪(snow) consists of ⻗(vapor) and 彐 (omitted form of 帚, means broom). It means snow that can be cleaned by broom. 霜 consists of ⻗(vapor), 木(tree) and 目(looks like the shape of fruit). It means frost, which causes plants and fruits to lose their vitality. 雷 consists of ⻗(vapor) and 田(looks like thunder resounding). It means thunder.

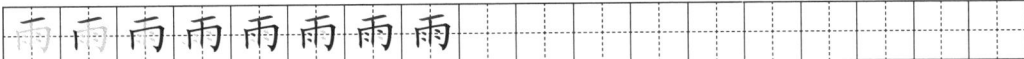

名 称:	戈字旁
本 义:	戈
例 字:	我、武、戎

记忆贴士

"戈"的金文字形像兵器，指的是古代一种横刃长柄的兵器。带"戈"的字意思往往和兵器有关。"我"的金文字形像一种带刺的兵器，现在用作第一人称代词。"武"由"戈"和"止"（脚，甲骨文字形为）组成，意思是出兵作战。"戎"由"戈"和"十"（盾牌）组成，意思是士兵的作战装备，包括戈和盾牌。

Name: gē zì páng
Original meaning: dagger-axe
Related characters: 我 (a weapon with spikes; I or me), 武 (military), 戎 (military affairs)

Memory tips

戈(bronze inscription is) is like a kind of ancient weapon named dagger-axe. The meanings of characters containing 戈 are usually related to weapon. 我(bronze inscription is) is like a weapon with spikes. Its original meaning is weapon. Now it is used as a first person pronoun(I, me). 武 consists of 戈(dagger-axe) and 止(oracle bone script is , meaning foot). It means to send troops to fight. 戎 consists of 戈(dagger-axe) and 十(shield). It means soldier's combat equipment, including dagger-axe and shield.

第十节

名　称：	酉字旁
本　义：	酒
例　字：	酒、醋、醉

记忆贴士

"酉"的金文字形  像一坛酒，本义是酒，现在指地支的第十位。"酒"由"氵"和"酉"组成，表示酒。"醋"由"酉"和"昔"（过去）组成，表明醋是放时间长的酒。"醉"由"酉"和"卒"（最后）组成，表示喝酒喝到最后就醉了。

Name: yǒu zì páng
Original meaning: liquor
Related characters: 酒 (liquor), 醋 (vinegar), 醉 (drunk)

Memory tips

酉(bronze inscription is) is like liquor in the jar. Its original meaning is liquor. Now it refers to the 10th terrestrial branch. 酒 consists of 氵 and 酉(liquor), meaning liquor. 醋 consists of 酉(liquor) and 昔(formerly), meaning that vinegar is liquor that has breathed for a long time. 醉 consists of 酉(liquor) and 卒(finally), meaning drunk.

名　称：	艮字旁
本　义：	回头看
例　字：	退、跟、根、痕

记忆贴士

"艮"的小篆字形 像一个扭头往后看的人，"见"的小篆字形 像一个往前看的人。带"艮"的字意思往往和往后看有关，或者以"艮"作为声旁。"退"由"辶"（走路）和"艮"（扭头往后看）组成，意思是往后走。"跟"由"足"（脚）和"艮"（扭头往后看）组成，意思是脚后跟。"根"由"木"（植物）和"艮"（脚跟，"跟"的省写，也作声旁）组成，意思是植物的根部。"痕"由"疒"（疾病）和"艮"（跟随，"跟"的省写，也作声旁）组成，意思是跟随着痛苦而来的疤痕。

Name: gèn zì páng
Original meaning: look back
Related characters: 退 (go back), 跟 (follow), 根 (root), 痕 (scar)

Memory tips

艮(xiaozhuan script is) is like a person who looks back. 见(xiaozhuan script is) looks like a person looking forward. The meanings of characters containing 艮 are usually related to looking back, or 艮 indicates the pronunciation. 退 consists of 辶(walk) and 艮(look back). It means to go backwards. 跟 consists of 𧾷(foot) and 艮(look back), meaning heel. 根 consists of 木(plant) and 艮(omitted form of 跟, means heal and also indicates pronunciation), meaning the root of plant. 痕 consists of 疒(disease) and 艮(omitted form of 跟, means to follow and also indicates pronunciation). It means scar that follows the pain.

名　称：	户字旁
本　义：	单扇门
例　字：	扇、扉、房

记忆贴士

"户"的甲骨文字形  像一扇门，本义是独扇门，现在常见的意思是家。"扇"由"户"和"羽"（像门扇的样子）组成，意思是门扇，现在的意思是扇子。"扉"由"户"和"非"组成，特指独扇门的门扇。"房"由"户"和"方"（旁边，也作声旁）组成，意思是旁边供妾住的房子，现在泛指所有的房子。

Name: hù zì páng
Original meaning: one-panelled door
Related characters: 扇 (door leaf, fan), 扉 (door leaf of one-panelled door), 房 (house)

Memory tips

户(oracle bone script is) is like an one-panelled door. Now it commonly means family. 扇 consists of 户(door) and 羽(looks like door leaves). It means door leaf. Now it commonly means fan. 扉 consists of 户(door) and 非(indicates pronunciation). It means the door leaf of one-panelled door. 房 consists of 户(door) and 方(side, also indicates pronunciation). It is used to refer to the house for concubines. Now it means house.

	名　称：衣字旁
	本　义：衣服
	例　字：初、袖、裙、补

记忆贴士

　　带"衤"的字意思往往和衣服有关。"初"（小篆字形为初）由"衤"（衣服）和"刀"（剪刀）组成，表示做衣服的第一步是剪裁，本义是起始。"袖"（小篆字形为袖）由"衤"（衣服）和"由"（穿过，也作声旁）组成，意思是衣服中胳膊穿过的位置。"裙"（小篆字形为裙）由"衤"（衣服）和"君"（声旁）组成，小篆字形中"衣"在"君"下面，意思是下装。"补"（繁体字为"補"，小篆字形为補）由"衤"和"卜"（繁体字部件为"甫"，"辅"的省写，意为辅助，也作声旁）组成，意思是缝补衣服。

Name:	yī zì páng
Original meaning:	clothes
Related characters:	初 (at first), 袖 (sleeve), 裙 (lower garment, skirt), 补 (sew)

Memory tips

　　The meanings of characters containing 衤 (clothes) are usually related to clothes. 初(xiaozhuan script is 初) consists of 衤 (clothes) and 刀(scissors). It means that the first step in making clothes is tailoring. Its original meaning is at first. 袖(xiaozhuan script is 袖) consists of 衤 (clothes) and 由 (pass through, also indicates pronunciation). It means sleeve. 裙(xiaozhuan script is 裙) consists of 衤 (clothes) and 君(indicates pronunciation). Xiaozhuan script shows that 衣 is under 君, meaning the lower garment. Now it commonly means skirt. 补(traditional character is 補, and xiaozhuan script is 補) consists of 衤 (clothes) and 卜 (the radical of the traditional character is 甫, meaning to assist and also indicating pronunciation). It means to sew clothes.

	名　称：干字旁
	本　义：武器（干）或主干（干）或劳动（幹）或缺乏水分（乾）
	例　字：肝、竿、秆、赶

记忆贴士

　　"干"有三个来源，分别是"干"（武器或主干）、"幹"（劳动）和"乾"（缺乏水分）。"肝"由"月"（肉，表示器官）和"干"（武器，动怒）组成，中国古人认为肝脏是发怒时容易受到损伤的器官，"肝"的意思是肝脏。"竿"由"竹"（竹子）和"干"（主干）组成，意思是竹子的主干。"秆"由"禾"（庄稼）和"干"（主干）组成，意思是庄稼的主茎。"赶"由"走"（跑）和"干"（武器）组成，意思是拿武器追赶、驱逐。

Name: gān zì páng
Original meaning: weapon (干) or trunk (干) or work (幹) or dry (乾)
Related characters: 肝 (liver), 竿 (bamboo pole), 秆 (crop stalk), 赶 (drive away)

Memory tips

干 has three sources, namely 干(weapon or trunk), 幹(work) and 乾(dry). 肝 consists of 月 (flesh) and 干(weapon, angry). Ancient Chinese believed that the liver is an organ that can be easily harmed when one is angry, so 肝 means liver. 竿 consists of ⺮(bamboo) and 干(trunk). It means bamboo pole. 秆 consists of 禾(crops) and 干(trunk). It means crop stalk. 赶 consists of 走 (run) and 干(weapon). It means to use weapon to chase or dispel.

名　称：鸟字旁
本　义：鸟
例　字：鸡、鸭、鹅

记忆贴士

"鸟"的甲骨文字形 像一只鸟，繁体字为"鳥"，带"鸟"的字意思往往和禽类有关。"鸡"（繁字体为"鷄"）由"又"（繁体字部件写作"奚"，作声旁）和"鸟"（禽类）组成，指一种能打鸣（公鸡）或生蛋（母鸡）的家禽。"鸭"由"甲"（声旁）和"鸟"（禽类）组成，通常指一种扁嘴短腿善游泳的家禽。"鹅"由"我"（声旁）和"鸟"（禽类）组成，指一种长颈、头部有肉质凸起、善游泳的家禽。

Name: niǎo zì páng
Original meaning: bird
Related characters: 鸡 (chicken), 鸭 (duck), 鹅 (goose)

Memory tips

鸟(oracle bone script is , and traditional character is 鳥) is like a bird, meaning bird. The meanings of characters containing 鸟 are usually related to bird. 鸡(traditional character is 鷄) consists of 又(the radical of the traditional character is 奚, indicating pronunciation) and 鸟(bird), meaning rooster or hen. 鸭 consists of 甲(indicates pronunciation) and 鸟(bird), meaning duck. 鹅 consists of 我 (indicates pronunciation) and 鸟(bird), meaning goose.

矢 矢	名 称：矢字旁
	本 义：箭
	例 字：知、短、矫

记忆贴士

"矢"的甲骨文字形像箭，本义是箭。"知"由"矢"（箭，像箭一样快）和"口"（说话）组成，表示知道的事物可以脱口而出，意思是知道、知识。"短"由"矢"（箭）和"豆"（声旁）组成，箭相对于弓来说不长，"短"的意思是长度小。"矫"由"矢"和"乔"（高，直）组成，意思是把箭弄直，现在的意思是矫正。

Name: shǐ zì páng

Original meaning: arrow

Related characters: 知 (know), 短 (short), 矫 (set right)

Memory tips

矢(oracle bone script is ↑) is like an arrow, meaning arrow. 知 consists of 矢(arrow, as fast as arrow) and 口(speak). It indicates that things that are known can be said quickly. It means to know and knowledge. 短 consists of 矢(arrow) and 豆(indicates pronunciation). The arrow is not long compared to the bow, so 短 means short. 矫 consists of 矢(arrow) and 乔(tall, straight). It originally means to straighten the arrow and now commonly means to set right.

饣	名 称：食字旁
	本 义：食物
	例 字：饭、饱、饥、饿

记忆贴士

带"饣"的字意思往往和食物有关。"饭"由"饣"（食物）和"反"（用手，小篆字形为⺈）组成，本义是吃饭，现在的意思是餐饭。"饱"由"饣"（食物）和"包"（肚子像孕妇，小篆字形为⺈，也作声旁）组成，意思是吃足。"饥"由"饣"（食物）和"几"（饭桌，小篆字形为⺈，也作声旁）组成，意思是到吃饭时候，肚子空了。"饿"由"饣"（食物）和"我"（人难受时发出的声音，也作声旁）组成，指很长时间没吃饭，发出难受的声音。"饿"的意思是肚子空，想吃东西。

Name: shí zì páng

Original meaning: food

Related characters: 饭 (meal), 饱 (full), 饥 (hungry), 饿 (hungry)

Memory tips

The meanings of characters containing 饣 are usually related to food. 饭 consists of 饣(food) and 反(use hand). It originally means to eat meal. Now it commonly means meal. 饱 consists of 饣(food) and 包(xiaozhuan script is ⟨img⟩, indicating that a person with a full stomach looks like a pregnant woman and also indicating pronunciation), meaning full. 饥 consists of 饣(food) and 几(dinner table, also indicates pronunciation). It means to feel hungry when it's time to eat. 饿 consists of 饣(food) and 我(indicates the sound made by people when feeling uncomfortable, and also indicates pronunciation). It indicates that a person hasn't eaten for a long time and makes uncomfortable sounds, meaning hungry.

名 称:	见字旁
本 义:	看到
例 字:	视、观、觅

记忆贴士

"见"的甲骨文字形 像一个有着大眼睛的人，本义是睁着眼睛看到。"视"由"礻"（启示）和"见"（看到）组成，表示祭祀时仔细查看神的启示。"观"的繁体字为"觀"（金文字形为 ），由"雚"（长着大眼睛的鸟，金文字形为 ）和"见"（看到）组成，表示仔细地看。"觅"由"爫"（用手摸索）和"见"（看到）组成，本义是寻找。

Name: jiàn zì páng
Original meaning: see
Related characters: 视 (look), 观 (observe), 觅 (look for)

Memory tips

见(oracle bone script is ⟨img⟩) is like a person with big eyes. It means to see. 视 consists of 礻(revelation) and 见(see). It means to look at heaven's revelation carefully during the sacrifice. Now it means to look. The traditional character of 观 is 觀. It consists of 雚(bronze inscription is ⟨img⟩, meaning bird with big eyes) and 见(see), meaning to observe. 觅 consists of 爫(grope with hands) and 见(see), meaning to look for.

弓	**名 称**：弓字旁
	本 义：射箭或发射弹丸的器械
	例 字：张、弦、引

记忆贴士

"弓"的甲骨文字形〔像一把弓,本义是射箭或发射弹丸的器械。"张"由"弓"和"长"(距离大)组成,本义是拉开弓。"弦"由"弓"和"玄"(丝线状物)组成,本义是绷在弓的两端用于射箭的牛筋。"引"由"弓"和"丨"(箭)组成,本义是拉开弓准备射箭,引申出带领的意思。

Name: gōng zì páng
Original meaning: bow
Related characters: 张 (pull the bow, open), 弦 (string), 引 (draw, lead)

Memory tips

弓(oracle bone script is 〔) is like a bow, meaning bow. 张 consists of 弓 and 长(long). It originally means to pull the bow. 弦 consists of 弓 and 玄(object like silk thread, string). It means bowstring. 引 consists of 弓 and 丨 (arrow). Its original meaning is to draw back the bowstring to prepare for shooting and extended to mean to lead.

弓	弓	弓																	

Part Two

500个常用汉字
500 Characters

第一节

昍 → 的 → 的
小篆　隶书　楷体

拼音：de；dí；dì　　**部件**：白、勺　　**部首**：白　　**结构**：左右
六书：形声　　　　**笔画**：8画　　　**本义**：明亮 bright
词语：①我的（de）mine　②的（dí）确 really　③目的（dì）goal
句子：①这本书是我的。This book is mine.
　　　　②他的确没有说谎。He really didn't lie.
　　　　③他不达目的不罢休。He won't stop until gets his goal.

记忆贴士

"的"（小篆字形为昍）由"白"（原本是"日"）和"勺"（声旁）组成，本义是明亮，引申为真实以及靶心等含义，现在常用作助词。

的(xiaozhuan script is 昍) consists of 白(original form is 日, meaning sun) and 勺(indicates pronunciation). Its original meaning is bright and extended to mean really, target and so on. It is now commonly used as an auxiliary word.

一 → 一 → 一 → 一
甲骨文　小篆　隶书　楷体

拼音：yī　　　**部件**：一　　　**部首**：一　　　**结构**：独体
六书：指事　　**笔画**：1画　　**本义**：最小的正整数 one
词语：①一个 one; a/an　②一直 always　③一起 together
句子：①这是一个故事。This is a story.
　　　　②他一直很忙。He is always very busy.
　　　　③我们一起去上课。We go to class together.

记忆贴士

"一"的甲骨文字形为一，只有一横，表示最小的正整数。

一(oracle bone script is 一) consists of only one horizontal stroke, meaning one.

 是 → 是 → 是 → 是

金文大篆　小篆　隶书　楷体

拼音：shì　　**部件**：日、疋　　**部首**：日　　**结构**：上下

六书：会意　　**笔画**：9画　　**本义**：正straight

词语：①于是therefore　②但是but　③总是always

句子：①雨太大了，于是裁判结束了比赛。The rain was too hard, therefore the referee ended the match.

②他数学很好，但是英语很差。He is good at math, but not good at English.

③他总是在抱怨。He is always complaining.

记忆贴士

"是"（小篆字形为是）由"日"和"疋"（正）组成，本义是正，即不偏斜，指太阳处于正中的位置，引申为对，正确。"是"现在常用作表示肯定判断的关系词。

是 consists of 日 and 疋(straight), and it refers to the position of the sun at high noon. Its original meaning is straight and extended to mean right or correct. Now 是 is commonly used as be.

 → → → 不 → 不

甲骨文　金文大篆　小篆　隶书　楷体

拼音：bù　　**部件**：不　　**部首**：一　　**结构**：独体

六书：象形　　**笔画**：4画　　**本义**：花萼calyx

词语：①不便inconvenience　②不安uneasy　③不必don't

句子：①多有不便，敬请谅解。We apologize for the inconvenience.

②他们为此感到不安。They felt uneasy for this.

③不必客气。Don't mention it.

记忆贴士

甲骨文字形像花萼，现在常用作否定副词。

不(oracle bone script is) is like calyx. Now it is usually used as a negative adverb.

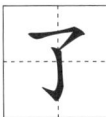 孑 → 了 → 了

小篆　隶书　楷体

拼音：liǎo；le　　**部件**：了　　**部首**：乛　　**结构**：独体

六书：象形　　**笔画**：2画　　**本义**：裹住了双臂的婴儿 wrapped baby

词语：①了（liǎo）解 know　②没完没了（liǎo）endlessly　③好了（le）it's done

句子：①你应该了解你客户的需求。You should know what your customer's wants.

②他没完没了地讲话。He spoke endlessly.

③好了。It's done.

记忆贴士

"了"的小篆字形孑像被裹住了双臂的婴儿，本义是婴儿。"了"假借为懂得、明白的意思。"了"还引申出结束的含义，现在也常用作助词。

了 (xiaozhuan script is 孑) is like a wrapped baby. Its original meaning is wrapped baby. It is used to mean to understand and extended to mean to end. Now it is also used as an auxiliary word.

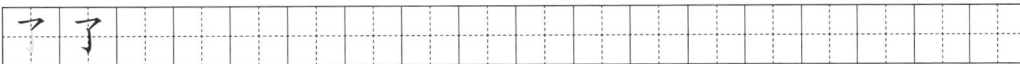

甲骨文　金文大篆　小篆　隶书　楷体

拼音：zài　　**部件**：𠂇、土　　**部首**：土　　**结构**：半包围

六书：形声　　**笔画**：6画

本义：存在 exist

词语：①现在 now　②存在 exist; have　③实在 really

句子：①现在你可以走了。Now you can go.

②这个产品存在质量问题。This product has quality problems.

③天气实在太热了。The weather is really hot.

记忆贴士

"在"的甲骨文字形𠂇像草木从土里长出来，表示草木生长在地上，本义为存在。

在 (oracle bone script is 𠂇) is like the grass growing out of the soil. It means that trees and grass grow on the ground. Its original meaning is to exist.

有

𠂇 → 㝵 → 㝵 → 有 → 有
甲骨文　金文大篆　小篆　　隶书　　楷体

拼音：yǒu　　**部件**：𠂇、月　　**部首**：月　　**结构**：半包围

六书：会意　　**笔画**：6画　　**本义**：拥有 have

词语：①有关 related　②有机 organic　③富有 wealthy

句子：①这是一个和数学有关的问题。This is a question related to math.
②这个商店出售有机食物。This shop sells organic food.
③他出生在一个富有的家庭。He was born in a wealthy family.

记忆贴士

"有"（金文字形为 ）由"𠂇"（手，金文字形为 ）和"月"（肉）组成，表示用手拿着肉，本义是拥有。

有(bronze inscription is) consists of 𠂇(bronze inscription is , meaning hand) and 月(meat). It means to hold meat with hand. Its original meaning is to have.

一 广 ナ 冇 有 有

人

𠆢 → 𠂉 → 尺 → 人 → 人
甲骨文　金文大篆　小篆　　隶书　　楷体

拼音：rén　　**部件**：人　　**部首**：人　　**结构**：独体

六书：象形　　**笔画**：2画　　**本义**：人 human being

词语：①敌人 enemy　②成年人 adult　③中国人 Chinese people

句子：①他是我们的敌人。He is our enemy.
②他现在是成年人了。He is now an adult.
③中国人热爱和平。Chinese people love peace.

记忆贴士

"人"的甲骨文字形 像站立的人形，本义是人。

人(oracle bone script is) looks like a standing person and its original meaning is human being.

人 人

这 → 這 → 这
隶书　楷体（繁体）　楷体（简体）

拼音：zhè　　**部件**：辶、文　　**部首**：辶　　**结构**：半包围
六书：会意　　**笔画**：7画　　**本义**：迎接 welcome
词语：①这个 this　②这些 these　③这边 this way
句子：①这个字怎么读？How to read this character?
　　　　②这些都是你的。These are all yours.
　　　　③请这边走。This way, please!

记忆贴士

"这"（繁体字为"這"）由"辶"（走路）和"文"（说话，繁体字部件为"言"）组成，表示一边走路一边说话，本义是迎接。"这"现在用作指示代词。

这(traditional character is 這) consists of 辶(walk) and 文(the radical of the traditional character is 言, meaning to speak). It indicates to speak while walking and the original meaning is to welcome. Now it is used as a demonstrative pronoun.

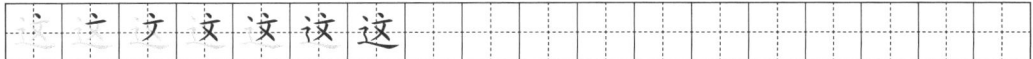

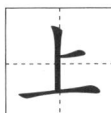
→ 二 → 上 → 上 → 上
甲骨文　金文大篆　小篆　隶书　楷体

拼音：shàng　　**部件**：上　　**部首**：一　　**结构**：独体
六书：指事　　**笔画**：3画　　**本义**：上面 upper
词语：①上午 morning　②上班 go to work　③晚上 night
句子：①我今天上午没有课。I have no class this morning.
　　　　②他去上班了。He went to work.
　　　　③你晚上有时间吗？Do you have time in the evening?

记忆贴士

"上"的甲骨文字形表示在某位置上方，本义是上面。

上 (oracle bone script is) means above a certain location. Its original meaning is upper.

第二节

甲骨文 金文大篆 小篆 隶书 楷体

拼音：dà　　　　　　**部件**：大　　　　　**部首**：大　　　　　**结构**：独体
六书：象形　　　　　**笔画**：3画　　　　　**本义**：成年人adult
词语：①大的the big one　②大学university　③大小size
句子：①我要大的。I want the big one.
　　　　②他在大学教书。He teaches in a university.
　　　　③这个大小合适。This size is suitable.

记忆贴士

"大"的甲骨文字形 ↑ 像一个张开双臂和双腿的人，本义是成年人，引申出和"小"相反的含义。

大(oracle bone script is ↑) looks like a person with arms and legs spread. Its original meaning is adult and extended to mean big.

甲骨文　金文大篆　小篆　隶书　楷体(繁体)　楷体(简体)

音：lái　　　　　　**部件**：来　　　　　**部首**：一　　　　　**结构**：独体
六书：象形　　　　　**笔画**：7画　　　　　**本义**：小麦wheat
词语：①过来come over　②回来be back　③将来in the future
句子：①请过来。Please come over.
　　　　②我回来了。I am back.
　　　　③将来我们要在这里建一所学校。We are going to build a school in this area in the future.

记忆贴士

"来"的甲骨文字形 像小麦，本义是小麦，小麦是外来物种，引申出过来的意思。

来(oracle bone script is) is like wheat. Its original meaning is wheat. Wheat is an introduced plant and 来 is extended to mean to come over.

第二部分 500个常用汉字

金文大篆 → **小篆** → **隶书** → **楷体**

拼音：hé　　**部件**：禾、口　　**部首**：禾　　**结构**：左右
六书：形声　　**笔画**：8画　　**本义**：声音协调 harmonious
词语：①和谐 harmonious　②和平 peace　③和睦 harmony
句子：①我们的目标是建设和谐社会。Our goal is to construct a harmonious society.
　　　　②他们将讨论一项和平协议。They will discuss a peace agreement.
　　　　③家庭和睦很重要。Family harmony is very important.

记忆贴士

　　"和"（金文字形为 ）由"禾"（芦管乐器）和"口"（吹奏）组成，表示吹奏芦管乐器，本义是声音协调，引申为应和和参与等含义，也用作连词，表示"和……一起"的意思。

　　和 consists of 禾(reed instrument) and 口(blow). It indicates to play the reed instrument and its original meaning is that the musical sound is harmonious. It is extended to mean to respond and participate. It is also used as a conjunction which means "and".

甲骨文 **金文大篆** **小篆** **隶书** **楷体**

拼音：wǒ　　**部件**：我　　**部首**：戈　　**结构**：独体
六书：象形　　**笔画**：7画　　**本义**：一种兵器 a kind of weapon
词语：①我们 we　②自我 myself　③我行我素 have one's own way
句子：①我们是大学生。We are university students.
　　　　②我要重塑自我。I will reinvent myself.
　　　　③他继续我行我素。He continues to have his own way.

记忆贴士

　　"我"的甲骨文字形 像一种兵器，小篆字形 也是像戈一样的兵器。"我"的本义是一种兵器，现在被用作第一人称代词。

　　The oracle bone script of 我 is . It is like a kind of weapon and xiaozhuan script 我 is also like a weapon which is similar to 戈. The original meaning of 我 is a kind of weapon. Now it is used as a first person pronoun.

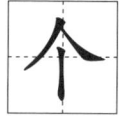 箇 → 個 → 个

隶书　　楷体（繁体）　　楷体（简体）

拼音：gè　　　　**部件**：个　　　　**部首**：人　　　　**结构**：独体
六书：形声　　　**笔画**：3画　　　**本义**：普通量词 common measure word
词语：①一个 one　②个性 character　③个人主义 individualism
句子：①这是一个安静的村庄。This is a quiet village.
　　　　②他的个性很倔强。He is man of an unbending character.
　　　　③他反对个人主义。He opposes individualism.

记忆贴士

"个"由"人"和"丨"组成，作为一个普通量词来使用。

个 consists of 人(person) and 丨. It is used as a common measure word.

甲骨文　金文大篆　小篆　　隶书　　楷体

拼音：zhōng；zhòng　**部件**：中　　**部首**：丨　　**结构**：独体
六书：指事　　　　　　**笔画**：4画　　**本义**：中间 middle
词语：①中（zhōng）国 China　②中（zhōng）间 middle
　　　　③中（zhòng）奖 win a prize
句子：①我爱中国。I love China.
　　　　②院子中间有一个喷泉。There is fountain in the center of the yard.
　　　　③我中奖了。I won a prize.

记忆贴士

"中"的甲骨文字形中间的一竖代表旗杆，表示旗帜立于中央，"中"的本义是中间。

中(oracle bone script is) is like a flag standing at the center of a place. Its original meaning is middle.

坤 → 地 → 地

小篆　　隶书　　楷体

拼音：dì；de　　**部件**：土、也　　**部首**：土　　**结构**：左右

六书：形声　　**笔画**：6画　　**本义**：大地 land

词语：①土地（dì）land　②地（dì）理 geography　③地（dì）方 place

句子：①所有土地都归国王所有。All the land belongs to the king.

②他最喜欢地理。He likes geography most.

③这是一个有趣的地方。This is a fun place.

记忆贴士

"地"（小篆字形为坤）由"土"（土地）和"也"（蛇，小篆字形为）组成，表示蛇在地面上爬行，本义是大地。"地"除了表示和"土地"有关的名词外，还可放在副词或副词短语后用作助词，读音为de。

地(xiaozhuan script is 坤) consists of 土(soil) and 也(xiaozhuan script is , meaning snake). It indicates that the snake crawls on the ground. The original meaning of 地 is land. Besides, 地 can also be used as an auxiliary word which is put after the adverb or the adverbial phrase. The pronunciation of auxiliang word 地 is neutral tone.

→ 爲 → 爲 → 为

甲骨文　　隶书　　楷体（繁体）　楷体（简体）

拼音：wèi；wéi　　**部件**：为　　**部首**：丶　　**结构**：独体

六书：会意　　**笔画**：4画　　**本义**：牵大象劳作 lead elephant to work in the field

词语：①因为（wèi）because　②以为（wéi）think　③行为（wéi）behavior

句子：①因为下雨，我们没有去公园。Because of the rain, we didn't go to the park.

②我以为你走了。I thought you were gone.

③他的行为是不理智的。His behavior is irrational.

记忆贴士

"为"的甲骨文字形像一只手牵着一头大象，本义是牵大象劳作。简体字"为"由繁体字"爲"的草书楷化而来。

The oracle bone script of 为 is . It is like a hand leading an elephant. Its original meaning is to lead elephant to work in the field. The simplified character 为 is the deformation of the cursive script of 爲.

他	他 → 他
	隶书　楷体

拼音：tā　　　**部件**：亻、也　　　**部首**：亻　　　**结构**：左右
六书：形声　　**笔画**：5画　　　　**本义**：其他 other
词语：①他们 they　②他人 others　③其他 other
句子：①他们是学生。They are students.
　　　　②不要总是抱怨他人。Don't always complain about others.
　　　　③我还需要买其他东西。I need to buy other things.

记忆贴士

"他"由"亻"（人，小篆字形为𠆢）和"也"（蛇，小篆字形为𠃑）组成，蛇跟人不是一类，所以"他"的本义是其他，"他"也作为第三人称代词。

他 consists of 亻(xiaozhuan script is 𠆢, meaning human) and 也(xiaozhuan script is 𠃑, meaning snake). Snake and human are of different species, so 他 originally means other. 他 is also used as a third person pronoun.

丿 亻 仂 佈 他

生	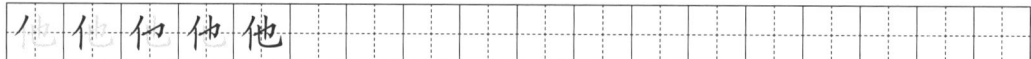 → → → 生 → 生
	甲骨文　金文大篆　小篆　隶书　楷体

拼音：shēng　**部件**：生　　　　**部首**：生　　　**结构**：独体
六书：会意　　**笔画**：5画　　　　**本义**：生长 grow
词语：①学生 student　②生命 life　③生词 new word
句子：①他们是学生。They are students.
　　　　②生命诚可贵。Life is really precious.
　　　　③本课有十个生词。There are ten new words in this lesson.

记忆贴士

"生"的金文字形 下面一横代表土地，上面部分代表初生草木。"生"的本义是生长。

The horizontal stroke at the bottom of 生(bronze inscription is) represents earth. The upper part represents young grass and trees. The original meaning of 生 is to grow.

丿 仁 仨 生 生

第三节

| 小篆 | 隶书 | 楷体 |

拼音：yào；yāo　　**部件**：西、女　　**部首**：西　　**结构**：上下
六书：象形　　**笔画**：9画　　**本义**：腰部waist
词语：①需要（yào）need　②重要（yào）important　③要（yāo）求demand
句子：①我需要一笔钱。I need a sum of money.
　　　　②这件事很重要。This is very important.
　　　　③顾客要求赔偿。The customer demands compensation.

记忆贴士

"要"的小篆字形 像一个人叉腰站立，本义是腰。"要"现在有求取之义，另外还有重要的意思。

The xiaozhuan script of 要 is . It is like a man with arms akimbo and its original meaning is waist. Now it means to ask for and important, etc.

| 隶书 | 楷体（繁体）| 楷体（简体）|

拼音：men　　**部件**：亻、门　　**部首**：亻　　**结构**：左右
六书：形声　　**笔画**：5画
本义：用在名词或代词后表示复数used after a noun or pronoun to indicate a plural
词语：①我们we　②孩子们children　③学生们students
句子：①我们是学生。We are students.
　　　　②孩子们在玩耍。Children are playing.
　　　　③学生们在写作业。Students are doing homework.

记忆贴士

"们"由"亻"（人）和"门"（声旁）组成，用在名词或代词后表示复数。

们 consists of 亻(person) and 门(indicates pronunciation). It is used after a noun or pronoun to indicate a plural.

79

| 甲骨文 | 金文大篆 | 小篆 | 隶书 | 楷体 |

拼音：yǐ　　　　**部件**：厶、人　　　　**部首**：人　　　　**结构**：左右

六书：会意　　　**笔画**：4画　　　　　**本义**：用 use

词语：①所以 so　②以为 think　③可以 can

句子：①雨太大了，裁判终止了比赛。The rain was too heavy, so the referee ended the match.
②我以为你走了。I thought you were gone.
③你可以这么说。You can say so.

记忆贴士

"以"（金文字形为 ）由"厶"（像物之形）和"人"组成，表示人用手提起一物，本义是用。"以"也可以用作介词和连词。

以(bronze inscription is) consists of 厶(something) and 人, meaning that a person uses a hand to lift something. Its original meaning is to use. It can also be used as a preposition or a conjunction.

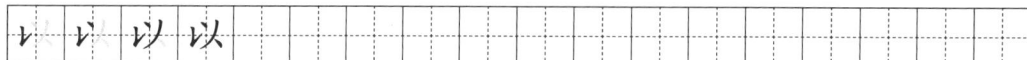

| 小篆 | 隶书 | 楷体 |

拼音：dào　　　　**部件**：至、刂　　　　**部首**：刂　　　　**结构**：左右

六书：形声　　　**笔画**：8画　　　　　**本义**：到达 arrive

词语：①到达 arrive　②迟到 late　③到处 everywhere

句子：①飞机九点到达。The air plane will arrive at 9 o'clock.
②快点，否则你就要迟到了。Hurry up, or you will be late.
③这里到处都是人。There are people everywhere.

记忆贴士

"到"（小篆字形为 ）由"至"（到达，小篆字形为 ）和"刂"（声旁）组成，本义是到达。

到(xiaozhuan script is) consists of 至(xiaozhuan script is , meaning arrive) and 刂 (indicates pronunciation). It originally means to arrive.

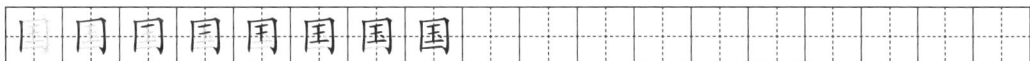
金文大篆　　小篆　　隶书　　楷体（繁体）　楷体（简体）

拼音：guó　　　**部件**：囗、玉　　**部首**：囗　　**结构**：全包围
六书：会意　　　**笔画**：8画　　　**本义**：国家country
词语：①中国China　②国家country　③国际international
句子：①中国有悠久的历史。China has a long history.
②这是一个有希望的国家。This is a hopeful country.
③今天是国际劳动节。Today is International Labor Day.

记忆贴士

"国"由"囗"和"玉"组成，"囗"表示国家的疆域，"玉"是国家财富和权力的象征。"国"的本义是国家。

国 consists of 囗(territory) and 玉(jade, symbol of national wealth and power). It originally means country.

小篆　　隶书　　楷体（繁体）　楷体（简体）

拼音：shí　　　**部件**：日、寸　　**部首**：日　　**结构**：左右
六书：形声　　　**笔画**：7画　　　**本义**：季节season
词语：①时间time　②及时timely　③时尚fashion
句子：①你明天有时间吗？Do you have time tomorrow?
②感谢你及时的帮助！Thank you for your timely help!
③学汉语是一种时尚。It is a fashion to learn Chinese.

记忆贴士

"时"的繁体字是"時"，由"日"（太阳）、"土"（走，本为"止"）和"寸"（手，劳动）组成，表示人们随着太阳的运行规律而劳作，本义是季节，引申出时间等含义。简体字"时"用"寸"取代了"寺"。

The traditional character of 时 is 時. It consists of 日(sun), 土(original form is 止, meaning walk) and 寸(xiaozhuan script is ㄎ, meaning to work with hand). It means that people work according to the rhythm of the sun. Its original meaning is season. Now it commonly means time. 土 is omitted in the simplified character.

 鼽 → 就 → 就
小篆　　隶书　　楷体

拼音：jiù　　**部件**：京、尤　　**部首**：亠　　**结构**：左右
六书：会意　　**笔画**：12画　　**本义**：到高处去住 move to heights
词语：①成就 achievement　②就业 get a job　③将就 make do with
句子：①他的成就让他的父亲很高兴。His achievement gratified his father.
　　　②就业对他来说不是问题。Getting a job is not a problem for him.
　　　③我们得在这里将就几天。We have to make do with the poor living condition for a few days.

记忆贴士

"就"由"京"（高，甲骨文字形为 ）和"尤"（特别）组成，本义是到高处去居住，引申出接近等含义。

就 consists of 京 (oracle bone script is , meaning high) and 尤 (special). Its original meaning is to move to a high place and extended to mean to approach, etc.

 𠈌 → 𠑹 → 屮屮 → 出 → 出
甲骨文　金文大篆　小篆　　隶书　　楷体

拼音：chū　　**部件**：出　　**部首**：凵　　**结构**：独体
六书：会意　　**笔画**：5画　　**本义**：出来 come out
词语：①杰出 outstanding　②出席 attend　③出口 exit
句子：①他是一名杰出的作家。He is an outstanding writer.
　　　②他出席了这次会议。He attended this meeting.
　　　③出口在那边。Exit is over there.

记忆贴士

"出"的甲骨文字形 𠈌 像一只脚从某个空间内出来，本义是出来。

The oracle bone script of 出 is 𠈌. It is like a foot coming out of a place and it originally means to come out.

说

小篆 → 说 → 说 → 说
小篆　　隶书　　楷体（繁体）楷体（简体）

拼音：shuō　　**部件**：讠、兑　　**部首**：讠　　**结构**：左右
六书：形声　　**笔画**：9画　　**本义**：说话speak
词语：①说话talk　②小说novel　③据说reputedly
句子：①不要说话。Don't talk!
②他喜欢读小说。He likes reading novels.
③据说他喜欢咖啡。Reputedly he likes drinking coffee.

记忆贴士

"说"由"讠"（说话）和"兑"（祷告）组成，"兑"的字形像一个人在祷告，"儿"是身体，"口"是嘴，"丷"表示说出来的话。"说"的本义是说话。

说 consists of 讠(speak) and 兑(looks like a person praying, meaning to pray). It originally means to speak. 兑 consists of 丷(abstract image of words), 口(mouth) and 儿(body). It means to pray.

会

 → 會 → 會 → 會 → 会
金文大篆　　小篆　　隶书　　楷体（繁体）楷体（简体）

拼音：huì　　**部件**：人、云　　**部首**：人　　**结构**：上下
六书：会意　　**笔画**：6画　　**本义**：会合get together
词语：①社会society　②机会opportunity　③会议meeting
句子：①这是我们社会的一个主要特点。This is a key feature of our society.
②这是一个绝佳的机会。This is a big opportunity.
③我来这里参加一场学术会议。I'm here for an academic conference.

记忆贴士

"会"由"人"和"云"组成，表示人像云一样聚集，本义是会合，引申出集会等含义。

会 consists of 人(person) and 云(xiaozhuan script is , meaning cloud), meaning that people are gathering like clouds. The original meaning of 会 is to get together and extended to mean to meet, etc.

第四节

 𦧇 → 也 → 也

　　　　小篆　　隶书　　楷体

拼音：yě　　**部件**：也　　**部首**：一　　**结构**：独体

六书：象形　　**笔画**：3画　　**本义**：蛇snake

词语：①也许perhaps　②也就是说in other words; that is to say

句子：①也许你是对的。Perhaps you are right.

　　　　②也就是说，你是对的。In other words, you are right.

记忆贴士

"也"的小篆字形𦧇像蛇，本义是蛇。"也"现在用作副词。

也(xiaozhuan script is 𦧇) is like a snake. Its original meaning is snake. Now it is commonly used as an adverb which means "also."

 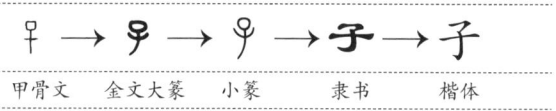 → 子 → 子

甲骨文　金文大篆　小篆　　隶书　　楷体

拼音：zǐ　　**部件**：子　　**部首**：子　　**结构**：独体

六书：象形　　**笔画**：3画　　**本义**：孩子child

词语：①儿子son　②椅子chair　③子弹bullet

句子：①他是你的儿子吗？Is he your son?

　　　　②我想买一把新椅子。I want to buy a new chair.

　　　　③一颗子弹击中了他的腿。A bullet hit him on the leg.

记忆贴士

"子"的甲骨文字形像一个小孩子的样子，有头、胳膊和身体。"子"的本义是孩子。

子(oracle bone script is) is like a child with a head, two arms and a body. It originally means child.

甲骨文　金文大篆　小篆　　隶书　　楷体（繁体）楷体（简体）

拼音：xué　　　　**部件**：⺍、子　　**部首**：子　　**结构**：上下
六书：会意　　　**笔画**：8画　　　　**本义**：学习study
词语：①学习learn　②学生student　③大学university
句子：①学习汉语使我很快乐。Learning Chinese makes me happy.
　　　②他是一个聪明的学生。He is a smart student.
　　　③他毕业于北京大学。He graduated from Peking University.

记忆贴士

"学"的甲骨文字形 ⚹ 由"×"（算筹）和"宀"（房子）组成，繁体字"學"加入了"臼（双手）"和"子（儿童）"表示孩子跟着老师学习，本义是学习。简体字"学"用"⺍"代替了"臼"。

The traditional character of 学 is 學 (oracle bone script is ⚹). It consists of 臼(hands and counting tools), 宀(house) and 子(child). It indicates that the child is following the teacher and its original meaning is to study. 臼 is replaced by ⺍ in simplified character.

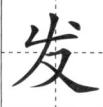

小篆　　隶书　　楷体（繁体）楷体（简体）　小篆　　隶书　　楷体（繁体）楷体（简体）

拼音：fā; fà　　　**部件**：发　　　**部首**：又　　**结构**：独体
六书：会意　　　**笔画**：5画　　　**本义**：1. 放箭shoot an arrow　2. 头发hair
词语：①发（fā）展development　②发（fā）明invent　③头发（fà）hair
句子：①国家非常重视经济的发展。The country pays attention to the economic development.
　　　②纸是在汉代发明的。Paper was invented in the Han dynasty.
　　　③我的头发是黑色的。My hair is black.

记忆贴士

简体字"发"有两个来源，一个是表示放箭的"發"，另一个是表示头发的"髮"。

"發"由"癶"（双脚）、"弓"（弓箭）和"殳"（使用）组成，合起来表示两脚站定，使用弓箭放箭，本义是放箭。

"髮"由"镸"（头，首）、"彡"（头发）和"犮"（翻山越岭，"跋"的省写）组成，意思是人长时间跋山涉水头发长得很长，本义是头发。

现在"發"和"髮"都写作"发"（由"髮"的草书字形楷化而来）。

发 has two sources.

發 consists of 癶(feet), 弓(bow) and 殳(use). It means to stand and shoot. Its original meaning is to shoot an arrow.

髮 consists of 镸(head), 彡(hair) and 犮(omitted form of 跋, means long arduous journey). It means people's hairs become long after a long journey. The original meaning of 髪 is hair.

Now both 發 and 髪 are written as 发(the deformation of the cursive script of 髪).

着 簫 → 著 → 著 → 着
小篆　　隶书　　楷体（繁体）　楷体（简体）

拼音：zhuó；zhe　　**部件**：䒑、目　　**部首**：䒑　　**结构**：半包围
六书：会意　　　　**笔画**：11　　　　**本义**：筷子 chopstick
词语：①着（zhuó）实 really　②穿着（zhuó）dress　③沉着（zhuó）calm
句子：①这让我着实高兴。It makes me feel really good.
　　　　②她独特的穿着引起了轩然大波。Her peculiar dress caused an uproar.
　　　　③他很沉着。He is a calm man.

记忆贴士

"着"的本字是"箸"（小篆字形为 簫），由"竹"（竹子）和"者"（祭品）组成，本义是祭祀时插在祭品上的筷子，引申出穿、接触等意思。"着"现在还用作助词，读音为 zhe。

The original character of 着 is 箸(xiaozhuan script is 簫). It consists of 竹(bamboo) and 者 (sacrifice). The original meaning is chopsticks that are inserted into the sacrificial offerings during the sacrifice. It is extended to mean to wear and touch, etc. Now it is also used as an auxiliary word. The pronunication of auxiliary word 着 is neutral tone.

对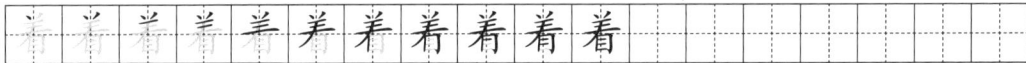
　　　　甲骨文　　金文大篆　　小篆　　隶书　　楷体（繁体）楷体（简体）

拼音：duì　　　　**部件**：又、寸　　**部首**：又　　**结构**：左右
六书：会意　　　**笔画**：5　　　　**本义**：两军对峙 military confrontation
词语：①绝对 definitely　②相对 relatively　③对称 symmetrical
句子：①他绝对不会这样做。He definitely won't do this.
　　　　②这里相对更安全。Here is relatively safer.
　　　　③这幅画的构图是对称的。The composition of the painting is symmetrical.

"对"的繁体字为"對"（甲骨文字形为 ），由"丵"（武器）和"寸"（手）组成，本义是两支军队对峙，引申出向着、正确等含义。简体字用"又"代替"丵"。

The traditional character of 对 is 對(oracle bone script is). It consists of 丵(weapon) and 寸

(hand). The original meaning is military confrontation and extended to mean to face and correct, etc. 丵 is replaced by 又 in simplified character.

拼音：zuò；zuō　　**部件**：亻、乍　　**部首**：亻　　**结构**：左右
六书：会意　　**笔画**：7画　　**本义**：劳作 labour
词语：①工作（zuò）work　②合作（zuò）cooperation
　　　　③自作（zuō）自受 suffer through one's own misdeeds
句子：①他在医院工作。He works in a hospital.
　　　　②谢谢您的合作。Thank you for your cooperation.
　　　　③他自作自受。He suffers through his own misdeeds.

记忆贴士

"作"由"亻"（人）和"乍"（用斧子砍木头，甲骨文字形为）组成，本义是劳作，引申出工作等含义。

作 consists of 亻(person) and 乍(oracle bone script is , meaning to chop the wood with an axe). Its original meaning is to labour and extended to mean to work and so on.

拼音：néng　　**部件**：厶、月、匕、匕　　**部首**：厶　　**结构**：左右
六书：象形　　**笔画**：10画　　**本义**：熊 bear
词语：①能力 ability　②性能 performance　③可能 probable
句子：①我相信他的能力。I trust in his ability.
　　　　②这是一辆高性能跑车。This is a high performance sports car.
　　　　③今天可能有雨。A rain is probable today.

记忆贴士

"能"的金文字形像熊，"能"由"厶"（像熊嘴巴）、"月"（熊肉）和两个"匕"（熊爪）组成，本义是熊。"能"现在表示能力、可能等含义。

能(bronze inscription is) is like a bear. 能 consists of 厶(mouth of bear), 月(flesh of bear) and two 匕(claw). Its original meaning is bear. Now it means ability and possibility, etc.

甲骨文　金文大篆　小篆　　隶书　　楷体

拼音：kě　　　　　**部件**：口、丁　　　**部首**：口　　　　**结构**：半包围
六书：会意　　　　**笔画**：5画　　　　**本义**：在神面前唱歌 sing in front of God
词语：①可以 can　②可爱 cute　③可怜 pitiful
句子：①你可以这么说。You can say so.
　　　　②这是一只可爱的狗。This is a cute dog.
　　　　③他真可怜。He is pitiful.

记忆贴士

"可"的甲骨文字形可由"口"（嘴）和"丁"（供桌）组成，本义是在神面前唱歌，引申出能够、值得等含义。

可 consists of 口(mouth) and 丁(sacrificial table). Its original meaning is to sing in front of God and extended to mean to be able to and worth, etc.

甲骨文　金文大篆　小篆　　隶书　　楷体

拼音：yú　　　　　**部件**：于　　　　**部首**：一　　　　**结构**：独体
六书：象形　　　　**笔画**：3画　　　　**本义**：超过 surpass
词语：①终于 finally　②关于 about　③善于 good at
句子：①我终于战胜了恐高症。I finally conquered the fear of height.
　　　　②这是一个关于狗的故事。This is a story about dog.
　　　　③他善于激励别人。He is good at motivating others.

记忆贴士

"于"的甲骨文字形 ㆑ 像气冲破阻碍，本义为超过，现在用作介词。

于(oracle bone script is ㆑) is like the gas breaking through the obstacle. Its original meaning is to surpass and now it is used as a preposition.

第五节

戌 → 戌 → 戌 → 成 → 成
甲骨文　金文大篆　　小篆　　　隶书　　　楷体

拼音：chéng　　**部件**：𠂉、戈　　**部首**：戈　　**结构**：半包围
六书：会意　　　**笔画**：6画　　　**本义**：完成accomplish
词语：①成功success　②成就achievement　③成绩result
句子：①一定能成功。Success is certain.
　　　　②这是他最伟大的成就。This is his greatest achievement.
　　　　③我希望你能考出好成绩。I hope you can get a good result.

记忆贴士

"成"的甲骨文字形戌由"𠂉"（城邑，和"口"相似）和"戈"（武器）组成，表示完成守城任务，本义为完成。

成(oracle bone script is 戌) consists of 𠂉(city, similar to 口) and 戈(weapon). It means to accomplish the task of guarding the city and its original meaning is to accomplish.

一	厂	厂	成	成	成								

用 → 用 → 用 → 用 → 用
甲骨文　金文大篆　　小篆　　　隶书　　　楷体

拼音：yòng　　**部件**：用　　**部首**：冂　　**结构**：独体
六书：象形　　**笔画**：5画　　**本义**：使用use
词语：①作用effect　②利用use　③信用credit
句子：①它的作用很小。Its effect is insignificant.
　　　　②我们需要在工作中利用新科技。We need to use new technologies in our work.
　　　　③信用体系很重要。Credit system is very important.

记忆贴士

"用"的甲骨文字形用像桶的形状，本义为使用。

用(oracle bone script is 用) is like a bucket. It originally means to use.

丿	冂	月	月	用									

过

甲骨文 → 隶书 → 楷体（繁体） → 楷体（简体）

拼音：guò　　**部件**：辶、寸　　**部首**：辶　　**结构**：半包围

六书：会意　　**笔画**：6画　　　　**本义**：经过 pass

词语：①过分 obsessively　②难过 feel bad　③度过 go through

句子：①他过分关注自己的外表。He has concentrated obsessively on his appearance.
　　　　②我为此感到难过。I feel bad for this.
　　　　③他度过了艰难的一年。He went through a tough year.

记忆贴士

"过"的繁体字为"過"，由"辶"（走路）和"咼"（旋涡）组成，表示从旋涡旁经过，本义是经过。简体字"过"用"寸"代替"咼"。

过 consists of 辶(walk) and 寸(the radical of the traditional character is 咼, meaning vortex). It indicates to bypass the vortex. It originally means to pass. 咼 is replaced by 寸 in simplified character.

一 寸 寸 辻 过 过

动

小篆 → 隶书 → 楷体（繁体） → 楷体（简体）

拼音：dòng　　**部件**：云、力　　**部首**：力　　**结构**：左右

六书：形声　　**笔画**：6画　　　　**本义**：行动 act

词语：①感动 moved　②激动 excited　③轰动 sensation

句子：①他被感动得落泪了。He is moved to tears.
　　　　②我很激动。I am excited.
　　　　③这次演出引起了轰动。This show caused a sensation.

记忆贴士

"动"的繁体字写作"動"，由"重"（负重）和"力"（力气）组成，本义是行动。简体字"动"用"云"代替"重"。

The traditional character of 动 is 動. It consists of 重(bear a heavy burden) and 力(strength). It originally means to act. 重 is replaced by 云 in simplified character.

动 动 动 动 动 动

拼音：zhǔ　　　部件：主　　　部首：丶　　　结构：独体
六书：象形　　　笔画：5画　　　本义：油灯灯芯lampwick
词语：①主要main　②主观subjective　③民主democracy
句子：①这是成功的主要原因。This is the main reason behind the success.
　　　②这是一个相当主观的方法。This is really a very subjective method.
　　　③我们为民主而奋斗。We fight for the democracy.

记忆贴士

"主"的小篆字形像油灯，下面的"王"表示油灯灯体，上面的一点表示灯芯，本义是油灯灯芯。"主"现在的意思是主要和主观等。

主 is like an oil lamp. 王 is like the body of lamp and 丶 is like the lampwick. The original meaning of 主 is lampwick. Now 主 commonly means main and subjective, etc.

拼音：xià　　　部件：下　　　部首：一　　　结构：独体
六书：指事　　　笔画：3画　　　本义：下面below
词语：①下课dismiss the class　②当下present　③下流obscene
句子：①快下课了。The class will be dismissed soon.
　　　②活在当下。Live in the present.
　　　③这是一个下流笑话。This is an obscene joke.

记忆贴士

"下"的甲骨文字形为，上面一弯横表示参照物，下面一点表示下面的意思，"下"的本义是下面。

The oracle bone script of 下 is. The upper stroke represents an object of reference, and the lower point indicates the meaning. Its original meaning is below.

| 甲骨文 | 金文大篆 | 小篆 | 隶书 | 楷体 |

拼音：ér　　　　**部件**：而　　　　**部首**：而　　　　**结构**：独体
六书：象形　　　**笔画**：6画　　　**本义**：胡须whisker
词语：①然而but　②而且and　③因而thus
句子：①然而你知道为什么吗？But do you know why?
　　　　②他长得高而且瘦。He is tall and thin.
　　　　③他起床晚了，因而错过了末班车。He got up late, thus missed the last bus.

记忆贴士

"而"的甲骨文字形为 𦥯，小篆字形为 而，其中一横表示鼻子，中间一竖表示人中，下面四个竖着的笔画，两侧两笔表示两腮的胡子，中间两笔表示嘴下的胡子。"而"的本义是胡须，现在用作连词。

The oracle bone script of 而 is 𦥯. It is like whiskers. The xiaozhuan script is 而. The horizontal represents the nose. The short vertical stroke in the middle represents the philtrum and the four vertical strokes indicate beards. Its original meaning is whisker and now it is used as a conjunction.

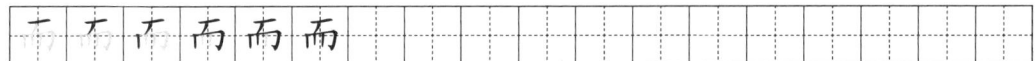

| 甲骨文 | 金文大篆 | 小篆 | 隶书 | 楷体 |

拼音：nián　　　**部件**：年　　　　**部首**：丿　　　　**结构**：独体
六书：形声　　　**笔画**：6画　　　**本义**：谷物成熟ripe
词语：①年轻young　②新年new year　③童年childhood
句子：①年轻人很快地受到新思想的影响。Young people are quickly influenced by new ideas.
　　　　②新年快乐！Happy new year!
　　　　③她有一个快乐的童年。She had a happy childhood.

记忆贴士

"年"的甲骨文字形 𠂤 上面是"禾"，下面是"人"，合起来是人搬运谷物，本义是谷物成熟。"年"现在表示年龄和时间单位等。

The oracle bone script of 年 is 𠂤. It consists of 禾(crop) and 人(person). It means a person moving crops and the original meaning is ripe. Now it means year and age, etc.

丿 → 少 → 分 → 分 → 分
甲骨文　金文大篆　小篆　隶书　楷体

拼音：fēn；fèn　　**部件**：八、刀　　**部首**：八　　**结构**：上下
六书：会意　　**笔画**：4画　　**本义**：切分 segment
词语：①分（fēn）析 analyze　②分（fēn）享 share　③过分（fèn）excessive
句子：①我们应该分析一下失败的原因。We should analyze the causes of our failure.
②我喜欢分享。I like to share.
③她的声音因过分激动而颤抖。Her voice trembles with excessive emotion.

记忆贴士

"分"由"八"（分）和"刀"组成，本义是切分，引申出成分等含义。

分 consists of 八(separate) and 刀(knife). Its original meaning is to segment and extended to mean component, etc.

微 → 得 → 得 → 得 → 得
甲骨文　金文大篆　小篆　隶书　楷体

拼音：dé；de　　**部件**：彳、日、一、寸　　**部首**：彳
结构：左右　　**六书**：会意　　**笔画**：11画　　**本义**：得到 get
词语：①得（dé）到 get　②得（dé）体 proper　③觉得（de）feel
句子：①你是如何得到它的？How did you get it?
②她的举止很得体。She has proper behavior.
③他觉得受到了歧视。He feels discriminated against.

记忆贴士

"得"（金文字形为 ）由"彳"（走路）"旦"（贝壳，原本是"贝"）"寸"（手）组成，表示在行走中有所得，本义是得到。

得(bronze inscription is) consists of 彳(walk), 旦(repleaces 贝, meaning shell) and 寸(hand). It indicates to get something while walking. It originally means to get.

第六节

家 → 家 → 家 → 家 → 家
甲骨文　金文大篆　小篆　　隶书　　楷体

拼音：jiā　　　　**部件**：宀、豕　　　**部首**：宀　　　**结构**：上下
六书：会意　　　**笔画**：10画　　　　**本义**：居所home
词语：①家具furniture　②家庭family　③国家country
句子：①我们需要一些家具。We need some furniture.
　　　　②这是一个大家庭。This is a big family.
　　　　③一个国家要想强盛必须团结一致。To be strong, a country must have unity.

记忆贴士

"家"由"宀"（房子）和"豕"（猪）组成，本义是居所。中国人在家中饲养猪有很久远的历史。

家 consists of 宀(house) and 豕(pig). It originally means home. Chinese have a long history of raising pigs at home.

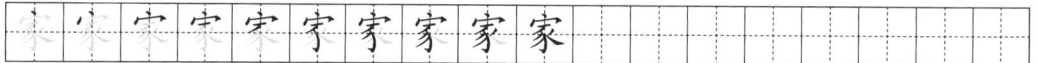

穜 → 種 → 種 → 种
小篆　隶书（繁体）　楷体（繁体）　楷体（简体）

拼音：zhòng；zhǒng　**部件**：禾、中　　**部首**：禾　　**结构**：左右
六书：形声　　　　　**笔画**：9画　　　　**本义**：种植cultivate
词语：①种（zhòng）植grow　②播种（zhǒng）seed　③种（zhǒng）类kind
句子：①我们今年种植水稻。We grow rice this year.
　　　　②现在是播种的季节。Now is the season of seeding.
　　　　③他们有不同种类的啤酒。They have different kinds of beers.

记忆贴士

"种"（繁体字为"種"）由"禾"（庄稼）和"中"（繁体字部件为"重"，意为负重，也作声旁）组成，本义是耕地、培育并收获庄稼，引申出种子、种类和品种等含义。

种(traditional character is 種) consists of 禾(crop) and 中(the radical of the traditional character is 重，meaning to bear a heavy burden，and also indicating pronunciation). Its original meaning is to cultivate and extended to mean seed, kind and variety, etc.

里 → 里 → 里 → 里　　🅘 → 裹 → 裏 → 裏 → 里
金文大篆　小篆　隶书　楷体　　金文大篆　小篆　隶书　楷体(繁体)　楷体(简体)

拼音：lǐ　　部件：里　　部首：里　　结构：独体
六书：会意　　笔画：7画

本义：有农田、房子的居民区 a living area with house and farm

词语：①公里 kilometer　②里面 inside　③哪里 where

句子：①学校离这儿10公里。School is 10 kilometers away from here.
　　　　②冰箱里面有什么？What is inside the refrigerator?
　　　　③他在哪里？Where is he?

> **记忆贴士**
>
> 简体字"里"有两个来源，一个是"里"，另一个是"裏"。
> "里"由"田"（农田）和"土"（房子）组成，本义是有农田、房子的居民区。
> "裏"由"衣"（衣服）和"里"（声旁）组成，本义是衣服的里层，引申出里面的含义。
> 现在"里"和"裏"都写作"里"。
>
> The simplified character 里 has two sources.
>
> 里 consists of 田(farm) and 土(residence). Its original meaning is a living area with house and farm.
>
> 裏 consists of 衣(clothes) and 里(indicates pronunciation). Its original meaning is the inner layer of clothes and extended to mean inside.
>
> Now both 里 and 裏 are written as 里.

丨 口 日 日 甲 里 里

🅐🅐 → 多 → 多 → 多
甲骨文　小篆　隶书　楷体

拼音：duō　　部件：夕　　部首：夕　　结构：上下
六书：会意　　笔画：6画　　本义：数量大 many

词语：①多少 how many　②许多 many　③多久 how long

句子：①房子里有多少人？How many people are there in the house?
　　　　②他知道许多故事。He knows many stories.
　　　　③你来中国多久了？How long have you been in China?

> **记忆贴士**
>
> "多"由两个"夕"（肉）组成，本义是数量大。
> 多 consists of two 夕(meat). It originally means many.

丿 夕 夕 多 多 多

經 → 經 → 經 → 經 → 经
金文大篆　　小篆　　　隶书　　楷体（繁体）楷体（简体）

拼音：jīng　　**部件**：纟、圣　　**部首**：纟　　**结构**：左右
六书：形声　　**笔画**：8画　　**本义**：织物的纵线 vertical line of fabric
词语：①经济 economy　②经验 experience　③经常 often
句子：①经济将要很快复苏。The economy will revive soon.
　　　　②我们没有任何管理经验。We have no experience of administration.
　　　　③我经常看故事书。I often read story books.

记忆贴士

"经"（繁体字为"經"）由"纟"（丝线）和"圣"（织布机，繁体字部件为"巠"）组成，本义是织物的纵线，引申出通过和持久不变等含义。

经(traditional character is 經) consists of 纟(silk) and 圣 (the radical of the traditional character is 巠, meaning loom). Its original meaning is the vertical line of fabric and extended to mean through and regular, etc.

| 纟 | 纟 | 纟 | 纪 | 红 | 经 | 经 | 经 | | | | | | |

自 → 自 → 自 → 自 → 自
甲骨文　金文大篆　小篆　　隶书　　楷体

拼音：zì　　**部件**：自　　**部首**：自　　**结构**：独体
六书：象形　　**笔画**：6画　　**本义**：鼻子 nose
词语：①自然 nature　②自由 freedom　③自豪 proud
句子：①自然的力量真大！What a giant impact of the nature!
　　　　②他没有自由。He has no freedom.
　　　　③我为你自豪。I am proud of you!

记忆贴士

"自"的甲骨文字形像鼻子，本义是鼻子。一个人指着自己的鼻子说自己，"自"用来指称自己。

自(oracle bone script is) is like a nose. It originally means nose. A man points at his own nose and talks about himself. 自 is used to refer to oneself.

| 自 | 自 | 自 | 自 | 自 | 自 | | | | | | | | |

现

现 → 现 → 现
隶书　楷体（繁体）楷体（简体）

拼音：xiàn　　**部件**：王、见　　**部首**：王　　**结构**：左右
六书：形声　　**笔画**：8画　　**本义**：出现 appear
词语：①现在now　②现代modern　③实现achieve
句子：①我们现在必须开始。We must begin now.
②他喜欢现代诗歌。He likes modern poetry.
③我将要实现我的目标。I will achieve my goal.

记忆贴士

"现"由"𤣩"（玉石）和"见"（使别人看见）组成，本义是出现，引申出现在的意思。

现 consists of 𤣩(jade) and 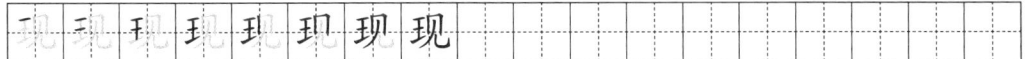见(show). Its original meaning is to appear and extended to mean now.

同

 → 同 → 同 → 同
金文大篆　小篆　隶书　楷体

拼音：tóng　　**部件**：冂、一、口　　**部首**：冂　　**结构**：半包围
六书：会意　　**笔画**：6画　　**本义**：会合 converge
词语：①同意agree　②同情sympathize　③同学classmate
句子：①我同意你的看法。I agree with you.
②我同情他。I sympathize with him.
③他是我大学同学。He is a college classmate of mine.

记忆贴士

"同"的金文字形像一个容器加一个盖子，本义是会合，引申出相同和一起等含义。

同(bronze inscription is) is like a container with a lid. Its original meaning is to converge and extended to mean to be the same as and to be with, etc.

 甲骨文 金文大篆 小篆 隶书 楷体 金文大篆 小篆 隶书 楷体（繁体）楷体（简体）

拼音： hòu　　**部件：** 厂、一、口　　**部首：** 厂　　**结构：** 半包围
六书： 会意　　**笔画：** 6画　　**本义：** 帝王monarch
词语： ①后代descendent　②后悔regret　③后来later
句子： ①他是维多利亚女王的后代。He is a descendent of Queen Victoria's.
　　　　②现在后悔已经来不及了。Now it's too late to regret it.
　　　　③后来我成了一名教师。Later I became a teacher.

记忆贴士

简体字"后"有两个来源，一个是"后"，另一个是"後"。"后"的金文字形像坐着的人，发号施令，表示君主、帝王的意思。"後"（金文字形为 ）由"彳"（走路）、"幺"（绳索，捆绑）和"夂"（脚）组成，本义是因行动迟缓而走在后面，引申出后面和后来等含义。现在"后"和"後"都写作"后"。

The simplified character 后 has two sources. 后(bronze inscription is) is like a seated person making a command. Its original meaning is monarch or emperor. 後(bronze inscription) consists of 彳(walk), 幺(rope, tie up) and 夂(foot). Its original meaning is to walk behind because of the slow pace. Now both 后 and 後 are written as 后.

 金文大篆 小篆 隶书 楷体（繁体）楷体（简体）

拼音： chǎn　　**部件：** 产　　**部首：** 立　　**结构：** 独体
六书： 形声　　**笔画：** 6画　　**本义：** 生育give birth to
词语： ①生产produce　②产品product　③特产specialty
句子： ①现在人们可以生产这种汽车。Now people can produce this kind of car.
　　　　②这种产品要卖到世界各地去。This product will be sold worldwide.
　　　　③龙井茶是杭州特产。Longjing Tea is a specialty of Hangzhou.

记忆贴士

"产"的繁体字"產"由"产"（声旁）和"生"（草木生长）组成，本义是生育，引申出生产和产品等含义。

The traditional character of 产 is 產. It consists of 产(indicates pronunciation) and 生(grass grows). Its original meaning is to give birth to and extended to mean to produce and product, etc. 生 is omitted in the simplified character.

第七节

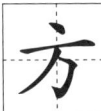

→ 方 → → 方 → 方

甲骨文　金文大篆　小篆　隶书　楷体

拼音：fāng　　**部件**：方　　**部首**：方　　**结构**：独体
六书：指事　　**笔画**：4画　　**本义**：刀的锋芒 knife edge
词语：①地方place　②大方generous　③方便easier
句子：①这不是一个普通的地方。This is not an ordinary place.
　　　②他非常大方。He is very generous.
　　　③纸币比硬币携带方便。Paper money is easier to carry than coins.

记忆贴士

"方"的甲骨文字形由"刀"和"一"（指事符号）组成，本义是刀的锋芒，后来指地方和方向等。

方(oracle bone script is) consists of 刀(knife) and 一(indicative symbol). Its original meaning is knife edge and used to mean place and direction, etc.

→ 工 → 工 → 工 → 工

甲骨文　金文大篆　小篆　隶书　楷体

拼音：gōng　　**部件**：工　　**部首**：工　　**结构**：独体
六书：象形　　**笔画**：3画　　**本义**：工具tool
词语：①工作job　②工人worker　③工具tool
句子：①我刚找到工作。I just found a job.
　　　②他是一个技术熟练的工人。He is a proficient worker.
　　　③这种工具很有用。This kind of tool is very useful.

记忆贴士

"工"的甲骨文字形像一个砸实地面用的工具，本义是工具，引申出工作的意思。

The oracle bone script of 工 is . It is like a tool for tamping the ground. Its original meaning is tool and extended to mean to work.

 彳 → 亍 → 行 → 行 → 行
甲骨文　金文大篆　小篆　隶书　楷体

拼音：xíng；háng　　**部件**：彳、丁　　**部首**：彳　　**结构**：左右
六书：象形　　**笔画**：6画　　**本义**：道路 road
词语：①行（xíng）政 administration　②行（xíng）为 behavior　③银行（háng）bank
句子：①这是行政办公室。This is administration office.
　　　②他的行为很不理智。His behavior is very irrational.
　　　③最近的银行在哪里？Where is the nearest bank?

记忆贴士

"行"的甲骨文字形 彳 像十字路口，本义是道路，引申出行走的意思。

行(oracle bone script is 彳) is like a crossroad. Its original meaning is road and extended to mean to walk.

 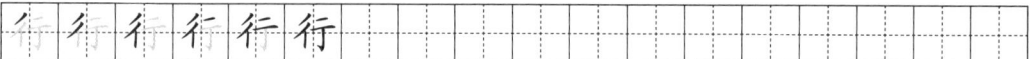
小篆　隶书　楷体　　隶书　楷体（繁体）楷体（简体）

拼音：miàn　　**部件**：面　　**部首**：面　　**结构**：独体
六书：象形　　**笔画**：9画　　**本义**：脸 face
词语：①里面 in; inside　②片面 one-sided　③全面 thoroughly
句子：①杯子里面有很多水。There is much water in the glass.
　　　②这种看法是片面的。This view is one-sided.
　　　③我们必须全面地看这个问题。We must thoroughly examine this issue.

记忆贴士

"面"的甲骨文字形 像人的脸，楷体的"面"由"页（头）"和"目（眼睛）"混合而成。"面"的本义是人的脸，引申出表面和方面等含义。简体字"面"合并了"麵"（面粉）的意思。

The oracle bone script of 面 is . It is like a face. Regular script 面 is a mixture of 页 (head) and 目 (eye). Its original meaning is face and extended to mean surface and aspect, etc. The meanings of simplified character 面 merges the meanings of 麵(flour).

那

那 → 那 → 那
小篆　　隶书　　楷体

拼音：nà　　**部件**：月、阝　　**部首**：阝　　**结构**：左右

六书：形声　　**笔画**：6画

本义：西域国名 the name of a country of the Western Regions

词语：①那里 there　②那个 that　③那么 so

句子：①他会觉得那里更安全。He would feel safer there.

②那个男孩是他弟弟。That boy is his younger brother.

③那么你的意见呢？So what about your opinion?

记忆贴士

"那"的小篆字形 由"月"（胡子，同"冉"）和"阝（邑）"组成，表示有大胡子男子的城邑，本义是西域国名。现在"那"用作指示代词。

那(xiaozhuan script is) consists of 月(beard, same as 冉) and 阝(city). It means the city with bearded men. The original meaning of 那 is the name of a country of the Western Regions. Now 那 is commonly used as a demonstrative pronoun and means "that."

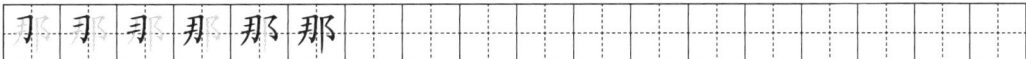

小

小 → 小 → 小 → 小 → 小
甲骨文　金文大篆　小篆　隶书　楷体

拼音：xiǎo　　**部件**：小　　**部首**：小　　**结构**：独体

六书：象形　　**笔画**：3画　　**本义**：细小 tiny

词语：①小气 stingy　②小学 primary school　③小姐 miss

句子：①他很小气。He is stingy.

②他是小学老师。He is primary school teacher.

③很高兴认识你，李小姐。It was nice meeting you, Miss Li.

记忆贴士

"小"的甲骨文字形 像沙砾，本义是细小、微小的意思。

小(oracle bone script is) is like tiny grains of sand. Its original meaning is tiny.

所

肵 → 斦 → 所 → 所
金文大篆　小篆　隶书　楷体

拼音：suǒ　　**部件**：户、斤　　**部首**：户　　**结构**：左右
六书：会意　　**笔画**：8画　　**本义**：守卫门户 guard the house
词语：①所以so　②所有all　③场所place
句子：①我去过那里了，所以我不想再去了。I've been there, so I don't want to go again.
　　　　②他吃了所有的苹果。He ate all the apples.
　　　　③图书馆是公共场所。Library is a public place.

记忆贴士

"所"由"户"（房子的门）和"斤"（斧子）组成，意思是守卫门户，引申为处所的意思。

所 consists of 户(the door of house) and 斤(axe). Its original meaning is to guard the house and extended to mean place.

起

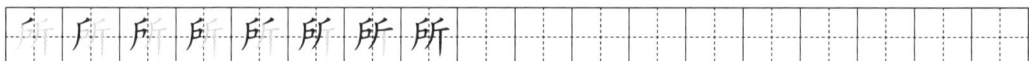 → 起 → 起
小篆　隶书　楷体

拼音：qǐ　　**部件**：走、己　　**部首**：走　　**结构**：半包围
六书：形声　　**笔画**：10画
本义：起立 stand up
词语：①一起together　②兴起rising　③起床get up
句子：①我们一起去学校。We go to school together.
　　　　②房地产业正在兴起 Real estate business is rising.
　　　　③你几点起床？When do you get up?

记忆贴士

"起"由"走"（走路）和"己"（声旁）组成，本义是起立，引申出升起等含义。

起 consists of 走(walk) and 己(indicates pronunciation). Its original meaning is to stand up and extended to mean to rise.

拼音：qù　　　　部件：土、厶　　　部首：土　　　　结构：上下
六书：会意　　　笔画：5画　　　　本义：离开leave
词语：①过去pass　②失去lose　③去年last year
句子：①一小时过去了。One hour passed.
　　　②他失去了所有的财产。He lost all his wealth.
　　　③去年他去了中国。Last year, he went to China.

记忆贴士

"去"的甲骨文字形像人离开坑穴，本义为离开，引申为"往……"。

去(oracle bone script is) is like a person leaving a pit. The original meaning is to leave and extended to mean to go.

拼音：zhī　　　　部件：之　　　　部首：丶　　　　结构：独体
六书：会意　　　笔画：3画　　　　本义：去某地go to a certain place
词语：①总之in a word　②之后after　③之前before
句子：①总之，结果令我满意。In a word, I'm satisfied with the result.
　　　②深思熟虑之后，他决定做这件事。After deliberation he decided to do it.
　　　③离开之前请关灯。Please turn off the light before leaving.

记忆贴士

"之"的甲骨文字形像一只脚在地面上，表示行走的意思，本义是去某地，也可以作为代词指示人或事物。

之(oracle bone script is) is like a foot on the ground. It means to walk. The original meaning is to go to a certain place and it can be used as a demonstrative pronoun.

第八节

都 → 䣇 → 都 → 都
金文大篆　小篆　隶书　楷体

拼音：dū；dōu　　**部件**：者、阝　　**部首**：阝　　**结构**：左右
六书：形声　　**笔画**：10画　　**本义**：建有宗庙的城市 city with the ancestral temple
词语：①首都（dū）capital　②都（dū）市 city　③都（dōu）不 neither
句子：①中国的首都是北京。China's capital is Beijing.
　　　②我喜欢都市生活。I like the life in city.
　　　③我们都不想出去。Neither of us felt like going out.

记忆贴士

"都"（金文字形为 䣇）由"者"（祭祀）和"阝"（城邑）组成，中国周代把有宗庙的城叫做都。"都"现在的意思是都市，也作副词。

都(bronze inscription is 䣇) consists of 者(sacrifice) and 阝(city). In the Zhou dynasty of China, the cities with ancestral temple were called 都. Now 都 commonly means big city and is also used as an adverb which means all.

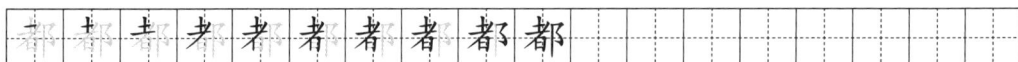

然 → 然 → 然 → 然
金文大篆　小篆　隶书　楷体

拼音：rán　　**部件**：肰、灬　　**部首**：灬　　**结构**：上下
六书：形声　　**笔画**：12画　　**本义**：燃烧 burn
词语：①然后 then　②自然 nature　③既然 now that
句子：①他关了灯，然后上床。He turned off the light, then went to bed.
　　　②艺术家从自然中获得灵感。Artists have drawn their inspiration from nature.
　　　③既然你来了，就住下吧。Now that you are here, you'd better stay.

记忆贴士

"然"由"夕"（肉）"犬"（狗）"灬"（火）组成，本义是燃烧，引申为同意等含义。

然 consists of 夕(meat), 犬(dog) and 灬(fire). The original meaning is to burn and extended to mean to agree, etc.

理 → 理 → 理
小篆　隶书　楷体

拼音：lǐ　　**部件**：王、里　　**部首**：王　　**结构**：左右
六书：形声　　**笔画**：11画　　**本义**：雕琢玉石 cut and polish jade
词语：①理想 ideal　②理解 understanding　③理论 theory
句子：①这跟理想差得很远。This is far from ideal.
　　　②友谊建立在互相理解的基础上。Friendship is based on mutual understanding.
　　　③这是一项新理论。This is a new theory.

记忆贴士

"理"由"王"（玉）和"里"（声旁）组成，意思是雕琢玉石，引申为解决问题。

理 consists of 王(jade) and 里(indicates pronunciation). Its original meaning is to cut and polish jade and extended to mean to solve problem.

進 → 進 → 進 → 進 → 进
金文大篆　小篆　隶书　楷体（繁体）　楷体（简体）

拼音：jìn　　**部件**：辶、井　　**部首**：辶　　**结构**：半包围
六书：会意　　**笔画**：7画　　**本义**：前进 move forward
词语：①前进 move forward　②先进 advanced　③改进 improve
句子：①我们朝首都前进。We move forward the capital.
　　　②这是世界上最先进的技术。This is the most advanced technology in the world.
　　　③我们要不断改进产品质量。We should constantly improve the product quality.

记忆贴士

"进"的繁体字为"進"，由"辶（行走）"和"隹"（鸟，鸟的脚只能前进不能后退）组成，本义是前进。简体字"进"用"井"代替"隹"。

The traditonal character of 进 is 進. It consists of 辶(walk) and 隹(bird, bird's feet can only move forward but not backward). Its original meaning is to move forward. 隹 is replaced by 井 in the simplified character.

体

鬱 → 體 → 體 → 体

金文大篆　小篆　楷体（繁体）楷体（简体）

拼音：tǐ　　**部件**：亻、本　　**部首**：亻　　**结构**：左右

六书：形声　　**笔画**：7画　　**本义**：躯干body

词语：①形声system　②体验try　③身体body

句子：①我们需要改革现行的教育体制。We need to fix the current education system.

②你想体验一下极限运动吗？Would you like to try any extreme sports?

③适当运动对你身体有好处。Proper exercise is good to your body.

记忆贴士

"体"由"亻（人）"和"本（本体）"组成，本义是人的躯干，引申为物体、体裁和体验等含义。

体 consists of 亻(person) and 本(body). Its original meaning is human body and extended to mean object, genre and experience, etc.

丿 亻 仁 什 休 体 体

还

 → 還 → 還 → 還 → 还

金文大篆　小篆　隶书　楷体（繁体）楷体（简体）

拼音：huán; hái　　**部件**：辶、不　　**部首**：辶　　**结构**：半包围

六书：形声　　**笔画**：7画　　**本义**：返回go back

词语：①还（huán）击counter　②归还（huán）return　③还（hái）在still

句子：①我打了他，他马上还击。I hit him and he quickly countered.

②如无法投递，则归还给寄件人。In case of nondelivery, return to the sender.

③他还在工作。He is still working.

记忆贴士

"还"（繁体字为"還"）由"辶"（行走）和"不"（繁体字部件为"睘"）组成，本义是返回。可以通过"不走了，就返回"帮助记忆。

还 consists of 辶(walk) and 不(the radical of the traditional character is 睘). Its original meaning is to go back. We can use the phrase "no more walk, go back" to facilitate memorization.

一 ア 不 不 还 还 还

第二部分　500个常用汉字

金文大篆　小篆　隶书　楷体

拼音：dìng　　**部件**：宀、疋　　**部首**：宀　　**结构**：上下
六书：会意　　**笔画**：8画　　**本义**：安定 steady
词语：①制定 make　②定金 deposit　③镇定 calm
句子：①我们需要制定一个计划。We need to make a plan.
　　　②我需要支付定金吗？Do I need to pay a deposit?
　　　③保持镇定！Remain calm!

记忆贴士

"定"（金文字形为）由"宀"（房子）和"疋"（征伐得胜，凯旋）组成，本义是安定，引申出固定等含义。

定(bronze inscription is ⍰) consists of 宀(house) and 疋(win the war and return home). Its original meaning is steady and extended to mean to fix, etc.

金文大篆　小篆　隶书　楷体（繁体）楷体（简体）

拼音：shí　　**部件**：宀、头　　**部首**：宀　　**结构**：上下
六书：会意　　**笔画**：8画　　**本义**：富足 wealthy
词语：①诚实 honest　②实验 experiment　③实在 really
句子：①他是一个诚实的男孩。He is honest boy.
　　　②实验证明了这个理论。The experiment confirmed the theory.
　　　③今天实在太冷了。It is really cold today.

记忆贴士

"实"的繁体字为"實"，由"宀"（房子）、"毌"（一串）和"贝"（钱）组成，本义是富足，引申为真实。简体字"实"用"头"代替"贯"。

The traditional character of 实 is 實. It consists of 宀(house), 毌(a string) and 贝(money). Its original meaning is wealthy and extended to mean real. 貫 is replaced by 头 in simplified character.

 金文大篆 → 小篆 → 隶书 → 楷体

拼音：rú　　**部件**：女、口　　**部首**：女　　**结构**：左右
六书：会意　　**笔画**：6画　　**本义**：遵从 follow
词语：①如果 if　②如何 how　③比如 such as
句子：①你如果作出承诺，就要做到。If you make a promise, abide by it.
②他不知道如何应付这些困难。He doesn't know how to cope with these difficulties.
③有些是必修课，比如：数学、物理和英语。Some subjects, such as mathematics, physics and English, are compulsory.

记忆贴士

"如"由"女"和"口"（命令）组成，表示女子听从命令，本义是遵从，引申出相似等含义。

如 consists of 女(female) and 口(order). It indicates that a woman following orders. Its original meaning is to follow and extended to mean similar, etc.

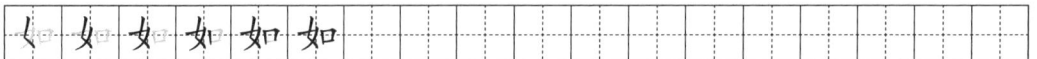

 麽 → 麽 → 么
隶书　　楷体（繁体）　　楷体（简体）

拼音：me　　**部件**：么　　**部首**：丿　　**结构**：独体
六书：形声　　**笔画**：3画　　**本义**：细小 tiny
词语：①什么 what　②怎么 how　③这么 so
句子：①我该对她说些什么？What should I say to her?
②你是怎么得出这个结论的？How did you make this conclution?
③我就是这么认为的。I just think so.

记忆贴士

"么"的繁体字"麽"由"麻"（麻线）和"么"（小）组成，本义是细小。"么"现在普遍用作词尾。

The traditional character of 么 is 麽. It consists of 麻(twine) and 么(small). Its original meaning is tiny. It is now commonly used as a suffix.

第九节

物 → 物 → 物
小篆　隶书　楷体

拼音：wù　　**部件**：牛、勿　　**部首**：牛　　**结构**：左右
六书：形声　　**笔画**：8画　　**本义**：万物object
词语：①礼物present　②物理physics　③事物things
句子：①我送给她一件漂亮的礼物。I gave her a beautiful present.
　　　②他对物理很感兴趣。He is very interested in physics.
　　　③许多新事物正在涌现。Many new things are springing up.

记忆贴士

"物"由"牛"（牛）和"勿"（声旁）组成，牛在先民眼里是重要的财物，"物"的本义是万事万物。

物 consists of 牛(cow) and 勿(indicates pronunciation). Cattle is an important property in the eyes of the ancient Chinese. The original meaning of 物 is object.

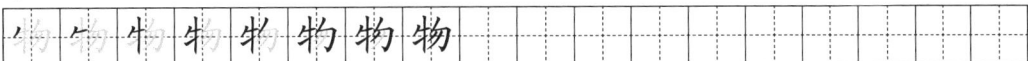

法 → 法
隶书　楷体

拼音：fǎ　　**部件**：氵、去　　**部首**：氵　　**结构**：左右
六书：会意　　**笔画**：8画　　**本义**：法律law
词语：①方法method　②法律law　③法院court
句子：①你试过那个新方法了吗？Have you tried the new method?
　　　②每个人都必须遵守法律。Everyone must abide by the law.
　　　③法院对裁决进行了复审。The court have reviewed the decision.

记忆贴士

"法"的古字是"灋"，"廌"是中国古代传说中的神兽，在审理案件的时候，用角去碰触理亏的人，"灋"的本义是法律。"法"字去掉"廌"，只留下"氵"和"去"两个部件。

The ancient character of 法 is 灋. 廌 means a kind of beast in ancient Chinese myths and legends. When the case is tried, the horn of the beast will touch the person who is inwardly guilty. The original meaning of 灋 is law. 廌 is removed in the simplified character 法.

你

你 → 你
隶书　楷体

拼音：nǐ　　**部件**：亻、尔　　**部首**：亻　　**结构**：左右
六书：形声　　**笔画**：7画　　**本义**：第二人称代词 second person pronoun
词语：①你好 hello　②你们 you　③迷你 mini
句子：①你好！Hello!
　　　　②你们有牛排吗？Do you have steak?
　　　　③她买了一条迷你裙。She bought a mini skirt.

记忆贴士

"你"中的"亻"表示词义和人有关，"尔"在古汉语中作第二人称代词使用。"你"在现代汉语中是第二人称代词。

你 consists of 亻(person) and 尔(you). It is a second person pronoun in modern Chinese.

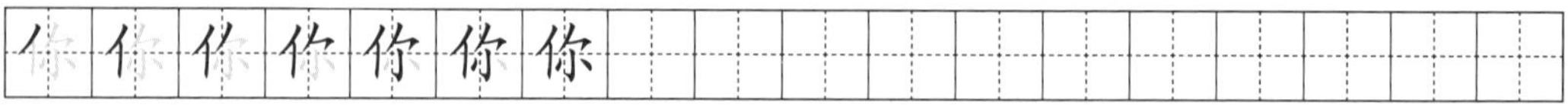

亅 亻 伱 你 你 你 你

好

𡥃 → 𡥃 → 好 → 好
甲骨文　小篆　隶书　楷体

拼音：hǎo；hào　　**部件**：女、子　　**部首**：女　　**结构**：左右
六书：会意　　**笔画**：6画　　**本义**：美好 good
词语：①你好（hǎo）hello　②爱好（hào）hobby　③好（hǎo）像 like
句子：①你好！Hello!
　　　　②你的爱好是什么？What's your hobby?
　　　　③这听起来好像神话故事。It sounds like a myth.

记忆贴士

好（甲骨文字形为 𡥃 ）由"女"（甲骨文字形为 ）和"子"（甲骨文字形为 ）组成，表示女子带着孩子，本义是美好。

好(oracle bone script is 𡥃) consists of 女(oracle bone script is , meaning woman) and 子(oracle bone script is , meaning child). It means that a woman with a child is good. Its original meaning is good.

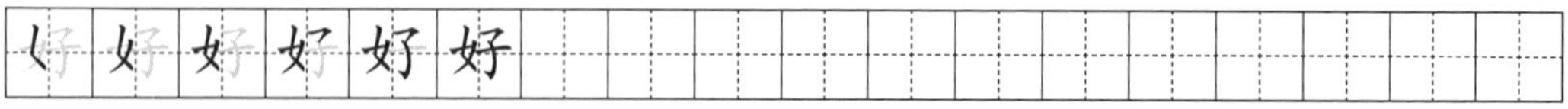

㇄ 女 女 好 好 好

小篆　　　隶书　　　楷体

拼音：xìng　　**部件**：忄、生　　**部首**：忄　　**结构**：左右

六书：形声　　**笔画**：8画　　**本义**：人的本性 human nature

词语：①性别 gender　②个性 character　③性质 nature

句子：①我们反对性别歧视。We object gender discrimination.
②他个性很强。He has a strong character.
③这是一个什么性质的组织？What's the nature of this organization?

记忆贴士

"性"由"忄"（心）和"生"（生长）组成，表示从人的内心生发出来的性质，本义是人的本性，引申出性别、性格等含义。

性 consists of 忄(heart) and 生(grow), meaning nature born out of the heart. Its original meaning is human nature and extended to mean gender and character, etc.

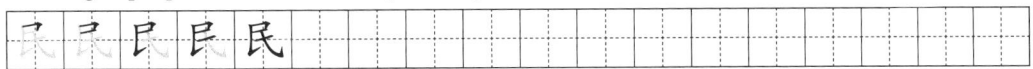

金文大篆　　小篆　　隶书　　楷体

拼音：mín　　**部件**：民　　**部首**：一　　**结构**：独体

六书：指事　　**笔画**：5画　　**本义**：平民 common people

词语：①人民 people　②民族 nation　③农民 farmer

句子：①为人民服务是我们的职责。To serve the people is our duty.
②这是一个感动了全民族的故事。It was a story that touched the nation's heart.
③农民将种植更多的小麦和大米。Farmer are growing more wheat and rice.

记忆贴士

"民"的金文字形像一个睁着大眼睛的人在寻找生存的地方，指为了生计不断奔波的人，本义是平民。

民(bronze inscription is) is like a person with big eyes looking for a place to live in, referring to people who are constantly rushing for their livelihood. The original meaning is civilian.

 从 → 从 → 从
　　　　　甲骨文　　隶书　　楷体

拼音：cóng　　**部件**：人、人　　**部首**：人　　**结构**：左右
六书：会意　　**笔画**：4画　　**本义**：随行follow
词语：①服从obey　②从不never　③从事work on
句子：①士兵必须服从命令。Soldier must obey orders.
　　　　②他从不怕任何事情。He is never afraid of anything.
　　　　③他主要从事新产品研发。He mainly worked on new products.

记忆贴士

"从"的字形是一个"人"跟着另一个"人",表示跟随,本义是随行。"从"也用作介词。

从 consists of two 人(person). It means that a person follows another person. The original meaning is to follow. It is also used as a preposition.

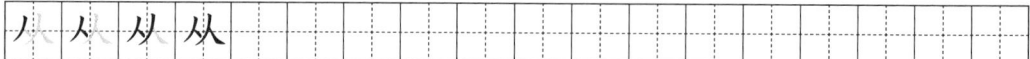

 　→ 天 → 天 → 天 → 天
　　　甲骨文　　金文大篆　　小篆　　隶书　　楷体

拼音：tiān　　**部件**：天　　**部首**：一　　**结构**：独体
六书：指事　　**笔画**：4画　　**本义**：天空sky
词语：①天使angel　②天赋gift, talent　③天真naive
句子：①多可爱的小天使！What a little angel!
　　　　②语言是人类独特的天赋。Language is a unique human gift.
　　　　③你太天真了！You're so naive!

记忆贴士

"天"的甲骨文字形像一个人,上面的"口"表示人头上的天空。"天"的本义是天空,引申为时间单位和上天。

The oracle bone script of 天 is . It is like a person with a square above his head. The square represents the sky above the head. The original meaning of 天 is sky and extended to mean day and heaven, etc.

112

甲骨文 → 金文大篆 → 小篆 → 隶书 → 楷体

拼音：huà　　**部件**：亻、匕　　**部首**：亻　　**结构**：左右
六书：会意　　**笔画**：4画　　**本义**：变化change
词语：①文化culture　②变化change　③化石fossil
句子：①他对中国的饮食文化感兴趣。He is interested in the culture of Chinese food.
②过去四十年间，中国变化很大。Chinese changed a lot in the past 40 years.
③石油是一种化石燃料。Petroleum is a kind of fossil fuel.

记忆贴士

"化"的甲骨文字形像一正一反两个人，本义是变化。

The oracle bone script of 化 is . It is like two people——one is normal and the other opposite. The original meaning of 化 is to change.

小篆 → 隶书 → 楷体

拼音：děng　　**部件**：⺮、寺　　**部首**：⺮　　**结构**：上下
六书：形声　　**笔画**：12画　　**本义**：整齐的竹简orderly bamboo slips
词语：①等待wait　②平等equality　③稍等wait a minute
句子：①我认为等待是明智之举。I think it advisable to wait.
②我们按照平等互利的原则进行贸易。Our trade is conducted on the basis of equality.
③请稍等！Wait a minute, please!

记忆贴士

"等"由"⺮"（竹简）和"寺"（古代官署，也是存放许多简册的地方）组成，本义是整齐的竹简，引申出等级和等待等含义。

等 consists of ⺮(bamboo slips) and 寺(government bureau in ancient China, and also a place where many bamboo slips are stored). Its original meaning is orderly bamboo slips and extended to mean rank and to wait, etc.

第十节

甲骨文　金文大篆　小篆　隶书　楷体

拼音：lì　　**部件**：力　　**部首**：力　　**结构**：独体
六书：象形　　**笔画**：2画　　**本义**：力气 strength
词语：①能力ability　②权力power　③智力intelligence
句子：①我们相信自己的能力。We believe in our own ability.
　　　②在民主政体中，权力必须分散。In a democracy, power must be divided.
　　　③他很聪明。He is of high intelligence.

记忆贴士

"力"的甲骨文字形 ♪ 像翻地的农具。在田里劳动需要花费力气，因此"力"的本义是力气。

力(oracle bone script is ♪) is like a farming tool. It takes a lot of effort to work in the field, so 力 originally means strength.

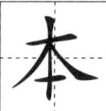

金文大篆　小篆　隶书　楷体

拼音：běn　　**部件**：本　　**部首**：一　　**结构**：独体
六书：指事　　**笔画**：5画　　**本义**：树根 tree root
词语：①根本fundamental　②本能instinct　③标本specimen
句子：①这是矛盾的根本原因。This is the fundamental cause of the contradiction.
　　　②这是人类的本能。This is human instinct.
　　　③这个标本只有一英寸长。The specimen is only an inch long.

记忆贴士

"本"（金文字形为 ）由"木"（树）和"一"（指事符号）组成，本义是树根，引申出根本等含义。

本(bronze inscription is) consists of 木(tree) and 一(indicative symbol). Its original meaning is tree root and extended to mean basic, etc.

 甲骨文　金文大篆　小篆　隶书　楷体（繁体）楷体（简体）

拼音：cháng；zhǎng　　**部件**：长　　**部首**：长　　**结构**：独体

六书：象形　　**笔画**：4画　　**本义**：老人 old person

词语：①特长（cháng）special talent　②擅长（cháng）good at　③长（zhǎng）大 grow up

句子：①你有什么特长？What special talent do you have?
②他擅长鉴别葡萄酒。He's good at judging wines.
③我已经长大了！I have grown up!

记忆贴士

"长"的甲骨文字形像挂着拐杖的长头发老人，本义是老人，引申出老的意思，又引申出距离大的意思。

The oracle bone script of 长 is . It is like a long-haired old person with a walking stick. Its original meaning is old person and extended to mean old. It also commonly means long.

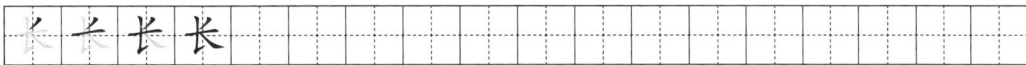

 甲骨文　金文大篆　小篆　隶书　楷体

拼音：xīn　　**部件**：心　　**部首**：心　　**结构**：独体

六书：象形　　**笔画**：4画　　**本义**：心脏 heart

词语：①关心 care about　②心情 mood　③伤心 sad

句子：①我们关心国家的前途。We care about the future of our country.
②他心情很好。He is in a good mood.
③他似乎很伤心。He seemed so sad.

记忆贴士

"心"的甲骨文字形像心脏，本义是心脏。

心(oracle bone script is) is like a heart. Its original meaning is heart.

把

把 → 把 → 把
小篆　　隶书　　楷体

拼音：bǎ　　**部件**：扌、巴　　**部首**：扌　　**结构**：左右
六书：形声　　**笔画**：7画　　**本义**：握住 hold

词语：①把握 seize　②拖把 mop　③把手 handle
句子：①你要把握机会。You have to seize the opportunity.
②我们需要买一把新拖把。We need to buy a new mop.
③他转动门把手去开门。He turned the handle to open the door.

记忆贴士

"把"由"扌"（手）和"巴"（一动不动，也作声旁）组成，本义是握住，引申出把手等含义。

把 consists of 扌 (hand) and 巴 (still, also indicates pronunciation). Its original meaning is to hold and extended to mean handle and so on.

部

部 → 部 → 部
小篆　　隶书　　楷体

拼音：bù　　**部件**：立、口、阝　　**部首**：阝　　**结构**：左右
六书：形声　　**笔画**：10画　　**本义**：古地名 the name of an ancient place

词语：①部分 part　②部队 troops　③全部 all
句子：①这个部分的功能是什么？What's the function of this part?
②部队就要出发了。The troops are about to set out.
③这项工作占去了我的全部时间。This job takes up all of my time.

记忆贴士

"阝"出现在字的右边，表示这个字和城邑有关。"部"的本义是古代的地名，现在指部位和部门等含义。

部 consists of 咅 and 阝(city). Its original meaning is the name of an ancient place. Now it refers to part and unit, etc.

羊 → 羛 → 羛 → 義 → 義 → 义

甲骨文　金文大篆　小篆　隶书（繁体）楷体（繁体）楷体（简体）

拼音：yì　　　　**部件**：义　　　　**部首**：丶　　　　**结构**：独体
六书：会意　　　**笔画**：3画　　　**本义**：正义 justice
词语：①意义 meaning　②义务 obligation　③正义 justice
句子：①这个故事的意义是什么？What's the meaning of this story?
　　　　②这是我的义务。This is my obligation.
　　　　③法官应有正义感。Judges should have a sense of justice.

记忆贴士

　　"义"的繁体字为"義"，由"羊"（祭祀用的牺牲）和"我"（武器）组成，本义是道德、行为等合乎正义，引申出意义的含义。

　　The traditional character of 义 is 義. It consists of 羊(sacrificial sheep) and 我(weapon). It means that morality and behavior are in line with justice. Its original meaning is justice and extended to mean significance.

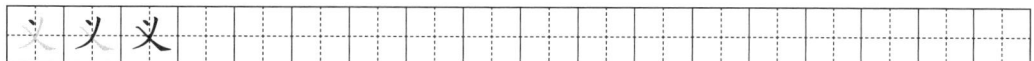

樣 → 樣 → 樣 → 样

小篆　　隶书　　楷体（繁体）楷体（简体）

拼音：yàng　　　**部件**：木、羊　　**部首**：木　　　**结构**：左右
六书：形声　　　**笔画**：10画　　　**本义**：柞木果实 Chinese oak fruit
词语：①榜样 example　②样式 style　③样子 looks
句子：①榜样的力量是无穷的。A fine example has infinite power.
　　　　②你喜欢这种样式吗？Do you like this style?
　　　　③我喜欢它的样子。I like how it looks.

记忆贴士

　　"样"由"木"（树）和"羊"（声旁）组成，本义是柞木果实，后借指样式。

　　样 consists of 木(tree) and 羊(indicates pronunciation). Its original meaning is Chinese oak fruit. 样 is borrowed to mean sample.

事

甲骨文 → 金文大篆 → 小篆 → 隶书 → 楷体

拼音：shì　　**部件**：事　　**部首**：一　　**结构**：独体

六书：会意　　**笔画**：8画　　**本义**：官职 governement post

词语：①故事 story　②从事 be engaged in　③事业 cause

句子：①我们都相信这个故事是真的。We all believe the story to be true.

②他从事科研工作。He is engaged in scientific research.

③这就是我们一直为之奋斗的事业。This is the cause for which we have been struggling.

记忆贴士

"事"的甲骨文字形由"手杖""口""手"组成，表示用手拿着手杖传递口令，本义是官职，引申出事情等含义。

The oracle bone script of 事 is . It consists of walking stick, mouth and hand. It indicates that a person has issued a decree with a cane. The original meaning is government post and extended to mean matter.

看

小篆 → 隶书 → 楷体

拼音：kàn；kān　　**部件**：龷、目　　**部首**：龷　　**结构**：半包围

六书：会意　　**笔画**：9画　　**本义**：远望 look into the distance

词语：①看（kàn）见 see　②好看（kàn）look fine　③看（kān）守 guard

句子：①你看见小王了吗？Did you see Xiaowang?

②这个杯子好看。This cup looks fine.

③他看守着一个仓库。He is guarding a storehouse.

记忆贴士

"看"由"龷"（手）和"目"（眼睛）组成，意思是用手搭在眼睛上方向远处看，本义是远望，引申出使视线接触人或物和看押等含义。

看 consists of 龷(hand) and 目(eye). It means to look into the distance with hand above eyes. Its original meaning is to look into the distance with hand above eyes and extended to mean to look and keep sombody or something under surveillance, etc.

第十一节

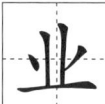 業 → 業 → 業 → 業 → 业
　　　　金文大篆　　小篆　　隶书　　楷体（繁体）楷体（简体）

拼音：yè　　　　**部件**：业　　　　**部首**：业　　　　**结构**：独体
六书：象形　　　**笔画**：5画
本义：古代用来悬挂钟鼓等乐器的板子 board used to hang the instrument in ancient times
词语：①专业 major　②事业 cause　③企业 enterprise
句子：①你的专业是什么？What's your major?
　　　　②他愿意为他们的崇高事业牺牲自己。He would immolate himself for their noble cause.
　　　　③这家企业有极好的前景。The enterprise has excellent prospects.

记忆贴士

"业"的金文字形为，本义是古代用来悬挂钟鼓等乐器的板子。"业"现在表示所从事的工作以及财产等含义。"业"的繁体字为"業"，简体字去掉了下面的部件，只保留"业"。

The original meaning of 业 (bronze inscription is ) is board used to hang instruments in ancient times. 业 now means the work undertaken and property, etc. The traditional character is 業, and the simplified character only retains 业.

丨	丬	业	业	业								

 當 → 當 → 當 → 当
　　　　小篆　　隶书　　楷体（繁体）楷体（简体）

拼音：dāng；dàng　　**部件**：⺌、彐　　**部首**：⺌　　**结构**：上下
六书：形声　　　**笔画**：6画　　**本义**：阻挡 obstruct
词语：①当（dāng）然 of course　②当（dāng）代 contemporary　③上当（dàng）be tricked
句子：①我当然不怕！Of course I'm not afraid!
　　　　②他是中国当代经济学家。He is a contemporary Chinese economist.
　　　　③我们上当了。We are tricked.

记忆贴士

"当"的繁体字为"當"，由"尚"（高）和"田"（田地）组成，意思是田地高出地面，挡住了路。"当"的本义是阻挡，引申出相当和"当……的时候"等含义。简体字"当"根据草书字形将下面的部件写成"彐"。

The traditional character of 当 is 當. It consists of 尚 (high) and 田 (land). It indicates that the field is high and blocks the road. The original meaning of 当 is to obstruct and extended to mean equal and when, etc. The complex lower parts are replaced by 彐 in simplified character.

丨	丷	业	当	当	当							

因 → 因 → 因 → 因 → 因
甲骨文　　金文大篆　　小篆　　隶书　　楷体

拼音： yīn　　**部件：** 囗、大　　**部首：** 囗　　**结构：** 全包围
六书： 会意　　**笔画：** 6画　　**本义：** 垫子mat
词语： ①因为because　②原因reason　③因此thus
句子： ①我喜欢和他一起工作，因为他性情沉着稳重。I like working with him because he's calm and equable.
②延误的原因是多方面的。The reasons for the delay were manifold.
③因此，这样做有三重好处。There are thus triple benefits.

记忆贴士

"因"由"囗"（垫子）和"大"（人）组成，像人坐在垫子上，本义为垫子，引申出依靠和原因等含义。

因 consists of 囗(mat) and 大(person). It looks like a person sitting on a mat. The original meaning is mat and extended to mean to rely on and reason, etc.

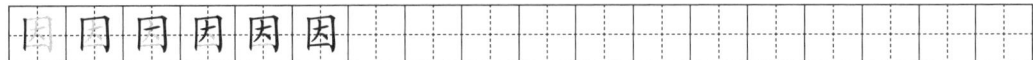

高 → 高 → 高 → 高 → 高
甲骨文　　金文大篆　　小篆　　隶书　　楷体

拼音： gāo　　**部件：** 亠、口、冋　　**部首：** 高　　**结构：** 上下
六书： 象形　　**笔画：** 10画　　**本义：** 由下到上距离远high
词语： ①高兴glad　②高效efficiently　③崇高lofty
句子： ①很高兴认识你！Glad to meet you!
②我可以高效地安排时间。I can organize my time efficiently.
③真正的爱情可以使一个人崇高。True love makes one lofty.

记忆贴士

"高"的金文字形像高楼的形状，本义是由下到上距离远，引申出超过一般标准和声音大等含义。

高(bronze inscription is 高) is like a tall building. Its original meaning is tall and extended to mean above the average and loud, etc.

隶书　　楷体

拼音：shí　　　　**部件**：十　　　　**部首**：十　　　　**结构**：独体

六书：指事　　　　**笔画**：2画　　　　**本义**：数字10 ten

词语：①十分quite　②十足very　③十字路口crossroad

句子：①对此我感到十分痛苦。I felt quite bitter about it.

②他是一个天赋十足的男孩。He is a very gifted boy.

③到第一个十字路口右转。Turn right at the first crossroad.

记忆贴士

"十"的甲骨文字形用"丨"表示"十"，金文在中间多了一点，后来一点变成了"一"。"十"的本义是数字10。

We can use Roman numeral X(ten) to help memorize Chinese characters 十(ten).

一　十

小篆　　　　隶书　　　　楷体（繁体）　楷体（简体）

拼音：kāi　　　　**部件**：一、廾　　　**部首**：一　　　　**结构**：独体

六书：会意　　　　**笔画**：4画　　　　**本义**：开门open the door

词语：①开心happy　②开会meeting　③开门open the door

句子：①我非常开心。I'm very happy.

②全体教师正在开会。The faculties are at a meeting.

③他有礼貌地给我开门。He courteously opened the door for me.

记忆贴士

"开"的繁体字为"開"，由"門"（门）和"开"（用手拉开门闩）组成，本义是开门。"廾"的小篆字形是一双手的形状，"一"表示门闩，"开"的本义是用手开门，引申出打开和驾驶等含义。

The traditional character of 开 is 開. It consists of 門(door) and 开(pull the latch with the hand). The xiaozhuan script of 廾 is , which looks like a pair of hands, and 一 means latch. Its original meaning is to open the door and extended to mean to open and drive, etc.

一　二　开　开

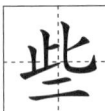 些 → 些 → 些
小篆　　隶书　　楷体

拼音：xiē　　**部件**：止、匕、二　　**部首**：止　　**结构**：上下
六书：会意　　**笔画**：8画　　**本义**：少许some
词语：①这些these　②有些some　③一些some
句子：①这些都是我的私人物品。These are all my personal items.
②有些专家看到了虚拟现实的前景。Some experts see the future in virtual reality.
③他给我了一些建议。He gave me some advice.

记忆贴士

"些"由"此"（踩踏）和"二"（两次）组成，表示不止一个，本义是少许的意思。

些 consists of 此(tread) and 二(twice). It means more than one and the original meaning is some.

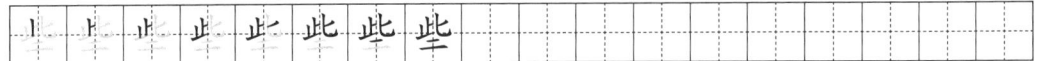

 社 → 社 → 社
小篆　　隶书　　楷体

拼音：shè　　**部件**：礻、土　　**部首**：礻　　**结构**：左右
六书：会意　　**笔画**：7画　　**本义**：土地神God of Land
词语：①社会society　②社区community　③社交social life
句子：①这是我们社会的一个主要特点。This is a key feature of our society.
②这个社区人口稠密。The community is densely populated.
③他忙于社交活动。He has a busy social life.

记忆贴士

"社"由"礻"（启示）和"土"（土地）组成，本义是土地神。"社"现在表示社会等含义。

社 consists of 礻 (revelation) and 土(land). It originally means God of Land. Now it means society and so on.

小篆　隶书　楷体

拼音：qián　　**部件**：丷、一、月、刂　　**部首**：丷　　**结构**：上下
六书：会意　　**笔画**：9画　　**本义**：前进 go forward
词语：①前途 future　②前提 precondition　③以前 before
句子：①我们的前途很光明。Our future is bright.
　　　　②和平是经济发展的前提。Peace is a precondition to economic development.
　　　　③我以前和他联系过。I contacted him before.

记忆贴士

"前"的小篆字形由"止（脚，小篆字形为 ）""舟（船，小篆字形为 ）""人（纤夫，小篆字形为 ）"组成，表示纤夫拉着船前进，本义是前进，引申出以前等含义。

前(xiaozhuan script is) consists of 止(xiaozhuan script is , meaning foot), 舟(xiaozhuan script is , meaning boat) and 人(xiaozhuan script is , meaning boat tracker). It indicates boat tracker pulling the boat. The original meaning is to go forward and extended to mean before and so on.

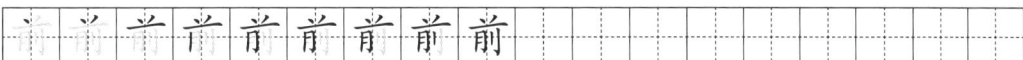

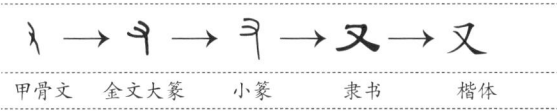

甲骨文　金文大篆　小篆　隶书　楷体

拼音：yòu　　**部件**：又　　**部首**：又　　**结构**：独体
六书：象形　　**笔画**：2画　　**本义**：右手 right hand
词语：①又来 come again　②又高又瘦 tall and thin　③又饥又渴 hungry and thirsty
句子：①他又来了。He came again.
　　　　②他又高又瘦。He is tall and thin.
　　　　③经过一天的行军，我们又饥又渴。After one day's march, we were both hungry and thirsty.

记忆贴士

"又"的甲骨文字形 像右手，本义是右手。现在"又"常用作副词，表示再的意思，或者表示几种情况或性质同时存在。

又(oracle bone script is) is like a right hand. The original meaning is right hand. It is now commonly used as an adverb and it means again or some situations occurring at the same time.

第十二节

 甲骨文 金文大篆 小篆 隶书 楷体

拼音：tā　　**部件**：宀、匕　　**部首**：宀　　**结构**：上下
六书：象形　　**笔画**：5画　　**本义**：蛇snake
词语：它们they
句子：它们的产量有限。They are produced in limited quantities.

记忆贴士

"它"的小篆字形像蛇，本义是蛇。后来"它"用作代词，指人以外的事物。

它(xiaozhuan script is) is like a snake. Its original meaning is snake. Now it is used as a pronoun that refers to things other than people.

甲骨文 金文大篆 小篆 隶书 楷体

拼音：shuǐ　　**部件**：水　　**部首**：水　　**结构**：独体
六书：象形　　**笔画**：4画　　**本义**：化学式是H_2O的液体water
词语：①水平level　②水晶crystal　③潜水diving
句子：①运动员都在同一个水平上。The players are on a level.
　　　②她戴着一串水晶珠子。She was wearing a strand of crystal beads.
　　　③我认为最好玩的就是潜水。I think the most interesting thing is scuba diving.

记忆贴士

"水"的甲骨文字形像水流，本义是一种无色无味无嗅的透明液体，化学式是H_2O。

水(oracle bone script is) is like the water flow. Its original meaning is water.

第二部分 500个常用汉字

其 → 其 → 其 → 其 → 其
甲骨文　金文大篆　小篆　隶书　楷体

拼音：qí　　**部件**：其　　**部首**：八　　**结构**：独体
六书：象形　　**笔画**：8画　　**本义**：簸箕dustpan
词语：①其实actually　②极其extremely　③其次secondly
句子：①我们的观点其实是一样的。Our views are actually the same.
　　　　②这个政策极其不合理。This policy was extremely irrational.
　　　　③其次，我们应该端正自己的态度。Secondly we should have a good attitude.

记忆贴士

"其"的甲骨文字形 其 像簸箕，本义是簸箕。在古汉语中，"其"被假借为代词，表示他、他们等，还可以作为加强语气的助词。

其(oracle bone script is 其) is like a dustpan. The original meaning is dustpan. It is used as a third person pronoun and an auxiliary word to strengthen the tone in ancient Chinese.

没 → 没
隶书　楷体

拼音：méi；mò　　**部件**：氵、殳　　**部首**：氵　　**结构**：左右
六书：会意　　**笔画**：7画　　**本义**：淹没submerge
词语：①沉没（mò）sink　②没（mò）收confiscate　③没（méi）有not have
句子：①一艘货船曾在这里沉没。A cargo ship sank here.
　　　　②他们没收了他的设备。They confiscated his equipments.
　　　　③他在美国没有亲戚。He doesn't have any relatives in America.

记忆贴士

"没"由"氵"（水）、"几"（旋涡）和"又"（手）组成，合起来表示人淹没在水中，本义是淹没，引申出没有等含义。

没 consists of 氵(water), 几(vortex) and 又(hand). It indicates that people are drowning in the water. The original meaning is to submerge and extended to mean no and so on.

小篆 → 隶书 → 楷体

拼音：xiǎng   **部件**：木、目、心   **部首**：心   **结构**：上下
六书：形声   **笔画**：13画   **本义**：想念 miss
词语：①理想 ideal   ②想象 imagine   ③想念 miss
句子：①这和他的理想相差甚远。This is far from his ideal.
②你能想象没有电的生活的吗？ Can you imagine life without electricity?
③我一直在想念你。I've been missing you.

记忆贴士

"想"由"相"（声旁）和"心"（心理活动，想要）组成，本义是想念，引申出思考和想要等含义。

想 consists of 相(indicates pronunciation), and 心(psychological activity, want). Its original meaning is to miss and extended to mean to think and want, etc.

一 十 木 木 相 机 相 相 相 相 想 想 想

小篆 → 隶书 → 楷体

拼音：yì   **部件**：立、日、心   **部首**：心   **结构**：上下
六书：会意   **笔画**：13画   **本义**：心思 idea
词语：①意思 meaning   ②意义 significance   ③意识 awareness
句子：①这个词是什么意思？What's the meaning of this word?
②这件事的意义是什么？What's the significance of it?
③他没有意识到自己的错误。He had no awareness of his mistakes.

记忆贴士

"意"由"音"（声音）和"心"组成，表示心的声音，本义是心思，引申出意思等含义。

意 consists of 音(sound) and 心(heart). It indicates the sound of heart. Its original meaning is idea and extended to mean significance, etc.

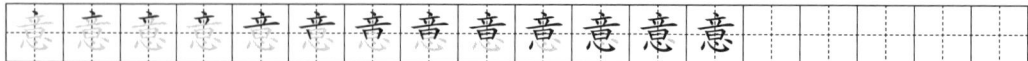

第二部分　500个常用汉字

丨 → 三 → 三 → 三
金文大篆　小篆　隶书　楷体

拼音：sān　　**部件**：一、一、一　　**部首**：一　　**结构**：独体
六书：指事　　**笔画**：3画　　**本义**：数字3 three
词语：①三个three　②第三third　③三角形triangle
句子：①这里有三栋房子。There are three houses.
　　　　②谁是第三名？Who is of the third place?
　　　　③旗子是三角形的。The shape of the flag is triangle.

记忆贴士

三横表示数字3。

三 consists of three 一(one). It originally means three.

 → 隻 → 隻 → 只　　只 → 只 → 只
甲骨文　隶书　繁体（楷体）楷体（简体）　金文大篆　隶书　楷体

拼音：zhī；zhǐ　　**部件**：口、八　　**部首**：口　　**结构**：上下
六书：指事　　**笔画**：5画
本义：古汉语中的语气词 modal particle in ancient Chinese
词语：①一只（zhī）one　②只（zhǐ）好have to　③只（zhǐ）有have only
句子：①我抓住了一只鸟。I captured a bird.
　　　　②我只好退出比赛。I have to quit the competition.
　　　　③我只有这一支笔。I have only this pen.

记忆贴士

简体字"只"有两个来源，一个是"只"，另一个是"隻"。

"只"由"口"（说话）和"八"（发出声音）组成，本义是古汉语中的语气词。

"隻"（甲骨文字形为）由"隹"（短尾鸟）和"又"（手）组成，本义是捕获一只鸟，引申出唯一的意思，也用作量词。

现在"只"和"隻"都写作"只"。

The simplified character 只 has two sources.

只 consists of 口(speak) and 八(voice). Its original meaning is modal particle in ancient Chinese.

隻 consists of 隹(bird) and 又(hand). It indicates to capture a bird. The original meaning is to capture a bird and extended to mean only. It is also used as a measure word.

Now both 只 and 隻 are written as 只.

重	重 → 𢕔 → 重 → 重
	金文大篆　小篆　隶书　楷体

拼音：zhòng；chóng　　**部件**：重　　**部首**：丿　　**结构**：独体
六书：会意　　**笔画**：9画　　**本义**：质量大heavy
词语：①重（zhòng）要important　②尊重（zhòng）respect　③重（chóng）复repeat
句子：①这件事很重要。It's very important.
　　　　②我们应该尊重他国文化。We need to respect foreign culture.
　　　　③他把那个词重复了好几遍。He repeated the word several times.

记忆贴士

"重"由"千"（人）和"里"（行囊和地面）组成，意思是人背着沉重的行囊走路。"重"的本义是质量大，引申出重复和再一次等含义。

重 consists of 千(man) and 里(bag and ground). It indicates that a man walk with a heavy bag. The original meaning is heavy and extended to mean to repeat and again, etc.

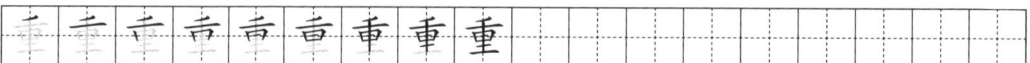

点	點 → 點 → 點 → 点
	小篆　　隶书　　楷体（繁体）　楷体（简体）

拼音：diǎn　　**部件**：占、灬　　**部首**：灬　　**结构**：上下
六书：形声　　**笔画**：9画　　**本义**：小黑点little black dot
词语：①优点merit　②焦点focus　③观点views
句子：①每个人都有优点和缺点。Everyone has merits and demerits.
　　　　②这将是此次报道的焦点。This will be the focus of the report.
　　　　③你应该让所有人知道你的观点。You should make your views known to everyone.

记忆贴士

"点"由"占"（沾染，"沾"的省写）和"灬"（墨水）组成，本义是小黑点，引申为地点和点击等含义。

点 consists of 占(omitted form of 沾, means to be stained with) and 灬(ink). Its original meaning is little black dot and extended to mean spot and to click, etc.

第十三节

鬯 → 與 → 與 → 与

小篆　　隶书　　楷体（繁体）楷体（简体）

拼音：yù；yǔ　　**部件**：与　　**部首**：一　　**结构**：独体
六书：会意　　**笔画**：3画　　**本义**：给予give
词语：①参与（yù）take part in　②与（yǔ）众不同different　③与（yǔ）生俱来innate
句子：①每个成员都可以参与管理。Every member may take part in the management.
　　　②这场表演与众不同。This show was different.
　　　③他有一种与生俱来的幽默感。He has an innate sense of humor.

记忆贴士

"与"（小篆字形为鬯）由"一"和"勺"组成，本义是将某物给予别人。"与"也用作连词。

与(xiaozhuan script is 鬯) consists of 一 and (spoon, 勺). Its original meaning is to give something to others. It is also used as a conjunction.

脾 → 使 → 使

小篆　　隶书　　楷体

拼音：shǐ　　**部件**：亻、吏　　**部首**：亻　　**结构**：左右
六书：形声　　**笔画**：8画　　**本义**：命令 order
词语：①即使even if　②使命mission　③大使ambassador
句子：①即使你不说，我也会知道。Even if you didn't tell me, I would know anyway.
　　　②这是我们的使命。This is our mission.
　　　③他是新任大使。He is the new ambassador.

记忆贴士

"使"由"亻"（与人事有关）和"吏"（使令）组成，本义是命令，引申出使用、致使等含义。

使 consists of 亻(related to people) and 吏(order). Its original meaning is to order and extended to mean to use and make, etc.

| 但 → 但 → 但 |
| 小篆　隶书　楷体 |

拼音：dàn　　**部件**：亻、旦　　**部首**：亻　　**结构**：左右
六书：形声　　**笔画**：7画
本义：脱去上衣，露出身体的一部分 take off the upper clothes and expose the upper body
词语：①但是 but　②不但 not only　③但愿 hope
句子：①电影还没结束，但是我得回去了。The movie is not finished, but I need to go back.
②他不但有才华，而且为人正直。He is not only very talented, but also very upright.
③但愿如此。I hope so.

记忆贴士

"但"由"亻"（人）和"旦"（声旁）组成，本义为脱去上衣，露出身体的一部分，后来本义由"袒"承担。"但"现在常用作连词，表示转折关系。

但 consists of 亻(person) and 旦(indicates pronunciation). It means to take off the upper clothes and expose the upper body. Later the original meaning is assumed by 袒. Now it is used as a conjunction, meaning but.

丿 亻 亻 但 但 但 但

| 庹 → 度 → 度 |
| 小篆　隶书　楷体 |

拼音：dù　　**部件**：广、廿、又　　**部首**：广　　**结构**：半包围
六书：形声　　**笔画**：9画　　**本义**：长度测量标准 linear measure
词语：①温度 temperature　②制度 system　③程度 extent
句子：①今天最高温度35℃。The highest temperature for today is 35 ℃.
②这个制度并不完美。This system is not perfect.
③他们对污染程度所知甚少。They have little information on the extent of the pollution.

记忆贴士

"度"由"庐"（"庶"的省写，声旁）和"又"（手）组成，表示用手臂来帮助计量长度，本义为长度测量标准，引申为程度和度过等含义。

度 consists of 庐(omitted form of 庶, indicates pronunciation) and 又(hand). It means to measure the length with arms. The original meaning is linear measure and extended to mean extent and to spend, etc.

庐 庐 广 庐 庐 庐 度 度 度

由 → 由 → 由
金文大篆　隶书　楷体

拼音：yóu　　**部件：**由　　**部首：**丨　　**结构：**独体
六书：会意　　**笔画：**5画　　**本义：**穿过 pass through
词语：①自由 freedom　②理由 reason　③由于 because of
句子：①我们享有言论自由。We have the freedom of speech.
　　　②他没有缺席的正当理由。He has no valid reason for his absence.
　　　③他们由于生活习惯不同分手了。They broke up because of different life styles.

记忆贴士

"由"的金文字形像一滴水穿过容器孔，本义是穿过，引申出理由等含义。

由(bronze inscription is) is like a drop of water through the opening of a container. Its original meaning is to pass through and extended to mean reason and so on.

→ → 道 → 道
金文大篆　小篆　隶书　楷体

拼音：dào　　**部件：**辶、首　　**部首：**辶　　**结构：**半包围
六书：形声　　**笔画：**12画　　**本义：**道路 road
词语：①道德 moral　②道理 reason　③报道 report
句子：①他们是一群有道德、有文化的人。They are a bunch of moral, educated people.
　　　②道理很简单。The reason is simple.
　　　③这是一篇失实的报道。This is a garbled report.

记忆贴士

"道"由"首"（人的头）和"辶"（走路）组成，本义是道路，引申出道德和说等含义。

道 consists of 首(human head) and 辶(walk). Its original meaning is road and extended to mean morality and to speak, etc.

全

小篆 → 隶书 → 楷体

拼音：quán　　**部件**：人、王　　**部首**：人　　**结构**：上下
六书：会意　　**笔画**：6画　　**本义**：纯色的玉 pure jade
词语：①安全 safety　②完全 entirely　③全面 thorough
句子：①安全第一！Safety first!　②他完全赞同。He agree entirely.
　　　　③他需要做一次全面体检。He needs a thorough physical examination.

记忆贴士

"全"由"人"和"王"（玉）组成，本义是纯色的玉，引申为完整无缺的意思。

全 consists of 人 and 王(jade). Its original meaning is pure jade and extended to mean intact.

制

金文大篆 → 小篆 → 隶书 → 楷体　　小篆 → 隶书 → 楷体（繁体）→ 楷体（简体）

拼音：zhì　　**部件**：、刂　　**部首**：刂　　**结构**：左右
六书：会意　　**笔画**：8画　　**本义**：修剪树木 trim trees
词语：①制裁 sanction　②制止 stop　③制造 make
句子：①美国对这个国家实施了制裁。The United States imposed sanction against this country.
　　　　②我们必须制止他。We must stop him.
　　　　③这个手机是中国制造的。This cell phone is made in China.

记忆贴士

简体字"制"有两个来源，一个是"制"，另一个是"製"。

"制"（小篆字形为 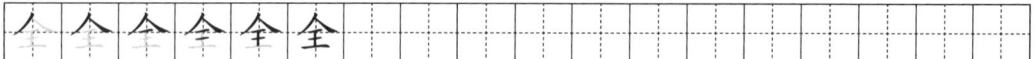）由"朱"（树木）和"刂"组成，本义是修剪树木，引申出限制等含义。

"製"（小篆字形为 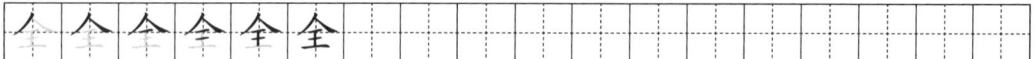）由"制"（裁剪）和"衣"组成，表示裁剪布料，本义是制作衣服，引申出制造等含义。

现在"制"和"製"都写作"制"。

The simplified character 制 has two sources.

制(xiaozhuan scrip is 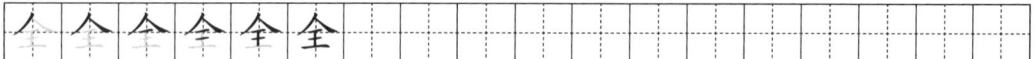) consists of 朱(tree) and 刂(knife). Its original meaning is to trim trees and extended to mean to restrict and so on.

製(xiaozhuan script is 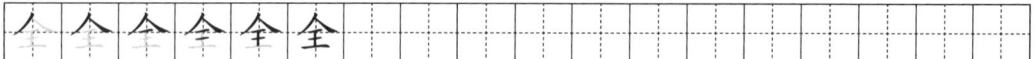) consists of 制(cut) and 衣(cloth). It means to cut fabrics and its original meaning is to make clothes. It is extended to mean to manufacture and so on.

Now both 制 and 製 are written as 制.

| 明 → 明 → 明 → 明 → 明 |
| 甲骨文　金文大篆　小篆　隶书　楷体 |

拼音：míng　　**部件**：日、月　　**部首**：日　　**结构**：左右
六书：会意　　**笔画**：8画　　**本义**：明亮 bright
词语：①聪明 clever　②声明 statement　③明白 see
句子：①这是一只聪明的海豚。It is a clever dolphin.
　　　②他否认了那个声明。He disowned the statement.
　　　③我明白了。I see.

记忆贴士

"明"由"日"（太阳）和"月"（月亮）组成，表示太阳和月亮把空间照亮，本义是明亮，引申出明白等含义。

明 consists of 日(sun) and 月(moon). It means that sunlight or moonlight illuminates the space. Its original meaning is bright and extended to mean to understand and so on.

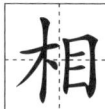

| 相 → 相 → 相 → 相 → 相 |
| 甲骨文　金文大篆　小篆　隶书　楷体 |

拼音：xiàng；xiāng　　**部件**：木、目　　**部首**：木　　**结构**：左右
六书：会意　　**笔画**：9画　　**本义**：看 look
词语：①相貌 facial feature　②相信 believe　③相对 relatively
句子：①他相貌端正。He has regular facial features.
　　　②他相信她。He believes her.
　　　③现在是相对平静的时期。Now it is a relatively calm period.

记忆贴士

"相"（甲骨文字形为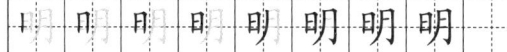）由"木"（树）和"目"（眼睛）组成，表示在树上向远处看，本义是看，引申出相貌和互相等含义。

相(oracle bone script is) consists of 木(tree) and 目(eye). It means to stand in the tree and look into the distance. Its original meaning is to look and extended to mean appearance and mutually, etc.

第十四节

两 → 两
隶书　楷体

拼音：liǎng　　**部件**：两　　**部首**：一　　**结构**：独体

六书：会意　　**笔画**：7画　　**本义**：车辆vehicle

词语：①两次twice　②两栖动物amphibian　③一两50g

句子：①我去年拜访过他两次。I visited him twice last year.

②青蛙是两栖动物。Frog is amphibian.

③一两等于50克。1 liang is equal to 50g.

记忆贴士

"两"的字形像两匹马拉的战车，本义是车辆。"两"现在表示数字2和重量单位等含义。

两 looks like a chariot drawn by two horses. Its original meaning is vehicle. Now it commonly means number two and a weight unit.

情 → 情 → 情

小篆　隶书　楷体

拼音：qíng　　**部件**：忄、青　　**部首**：忄　　**结构**：左右

六书：形声　　**笔画**：11画　　**本义**：喜爱之情affection

词语：①爱情love　②感情feeling　③亲情family affection

句子：①这是一首爱情歌曲。This is a song about love.

②他伤害了她的感情。He hurts her feelings.

③亲情是与生俱来的。Family affection is innate.

记忆贴士

"情"由"忄"（心）和"青"（漂亮，"倩"的省写）组成，表示美好的情绪，本义是喜爱之情，引申出感情等含义。

情 consists of 忄(heart) and 青(omitted form of 倩, means beautiful). It means wonderful emotion. Its original meaning is affection and extended to mean feeling, etc.

外

甲骨大篆 → 小篆 → 隶书 → 楷体

拼音：wài　　**部件**：夕、卜　　**部首**：夕　　**结构**：左右
六书：会意　　**笔画**：5画　　**本义**：外面 outside
词语：①外面 outside　②外语 foreign language　③例外 exception
句子：①外面的温度降到了零度以下。The temperature outside dropped below zero.
　　　　②我可以说多种外语。I can speak many foreign languages.
　　　　③他是个例外。He is an exception.

记忆贴士

"外"由"夕"（月亮）和"卜"（占卜）组成，表示在户外月下占卜，本义为外面。

外 consists of 夕(moon) and 卜(divine). It means to divine outdoors at night. Its original meaning is outside.

丿 ク 夕 夘 外

间

隶书 → 楷体（繁体）→ 楷体（简体）

拼音：jiān；jiàn　　**部件**：门、日　　**部首**：门　　**结构**：半包围
六书：会意　　**笔画**：7画　　**本义**：门缝 a crack between a door and its frame
词语：①空间（jiān）space　②时间（jiān）time　③间（jiàn）接 indirect
句子：①它的储物空间有限。It has limited storage space.
　　　　②我需要更多思考时间。I need more time to think.
　　　　③那是对这一问题的间接回复。That is an indirect answer to the question.

记忆贴士

"间"由"门"和"日"（太阳）组成，表示在门缝中看到日光，本义是门缝，引申为空间等含义。

间 consists of 门(door) and 日(sun). It means to see daylight through the crack of the door. The original meaning of 间 is a crack between a door and its frame and extended to mean space, etc.

丶 丨 门 闩 闫 间 间

二

甲骨文 → 金文大篆 → 小篆 → 隶书 → 楷体

拼音：èr　　**部件**：二　　**部首**：一　　**结构**：独体

六书：指事　　**笔画**：2画　　**本义**：数字2 two

词语：①二进制 binary　②二胡 erhu (an instrument for Chinese traditional music and drama)
　　　　③二等 second-class

句子：①计算机使用二进制。Computer does the calculations on binary.
　　　　②他演奏了二胡。He played the erhu.
　　　　③我要买一张二等座票。I would like to buy a second-class ticket.

记忆贴士

两横表示数字2。

二 consists of two 一，meaning two.

关

關 → 關 → 关

隶书　楷体（繁体）　楷体（简体）

拼音：guān　　**部件**：丷、天　　**部首**：丷　　**结构**：上下

六书：形声　　**笔画**：6画　　**本义**：门闩 bolt

词语：①关门 closed　②关心 be concerned about　③关系 relation

句子：①商店关门了。The shop is closed.
　　　　②每个人都关心自己的前途。Everybody is concerned about their own future.
　　　　③我们必须和中国保持友好关系。We must maintain friendly relations with China.

记忆贴士

"关"的繁体字为"關"，由"門"和"䰜"（用手上门闩）组成，本义是门闩，引申出关闭和关卡等含义。

The traditional character of 关 is 關. It consists of 門(door) and 䰜(latch with hand). The original meaning of 關 is bolt and extended to mean to close and barrier, etc.

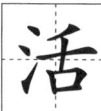 

拼音：huó **部件**：氵、舌 **部首**：氵 **结构**：左右
六书：形声 **笔画**：9画 **本义**：流水声 the sound of water flow
词语：①生活 life ②活泼 lively ③活动 activity
句子：①我喜欢校园生活。I like campus life.
②她性格活泼。She has a lively personality.
③他愿意参加这个活动。He likes to join in this activity.

记忆贴士

"活"由"氵"（水）和"舌"（舌头，表示说话的意思）组成，本义是流水声，引申出活动和生活等含义。

活 consists of 氵(water) and 舌(tongue, indicates to speak). Its original meaning is the sound of water flow and extended to mean to live and life, etc.

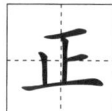 

拼音：zhèng **部件**：正 **部首**：一 **结构**：独体
六书：会意 **笔画**：5画 **本义**：征伐 send troops to a just war
词语：①正直 integrity ②正义 justice ③正方形 square
句子：①他很正直。He has integrity.
②他很有正义感。He has a good sense of justice.
③正方形是一种特殊的四边形。A square is a special quadrilateral.

记忆贴士

"正"（甲骨文字形为 ）由"一"（城邑）和"止"（脚）组成，本义是征伐，引申出正义和不偏斜等含义。

正(oracle bone script is) consists of 一(city) and 止(foot). Its original meaning is to send troops to a just war and extended to mean just and straight, etc.

| 甲骨文 | 金文大篆 | 小篆 | 隶书 | 楷体 |

拼音：hé **部件**：人、一、口 **部首**：人 **结构**：上下

六书：会意 **笔画**：6画 **本义**：闭合 close

词语：①合作 cooperation ②符合 suit ③合算 worthwhile

句子：①感谢您的合作！Thank you for your cooperation!
②这双鞋符合你的要求。This pair of shoes suits your needs.
③买这种表很合算。Buying such a watch is worthwhile.

记忆贴士

"合"的甲骨文字形像一个容器上加一个盖子，表示闭合、合拢的意思，本义为闭合，引申出结合和合适等含义。

合(oracle bone script is) consists of 人(lid) and 口(container). Its original meaning is to close and extended to mean to combine and proper, etc.

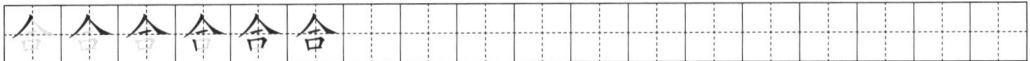

| 金文大篆 | 小篆 | 隶书 | 楷体 |

拼音：zhě **部件**：耂、日 **部首**：耂 **结构**：半包围

六书：形声 **笔画**：8画

本义：众人在火上煮食物并聊天 people cook food on the fire and chat with each other

词语：①或者 or ②学者 scholar ③记者 reporter

句子：①你有信用卡或者借记卡吗？Do you have any credit card or debit card?
②他是一位受人尊重的学者。He is a respected scholar.
③她是一名记者。She is a reporter.

记忆贴士

"者"（金文字形为 ）由"耂"（火）和"日"（说话）组成，本义是众人在火上煮食物并聊天，引申出代表特定的人或事物的意思。

者 consists of 耂(fire) and 日(speak). Its original meaning is that people cook food on the fire and chat with each other and extended to mean to represent certain people or things.

第十五节

形 → 形 → 形
小篆　　隶书　　楷体

拼音：xíng　　**部件**：开、彡　　**部首**：彡　　**结构**：左右
六书：形声　　**笔画**：7画　　**本义**：绘画实物形象 paint the image of an object
词语：①形状 shape　②形式 form　③形象 image
句子：①请描述一下它的形状和大小。Please describe its shape and size.
　　　②我反对任何形式的狩猎。I'm against hunting in any form.
　　　③这个公司的形象已经受损。The image of this company has been hurt.

记忆贴士

"形"由"开"（研磨颜料，"研"的省写）和"彡"（光彩）组成，本义是绘画实物形象，引申出外观的意思。

形 consists of 开(omitted form of 研, means to grind pigments) and 彡(color). Its original meaning is to paint the image of an object and extended to mean facade.

應 → 應 → 應 → 应
小篆　　隶书　　楷体（繁体）　楷体（简体）

拼音：yīng；yìng　　**部件**：广、丷、一　　**部首**：广　　**结构**：半包围
六书：形声　　**笔画**：7画　　**本义**：应当 should
词语：①应（yīng）该 should　②答应（yìng）promise　③适应（yìng）adjust
句子：①你应该早点起床。You should get up early.　②我答应你。I promise you.　③我们得适应新环境。We have to adjust to the new environment.

记忆贴士

"应"的繁体字"應"由"广""亻""隹""心"组成，可以理解为在广阔的天空，排成人字形飞翔的大雁，相互之间有心灵感应。本义为应当，引申出响应和答应等含义。简体字"应"由繁体字的草书楷化而成。

The traditional character of 应 is 應. It consists of 广(vast), 亻(person), 隹(bird) and 心(heart). It can be construed that in the vast sky, the wild geese fly in herringbone formation, who have telepathy with one another. The original meaning is should and extended to mean to respond and promise, etc. The simplified character 应 is the deformation of the cursive script of 應.

139

 甹 → 頯 → 頭 → 頭 → 头

金文大篆　　小篆　　隶书　　楷体（繁体）楷体（简体）

拼音：tóu　　　　**部件**：头　　　　**部首**：大　　　　**结构**：独体
六书：形声　　　**笔画**：5画　　　　**本义**：人头 head
词语：①头发 hair　②指头 finger　③头等舱 first-class cabin
句子：①他的头发是黑色的。His hair is black.
　　　　②她割伤了手指。She cut her finger.
　　　　③我买一张头等舱票。I would like to buy a ticket for the first-class cabin.

记忆贴士

"头"由"大"（人）和"丶"（头的位置，指事符号）组成，本义是人的头。

头 consists of 大(person) and 丶(indicative symbol, showing the position of head). It originally means head.

 無 → 無 → 无

隶书　　楷体（繁体）楷体（简体）

拼音：wú　　　　**部件**：无　　　　**部首**：无　　　　**结构**：独体
六书：象形　　　**笔画**：4画　　　　**本义**：跳舞 dance
词语：①无线 wireless　②无耻 shameless　③无偿 for free
句子：①你们有无线话筒吗？Do you have a wireless microphone?
　　　　②这是一种无耻的行为。It is a shameless behavior.
　　　　③你可以无偿获得这本书。You can get this book for free.

记忆贴士

"无"的字形像一个在跳舞的人，本义是跳舞。现在表示没有等含义。

无 is like a person dancing. Its original meaning is dance. It now means not have, etc.

拼音：liáng；liàng　　**部件**：日、一、里　　**部首**：日　　**结构**：上中下
六书：会意　　**笔画**：12画　　**本义**：称量measure
词语：①测量（liáng）measure　②质量（liàng）quality　③量（liàng）化quantify
句子：①我们要测量它的长度。We should measure its length.
②这家公司非常注重质量。This company cares about quality.
③它们的关系可以量化。Their relations can be quantified.

记忆贴士

"量"的金文字形 像一个圆口的容器，用来称量东西，本义是称量，引申出容量、数量等含义。

量(bronze inscription is) is like a round-mouthed container, which is used to measure things. Its original meaning is to measure and extended to mean amount, etc.

拼音：biǎo　　**部件**：圭、⿰　　**部首**：一　　**结构**：上下
六书：会意　　**笔画**：8画　　**本义**：外衣coat
词语：①手表watch　②表达express　③表扬praise
句子：①我喜欢这只手表。I like this watch.
②他表达了自己的观点。He expressed his views.
③我们受到了表扬。We are praised.

记忆贴士

"表"的小篆字形 由"衣"（小篆字形为 ）和"毛"（小篆字形为 ）组成，古人穿皮衣将毛朝外面，"表"的本义是外衣，引申出表面和显示等含义。

The xiaozhuan script of 表 is . It consists of (coat) and (fur). The ancients wore leather to put the hair outward, and the original meaning of 表 is coat. It is extended to mean surface and to express, etc.

象

甲骨文 → 金文大篆 → 小篆 → 隶书 → 楷体

拼音：xiàng　　**部件**：象　　**部首**：⺈　　**结构**：独体

六书：象形　　**笔画**：11画　　**本义**：大象 elephant

词语：①想象 imagine　②大象 elephant　③抽象 abstract

句子：①你能想象没有手机的生活吗？Can you imagine life without cell phones?
　　　　②孩子们喜欢大象。Kids like elephant.
　　　　③这是一幅抽象画。This is an abstract painting.

记忆贴士

"象"的甲骨文字形像大象，本义是大象，引申出形状和样子等含义。

象 (oracle bone script is) is like an elephant. It originally means elephant. It is extended to mean shape and appearance, etc.

气

甲骨文 → 金文大篆 → 小篆 → 隶书 → 楷体（繁体）楷体（简体）

拼音：qì　　**部件**：气　　**部首**：气　　**结构**：独体

六书：象形　　**笔画**：4画　　**本义**：云 cloud

词语：①天气 weather　②生气 angry　③气氛 atmosphere

句子：①他讨厌闷热的天气。He hates sultry weather.
　　　　②我非常生气。I am very angry.
　　　　③屋子里有一股紧张的气氛。There's an atmosphere of tension in the room.

记忆贴士

"气"的金文字形像云气蒸腾的样子，本义是云，引申出气体和发怒等含义。

气 (bronze inscription is) is like rising clouds. Its original meaning is cloud and extended to mean gas and angry, etc.

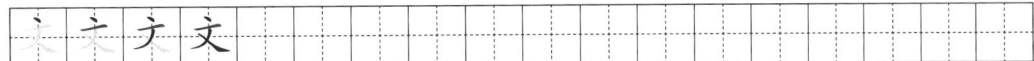

拼音：wén　　　　**部件**：文　　　　**部首**：文　　　　**结构**：独体
六书：象形　　　　**笔画**：4　　　　**本义**：文身 tattoo
词语：①文化 culture　②文学 literature　③中文 Chinese
句子：①他对中国饮食文化很感兴趣。He is very interested in Chinese food culture.
　　　②他精通中国文学。He is conversant with Chinese literature.
　　　③他们为电影制作中文字幕。They make Chinese subtitles for the movies.

记忆贴士

"文"的甲骨文字形 像一个胸前有文身的人，"文"的本义是文身，引申出文章和语言等含义。

文(oracle bone script is) is like a person with tattoo on the chest. Its original meaning is tattoo and extended to mean article and written language, etc.

拼音：zhǎn　　　　**部件**：尸、㠭　　　**部首**：尸　　　**结构**：半包围
六书：形声　　　　**笔画**：10　　　**本义**：展开 unfold
词语：①发展 develop　②展示 demonstrate　③展览 exhibition
句子：①政府决定发展旅游业。The government decided to develop tourism.
　　　②学生们展示了他们的技能。Students demonstrated their skills.
　　　③学校定期组织专场展览。School regularly organizes special exhibitions.

记忆贴士

"展"的小篆字形 由"尸"（身体）、四个"工"（玉片）和"衣"组成，表示展开衣服穿上，本义是展开，引申出展览等含义。

The xiaozhuan script of 展 is . It consists of 尸(body), four 工(jade) and 衣(clothes). It means to unfold the clothes and put them on. The original meaning is to unfold and extended to mean to exhibit and so on.

第十六节

系 → 系 → 系
小篆　隶书　楷体

拼音：xì；jì　　**部件**：丿、糸　　**部首**：丿　　**结构**：上下
六书：会意　　**笔画**：7画　　**本义**：悬hang
词语：①系（xì）统system　②联系（xì）contact　③系（jì）紧fasten
句子：①他更换了操作系统。He changed the operating system.
　　　②他以前和我联系过。He contacted me before.
　　　③请系紧安全带。Please fasten the safty belt.

记忆贴士

"系"（小篆字形为 系）由"丿"（手，小篆字形为 爪）和"糸"（丝，小篆字形为 糸）组成，表示丝在手中下垂悬在空中，本义是悬，引申出打结和联系等含义。

系(xiaozhuan script is 系) consists of 丿 (xiaozhuan script is 爪, meaning hand) and 糸 (xiaozhuan script is 糸, meaning silk). It indicates silk hanging in the hand. Its original meaning is to hang and extended to mean to tie and connect, etc.

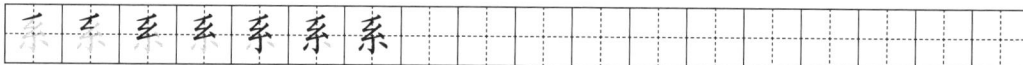

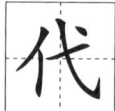

代 → 代 → 代
小篆　隶书　楷体

拼音：dài　　**部件**：亻、弋　　**部首**：亻　　**结构**：左右
六书：形声　　**笔画**：5画　　**本义**：做事时人互相替换change shifts at work
词语：①现代modern　②代表represent　③代价price
句子：①我们将要学习现代汉语。We will learn modern Chinese.
　　　②他们代表中国。They represent China.
　　　③他们为此付出了高昂的代价。They paid a high price for that.

记忆贴士

"代"由"亻"（人）和"弋"（带有绳子的箭，用于射鸟，可循环使用，金文字形为 弋）组成，本义是做事时人互相替换，引申为人代际间的更迭和历史上的时期等。

代 consists of 亻(person) and 弋(bronze inscription is 弋, meaning reusable arrow with rope for shooting birds). Its original meaning is to change shifts at work and extended to mean generation and historical period, etc.

第二部分 500个常用汉字

拼音：jiā　　**部件**：力、口　　**部首**：力　　**结构**：左右
六书：会意　　**笔画**：5画　　**本义**：说超出事实的话 exaggerate the fact
词语：①增加 increase　②参加 attend　③加强 enhance
句子：①他通过兼职增加收入。He increased his income by doing part-time job.
　　　　②许多人参加了那场讲座。Many people attended the lecture.
　　　　③我们应该加强合作。We should enhance cooperation.

记忆贴士

"加"由"力"（力气）和"口"（说话）组成，表示用力说话，本义是说超出事实的话，引申出增加等含义。

加 consists of 力(strength) and 口(speak). It means to speak hard. The original meaning is to exaggerate the fact and extended to mean to increase.

拼音：gè　　**部件**：夂、口　　**部首**：夂　　**结构**：上下
六书：会意　　**笔画**：6画　　**本义**：到来 arrive
词语：①各自 respective　②各种 various　③各位 everybody
句子：①我们有各自的研究领域。We have respective research fields.
　　　　②他们销售各种奶酪。They sell various cheeses.
　　　　③各位请随我来。Everybody, please follow me.

记忆贴士

"各"的甲骨文字形 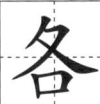 像脚朝城邑走来，表示人来到和进入的意思。"各"的本义是到来，现在表示每个等含义。

各(oracle bone script is ) consists of 夂(foot) and 口(city). It is like a foot walking towards the city. It indicates to come and enter. Its original meaning is to arrive and now it means each and every, etc.

145

很

很 → 很 → 很
小篆　　隶书　　楷体

拼音：hěn　　**部件**：彳、艮　　**部首**：彳　　**结构**：左右
六书：形声　　**笔画**：9画　　**本义**：不听从 disobey
词语：①很好 very well　②很热 very hot　③很高兴 very glad
句子：①他汉语说得很好。He speaks Chinese very well.
　　　　②今天很热。It's hot today.
　　　　③很高兴见到你。I'm very glad to see you.

记忆贴士

"很"由"彳"（道路，"行"的省写）和"艮"（回头看，小篆字形为 ）组成，表示走在后面的人回头看路不听从指挥，本义是不听从。"很"现在是程度副词。

很 consists of 彳(omitted form of 行, means road) and 艮(xiaozhuan script is , meaning look back). It means that the person who walks behind looks back and does not obey the command. Its original meaning is to disobey. Now it is used as an adverb which means very.

教

教 → 教 → 教 → 教
金文大篆　　小篆　　隶书　　楷体

拼音：jiào；jiāo　　**部件**：孝、攵　　**部首**：攵　　**结构**：左右
六书：形声　　**笔画**：11画　　**本义**：教学 instruct
词语：①教（jiào）育 education　②教（jiào）师 teacher　③教（jiāo）书 teach
句子：①他献身教育事业。He dedicated his life to education.
　　　　②她是一名教师。She is a teacher.
　　　　③我在一所大学教书。I teach at a university.

记忆贴士

"教"（小篆字形为教）由"爻"（算筹，"爻"的变形）"子"（孩子）"攵"（手拿着小棍儿）组成，本义是教学。

教(xiaozhuan script is 教) consists of 爻(deformation of 爻, meaning count rods), 子(xiaozhuan script is 子, meaning child) and 攵(hold a stick). Its original meaning is to instruct.

甲骨文　金文大篆　小篆　隶书　楷体

拼音：xīn　　**部件**：亲、斤　　**部首**：斤　　**结构**：左右
六书：形声　　**笔画**：13画　　**本义**：砍伐树木 chop the tree
词语：①新鲜 fresh　②创新 innovate　③新闻 news
句子：①这些鱼很新鲜。These fish are fresh.
　　　②我们应该培养学生的创新能力。We should foster students' innovation ability.
　　　③这是一个重大的新闻。This is big news.

记忆贴士

"新"的甲骨文字形 像斧子砍树，本义是砍伐树木，由刚砍伐的树木引申出刚得到的意思（和"旧"相对）。

新(oracle bone script is) consists of 亲(tree) and 斤(axe). Its original meaning is to chop the tree and extended to mean new.

甲骨文　金文大篆　小篆　隶书　楷体

拼音：xiàng　　**部件**：冂、口　　**部首**：口　　**结构**：半包围
六书：会意　　**笔画**：6画　　**本义**：朝北的窗子 the north-facing window
词语：①方向 direction　②向往 yearn for　③内向 introvert
句子：①他给我指了一个错误的方向。He gave me a wrong direction.
　　　②这正是我向往的地方。It is the place that I yearned for.
　　　③他性格内向。He is introvert.

记忆贴士

"向"的甲骨文字形 像房屋的一面墙上有窗户，本义是朝北的窗户，引申为朝向等含义。

向(oracle bone script is) is like a house with a window. The original meaning of 向 is the north-facing window and extended to mean towards and so on.

檆 → 機 → 機 → 机
小篆　　隶书　　楷体（繁体）楷体（简体）

拼音：jī　　**部件**：木、几　　**部首**：木　　**结构**：左右
六书：形声　　**笔画**：6画
本义：弓弩上的发射机关 the launching mechanism on the bow
词语：①飞机 plane　②机会 chance　③生机 vitality
句子：①我坐飞机去北京。I go to Beijing by plane.
　　　　②我们有获胜的机会。We have the chance of winning.
　　　　③绿色代表生机。The color green represents vitality.

记忆贴士

"机"的繁体字"機"由"木"和"幾"组成，"幾"（小篆字形为 ）由"糸"（弓弦，小篆字形为 ）、"戈"（兵器，小篆字形为 ）和"人"（箭的形状）组成，"機"的本义是弓弩上的发射机关。

The traditional character of 机 is 機(xiaozhuan script is). It consists of 木(xiaozhuan script is , meaning wood) and 幾(xiaozhuan script is). Its original meaning is the launching mechanism on the bow.

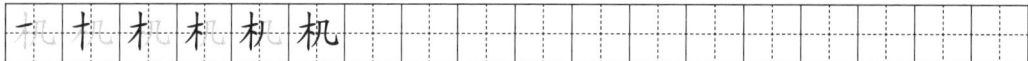

她 → 她
隶书　　楷体

拼音：tā　　**部件**：女、也　　**部首**：女　　**结构**：左右
六书：形声　　**笔画**：6画
本义：指称女性的第三人称代词 the third person pronoun referring to female
词语：她的 her
句子：她的爸爸是工程师。Her dad is an engineer.

记忆贴士

"她"由"女"（女性，小篆字形为 ）和"也"（蛇，小篆字形为 ）组成，本义是指称女性的第三人称代词。

她 consists of 女(xiaozhuan script is , meaning female) and 也(xiaozhuan script is , meaning snake). It originally means the third person pronoun referring to woman.

第十七节

内 → 内 → 内

甲骨文　隶书　楷体

拼音：nèi　　　　**部件：**内　　　　**部首：**｜　　　　**结构：**独体
六书：会意　　　　**笔画：**4画　　　　**本义：**进入enter
词语：①内容content　②内疚guilty　③内部inside
句子：①这本书内容很丰富。This book is rich in content.
　　　　②我感到很内疚。I felt so guilty.
　　　　③让我们看一下它的内部结构。Let's look inside it.

记忆贴士

"内"的甲骨文字形像人走入一个三面合围的空间，"内"的本义是进入，引申为内部。

内(oracle bone script is) is like a person walking into a space enclosed on three sides. The original meaning of 内 is to enter and extended to mean inside.

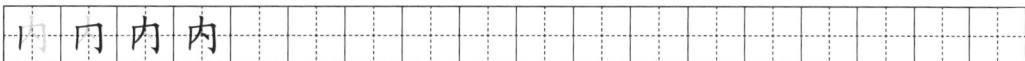

此 → 此 → 此 → 此

金文大篆　小篆　隶书　楷体

拼音：cǐ　　　　**部件：**止、匕　　　　**部首：**止　　　　**结构：**左右
六书：会意　　　　**笔画：**6画　　　　**本义：**踩踏step on
词语：①因此so　②此外moreover　③彼此each other
句子：①因此我们来到了这里。So we came here.
　　　　②此外，轮胎已经老化了。Moreover, the tire is wornout.
　　　　③他们彼此相爱了。They loved each other.

记忆贴士

"此"（金文字形为 ）由"止"（脚，金文字形为 ）和"匕"（人，金文字形为 ）组成，表示一只脚踩在人身上，本义为踩踏。"此"被借用为指示代词，表示"这"的意思。

此(bronze inscription is) consists of 止(bronze inscription is , meaning foot) and 匕(bronze inscription is , meaning person). It means to step on a person. Its original meaning is to step on. Now it is used as a demonstrative pronoun and means "this."

拼音：lǎo　　部件：耂、匕　　部首：老　　结构：上下
六书：会意　　笔画：6画　　本义：衰老 old
词语：①老实 honest　②老人 old man　③老板 boss
句子：①他一向很老实。He is always honest.
　　　②他是个令人尊敬的老人。He is a venerable old man.
　　　③她是我老板。She is my boss.

记忆贴士

"老"的甲骨文字形像一个手拿拐杖的老人，本义为衰老。

老(oracle bone script is) is like an old man with a walking stick. Its original meaning is old.

拼音：biàn　　部件：亦、又　　部首：又　　结构：上下
六书：形声　　笔画：8画　　本义：变化 change
词语：①变化 change　②改变 change　③变质 bad
句子：①他们的生活变化很大。Their life changed a lot.
　　　②该做出一些改变了。It is time to make some changes.
　　　③食物在夏天容易变质。Food is apt to go bad in summer.

记忆贴士

"变"的繁体字为"變"。上面的部件"䜌"由"糹"（丝）和"言"（语言）组成，意思是诺言。下面的部件"攵"表示手持棍子。"變"表示用武力强制改变，本义为变化。简体字"变"用简单的部件代替之前复杂的部件，上面保留原部件的轮廓，下面用"又"（手）代替"攵"（手持棍子）。

The traditional character of 变 is 變. The upper radical is 䜌. It consists of 糹(silk) and 言 (word), meaning promise. The lower radical is 攵. It means to hold a stick. 變 means to force to change. Its original meaning is to change. The simplified character 变 consists of 亦(replaces 䜌) and 又(replaces 攵, meaning hand).

 原 → 原 → 原
小篆　　隶书　　楷体

拼音：yuán　　**部件**：厂、白、小　　**部首**：厂　　**结构**：半包围
六书：会意　　**笔画**：10画　　**本义**：水源source of a river
词语：①原则principle　②原谅forgive　③原因reason
句子：①他们破坏了原则。They infringed the principle.
②请原谅他们吧！Please forgive them!
③你找到失败的原因了吗？Have you found the cause of failure?

记忆贴士

"原"由"厂（山崖，金文字形为厂）"和"氺"（泉，"泉"的变形）组成，本义是水源，引申出最初和基本等含义。

原 consists of 厂(bronze inscription is 厂, meaning cliff) and 氺 (deformation of 泉, means fountain). It is like water flowing from the source. The original meaning of 原 is the source of water and extended to mean original and primary, etc.

 結 → 結 → 结
隶书　　楷体（繁体）　楷体（简体）

拼音：jié；jiē　　**部件**：纟、吉　　**部首**：纟　　**结构**：左右
六书：形声　　**笔画**：9画　　**本义**：系tie up
词语：①结（jié）构structure　②结（jié）婚marry　③结（jiē）实strong
句子：①什么是房子的基本结构？What is the basic structure of a house?
②你结婚了吗？Are you married?
③他的身体相当结实。His body is fairly strong.

记忆贴士

"结"由"纟"（丝）和"吉"（声旁）组成，表示把东西系在一起，本义为系，引申出结束和结果等含义。

结 consists of 纟(silk, thread) and 吉(indicates pronunciation). Its original meaning is to tie up and extended to mean to end and to bear(fruit), etc.

 閂 → 閂 → 閒 → 問 → 问

甲骨文　金文大篆　　小篆　　楷体（繁体）楷体（简体）

拼音：wèn　　**部件**：门、口　　**部首**：门　　**结构**：半包围
六书：形声　　**笔画**：6画　　　　**本义**：询问inquire
词语：①问题question　②学问knowledge　③顾问counselor
句子：①这个问题很好。This is a good question.
　　　　②他是一个很有学问的人。He is really a man of knowledge.
　　　　③我们需要一个高级顾问。We need a senior counselor.

记忆贴士

"问"由"门"（大门）和"口"（说话）组成，意思是在门口向别人询问外面的事情，本义是询问。

问 consists of 门(door) and 口(speak). It means to ask someone at the door about what happened outside. The original meaning of 问 is to inquire.

 ᖵ → ᖵ → 手 → 手

　　　　金文大篆　　小篆　　隶书　　楷体

拼音：shǒu　　**部件**：手　　**部首**：手　　**结构**：独体
六书：象形　　**笔画**：4画　　**本义**：手hand
词语：①手机cell phone　②手段means　③分手break up
句子：①我的手机在哪儿？Where is my cell phone?
　　　　②他们利用不正当手段获胜。They won by unfair means.
　　　　③他们昨天分手了。They broke up yesterday.

记忆贴士

"手"的金文字形 ᖵ 像一只手，本义是手。

手(bronze inscription is ᖵ) is like a hand and its original meaning is hand.

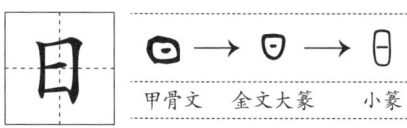

拼音：rì　　　　**部件**：日　　　　**部首**：日　　　　**结构**：独体
六书：象形　　　**笔画**：4画　　　**本义**：太阳sun
词语：①生日birthday　②节日festival　③日记diary
句子：①今天是我的生日。Today is my birthday.
　　　　②春节是中国最重要的节日。Spring Festival is the most important holiday in China.
　　　　③日记可以记录你生活中每天发生的事情。Diary can record what happens in your daily life.

记忆贴士

"日"的甲骨文字形  像太阳，本义是太阳，引申为天和日期等含义。

日(oracle bone script is ) is like the sun. Its original meaning is sun and extended to mean day and date, etc.

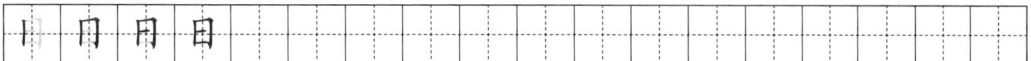

拼音：lì　　　　**部件**：禾、刂　　**部首**：刂　　　**结构**：左右
六书：会意　　　**笔画**：7画　　　**本义**：锋利sharp
词语：①胜利victory　②利益interests　③顺利go well
句子：①我们一起庆祝胜利。We celebrated the victory together.
　　　　②这符合双方利益。It is in the interests of both sides.
　　　　③一切进展顺利。Everything goes well.

记忆贴士

"利"由"禾"（庄稼）和"刂"（刀）组成，表示用锋利的刀割庄稼，本义是锋利，引申出好处等含义。

利 consists of 禾(crop) and 刂(knife). It means to reap crops with a sharp knife. The original meaning of 利 is sharp and extended to mean benefit, etc.

第十八节

甲骨文 → 金文大篆 → 隶书 → 楷体（繁体）→ 楷体（简体）

拼音： zhì　　**部件：** 厂、十、贝　　**部首：** 贝　　**结构：** 半包围

六书： 形声　　**笔画：** 8画　　**本义：** 抵押mortgage

词语： ①质量quality　②素质quality　③性质nature

句子： ①这些衣服质量很好。These clothes are of good quality.

②运动员需要好的心理素质。Athletes should have good mental qualities.

③这是一个人道主义性质的组织。This is a group of humanitarian nature.

记忆贴士

"质"的繁体字为"質"，由"斤"（两把斧子）和"貝"（钱，繁体字部件为"貝"）组成，表示用两把斧子作为抵押得到钱，本义是抵押，引申为性质和质量等含义。简体字"质"保留了一个"斤"，并且将"貝"简化为"贝"。

The traditional character of 质 is 質. It consists of 斦(two axes) and 貝(the radical of the traditional character is 貝, meaning money). It means to get money with two axes as mortgage. The original meaning of 質 is mortgage and extended to mean nature and quality, etc. The simplified character 质 retains one 斤 and simplifies 貝 to 贝.

→ 已 → 已

小篆　　隶书　　楷体

拼音： yǐ　　**部件：** 已　　**部首：** 已　　**结构：** 独体

六书： 象形　　**笔画：** 3画　　**本义：** 停止stop

词语： ①已经already　②不得已have no alternative　③已婚married

句子： ①我已经找到它了。I have found it.

②我不得已只能熬夜工作。I had no alternative but to work late into the night.

③他是一个已婚男人。He is a married man.

记忆贴士

"已"的小篆字形像初生的婴儿，表示怀胎结束，本义是停止，引申出已经等含义。

已(xiaozhuan script is 𢀖) is like a newborn baby, meaning the end of pregnancy. The original meaning is to stop and extended to mean already, etc.

冣 → 最 → 最
小篆　隶书　楷体

拼音：zuì　　**部件**：曰、取　　**部首**：曰　　**结构**：上下
六书：会意　　**笔画**：12画　　**本义**：军功最高 the highest military merit
词语：①最终at last　②最近lately　③最初initial
句子：①我们最终达成了一致。We reached an agreement at last.
②我最近犯了一个可笑的错误。I made a laughable mistake lately.
③最初的想法非常好。The initial idea was excellent.

记忆贴士

"最"（小篆字形为冣）由"冃"（冒犯敌人）和"取"（割取敌人左耳）组成，本义为军功最高。现在"最"作为副词，意思是极。

最(xiaozhuan script is 冣) consists of 冃(offend the enemy) and 取(cut off the left ear of the enemy). Its original meaning is the highest military merit. Now it is used as an adverb which means the most.

政 → 政 → 政 → 政
金文大篆　小篆　隶书　楷体

拼音：zhèng　　**部件**：正、攵　　**部首**：攵　　**结构**：左右
六书：形声　　**笔画**：9画　　**本义**：统治govern
词语：①政治politics　②政策policy　③行政administrative
句子：①他对政治不感兴趣。He has no interest in politics.
②他们调整了外交政策。They changed the foreign policy.
③他在行政岗位上工作。He works in an administrative position.

记忆贴士

"政"由"正"（匡正）和"攵"（使用棍棒强制）组成，表示统治者使用棍棒匡正（治理）天下，本义是统治，引申为政治等含义。

政 consists of 正(redress) and 攵(force with a club). It means that the ruler uses the club to redress (govern) the world. The original meaning is to govern and extended to mean politics, etc.

 → 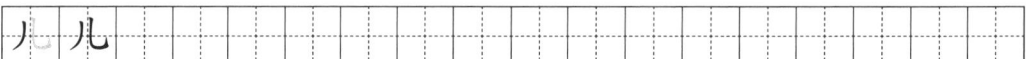 兒 → 兒 → 儿

金文大篆　小篆　　隶书　楷体（繁体）楷体（简体）

拼音：ér　　　　**部件**：儿　　　　**部首**：儿　　　　**结构**：独体
六书：象形　　　**笔画**：2画　　　　**本义**：儿童 child
词语：①儿童 child　②儿女 sons and daughters　③婴儿 infant
句子：①他研究儿童文学。He studies children's literature.
　　　　②他很爱他的儿女。He loves his sons and daughters very much.
　　　　③她把婴儿抱在手里。She is holding the infant in her arms.

记忆贴士

"儿"的繁体字为"兒"，其金文字形像小孩张口笑，本义是儿童。"儿"由繁体字"兒"去掉上面的部件简化而成。

The traditional character of 儿 is 兒. Its bronze inscription is , which is like a child who is laughing. Its original meaning is child. The simplified character 儿 only retains the lower component of 兒.

 → → → 見 → 見 → 见

甲骨文　金文大篆　小篆　　隶书　楷体（繁体）楷体（简体）

拼音：jiàn　　　**部件**：见　　　　**部首**：见　　　　**结构**：独体
六书：会意　　　**笔画**：4画　　　　**本义**：看见 see
词语：①看见 see　②意见 opinion　③偏见 prejudice
句子：①你看见我的笔了吗？Did you see my pen?
　　　　②你应该寻求专家的意见。You should seek experts' opinions.
　　　　③他们之间有很深的偏见。There was a deep-rooted prejudice between them.

记忆贴士

"见"的甲骨文字形由"目"（眼睛，甲骨文字形为　）和"人"（甲骨文字形为　）组成，"目"作为眼睛被突出，本义是看见。

见(oracle bone script is) consists of 目(oracle bone script is , meaning eye) and 人(oracle bone script is , meaning person), with 目 standing out. Its original meaning is to see.

甲骨文 金文大篆 小篆 隶书 楷体

拼音：bìng　　**部件**：丷、开　　**部首**：丷　　**结构**：上下
六书：象形　　**笔画**：6画　　**本义**：合并 combine
词语：①并且 and　②兼并 merge　③肩并肩 side by side
句子：①这个房间大并且干净。This room is big and clean.
②这家大公司兼并了很多小公司。The big company merged various small businesses.
③我们肩并肩坐着。We sat side by side.

记忆贴士

"并"的甲骨文字形 像把两个人的腿部绑在一起，本义是合并。

并(oracle bone script is) is like tying the legs of two people together. Its original meaning is to combine.

金文大篆 小篆 隶书 楷体

拼音：píng　　**部件**：平　　**部首**：干　　**结构**：独体
六书：会意　　**笔画**：5画　　**本义**：语气平和舒缓 the tone is calm and soothing
词语：①平凡 ordinary　②平安 safe　③平衡 balance
句子：①他过着平凡的生活。He lives an ordinary life.
②他们平安归来。They came home safely.
③骑自行车时要保持平衡。You should keep balance when you ride a bike.

记忆贴士

"平"由"干"（气流受到阻碍而能越过）和"丷"（分开）组成，表示气流越过阻碍而分散，本义是语气平和舒缓，引申为普通和安定等含义。

平 consists of 干(airflow meets an obstacle and is able to cross it) and 丷(disperse). It means that the airflow is dispersed after hitting the obstacle. Its original meaning is that the tone is calm and soothing and extended to mean ordinary and peaceful, etc.

篆 → 資 → 資 → 资

小篆　　隶书　　楷体（繁体）　楷体（简体）

拼音：zī　　　**部件**：次、贝　　**部首**：贝　　**结构**：上下
六书：形声　　**笔画**：10画　　**本义**：钱财 money
词语：①资源resource　②工资salary　③资料information
句子：①我们需要保护自然资源。We should protect natural resources.
　　　　②你发工资了吗？ Did you get your salary?
　　　　③我需要一些关于鸟类的资料。I need some information about birds.

记忆贴士

"资"由"次"（声旁）和"贝"（钱）组成，本义是钱财，引申出费用等含义。

资 consists of 次(indicates pronunciation) and 贝(money). The original meaning is money and extended to mean expense, etc.

꿔 → 꿔 → 𝕳 → 比 → 比

甲骨文　金文大篆　小篆　　隶书　　楷体

拼音：bǐ　　　**部件**：匕、匕　　**部首**：比　　**结构**：左右
六书：会意　　**笔画**：4画　　**本义**：挨着 next to
词语：①比赛game　②比例percentage　③比较compare
句子：①我们在比赛中获得了三枚金牌。We won three gold medals in the games.
　　　　②每个班级男生的比例增加了。The percentage of boys increased in every class.
　　　　③他比较了两个电脑的配置。He compared the configurations of two computers.

记忆贴士

"比"的甲骨文字形 꿔 是两个人肩并肩站立，本义为挨着，引申为较量和比率等含义。

比(oracle bone script is 꿔) is like two people standing next to each other. Its original meaning is next to and extended to mean to compete and ratio, etc.

第十九节

𤿡 → 特 → 特
小篆　隶书　楷体

拼音：tè　　**部件**：牜、寺　　**部首**：牜　　**结构**：左右
六书：形声　　**笔画**：10画　　**本义**：公牛 ox
词语：①特点 characteristic　②特长 specialty　③特殊 special
句子：①慷慨是王先生的一大特点。Generosity is a special characteristic of Mr. Wang's.
②唱歌是我的特长。Singing is my specialty.
③他没有特殊的要求。He has no special requirement.

记忆贴士

"特"由"牜"（牛）和"寺"（祭祀的场所）组成，表示用来祭祀的公牛，本义是公牛，引申出特别等含义。

特 consists of 牜(ox) and 寺(place of sacrifice). It means the ox used for sacrifice. Its original meaning is ox and extended to mean special, etc.

果 → 果 → 果 → 果 → 果
甲骨文　金文大篆　小篆　隶书　楷体

拼音：guǒ　　**部件**：果　　**部首**：丨　　**结构**：独体
六书：象形　　**笔画**：8画　　**本义**：果实 fruit
词语：①水果 fruit　②如果 if　③效果 effect
句子：①苹果是我最喜欢的水果。Apple is my favorite fruit.
②如果你修改一下这篇文章，我们就把它发表在报纸上。If you modify this article, we will publish it in the newspaper.
③这是最理想的效果。This is the most ideal effect.

记忆贴士

"果"的甲骨文字形 果 像树上结满了果实，本义为果实，引申为结果等含义。

果(oracle bone script is 果) is like a tree full of fruit. Its original meaning is fruit and extended to mean result, etc.

什

什 → 什 → 什
小篆　　隶书　　楷体

拼音：shí；shén　　**部件**：亻、十　　**部首**：亻　　**结构**：左右
六书：形声　　**笔画**：4画　　**本义**：十个事物形成的集体 a collection of ten things
词语：①什（shí）锦 assorted　②什（shén）么 what　③什（shén）么地方 where
句子：①这家店出售什锦奶糖。This shop sells assorted toffee.
②你要考虑下一步做什么。You should consider what to do next.
③他们不知道他们在什么地方。They don't know where they are.

记忆贴士

"什"由"亻"（人）和"十"组成，表示十个人，本义为十个事物形成的一个集体。现在"什"和"么"合起来构成一个疑问代词。

什 consists of 亻(person) and 十(ten). It means ten people. Its original meaning is a collection of ten articles. Now it is used to form an interrogative pronoun 什么(what) with 么.

建

金文大篆　　小篆　　隶书　　楷体

拼音：jiàn　　**部件**：廴、聿　　**部首**：廴　　**结构**：半包围
六书：会意　　**笔画**：8画　　**本义**：树立 erect
词语：①建议 suggest　②建筑 building　③建设 build
句子：①您对此有什么建议？Do you have any suggestion about that?
②那栋建筑是图书馆。That building is a library.
③他们要建设一个新医院。They are building a new hospital.

记忆贴士

"建"的金文字形像一只手拿着木柱立于庭院，本义是树立，引申出建立和提出等含义。

The bronze inscription of 建 is. It is like a hand holding a wooden pillar in the courtyard. Its original meaning is to erect and extended to mean to establish and propose, etc.

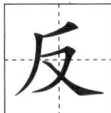 month → 月 → 反 → 反
金文大篆　　小篆　　隶书　　楷体

拼音：fǎn　　**部件**：厂、又　　**部首**：厂　　**结构**：半包围
六书：会意　　**笔画**：4画　　**本义**：手反转 flip hand
词语：①反映 reflect　②反应 respond　③反思 rethink
句子：①我们的论文应该反映这些变化。Our paper should reflect these change.
　　　　②他对我们的建议有什么反应？How did they respond to our suggestion?
　　　　③我正在反思这种策略。I'm rethinking this strategy.

记忆贴士

"反"由"厂"（石崖）和"又"（手）组成，表示手心翻转摸着石崖顶部，本义为手翻转，引申出回和还等含义。

反 consists of 厂(cliff) and 又(hand). It means that the palm of the hand touches the top of the stone cliff. The original meaning is to flip hand and extended to mean to return and so on.

 常 → 常 → 常
小篆　　隶书　　楷体

拼音：cháng　　**部件**：尚、巾　　**部首**：巾　　**结构**：上下
六书：形声　　**笔画**：11画　　**本义**：下裙 skirt
词语：①非常 very　②经常 often　③常识 common sense
句子：①他非常生气。He is very angry.
　　　　②你应该经常备份数据。You should backup your data often.
　　　　③这对于我们来说是常识。This is common sense to us.

记忆贴士

"常"由"尚"（流行）和"巾"（布）组成，表示流行的服饰，汉代以前中国无论男女都穿裙子，本义是下裙，引申出一般和普遍等含义。

常 consists of 尚(popular) and 巾(cloth), meaning popular clothing. Before the Han dynasty, both men and women wore skirts in China. The original meaning of 常 is the lower skirt and extended to mean general and common, etc.

知 → 知 → 知
小篆　隶书　楷体

拼音：zhī　　**部件**：矢、口　　**部首**：矢　　**结构**：左右
六书：会意　　**笔画**：8画　　**本义**：知道know

词语：①知道know　②知识knowledge　③无知ignorance
句子：①我不知道她的名字。I don't know her name.
②我们需要一些专业知识。We require some professional knowledge.
③我们必须原谅他的无知。We must make allowance for his ignorance.

记忆贴士

"知"由"矢"（箭，和箭一样快）和"口"（说话）组成，表示知道的事物可以脱口而出，本义是知道，引申出知识等含义。

知 consists of 矢(arrow, as fast as arrow) and 口(speak). It means things that are known can be said quickly. The original meaning is to know and extended to mean knowledge, etc.

第 → 第
隶书　楷体

拼音：dì　　**部件**：𥫗、弟　　**部首**：𥫗　　**结构**：上下
六书：会意　　**笔画**：11　　**本义**：次序order

词语：①第一first　②第二职业second job　③第三人称third-person
句子：①这是我的第一份工作。This is my first job.
②除了本职工作，你还有第二职业吗？Do you have a second job in addition to your full-time job?
③这本书采用第三人称叙述。This book adopts the third-person narrative.

记忆贴士

"第"由"𥫗"（竹子）和"弟"（线次第缠绕），表示将竹简按照次序编起来，本义是次序。现在"第"用在整数前形成序数词。

第 consists of 𥫗(bamboo) and 弟(like the line winding). It means that the bamboo slips are compiled in order. Its original meaning is order. Now it is used before integers to form ordinal numbers.

第二部分 500个常用汉字

电 → 電 → 電 → 電 → 电
甲骨文　小篆　隶书　楷体（繁体）楷体（简体）

拼音：diàn　　**部件**：电　　**部首**：｜　　**结构**：独体
六书：形声　　**笔画**：5画　　**本义**：闪电lightning
词语：①电脑computer　②电池battery　③电子electronic
句子：①我喜欢这台电脑。I like this computer.
　　　　②你需要一块新电池。You need a new battery.
　　　　③我是一个电子产品发烧友。I am a fan of electronic products.

记忆贴士

"电"的繁体字为"電"，其甲骨文字形  上面是雨，下面是闪电，本义是闪电，现在指一种能使电灯发光、机械转动的能量。

The tradition character of 电 is 電. Its oracle bone script is . The upper part is rain and the lower part lightning. The original meaning is lightning. Now it refers to a kind of energy that can make the light and make machines work.

| 丨 | 冂 | 冋 | 日 | 电 | | | | | | | | | | | | | |

→ 思 → 思
小篆　隶书　楷体

拼音：sī　　**部件**：田、心　　**部首**：田　　**结构**：上下
六书：会意　　**笔画**：9画　　**本义**：思考think
词语：①思考think　②意思mean　③沉思meditate
句子：①我们需要学习如何思考。We need to learn how to think.
　　　　②我不知道你什么意思。I don't know what you mean.
　　　　③我正在沉思。I am meditating.

记忆贴士

"思"（小篆字形为 ）由"田"（脑子，小篆字形为 ）和"心"（心脏，小篆字形为 ）组成，古人认为思考是脑子和心共同作用的结果，"思"的本义是思考。

思(xiaozhuan script is) consists of 田(xiaozhuan script is , meaning brain) and 心(xiaozhuan script is , meaning heart). Ancient Chinese thought that thinking is the result of the joint action of the brain and the heart. The original meaning of 思 is to think.

| 思 | 田 | 思 | 思 | 思 | 思 | 思 | 思 | 思 | | | | | | | | | |

第二十节

金文大篆 → 小篆 → 隶书 → 楷体

拼音：lì　　**部件**：立　　**部首**：立　　**结构**：独体
六书：会意　　**笔画**：5画　　**本义**：站立 stand
词语：①独立 independence　②立刻 immediately　③树立 set
句子：①他们为独立而战。They fight for independence.
　　　　②立刻关掉水龙头。Turn the tap off immediately.
　　　　③他为我们树立了一个好榜样。He set a good example to us.

记忆贴士

"立"的甲骨文字形 像一个人站立在地面上，本义是站立，引申出生存和立刻等含义。

立 (oracle bone script is) is like a person standing on the ground. The original meaning is to stand and extended to mean to live and immediately, etc.

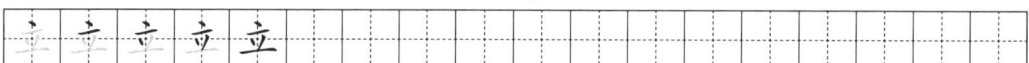

小篆 → 隶书 → 楷体

拼音：tí　　**部件**：扌、是　　**部首**：扌　　**结构**：左右
六书：形声　　**笔画**：12画
本义：手臂垂悬持拿物品 carry (in one's hand with the arm drooped)
词语：①提高 improve　②提倡 advocate　③提醒 remind
句子：①你是怎么提高汉语水平的？How did you improve your Chinese?
　　　　②我们应该提倡节约用水。We should advocate water conservation.
　　　　③请提醒我下车。Please remind me to get off.

记忆贴士

"提"由"扌"（手）和"是"（声旁）组成，本义是手臂垂悬持拿物品，引申出提升和说起等含义。

提 consists of 扌 (hand) and 是 (indicates pronunciation). Its original meaning is to carry something in one's hand with the arm drooped and extended to mean to raise and mention, etc.

164

或 → 或 → 或 → 或
金文大篆　小篆　隶书　楷体

拼音：huò　　**部件**：戈、口、一　　**部首**：戈　　**结构**：半包围
六书：会意　　**笔画**：8画　　**本义**：国家country
词语：①或者or　②或许perhaps　③或多或少more or less
句子：①我们九月或者十月去北京。We are going to Beijing on September or October.
②或许你是对的。Perhaps you are right.
③他们或多或少能讲点汉语。They can speak Chinese more or less.

记忆贴士

"或"由"口"（城邑）"一"（城墙）"戈"（武器）组成，表示武装守卫的疆域。"或"的本义是国家，后借用为代词，表示有的人或事物。

或 consists of 口(city), 一(city wall) and 戈(weapon). It means the territory which has armed guards. The original meaning of 或 is country, and later it's used as a pronoun to mean some people or things.

→ → → 通 → 通
甲骨文　金文大篆　小篆　隶书　楷体

拼音：tōng　　**部件**：辶、甬　　**部首**：辶　　**结构**：半包围
六书：形声　　**笔画**：10画　　**本义**：无阻碍通过pass without hindrance
词语：①沟通communication　②交通traffic　③通知notification
句子：①大学生要学习一些沟通技巧。College students should learn some communication skills.
②我们不能违反交通规则。We shouldn't violate traffic regulations.
③请等待我们的通知。Please wait for our notification.

记忆贴士

"通"由"辶"（行走）和"甬"（钟，钟声可以不受阻挡地传递到很远的地方）组成，本义为没有阻碍地通过，引申出连接和整个等含义。

通 consists of 辶(walk) and 甬(bell, whose sound can be heard far away). The original meaning of 通 is to pass without hindrance and extended to mean to connect and whole, etc.

解 → 解 → 解 → 解
金文大篆　小篆　隶书　楷体

拼音：jiě　　**部件**：角、刀、牛　　**部首**：角　　**结构**：左右
六书：会意　　**笔画**：13画　　**本义**：分解牛 dismember a cow
词语：①解释 explain　②了解 know　③理解 understand
句子：①我会和他解释。I'll explain it to him.
　　　　②我对艺术了解不多。I don't know much about the art.
　　　　③这个句子很难理解。This sentence is hard to understand.

记忆贴士

"解"由"牛""角""刀"组成，意思是抓住牛角，用刀把牛剖开，本义是分解牛，引申为懂得和解释等含义。

解 consists of 牛(cow), 角(horn) and 刀(knife). It means to grab the horns and dismember a cow with knife. The original meaning is to dismember a cow and extended to mean to know and explain, etc.

身 → 身 → 身 → 身 → 身
甲骨文　金文大篆　小篆　隶书　楷体

拼音：shēn　　**部件**：身　　**部首**：身　　**结构**：独体
六书：象形　　**笔画**：7画　　**本义**：人体躯干 human torso
词语：①身体 body　②终身 lifelong　③文身 tattoo
句子：①他身体很健壮。He has a strong body.
　　　　②现代社会提倡终身学习。Lifelong learning is encouraged in modern society.
　　　　③他想除去自己的文身。He wants to remove his tattoos.

记忆贴士

"身"的甲骨文字形像一个大肚子的人，表示脖子以下、屁股以上的身体。"身"的本义是人体躯干，引申出生命等含义。

The oracle bone script of 身 is . It is like a man with a big belly and it means the body below the neck and above the buttocks. The original meaning of 身 is the human torso and extended to mean life and so on.

| 甲骨文 | 金文大篆 | 小篆 | 隶书 | 楷体 |

拼音：sì　　　　**部件**：四　　　　**部首**：囗　　　　**结构**：独体
六书：会意　　　**笔画**：5画　　　**本义**：数字4 four
词语：①四季four seasons　②五湖四海all corners of the country　③四面八方all directions
句子：①中国一年有四季。There are four seasons in China.
②学生们来自五湖四海。Students come from all corners of the country.
③大火向四面八方蔓延。The fires were spreading in all directions.

记忆贴士

"四"的甲骨文字形 ☰ 是四个"一"，本义是数字4。"四"是"二"的倍数，把四个一竖写以后再加上一个二。

The oracle bone script of 四 is ☰. The original meaning is 4. 四 is twice as many as 二. 四 consists of four vertical 一 and a 二.

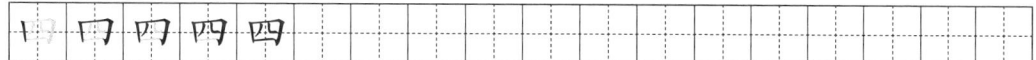

| 甲骨文 | 金文大篆 | 小篆 | 隶书 | 楷体 |

拼音：pǐn　　　　**部件**：口、口、口　　**部首**：口　　　**结构**：上下
六书：会意　　　**笔画**：9画　　　**本义**：众多numerous
词语：①品位taste　②品质quality　③品牌brand
句子：①他很有品位。He has a good taste.
②善良是她的主要品质。Her most essential quality is kindheartedness.
③我买了一个知名品牌电脑。I bought a famous-brand computer.

记忆贴士

"口"表示器物，三个"口"表示众多器物，"品"的本义是众多，引申出辨别好坏和品质等含义。

品 consists of three 口(artifact). It means a large number of artifacts. The original meaning of 品 is numerous and extended to mean sample and quality, etc.

167

几

篆 → 幾 → 几　　∩ → 几 → 几
小篆　　隶书　楷体(简体)　　金文大篆　隶书　楷体

拼音：jī；jǐ　　**部件**：几　　**部首**：几　　**结构**：独体
六书：象形　　**笔画**：2画　　**本义**：小桌子 small table
词语：①茶几(jī) tea table　②几(jī)乎 almost　③几(jǐ)天 several days
句子：①这个茶几面是钢化玻璃的。The surface of this tea table is made of tempered glass.
②几乎每个人都喜欢中国菜。Almost everybody appreciates Chinese food.
③几天过去了，什么都没发生。Several days passed and nothing happened.

记忆贴士

简体字"几"有两个来源，一个是"几"，另一个是"幾"。

"几"的金文字形 ∩ 像茶几的形状，本义是小桌子。

"幾"由两个"幺"（丝）和"戍"（守卫）组成，表示发现有细微的敌情而派兵把守，本义是细微。

现在"几"和"幾"都写作"几"。

The simplified character 几 has two sources.

几(bronze inscription is ∩) is like a table. Its original meaning is small table.

幾 consists of two 幺(silk) and 戍(guard). It means to send troops to guard after discovering slight enemy activities. The original meaning of 幾 is slight.

Now both 几 and 幾 are written as 几.

| 丿 | 几 | | | | | | | | | | | | | | | | | | |

位

位 → 位 → 位
小篆　隶书　楷体

拼音：wèi　　**部件**：亻、立　　**部首**：亻　　**结构**：左右
六书：会意　　**笔画**：7画　　**本义**：站立的位置 standing position
词语：①品位 taste　②职位 position　③位置 seat
句子：①你很有品位。You have a good taste.
②这个公司还空缺一个工程师职位。The position for engineer is still open in this company.
③他抢到了靠近门的位置。He grabbed the seat near the door.

记忆贴士

"位"由"亻"（人）和"立"（站立）组成，本义是站立的位置。

位 consists of 亻(person) and 立(stand). It originally means the position of standing.

第二十一节

别 → 别
隶书　　楷体

拼音：bié　　**部件**：口、力、刂　　**部首**：刂　　**结构**：左右
六书：会意　　**笔画**：7画　　**本义**：分解 cut apart
词语：①特别 especially　②别致 exquisite　③分别 separately
句子：①他特别理想化。He is especially idealistic.
　　　　②这个帽子看起来很别致。This hat looks exquisite.
　　　　③请分别给我们开发票。Please invoice us separately.

记忆贴士

"别"由"另"（骨头）和"刂"（刀）组成，表示将动物的肉从骨头上剔除，本义是分解，引申出分离和差别等含义。

别 consists of 另(bone) and 刂(knife). It means to remove meat from animal bones. Its original meaning is to cut apart and extended to mean to leave and different, etc.

论 → 論 → 論 → 论
小篆　　隶书　　楷体（繁体）　　楷体（简体）

拼音：lùn　　**部件**：讠、仑　　**部首**：讠　　**结构**：左右
六书：形声　　**笔画**：6画　　**本义**：议论 discuss
词语：①理论 theory　②讨论 discuss　③争论 argue
句子：①这在理论上是可行的。It is possible in theory.
　　　　②我们需要讨论现在做什么。We need to discuss what to do now.
　　　　③他们就此问题争论了多年。They have argued for years about this.

记忆贴士

"论"由"讠"（说话）和"仑"（评述典籍，繁体字部件为"侖"）组成，本义是议论。"侖"由"亼"（口，评说）和"冊"（册，典籍）组成，本义是评述典籍。

论 consists of 讠(speak) and 仑(the radical of the traditional character is 侖, meaning to comment on classics). It means to discuss. 侖 consists of 亼(speak, comment) and 冊(looks like books, meaning classics). It originally means to comment on classics.

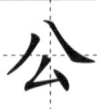

甲骨文　金文大篆　小篆　隶书　楷体

拼音：gōng　　**部件**：八、厶　　**部首**：八　　**结构**：上下
六书：会意　　**笔画**：4画　　**本义**：无私 selfless
词语：①公司 company　②公寓 flat　③公益 public welfare
句子：①他在一家中国公司工作。He works for a Chinese company.
　　　②我住在市中心的公寓里。I live in a flat in the downtown.
　　　③这次捐赠全部用于公益事业。This donation is all used for public welfare.

记忆贴士

"公"由"八"（相背）和"厶"（自私）组成，表示与自私相背，本义为无私。

公(xiaozhuan script is 公) consists of 八(xiaozhuan script is 八, meaning contrary) and 厶 (selfish). It means contrary to selfishness and its original meaning is selfless.

小篆　隶书　楷体（繁体）　楷体（简体）

拼音：jǐ；gěi　　**部件**：纟、合　　**部首**：纟　　**结构**：左右
六书：形声　　**笔画**：9画　　**本义**：充足 ample
词语：①给（jǐ）予 afford　②供给（jǐ）supply　③送给（gěi）give
句子：①他们给予我慷慨的帮助。They generously afforded us assistance.
　　　②食品供给超过了需求。The food supply exceeds the demand.
　　　③我送给他一本书。I gave him a book.

记忆贴士

"给"由"纟"（丝线）和"合"（连接）组成，表示将丝线接上，本义是充足，引申出供给和给等含义。

给 consists of 纟(silk thread) and 合(connect). It means to connect silk thread. The original meaning is ample and extended to mean to supply and give, etc.

 甲骨文 → 金文大篆 → 小篆 → 隶书 → 楷体

拼音：shǎo；shào　　**部件**：少　　**部首**：小　　**结构**：独体
六书：形声　　**笔画**：4画　　**本义**：数量小 few
词语：①多少（shǎo）how many　②至少（shǎo）at least　③青少（shào）年 juvenile
句子：①你看到多少只狗？How many dogs do you see?
　　　②我们至少需要十天时间。We need ten days at least.
　　　③青少年犯罪是一个社会问题。Juvenile delinquency is a social problem.

记忆贴士

"少"由"小"（沙子，甲骨文字形为⨀）和"丿"组成，本义是数量小，引申出缺少和年轻等含义。

少 consists of 小(oracle bone script is ⨀, meaning sand) and 丿. Its original meaning is few and extended to mean to lack and young, etc.

 金文大篆 → 隶书 → 楷体（繁体）→ 楷体（简体）

拼音：tiáo　　**部件**：夂、木　　**部首**：夂　　**结构**：上下
六书：形声　　**笔画**：7画　　**本义**：树枝 branch
词语：①条件 requirement　②苗条 slim　③教条 dogma
句子：①你们有什么条件？What are your requirements?
　　　②女性都渴望身材苗条。Females crave to stay slim.
　　　③放弃这死板的教条吧。Give up the rigid dogma.

记忆贴士

"条"由"夂"（手拿）和"木"（木）组成，表示可以做拐杖的树枝，本义是树枝，引申为项目等含义。

条 consists of 夂(hold) and 木(tree). It means branch that can be used as cane. Its original meaning is branch and extended to mean item and so on.

观

观 → 觀 → 觀 → 觀 → 观
甲骨文　小篆　隶书　楷体（繁体）楷体（简体）

拼音：guān　　**部件**：又、见　　**部首**：见　　**结构**：左右
六书：形声　　**笔画**：6画　　**本义**：仔细看 watch carefully
词语：①观察 observe　②客观 objective　③乐观 optimistic
句子：①这值得仔细观察。This is worth observing closely.
②这篇新闻很客观。This news is very objective.
③我对此并不乐观。I'm not optimistic about this.

记忆贴士

"观"的繁体字为"觀"（甲骨文字形为 ），由"藋"（长着大眼的鸟）和"见"（看见）组成，本义是仔细看。简体字"观"用"又"和"见"分别取代"藋"和"见"。

The traditional character of 观 is 觀(oracle bone script is). It consists of 藋(a kind of bird with big eyes) and 见(see). The original meaning of 觀 is to watch carefully. 藋 and 见 are replaced by 又 and 见 separately in simplified character 观.

フ　又　邓　观　观　观

回

 → 回 → 回
小篆　隶书　楷体

拼音：huí　　**部件**：口、口　　**部首**：口　　**结构**：全包围
六书：象形　　**笔画**：6画　　**本义**：回旋 whirl
词语：①回忆 memory　②回顾 look back　③回报 repay
句子：①我们在这座城市有美好的回忆。We had sweet memories in this city.
②我们回顾了中国的发展历程。We looked back on the development of China.
③我们该怎么回报你？How can we repay you?

记忆贴士

"回"的小篆字形 像水回旋的样子，本义是回旋，引申出回答和回去等含义。

回(xiaozhuan script is) is like a water whirl. The original meaning is whirl and extended to mean to answer and go back, etc.

丨　冂　冋　回　回　回

金文大篆 → 小篆 → 楷体

拼音：hǎi　　**部件**：氵、每　　**部首**：氵　　**结构**：左右
六书：形声　　**笔画**：10画
本义：河流发源的大湖 great lake where the river originates
词语：①海洋 ocean　②海拔 altitude　③海报 poster
句子：①海洋中有丰富的资源。The ocean is rich in resource.
　　　②这座城市海拔1700米。This city is at the altitude of 1,700 meters.
　　　③把旧海报撕下来。Tear down the old poster.

记忆贴士

"海"由"氵"（河流）和"每"（妇女生育）组成，表示河流的源头，本义是河流发源的大湖，现在的意思是海洋。

海 consists of 氵(river) and 每(woman gives birth). Its original meaning is great lake where the river originates and now it means ocean.

金文大篆 → 小篆 → 隶书 → 楷体

拼音：jī　　**部件**：其、土　　**部首**：土　　**结构**：上下
六书：形声　　**笔画**：11画　　**本义**：墙脚 foot of a wall
词语：①基础 basis　②基本 basic　③基金 fund
句子：①我们已经为合作奠定了坚实的基础。We have constituted a solid basis for cooperation.
　　　②这是汽车的一项基本功能。This is a basic function for cars.
　　　③我们必须建立一个储备基金。We must build up a reserve fund.

记忆贴士

"基"由"其"（土箕，一种装土的建筑工具）和"土"（土块）组成，本义是墙脚，引申为基础等含义。

基 consists of 其(a kind of construction tool for loading soil) and 土(clod). Its original meaning is foot of a wall and extended to mean foundation, etc.

第二十二节

癶 → 㳄 → 次 → 次
金文大篆　小篆　隶书　楷体

拼音：cì　　**部件**：冫、欠　　**部首**：冫　　**结构**：左右
六书：会意　　**笔画**：6画　　**本义**：旅途中停下来休息 stop and rest during the trip
词语：①层次 level　②次序 order　③次品 defective
句子：①这是一次多层次的合作。It is a multi-level cooperation.
　　　②词汇表按字母表次序排列。The vocabulary is arranged in the alphabetical order.
　　　③我昨天买的衣服是次品。The clothes I bought yesterday are defective.

记忆贴士

"次"由"冫"（冷）和"欠"（打哈欠）组成，表示又冷又困，本义是旅途中停下来休息，引申出质量差和次序等含义。

次 consists of 冫(cold) and 欠(yawn). It means to stop and rest for being cold and sleepy during the trip. The original meaning of 次 is to stop and rest during the trip and extended to mean order and inferior, etc.

襣 → 被 → 被
小篆　隶书　楷体

拼音：bèi　　**部件**：衤、皮　　**部首**：衤　　**结构**：左右
六书：形声　　**笔画**：10画　　**本义**：被子 quilt
词语：①被子 quilt　②被动 passively　③植被 vegetation
句子：①他把旧被子扔了。He threw his old quilt away.
　　　②我只能被动地接受决定。I can't do anything except passively accept the decision.
　　　③这个湖被热带植被环绕。This lake is surrounded by tropical vegetation.

记忆贴士

"被"由"衤"（衣服）和"皮"（动物皮）组成，表示睡觉时穿的衣服，本义为被子，引申出覆盖和被动等含义。

被 consists of 衤(clothes) and 皮(leather). It means clothes worn during the sleeping time. Its original meaning is quilt and extended to mean to cover and passive, etc.

拼音：shān	部件：山	部首：山	结构：独体
六书：象形	笔画：3画	本义：地面上土石隆起的地貌mountain	

词语：①山脉mountain range ②山顶mountaintop ③山脚foot of maintain

句子：①这里是世界上最长的山脉。This is the longest mountain range in the world.

②这个寺庙坐落在山顶。This temple lies on the mountaintop.

③我们下午一点半在山脚下集合。We shall assemble at 1:30 p.m. at the foot of the mountain.

记忆贴士

"山"的甲骨文字形 像山峰，本义为地面上土石隆起所形成的地貌。

山(oracle bone script is) is like a mountain. Its original meaning is mountain.

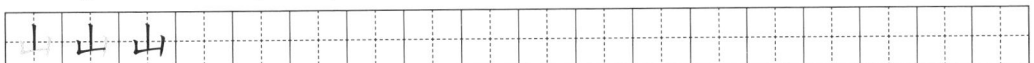

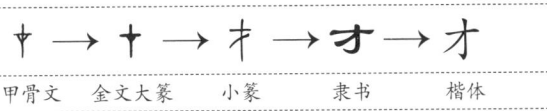

拼音：cái	部件：才	部首：一	结构：独体
六书：象形	笔画：3画	本义：初生草木sprouting plant	

词语：①人才talent ②才能ability ③刚才just now

句子：①这家公司用高薪吸引人才。This company attracts talents with high salary.

②我从没有怀疑过你的才能。I have never doubted about your ability.

③我刚才在打电话。I was on the phone just now.

记忆贴士

"才"的甲骨文字形 像刚长出来的草木，"一"表示地面，本义是初生的草木，引申出才能和刚才等含义。

才(oracle bone script is) is like a sprouting grass or tree. Its original meaning is sprouting plant and extended to mean ability and just now, etc.

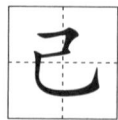

己

己 → 己 → 己 → 己 → 己
甲骨文　金文大篆　小篆　隶书　楷体

拼音：jǐ　　**部件**：己　　**部首**：己　　**结构**：独体
六书：象形　　**笔画**：3画　　**本义**：丝的头绪 main thread
词语：①自己 own　②知己 intimate friends　③各抒己见 freely express views
句子：①我们有自己的理由。We have our own reasons.
　　　　②他们是知己。They are intimate friends.
　　　　③大家可以各抒己见。Everybody can freely express personal views.

记忆贴士

"己"的甲骨文字形己像丝线，本义是丝线的头绪，用来缠束丝，后借指自己。

己 (oracle bone script is 己) is like silk thread. Its original meaning is main thread used to twine the silks. Now it is used to refer to oneself.

期

期 → 期 → 期 → 期
金文大篆　小篆　隶书　楷体

拼音：qī　　**部件**：其、月　　**部首**：月　　**结构**：左右
六书：形声　　**笔画**：12画　　**本义**：约定时间 make an appointment
词语：①期待 anticipate　②日期 date　③期间 during
句子：①我们期待您的回信。We are anticipating your reply.
　　　　②他看错了通知上的日期。He misread the date in the notice.
　　　　③节日期间我们不上课。We have no class during festivals.

记忆贴士

"期"由"其"（簸箕，用来积累）和"月"（月亮，表示时间）组成，意思是约好时间后需要积攒时间来实现约定，本义为约定时间，引申出盼望和一段时间等含义。

期 consists of 其 (loading tool, means to accumulate) and 月 (moon, means time). It means to accumulate time after an appointment. The original meaning of 期 is to make an appointment and extended to mean to expect and a period of time, etc.

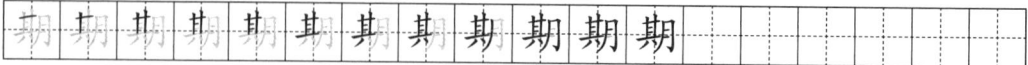

第二部分 500个常用汉字

金文大篆 → 小篆 → 隶书 → 楷体

拼音：xī　　**部件**：西　　**部首**：西　　**结构**：独体
六书：象形　　**笔画**：6画　　**本义**：鸟巢 bird nest
词语：①东西 thing　②西瓜 watermelon　③西方 western
句子：①我要去买食物和其他东西。I am going to buy food and other things.
　　　②西瓜是一种常见水果。Watermelon is a kind of common fruit.
　　　③我们从西方国家进口设备。We import equipments from western countries.

记忆贴士

"西"的金文字形像鸟巢，本义是鸟巢。日落西方，鸟儿归巢，"西"引申出西方的含义。

西 (bronze inscription is) is like a bird nest. The original meaning is bird nest. When the sun sets in the west, birds return home. 西 is extended to mean west.

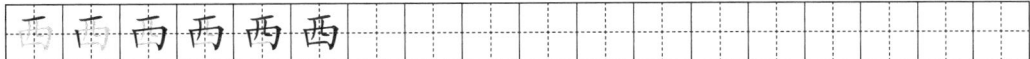

金文大篆 → 隶书 → 楷体（繁体）楷体（简体）

拼音：shù　　**部件**：术　　**部首**：木　　**结构**：独体
六书：会意　　**笔画**：5画　　**本义**：城中的道路 road in the city
词语：①艺术 art　②技术 technology　③战术 tactic
句子：①他擅长艺术和体育。He excels in art and sports.
　　　②科学为现代技术作出了巨大贡献。Science has contributed much to modern technology.
　　　③教练讲解了他的战术。Coach explained his tactics.

记忆贴士

"术"的繁体字"術"由"行"（道路，金文字形为 ）和"术"（编织篱笆）组成，意思是两边有篱笆的路，本义为城中的道路，引申为途径、方法。

術 (traditional character of 术) consists of 行 (bronze inscription is , meaning road) and 术 (weave fence). It means fenced road. The original meaning of 術 is road in the city and extended to mean way and method.

177

 濟 → 濟 → 濟 → 濟 → 济

甲骨文　小篆　隶书　楷体（繁体）　楷体（简体）

拼音：jì　　**部件**：氵、齐　　**部首**：氵　　**结构**：左右
六书：形声　　**笔画**：9画
本义：齐心协力划船渡河 paddle a boat together to cross the river
词语：①经济 economy　②救济 relief　③接济 offer financial help
句子：①这个国家经济发展很快。The economy of the country developed quickly.
　　　　②他靠救济生活。He lives on relief.
　　　　③他经常接济他的弟弟。He often offers financial help to his younger brother.

记忆贴士

"济"的繁体字为"濟"（甲骨文字形为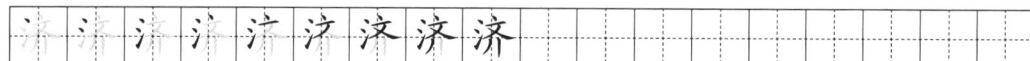），由"氵"（河）和"齊"（齐心协力）组成，本义是齐心协力划船渡河，引申为救助等含义。简体字"济"用"齐"代替"齊"。

The traditional character of 济 is 濟 (oracle bone script is). It consists of 氵 (river) and 齊 (make concerted efforts). Its original meaning is to paddle a boat together to cross the river and extended to mean to relieve, etc. 齊 is replaced by 齐 in simplified character 济.

 認 → 認 → 认

隶书　楷体（繁体）　楷体（简体）

拼音：rèn　　**部件**：讠、人　　**部首**：讠　　**结构**：左右
六书：形声　　**笔画**：4画　　**本义**：识别 recognize
词语：①认识 know　②认真 conscientious　③认为 think
句子：①你认识他吗？Do you know him?
　　　　②他办事很认真。He is very conscientious.
　　　　③你认为哪一个最好？Which do you think is the best one?

记忆贴士

"认"的繁体字为"認"，由"言"（说话）和"忍"（声旁）组成，本义是识别，引申出承认等含义。简体字"认"用"讠"代替"言"，用"人"代替"忍"。

The traditional character of 认 is 認. It consists of 言 (speak) and 忍 (indicates pronunciation). The original meaning is to recognize and extended to mean to admit, etc. 言 is replaced by 讠 and 忍 is replaced by 人 in simplified character 认.

第二十三节

甲骨文　金文大篆　小篆　隶书　楷体

拼音：xiān　　**部件**：⺧、儿　　**部首**：儿　　**结构**：上下
六书：会意　　**笔画**：6画　　**本义**：走在别人前面 walk in front of others
词语：①先生 sir　②先进 advanced　③祖先 ancestor
句子：①我们和李先生有约。We have an appointment with Mr. Li.
　　　②他们有最先进的机器。They have the most advanced machines.
　　　③我们的祖先创造了伟大的文明。Our ancestors created a great civilization.

记忆贴士

"先"的甲骨文字形由"脚"（甲骨文字形为）和"人"（甲骨文字形为）组成，"脚"在"人"前，本义是走在别人前面，引申出时间或次序在……前等含义。

先(oracle bone script is) consists of (oracle bone script is , meaning foot) and 儿(oracle bone script is , meaning person). The foot is in front of the person. The original meaning is to walk in front of others and extended to mean before, etc.

金文大篆　小篆　隶书　楷体

拼音：mìng　　**部件**：亼、叩　　**部首**：人　　**结构**：上下
六书：会意　　**笔画**：8画　　**本义**：口头命令 give verbal order
词语：①生命 life　②使命 mission　③革命 revolution
句子：①他冒着生命危险去救那个男孩。He risked his life in trying to save the boy.
　　　②这是我们的使命。This is our mission.
　　　③你读了有关信息革命那本书没有？Have you read the book on information revolution?

记忆贴士

"命"的金文字形由"令"（命令，金文字形为）和"口"（口头）组成，表示用口头发号命令，本义为口头命令，引申出动植物的生活能力等含义。

命(bronze inscription is) consists of 令(bronze inscription is , meaning order) and 口 (speak). The original meaning is to give verbal order and extended to mean life, etc.

走

金文大篆 → 小篆 → 隶书 → 楷体

拼音：zǒu　　**部件**：土、龰　　**部首**：走　　**结构**：上下
六书：会意　　**笔画**：7画　　**本义**：跑run
词语：①走路walk　②走俏sell well　③走廊corridor
句子：①我每天走路上班。I walk to work everyday.
②SUV在中国市场很走俏。The SUV sells well in China.
③走廊两边都有门。There are doors on both sides of the corridor.

记忆贴士

"走"的金文字形上面像人摆动双臂跑步，下面是脚，本义是跑，现在是步行的意思。

走(bronze inscription is ) is like a person running with the arms swinging. The lower part is foot. The original meaning is to run. Now it means to walk.

真

真 → 真 → 真

小篆　隶书　楷体

拼音：zhēn　　**部件**：十、具、八　　**部首**：十　　**结构**：上下
六书：会意　　**笔画**：10画
本义：探求事物的本真explore the true nature of things
词语：①真诚sincerely　②天真naive　③真理truth
句子：①我真诚地向你道歉。I apologize to you sincerely.
②这个想法很天真。This idea is naive.
③他在寻找真理。He is searching after truth.

记忆贴士

"真"和"贞"同源，都是用神鼎占卜，"真"的意思侧重于求得真相，"贞"的意思侧重于观察神迹。"真"的本义为探求事物的本真，引申为真实。

The meanings of 真 and 贞 are derived from divination using the sacred tripod. The meaning of 真 focuses on seeking truth, and the meaning of 贞 focuses on observing miracles. The original meaning of 真 is to explore the true nature of things and extended to mean real.

员 → 员 → 员
小篆　　隶书　　楷体（简体）

拼音：yuán　　**部件**：口、贝　　**部首**：口　　**结构**：上下
六书：会意　　**笔画**：7画　　**本义**：圆形round
词语：①动员mobilize　②员工staff　③服务员waiter
句子：①他动员许多人搜寻失踪男孩。He mobilized many people to search for the missing boy.
②他裁掉了15%的员工。He laid off 15% of the staff.
③他是一名服务员。He is a waiter.

记忆贴士

"员"的甲骨文字形 由"鼎"（甲骨文字形为 ）和圆形符号组成，表示鼎口的圆形形状，本义是圆形。"员"现在表示团队中的成员。

员(oracle bone script is) consists of "鼎"(oracle bone script is) and a circle. It means the circular shape of the tripod mouth. The original meaning of 员 is round. Now it means the member of a group.

→ → → 及 → 及
甲骨文　金文大篆　小篆　隶书　楷体

拼音：jí　　**部件**：及　　**部首**：丿　　**结构**：独体
六书：会意　　**笔画**：3画　　**本义**：追赶上catch up
词语：①及时timely　②以及and　③普及popular
句子：①我们感谢你及时的帮助。We are grateful to you for your timely help.
②他向我们提供了水以及食物。He provided water and food to us.
③这儿最普及的运动是篮球。The most popular sport here is basketball.

记忆贴士

"及"的金文字形 像用手抓住前面的人，本义是追赶上，引申出到达等含义。"及"也可以作连词，表示"和"。

The bronze inscription of 及 is . It is like grabbing people with hand. The original meaning is to catch up and extended to mean to arrive, etc. It is also used as a conjunction.

 纂 → 數 → 數 → 数
金文大篆　　隶书　　楷体（繁体）楷体（简体）

拼音：shǔ；shù　　　**部件**：米、女、攵　　**部首**：攵　　　**结构**：左右
六书：形声　　　　　**笔画**：13　　　　　　**本义**：计数 count
词语：①数（shǔ）落 scold　②参数（shù）parameter　③数（shù）据 data
句子：①爸爸数落我，说我不负责任。Dad has scold me, saying I am irresponsible.
　　　　②我们需要一个关键参数。We need a key parameter.
　　　　③这些观测数据非常重要。These observational data are very important.

记忆贴士

"数"由"娄"（连续）和"攵"（用手操作）组成，本义是计数，引申出数字等含义。

数 consists of 娄(consecutive) and 攵(with hand). Its original meaning is to count and extended to mean number, etc.

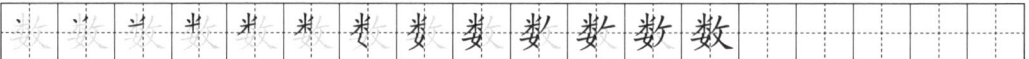

 話 → 話 → 话 → 话
小篆　　隶书　　楷体（繁体）楷体（简体）

拼音：huà　　　　　　**部件**：讠、舌　　　　**部首**：讠　　　**结构**：左右
六书：形声　　　　　**笔画**：8画　　　　　　**本义**：交谈 have a conversation
词语：①电话 telephone　②话题 topic　③神话 myth
句子：①你能告诉我校长办公室的电话号码吗？Could you tell me the telephone number for the principle office?
　　　　②这是今天讨论的话题。This is the topic of discussion today.
　　　　③这听起来像个神话。It sounds like a myth.

记忆贴士

"话"由"讠"（说话）和"舌"（舌头）组成，本义是交谈，引申出话语的含义。

话 consists of 讠(speak) and 舌(tongue). Its original meaning is to have a conversation and extended to mean word.

 門 → 門 → 門 → 門 → 門 → 门

甲骨文　金文大篆　小篆　隶书　楷体（繁体）楷体（简体）

拼音：mén　　**部件**：门　　**部首**：门　　**结构**：独体
六书：象形　　**笔画**：3画　　**本义**：双扇门 double-leaf door
词语：①大门 gate　②门口 at the gate　③门票 ticket
句子：①他们正在为大学建一座新大门。They are building a new gate for the university.
　　　　②让我们在门口见面吧。Let's meet at the gate.
　　　　③博物馆门票多少钱？How much is the museum ticket?

记忆贴士

"门"的繁体字为"門"，其甲骨文字形  像双扇门，本义是双扇门。简体字"门"只保留了"門"的轮廓。

The traditional character of 门 is 門. Its oracle bone script is , which is like a double-leaf door and it originally means double-leaf door. The simplified character 门 only retains the contour of 門.

 級 → 级 → 级 → 级

小篆　隶书　楷体（繁体）楷体（简体）

拼音：jí　　**部件**：纟、及　　**部首**：纟　　**结构**：左右
六书：形声　　**笔画**：6画　　**本义**：丝的等级 rating of silk
词语：①高级 senior　②阶级 class　③上级 superior
句子：①他是一名高级工程师。He is a senior engineer.
　　　　②阶级矛盾是社会动乱的征兆。Class conflict is a symptom of anomie.
　　　　③他得到了上级的表彰。He was praised by his superior.

记忆贴士

"级"由"纟"（丝）和"及"（声旁）组成，本义是丝的等级。

级 consists of 纟(silk) and 及(indicates pronunciation). Its original meaning is the rating of silk.

第二十四节

军 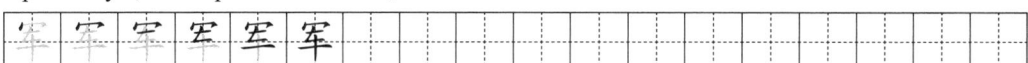 → 車 → 軍 → 軍 → 军

金文大篆　　小篆　　隶书　　楷体（繁体）　楷体（简体）

拼音：jūn　　　　**部件**：冖、车　　　**部首**：冖　　　**结构**：上下
六书：会意　　　**笔画**：6画　　　　**本义**：用战车围成营垒 encircle with chariot
词语：①军人 soldier　②敌军 enemy troops　③军队 army
句子：①他是一名军人。He is a soldier.
　　　　②敌军已经撤退。The enemy has retreated.
　　　　③这里有一支军队。There is an army.

记忆贴士

"军"的繁体字为"軍"，其金文字形外面是"冖"，里面是"車"。古代军队驻扎用车围成营垒。"軍"的本义是用战车围成营垒，引申为军队。简体字"军"用"车"代替"車"。

The traditional character of 军 is 軍(bronze inscription is ). It consists of 冖(encircle) and 車(chariot). The original meaning of 軍 is to encircle with chariot and extended to mean army. 車 is replaced by 车 in simplified character 军.

统　統 → 統 → 統 → 统

小篆　　隶书　　楷体（繁体）　楷体（简体）

拼音：tǒng　　　**部件**：纟、充　　　**部首**：纟　　　**结构**：左右
六书：形声　　　**笔画**：9画　　　　**本义**：丝的头绪 main threads of silk
词语：①统治 rule　②系统 system　③总统 president
句子：①他统治这地方。He rules this place.
　　　　②他在给电脑装操作系统。He is installing operating system to the computer.
　　　　③他是新总统。He is the new president.

记忆贴士

"统"由"纟"（丝线）和"充"（声旁）组成，本义是丝的头绪，引申出控制和全部等含义。

统 consists of 纟(silk thread) and 充(indicates pronunciation). Its original meaning is to tie all threads together and extended to mean to control and all, etc.

光

甲骨文 → 金文大篆 → 小篆 → 隶书 → 楷体

拼音：guāng　　**部件**：⺌、兀　　**部首**：⺌　　**结构**：上下
六书：会意　　**笔画**：6画　　**本义**：光亮light
词语：①光明bright　②风光landscape　③光滑smooth
句子：①前途是光明的。The prospects are bright.
②我们欣赏沿途的自然风光。We enjoyed the landscape along the road.
③它的表面像镜子一样光滑。Its surface is as smooth as that of a mirror.

记忆贴士

"光"的甲骨文字形 上面是"火"（甲骨文字形为 ），下面是"人"，表示人拿着火炬，本义是光亮，引申出光线和光滑等含义。

光(oracle bone script is) consists of ⺌(oracle bone script is , meaning fire) and 兀(person). It means a man holding a torch. Its original meaning is light and extended to mean ray and smooth, etc.

光 光 光 光 光 光

声

小篆 → 隶书 → 楷体（繁体）→ 楷体（简体）

拼音：shēng　　**部件**：士、尸　　**部首**：士　　**结构**：上下
六书：形声　　**笔画**：7画　　**本义**：声音sound
词语：①声音sound　②名声reputation　③声调tone
句子：①声音太大。The sound is too loud.
②他的名声很好。He has a good reputation.
③汉语中的声调很重要。Tone is very important in Chinese language.

记忆贴士

"声"的繁体字为"聲"。它由"殸"（击磬）和"耳"（耳朵）组成，本义是声音。简体字"声"只保留了繁体字左上角的部件。

The traditional character of 声 is 聲. It consists of 殸(hit chime) and 耳(ear). Its original meaning is sound. The simplified character 声 retains the upper left corner radical of the traditional character 聲.

一 十 圭 声 声 声 声

颗 → 題 → 題 → 题
小篆　　　隶书　　楷体（繁体）楷体（简体）

拼音：tí　　**部件**：是、页　　**部首**：页　　**结构**：半包围
六书：形声　　**笔画**：15画　　**本义**：额头forehead
词语：①标题title　②试题examination question　③话题topic
句子：①这篇文章没有标题。This article has no title.
　　　　②一共15道试题。There are 15 examination questions in total.
　　　　③他们在谈论这个话题。They are talking about this topic.

记忆贴士

"题"由"是"（上）和"页"（头）组成，本义是额头。现在的意思是书写和题目等含义。

题 consists of 是(upper) and 页(head). It originally means forehead. Now it means to inscribe and title, etc.

∧ → 人 → 人 → 入 → 入
甲骨文　金文大篆　小篆　　隶书　　楷体

拼音：rù　　**部件**：入　　**部首**：入　　**结构**：独体
六书：象形　　**笔画**：2　　**本义**：进去go into
词语：①进入go into　②加入join　③收入income
句子：①他一个人进入房间。He went into the room alone.
　　　　②欢迎加入我们。Welcome to join us.
　　　　③我今年的收入增加了。My income of this year has increased.

记忆贴士

"入"的甲骨文字形∧像一个尖头的东西，容易戳进别的东西。"入"的本义是进去。

入(oracle bone script is ∧) is like something with a sharp tip, which makes it easy to stab into other things. The original meaning of 入 is to go into somewhere or something.

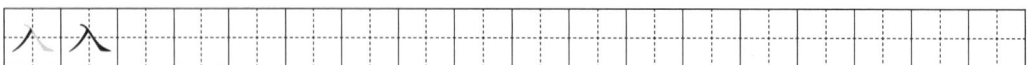

 羊 → 美 → 美 → 美 → 美
甲骨文　金文大篆　小篆　隶书　楷体

拼音：měi　　**部件**：羊、大　　**部首**：羊　　**结构**：上下
六书：会意　　**笔画**：9画　　**本义**：味美delicious
词语：①美味delicious　②美丽beautiful　③完美perfect
句子：①这里的食物极其美味。The food here is extremely delicious.
　　　②她是个美丽的姑娘。She is a beautiful girl.
　　　③这是件完美的作品。This is a perfect piece of work.

记忆贴士

"美"由"羊"（羊）和"大"组成。古人认为肥羊味美。"美"的本义是味美，引申出漂亮等含义。

美 consists of 羊(sheep) and 大(big, fat). Its original meaning is delicious and extended to mean beautiful, etc.

 ⊌ → ⊌ → ⊎ → 口 → 口
甲骨文　金文大篆　小篆　隶书　楷体

拼音：kǒu　　**部件**：口　　**部首**：口　　**结构**：独体
六书：象形　　**笔画**：3画　　**本义**：嘴mouth
词语：①借口excuse　②口碑reputation　③人口population
句子：①不要再找借口了。No more excuses.
　　　②这个品牌有很好的口碑。This brand has a good reputation.
　　　③这个国家大多数人口生活在城市。The majority of this country's population lives in the city.

记忆贴士

"口"的甲骨文字形 ⊌ 像人嘴，本义是嘴，引申出出入通过的地方等含义。

口(oracle bone script is ⊌) is like a mouth. Its original meaning is mouth and extended to mean place to pass through, etc.

 感 → 感 → 感
小篆　　隶书　　楷体

拼音：gǎn　　**部件**：咸、心　　**部首**：心　　**结构**：上下
六书：形声　　**笔画**：13画　　**本义**：感动 move
词语：①感动 move　②感情 emotion　③敏感 sensitive
句子：①他的话感动了每个人。His words moved everyone.
　　　　②男人表达感情的方式和女人不同。Men express emotions differently than women.
　　　　③我们最好别谈敏感话题。We'd better keep off the sensitive topic.

记忆贴士

"感"由"咸"（全，都）和"心"（心情）组成，表示心完全被触动，本义是感动，引申出感觉等含义。

感 consists of 咸(completely) and 心(heart). It means that the heart is completely touched. Its original meaning is to move and extended to mean to feel, etc.

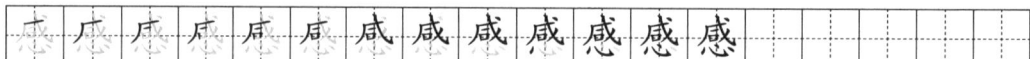

 戰 → 戰 → 戰 → 戰 → 战
金文大篆　小篆　隶书　楷体（繁体）　楷体（简体）

拼音：zhàn　　**部件**：占、戈　　**部首**：戈　　**结构**：左右
六书：形声　　**笔画**：9画　　**本义**：打仗 fight
词语：①战略 strategy　②战争 war　③挑战 challenge
句子：①战术不同于战略。Tactics differ from strategies.
　　　　②许多人在这场战争中丧生。A lot of people died in this war.
　　　　③我们要面对一些巨大的挑战。There are some big challenges before us.

记忆贴士

"战"由"占"（声旁）和"戈"（武器）组成，本义是打仗，引申出战争等含义。

战 consists of 占(indicates pronunciation) and 戈(weapon). Its original meaning is to fight and extended to mean war, etc.

188

第二十五节

科 → 科 → 科
小篆　隶书　楷体

拼音：kē　　**部件**：禾、斗　　**部首**：禾　　**结构**：左右
六书：会意　　**笔画**：9画　　**本义**：品类 sort
词语：①科学 science　②科目 course　③学科 subject
句子：①我爱科学。I love science.
②我的主修科目是汉语。My major course is Chinese.
③哲学是一门重要的学科。Philosophy is an important subject.

记忆贴士

"科"由"禾"（农作物）和"斗"（称量的器具）组成，合起来表示分别农作物的品类，本义是品类。

科 consists of 禾(crop) and 斗(a kind of measuring implement). It means to identify the sort of crops. Its original meaning is sort.

一 二 千 禾 禾 禾 禾 科 科

程 → 程 → 程
小篆　隶书　楷体

拼音：chéng　　**部件**：禾、口、王　　**部首**：禾　　**结构**：左右
六书：形声　　**笔画**：12画　　**本义**：称量粮食 measure crops
词语：①工程 project　②程序 procedure　③程度 extent
句子：①这项工程需要延长两个月才能完工。The project should be extended for two months.
②他熟悉招聘程序。He is familiar with recruitment procedure.
③我们想知道毁坏的程度。We want to know the extent of the damage.

记忆贴士

"程"由"禾"（庄稼）和"呈"（声旁）组成，本义是称量粮食，引申出时间安排和程度等含义。

程 consists of 禾(crop) and 呈(indicates pronunciation). Its original meaning is to measure crops and extended to mean schedule and extent, etc.

一 二 千 禾 禾 禾 秆 秆 程 程 程 程

式

式 → 式 → 式
小篆　隶书　楷体

拼音：shì　　**部件**：工、弋　　**部首**：弋　　**结构**：半包围
六书：形声　　**笔画**：6画　　**本义**：规矩 rule
词语：①方式 way　②仪式 ceremony　③格式 format
句子：①我喜欢他的教学方式。I like his way of teaching.
②他出席了一个官方的仪式。He attended an official ceremony.
③这篇文章有各种格式供下载。This article is available for downloading in various formats.

记忆贴士

"式"由"弋"（带绳子的箭，可画圆）和"工"（尺子，可画方）组成，表示做事的尺度，本义为规矩，引申出方法、类型等含义。

式 consists of 弋(an arrow with rope, used to draw a circle) and 工(ruler, used to draw square). It means to do things according to the rule. Its original meaning is rule and extended to mean method and type, etc.

指

指 → 指 → 指 → 指
金文大篆　小篆　隶书　楷体

拼音：zhǐ　　**部件**：扌、匕、日　　**部首**：扌　　**结构**：左右
六书：形声　　**笔画**：9画　　**本义**：手指 finger
词语：①指导 guide　②指令 instruction　③指挥 command
句子：①你的老师应该能指导你。Your teacher should be able to guide you.
②我们得执行那个指令。We need to execute that instruction.
③谁在指挥这支军队？Who is commanding this army?

记忆贴士

"指"由"扌"（手）和"旨"（声旁）组成，本义是手指，引申出指导和指挥等含义。

指 consists of 扌 (hand) and 旨(indicates pronunciation). Its original meaning is finger and extended to mean to guide and command, etc.

金文大篆　小篆　隶书　楷体

拼音：shì　　**部件**：世　　**部首**：一　　**结构**：独体
六书：指事　　**笔画**：5画　　**本义**：三十年 thirty years
词语：①世界 word　②世故 sophisticated　③世纪 century
句子：①他是世界上最好的足球门将。He is the best goalkeeper in the world.
　　　②我们不愿意和世故的人打交道。We hate to deal with a sophisticated man.
　　　③他是20世纪最伟大的作家之一。He is one of the greatest writers in the 20th century.

记忆贴士

"世"的金文字形为 ↓，它在 ↓（止）上加三个点，表示三十年。"世"的本义为三十年，引申出人的一生和世界等含义。

The bronze inscription of 世 is ↓. It consists of ↓ (止) and three dots. The original meaning of 世 is thirty years and extended to mean lifetime, world, etc.

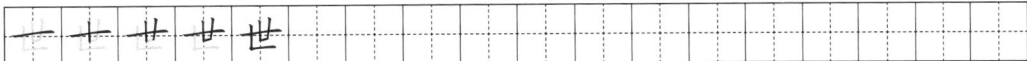

金文大篆　小篆　隶书　楷体

拼音：bì　　**部件**：必　　**部首**：丶　　**结构**：独体
六书：形声　　**笔画**：5画
本义：兵器的手柄 handle of weapon
词语：①必须 must　②必然 inevitable　③必要 necessary
句子：①我们必须马上出发。We must set off at once.
　　　②那是必然的。It is inevitable.
　　　③进一步的检查是必要的。A further examination is necessary.

记忆贴士

"必"的金文字形 ↓ 由"戈"（兵器）和"八"（声旁）组成，本义是兵器的手柄，现在表示必须等含义。

必 consists of 戈(weapon) and 八(indicates pronunciation). Its original meaning is the handle of weapon. Now it means must, etc.

放

拼音：fàng　　**部件**：方、攵　　**部首**：方　　**结构**：左右
六书：形声　　**笔画**：8画　　**本义**：流放 exile
词语：①放弃 give up　②开放 open　③释放 release
句子：①他放弃了考试。He gave up the exam.
②这所大学图书馆对所有人开放。This university library is open to all.
③他从狱中被释放出来了。He was released from prison.

记忆贴士

"放"（小篆字形为 𣬉）由"方"（远方）和"攵"（手拿棍棒驱赶）组成，本义是驱逐、流放，引申出释放和放置等含义。

放 consists of 方(distant place) and 攵(hold a club to expel). Its original meaning is to exile and extended to mean to release and put, etc.

打

拼音：dǎ　　**部件**：扌、丁　　**部首**：扌　　**结构**：左右
六书：形声　　**笔画**：5画　　**本义**：击 hit
词语：①打扰 disturb　②打算 intend　③殴打 beat
句子：①请不要打扰我们。Please do not disturb us.
②我打算立刻做这件事。I intend to do it at once.
③防暴警察用警棍殴打了抗议者。Riot police beat protesters with batons.

记忆贴士

"打"由"扌"（手）和"丁"（钉子）组成，本义是击，引申出做等含义。

打 consists of 扌(hand) and 丁(nail). Its original meaning is to hit and extended to mean to do, etc.

 接 → 接 → 接
小篆　　隶书　　楷体

拼音：jiē　　**部件**：扌、立、女　　**部首**：扌　　**结构**：左右
六书：形声　　**笔画**：11画　　**本义**：两手相触交会 two hands contact
词语：①连接connect　②接受accept　③直接direct
句子：①这条铁路连接了两个国家。The railroad connects two countries.
　　　　②请接受我最美好的祝愿。Please accept my best wishes.
　　　　③这对他们的利益造成了直接威胁。It poses a direct threat to their interests.

记忆贴士

"接"由"扌"（手）和"妾"（声旁）组成，本义是两手相触交会，引申为接连、接触等含义。

接 consists of 扌 (hand) and 妾(indicates pronunciation). Its original meaning is that two hands contact and extended to mean to connect and touch, etc.

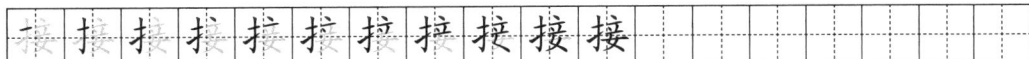

 總 → 總 → 總 → 总
小篆　　隶书　　楷体（繁体）　楷体（简体）

拼音：zǒng　　**部件**：丷、口、心　　**部首**：心　　**结构**：上下
六书：形声　　**笔画**：9画　　**本义**：束扎丝线 bundle silk threads
词语：①总结summary　②总理premier　③总是always
句子：①最后一段是简短的总结。The last paragraph is a short summary.
　　　　②总理主持了这次会议。The premier chaired the meeting.
　　　　③他们周末总是在外面吃饭。They always dine out on weekend.

记忆贴士

"总"的繁体字是"總"，由"糹"（丝线）和"悤"（声旁）组成，本义是束扎丝线，引申出概括和全体等含义。

The traditional character of 总 is 總. It consists of 糹 (silk) and 悤(indicates pronunciation). Its original meaning is to bundle silk threads and extended to mean to generalize and whole, etc.

193

第二十六节

做 → 做
隶书　　楷体

拼音：zuò　　**部件**：亻、古、夂　　**部首**：亻　　**结构**：左右

六书：会意　　**笔画**：11画　　**本义**：从事某种工作 do a certain job

词语：①做梦 dream　②做工 workmanship　③当做 as

句子：①我是不是在做梦？Am I dreaming?
②我想要一套做工精细的服装。I want a suit of fine workmanship.
③他养了两条蛇当做宠物。He has two snakes as pets.

记忆贴士

"做"由"亻"（人）和"故"（前人做过的事）组成，本义是人从事某种工作，引申出制作和用做等含义。

做 consists of 亻(person) and 故(things done by the predecessors). Its original meaning is to do certain job and extended to mean to make and as, etc.

东

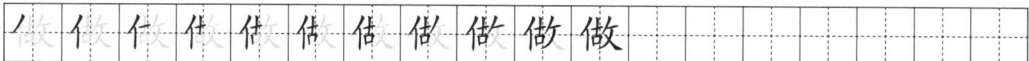

甲骨文　　金文大篆　　小篆　　隶书　　楷体（繁体）　　楷体（简体）

拼音：dōng　　**部件**：一　　**部首**：一　　**结构**：独体

六书：会意　　**笔画**：5画　　**本义**：东方 east

词语：①东方 east　②东西 thing　③东道主 host

句子：①寺庙朝着正东方。The temple faces due east.
②我想去买蔬菜和其他东西。I want to buy vegetables and other things.
③中国是这届比赛的东道主。This match is hosted by China.

记忆贴士

"东"的繁体字"東"由"木"（树）和"日"（太阳）组成，可以理解为树木位于日出的方向，本义是东方。

The traditional character of 东 is 東. It consists of 木(tree) and 日(sun). It can be construed that the tree is in the direction of sunrise. Its original meaning is east.

甲骨大篆 → 小篆 → 隶书 → 楷体(繁体) → 楷体(简体)

拼音：qū　　**部件**：匚、乂　　**部首**：匚　　**结构**：半包围
六书：会意　　**笔画**：4画　　**本义**：区分 distinguish
词语：①区别 difference　②郊区 suburb　③社区 community
句子：①这是非常重要的区别。This is a very significant difference.
②他住在郊区。He lives at the suburb.
③我在一个社区做志愿者。I am doing volunteer work for a community.

记忆贴士

"区"的小篆字形區，由"匚"（盛物的器具）和"品"（许多物品）组成，本义是区分，引申出区域等含义。简体字"区"用"乂"代替了"品"。

The xiaozhuan script of 区 is 區. It consists of 匚(container) and 品(things). Its original meaning is to distinguish things and extended to mean area, etc. 品 is replaced by 乂 in simplified character 区.

小篆 → 隶书 → 楷体(繁体) → 楷体(简体)

拼音：nóng　　**部件**：农　　**部首**：丶　　**结构**：独体
六书：会意　　**笔画**：6画　　**本义**：在农田里劳动 work in the field
词语：①农民 farmer　②农业 agriculture　③农场 farm
句子：①农民希望过上富裕的生活。Farmers want to have a prosperous life.
②他是主管农业的副市长。He is the deputy mayor who is in charge of agriculture.
③20岁之前我在农场工作。I had worked on a farm before I was twenty.

记忆贴士

"农"的小篆字形为農，由"𦥑"（双手）"囟"（农田，"田"的变形）"辰"（使用工具劳动）组成，合起来表示在田里劳动。"农"的本义是在田里劳动，引申出和农业有关的含义。繁体字写作"農"，简体字"农"保留了"農"的轮廓。

The xiaozhuan script of 农 is 農. It consists of 𦥑(two hands), 囟(deformation of 田, means field) and 辰(work with tools). Its original meaning is to work in the field and extended to meanings related to agriculture. The simplified character 农 retains the contour of the traditional character 農.

强

強 → 强 → 強 → 强

小篆　　隶书　　楷体（繁体）楷体（简体）

拼音：qiáng；jiàng；qiǎng　　**部件**：弓、虽　　**部首**：弓

结构：左右　　**六书**：会意　　**笔画**：12画

本义：米中的小黑虫 black insect in the rice

词语：①顽强（qiáng）tenacious　②倔强（jiàng）stubborn　③强（qiǎng）迫 force

句子：①运动员需要有顽强的意志。Athlete should have tenacious spirit.

②他是一个很倔强的男孩。He is a stubborn boy.

③我们被强迫着做这件事。We are forced to do this.

记忆贴士

"强"的繁体字为"強"由"弘"（声旁）和"虫"（昆虫）组成，本义是米中的小黑虫，后被借用来表示有力等含义。

強(traditional character is 强) consists of 弘(indicates pronunciation) and 虫(insect). Its original meaning is black insect in the rice. It is borrowed to mean powerful, etc.

造

𠧢 → 諧 → 造 → 造

金文大篆　　小篆　　隶书　　楷体

拼音：zào　　**部件**：辶、告　　**部首**：辶　　**结构**：半包围

六书：形声　　**笔画**：10画　　**本义**：到 arrive

词语：①创造 create　②制造 make　③建造 build

句子：①我们努力为合作创造条件。We tried to create conditions for cooperation.

②这支铅笔是中国制造的。This pencil is made in China.

③为了纪念英雄，人们建造了一座纪念碑。A monument was built to commemorate heroes.

记忆贴士

"造"由"辶"（走路）和"告"（声旁）组成，本义是到。后来"造"承担了"艁"的"制造"含义。

造 consists of 辶(walk) and 告(indicates pronunciation). Its original meaning is to arrive. 造 assumes the meaning of to make from 艁.

类 → 類 → 類 → 类
小篆　　隶书　　楷体（繁体）楷体（简体）

拼音：lèi　　**部件**：米、大　　**部首**：米　　**结构**：上下
六书：形声　　**笔画**：9画　　**本义**：种类category
词语：①类型type　②人类human being　③分类classify
句子：①你们需要什么类型的文件？What types of files do you need?
　　　②人类有很强的适应能力。Human being can be very adaptable.
　　　③请按国籍将学生分类。Please classify students by nationality.

记忆贴士

"类"的繁体字为"類"，由"米"（像动物脚印）"犬"（狗和其他动物）"頁"（头）组成，表示通过头和脚印来判断动物的类别，本义为种类。简体字"类"去掉了繁体字中的"頁"和"犬"的一点。

The traditional character of 类 is 類. It consists of 米(like the footprint of the animal), 犬(dog and other animals) and 頁(head). It means that the category of the animal is judged by the head and the footprint. The original meaning of 類 is category. 頁 and 、are removed in simplified character 类.

受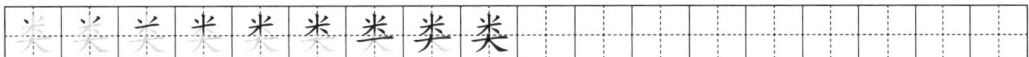
甲骨文　金文大篆　小篆　隶书　楷体

拼音：shòu　　**部件**：爫、冖、又　　**部首**：又　　**结构**：上下
六书：会意　　**笔画**：8画　　**本义**：接受receive
词语：①享受enjoy　②接受accept　③感受feel
句子：①他很享受朋友陪伴的乐趣。He enjoyed the company of friends.
　　　②我接受了他的邀请。I accepted his invitation.
　　　③他们感受到了社会的压力。They felt social pressure.

记忆贴士

"受"的金文字形像两只手中间有一个舟，表示传递东西，本义为接受。

受(bronze inscription is ) is like a boat between two hands. It means to pass things. The original meaning of 受 is to receive.

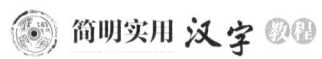

场 → 場 → 場 → 场
小篆　　隶书　　楷体（繁体）　楷体（简体）

拼音：chǎng　　**部件**：土、𦥑　　**部首**：土　　**结构**：左右
六书：形声　　**笔画**：6画
本义：祭神用的平地 flat land used for sacrifice
词语：①市场market　②立场position　③广场square
句子：①国外市场越来越重要。The foreign market was increasingly crucial.
②他已经清楚地表明了立场。He has shown his position clearly.
③这就是中央广场。This is the central square.

记忆贴士

"场"由"土"（土地）和"𦥑"（太阳），本义是祭神用的平地，引申出场地和位置等含义。

场 consists of 土(land) and 𦥑(sun). Its original meaning is the flat land used for sacrifice and extended to mean field and position, etc.

五 → 五 → 五 → 五 → 五
甲骨文　金文大篆　小篆　　隶书　　楷体

拼音：wǔ　　**部件**：五　　**部首**：一　　**结构**：独体
六书：会意　　**笔画**：4画　　**本义**：交叉cross
词语：①五官端正well-featured　②五角星 five-pointed star　③五岳the Five Mountains
句子：①这个小伙子五官端正。He is a well-featured young man.
②这是一个五角星。This is a five-pointed star.
③泰山是五岳之首。Mount Tai is the first of China's Five Mountains.

记忆贴士

"五"的甲骨文字形由"二"（天地）和"乂"（交错）组成，表示阴阳在天地间交错。"五"的本义是交错，现在的意思是数字5。

The oracle bone script of 五 is . It consists of 二(heaven and earth) and 乂(cross), meaning that *yin* and *yang* are intertwined between heaven and earth. Its original meaning is to cross and now it means five.

第二十七节

直 → 直 → 直 → 直

金文大篆　小篆　隶书　楷体

拼音： zhí　　**部件：** 十、且　　**部首：** 十　　**结构：** 上下
六书： 会意　　**笔画：** 8画　　**本义：** 不弯曲straight
词语： ①直径diameter　②正直upright　③直接immediate
句子： ①这是一棵直径约一米的大树。It is a big tree about one meter in diameter.
　　　②他是一个正直的官员。He is an upright official.
　　　③直接原因是什么？What is the direct cause?

记忆贴士

"直"的金文字形 包括了"十"（手）、"目"（眼睛）和"乚"（线），表示木匠用线测量木头直不直，本义是不弯曲。

The bronze inscription of 直 is . It consists of 十(hand), 目(eyes) and 乚(wire). It means that carpenter uses wire to measure the straightness of wood and its original meaning is straight.

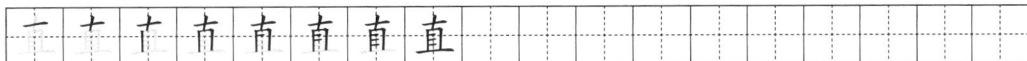

月 → 月 → 月 → 月 → 月

甲骨文　金文大篆　小篆　隶书　楷体

拼音： yuè　　**部件：** 月　　**部首：** 月　　**结构：** 独体
六书： 象形　　**笔画：** 4画　　**本义：** 月亮moon
词语： ①月亮moon　②月牙crescent moon　③岁月age
句子： ①月亮被云遮住了。The moon was obscured by clouds.
　　　②你能看到月牙吗？Can you see the crescent moon?
　　　③岁月在他脸上留下了痕迹。Age stamped his face with lines.

记忆贴士

"月"的甲骨文字形 形像月亮，本义为月亮，引申为计时单位。

月(oracle bone script is) is like the moon and its original meaning is moon and extended to mean month, etc.

流

金文大篆 → 小篆 → 隶书 → 楷体

拼音：liú **部件**：氵、㐬 **部首**：氵 **结构**：左右
六书：会意 **笔画**：10画 **本义**：水流动 flow
词语：①流行popular ②交流exchange ③流氓hooligan
句子：①我喜欢流行音乐。I like popular music.
②我们加强了与其他国家的文化交流。We strengthened the cultural exchanges with other countries.
③他们采取强硬手段对付足球流氓。They got tough with football hooligans.

记忆贴士

"流"（小篆字形为 㳅）由"氵"（水）和"㐬"（上面是胎儿，下面是羊水，意思是胎儿随羊水出来）组成，本义是水流动。

流 consists of 氵(water) and 㐬(the upper radical is fetus and the lower part is amniotic fluid, meaning that the fetus comes out with the amniotic fluid). Its original meaning is to flow.

决

小篆 → 隶书 → 楷体

拼音：jué **部件**：冫、夬 **部首**：冫 **结构**：左右
六书：形声 **笔画**：6画 **本义**：水决堤 overflow
词语：①决定decide ②决心determination ③坚决resolutely
句子：①我决定退出俱乐部。I've decided to quit the club.
②没有人可以动摇我的决心。No one can shake my determination.
③我坚决反对这个想法。I resolutely oppose this idea.

记忆贴士

"决"由"冫"（水）和"夬"（因开口而通畅）组成，本义是水决堤，引申出决定和一定（用在否定词前）等含义。

决 consists of 冫(water) and 夬(unobstructed because of the opening). Its original meaning is to overflow and extended to mean to decide and definitely(used before negative adverbs).

第二部分　500个常用汉字

金文大篆　　隶书　　楷体　　　　　　小篆　　隶书　　楷体（繁体）楷体（简体）

𩙿 → 乾 → 乾 → 干
小篆　　隶书　　楷体（繁体）楷体（简体）

拼音：gān；gàn　　　**部件**：干　　　**部首**：干　　　**结构**：独体
六书：形声　　　　　**笔画**：3画　　　**本义**：盾牌 shield
词语：①干（gān）预 intervene　②干（gān）旱 drought　③树干（gàn）trunk
句子：①在联合国的干预下，局势变得缓和。The situation calmed down when the UN intervened.
　　　　②干旱造成了饥荒。Food is scarce because of drought.
　　　　③箭射中了树干。Arrow hit the trunk.

记忆贴士

简体字"干"有三个来源，分别是"干""幹""乾"。

"干"的金文字形 丫 像防御武器，本义是盾牌。

"幹"由"𠦝"（日出，"朝"的省写）"人""干"（捕猎工具）组成，本义是日出而作。

"乾"由"𠦝"（日出，"朝"的省写）和"乞"（蒸汽）组成，本义是因水汽蒸发而缺少水分。

现在"干""幹""乾"都写作"干"。

The simplified character 干 has three sources.

干(bronze inscription is 丫) is like a defensive weapon. Its original meaning is shield.

幹 consists of 𠦝(omitted form of 朝, means sunrise), 人(people) and 干(hunting tool). Its original meaning is to start to work after sunrise.

乾 consists of 𠦝(omitted form of 朝, means sunrise) and 乞(vapor). Its original meaning is lack of moisture due to water evaporation.

Now 干, 幹 and 乾 are all written as 干.

则

则 → 则 → 则 → 則 → 则
金文大篆　小篆　隶书　楷体（繁体）楷体（简体）

拼音：zé　　**部件**：贝、刂　　**部首**：贝　　**结构**：左右
六书：会意　　**笔画**：6画　　**本义**：法则 rule
词语：①原则 principle　②准则 norm　③否则 or
句子：①这是原则性问题。This is a matter of principle.
　　　②这些法律反映了宪法准则。These laws reflect constitutional norms.
　　　③我们必须马上出发，否则就会迟到。We should leave at once, or we'll be late.

记忆贴士

"则"的金文字形由"鼎"和"刀"组成，表示在鼎上铸法律条文，让人遵守，本义是法则。繁体字为"則"，这里的"貝"实际上是"鼎"。简体字"则"用"贝"代替"貝"。

The traditional character of 则 is 則. Its bronze inscription is , which consists of 鼎(an ancient cooking vessel which is the symbol of dynasty) and 刂(knife). It indicates to cast legal provisions on an ancient cooking vessel which is the symbol of dynasty. Its original meaning is rule. 貝 in the traditional character is actually the deformation of 鼎, and is replaced by 贝 in the simplified character.

丨 冂 贝 贝 则 则

更

更 → 更 → 更 → 更
金文大篆　小篆　隶书　楷体

拼音：gēng；gèng　　**部件**：更　　**部首**：一　　**结构**：独体
六书：形声　　**笔画**：7画　　**本义**：敲钟报时 ring the bell to tell time
词语：①更（gēng）新 update　②更（gēng）换 change　③更（gèng）加 more
句子：①他在计算机上更新了数据。He updated the data on the computer.
　　　②他们仅仅更换了一根保险丝。They only changed a fuse.
　　　③我更加迷惑不解了。I was more confused.

记忆贴士

"更"的小篆字形为更，由"丙"（石钟）和"攴"（拿棍子敲）组成，本义是敲钟报时，引申为改变和替换等含义。"更"也可用作表示加深程度的副词。

The xiaozhuan script of 更 is 更. It consists of 丙(stone bell) and 攴(hit with stick). Its original meaning is to ring the bell to tell time and extended to mean to change and replace, etc. It is also used as an adverb which means even more.

一 一 一 一 更 更 更

 甴 → 色 → 色
小篆　　隶书　　楷体

拼音：sè　　**部件**：⺈、巴　　**部首**：色　　**结构**：上下
六书：会意　　**笔画**：6画　　**本义**：脸色 countenance
词语：①角色 role　②颜色 color　③特色 feature
句子：①他在片中扮演一个重要角色。He played an important role in the film.
②车是什么颜色的？ What color is the car?
③每个少数民族都有自己的特色。 Each minority ethnic group has its own feature.

记忆贴士

"色"的小篆字形 甴 包含两个人，像一个人驮着另一个人，看其脸色。本义为脸色，引申出颜色和特色等含义。

色 (xiaozhuan script is 甴) is like a person staring at another person and watching his countenance. The original meaning is countenance and extended to mean color and feature, etc.

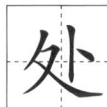 𠀎 → 𠬛 → 處 → 處 → 处
金文大篆　小篆　　隶书　　楷体（繁体）楷体（简体）

拼音：chǔ；chù　　**部件**：夂、卜　　**部首**：夂　　**结构**：半包围
六书：会意　　**笔画**：5画　　**本义**：停下来休息 stop to have a rest
词语：①处（chǔ）理 dispose　②处（chǔ）分 discipline　③住处（chù）residence
句子：①我该如何处理废纸？ How should I dispose the used paper?
②他受到了严厉的处分。 He has been disciplined severely.
③我们回到了住处。 We returned to the residence.

记忆贴士

"处"的繁体字为"處"，由"虍"和"夂（脚）"组成，表示老虎蹲踞着休息，本义是停下来休息，引申出地点和处理等含义。简体字"处"用"卜"代替"虍"。

The traditional character of 处 is 處. It consists of 虍(tiger) and 夂(foot). It means that the tiger is resting. Its original meaning is to stop to have a rest and extended to mean place and to treat, etc. 虍 is replaced by 卜 in simplified character 处.

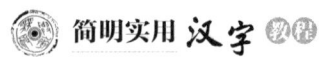

路 → 路 → 路 → 路

金文大篆　　小篆　　隶书　　楷体

拼音：lù　　　　**部件**：𧾷、各　　　　**部首**：𧾷　　　　**结构**：左右

六书：形声　　　**笔画**：13画　　　　**本义**：道路 road

词语：①道路road　②马路street　③路标signpost

句子：①这是条艰险的道路。This road is hard and steep.

②我想去马路对面的那家餐厅。I'd like to go to the restaurant that is across the street.

③这个路标指示去首都的方向。This signpost tells the way to the capital.

记忆贴士

"路"由"𧾷"（脚）和"各"（到来）组成，本义是道路。

路 consists of 𧾷(foot) and 各(arrive). Its original meaning is road.

𠃌	口	口	무	무	묘	𧾷	𧾷丶	𧾷夂	𧾷夂	路	路	路						

第二十八节

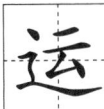

籆 → 運 → 運 → 运
小篆　　隶书　　楷体（繁体）楷体（简体）

拼音： yùn　　**部件：** 辶、云　　**部首：** 辶　　**结构：** 半包围
六书： 形声　　**笔画：** 7画　　**本义：** 移动 move
词语： ①幸运 lucky　②运用 apply　③运动 sports
句子： ①我很幸运赶上了最后一班公交车。I was lucky enough to catch the last bus.
　　　②我们要把理论应用到实践当中。We should apply the theory to practice.
　　　③你最喜欢什么运动？What is your favorite sports?

记忆贴士

"运"的繁体字为"運"，由"辶"（走）和"軍"（军队）组成，表示军队转移，本义是移动。

The traditional character of 运 is 運. It consists of 辶(walk) and 軍(army). It means that army transfer. Its original meaning is to move.

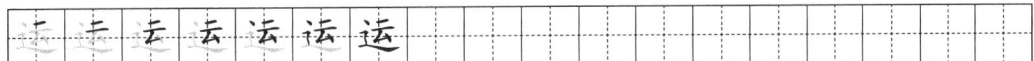

忹 → 玊 → 任 → 任 → 任
甲骨文　金文大篆　小篆　　隶书　　楷体

拼音： rèn　　**部件：** 亻、壬　　**部首：** 亻　　**结构：** 左右
六书： 形声　　**笔画：** 6画　　**本义：** 挑重物 shoulder heavy goods
词语： ①责任 responsibility　②信任 trust　③任何 any
句子： ①他拒绝承担责任。He disclaimed responsibility.
　　　②我完全信任你。I trust you completely.
　　　③我们应该准备好应对任何紧急情况。We should be prepared for any contingency.

记忆贴士

"任"（甲骨文字形为忹）由"亻"（人）和"壬"（承受）组成，像人挑着担子，本义是挑重物，引申出承担和责任等含义。

任(oracle bone script is 忹) consists of 亻(person) and 壬(bear). It is like a person shouldering a burden. Its original meaning is to shoulder heavy goods and extended to mean to assume and responsibility, etc.

 鼎 → 鼎 → 具

金文大篆　　小篆　　楷体

拼音：jù　　**部件**：且、八　　**部首**：八　　**结构**：上下
六书：会意　　**笔画**：8画　　**本义**：准备饭食prepare meal
词语：①工具tool　②具体specific　③玩具toy
句子：①你需要一套新工具。You need a set of new tools.
　　　　②我们需要根据具体情况做决定。We should make decision in accordance with specific conditions.
　　　　③你应该给他买个玩具。You should buy him a toy.

记忆贴士

"具"的金文字形 鼎 上面是"鼎"下面是"双手"，表示双手捧着盛食物的餐具，本义为准备饭食，引申出具体和用具等含义。

具(bronze inscription is 鼎) is like two hands carrying a food vessel. Its original meaning is to prepare meal and extended to mean detail and utensil, etc.

 ◐ → ◐ → 目 → 目 → 目

甲骨文　　金文大篆　　小篆　　隶书　　楷体

拼音：mù　　**部件**：目　　**部首**：目　　**结构**：独体
六书：象形　　**笔画**：5画　　**本义**：眼睛eye
词语：①目标goal　②目的purpose　③醒目striking
句子：①我将实现我的目标。I will achieve my goal.
　　　　②你的目的是什么？What is your purpose?
　　　　③这个标志很醒目。This sign is striking.

记忆贴士

"目"的甲骨文字形 ◐ 像眼睛，有眼眶和瞳孔，本义是眼睛，引申出看等含义。

目(oracle bone script is ◐) is like an eye. Its original meaning is eye and extended to mean to look.

 再 → 再 → 再
　　　　　小篆　　隶书　　楷体

拼音：zài　　**部件**：再　　**部首**：一　　**结构**：独体
六书：会意　　**笔画**：6画　　**本义**：第二次 again

词语：①再见 goodbye　②再次 again　③再三 repeatedly
句子：①我必须得说再见了。I have to say goodbye.
　　　　②再次感谢您！Thank you again!
　　　　③他再三向我们道歉。He apologized repeatedly to us.

记忆贴士

"再"的小篆字形 再 像手拿渔网，表示重复撒网的动作，本义是第二次做某事。
再(xiaozhuan script is 再) is like a hand carrying the fishing net. It means to repeat the action of casting the fishing net. The original meaning is to do something once again.

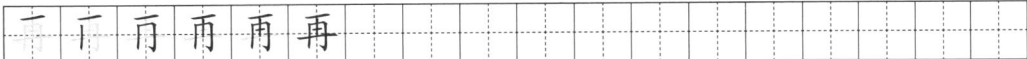

 治 → 治 → 治
　　　　　小篆　　隶书　　楷体

拼音：zhì　　**部件**：氵、台　　**部首**：氵　　**结构**：左右
六书：形声　　**笔画**：8画　　**本义**：控制河水不泛滥 prevent flood

词语：①政治 politics　②法治 rule of law　③统治 rule
句子：①他从小就对政治感兴趣。He has been interested in politics since a young age.
　　　　②在一个社会中法治是至关重要的。The rule of law is critical in a society.
　　　　③他统治这个国家30年。He ruled this country for 30 years.

记忆贴士

"治"由"氵"（水，河）和"台"（胎儿）组成，意思是像接生一样让水顺河道流走，本义是控制河水不泛滥，引申出管理等含义。
治 consists of 氵(river) and 台(fetus). It means to let the water flow along the river like a delivery. The original meaning is to keep the river from flooding and extended to mean to govern, etc.

 祏 → 褍 → 神 → 神
金文大篆　小篆　隶书　楷体

拼音：shén　　**部件**：礻、申　　**部首**：礻　　**结构**：左右
六书：形声　　**笔画**：9画　　**本义**：神灵deity
词语：①精神spirit　②神秘mysterious　③神圣holy
句子：①我喜欢他乐观向上的精神。I like his upbeat spirit.
②神秘的来访者不见了。The mysterious visitor vanished.
③对他们来说，这里是个神圣的地方。This is a holy place to them.

记忆贴士

"神"（金文字形为祏）由"礻"（启示）和"申"（字形像闪电）组成，本义是神灵，引申出令人惊异的和心思等含义。

神(bronze inscription is 祏) consists of 礻 (revelation) and 申(looks like lightning). Its original meaning is deity and extended to mean supernatural and mind, etc.

 𠂹 → 裘 → 求 → 求
金文大篆　小篆　隶书　楷体

拼音：qiú　　**部件**：求　　**部首**：一　　**结构**：独体
六书：象形　　**笔画**：7画　　**本义**：皮衣fur coat
词语：①追求pursue　②要求require　③请求request
句子：①我们有勇气追求梦想。We have the courage to pursue dream.
②协议要求学校提供网络。The agreement requires the school to provide network.
③我们请求他离开。We request that he should leave.

记忆贴士

"求"的小篆字形裘像毛朝外翻的皮袄，本义是皮衣，引申出设法得到和恳请等含义。

求(xiaozhuan script is 裘) is like a fur coat with the fur outside. Its original meaning is fur coat and extended to mean to try to get and request, etc.

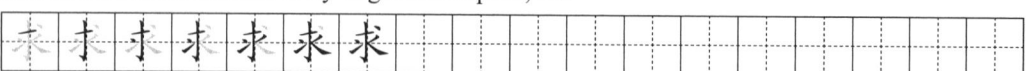

件 → 件 → 件
小篆　隶书　楷体

拼音：jiàn　　**部件**：亻、牛　　**部首**：亻　　**结构**：左右
六书：会意　　**笔画**：6画　　**本义**：分解dismember
词语：①条件condition　②软件software　③文件document
句子：①我们的居住条件比过去好了很多。Our living conditions are much better than before.
②你用什么杀毒软件？What anti-virus software do you use?
③这个文件是一个官方声明。This document is an official statement.

记忆贴士

"件"（小篆字形为件）由"人"和"牛"组成，表示人分解牛，本义是分解，引申出小而独立的事物等含义。

件(xiaozhuan script is 件) consists of 亻(person) and 牛(cow). It means a person dismembering a cow. The original meaning is to disintegrate and extended to mean tiny and independent things.

管 → 管 → 管
小篆　隶书　楷体

拼音：guǎn　　**部件**：⺮、官　　**部首**：⺮　　**结构**：上下
六书：形声　　**笔画**：14画
本义：一种类似于笛子的乐器 a kind of musical instrument like flute
词语：①尽管although　②主管director　③管家butler
句子：①尽管他可能是对的，但我还是不能同意他的意见。Although he might be right, I don't agree with him.
②他是这个单位的主管。He is the director of this unit.
③管家认识他。The butler knew him.

记忆贴士

"管"由"⺮"（竹子）和"官"（声旁）组成，本义是一种类似于笛子的乐器，引申出管道和管理等含义。

管 consists of ⺮(bamboo) and 官(indicates pronunciation). Its original meaning is a kind of musical instrument like flute and extended to mean tube and to govern, etc.

第二十九节

组 → 組 → 組 → 組 → 组
金文大篆　小篆　隶书　楷体（繁体）楷体（简体）

拼音：zǔ　　**部件**：纟、且　　**部首**：纟　　**结构**：左右
六书：形声　　**笔画**：8画　　**本义**：宽丝带 wide silk band
词语：①组织organization　②组成form　③组建organize
句子：①政府解散了这个非法组织。The government disbanded the illegal organization.
　　　　②他们组成了一个班级。They formed a class.
　　　　③他们组建了一支军队。They set up an army.

记忆贴士

"组"由"纟"（丝线）和"且"（声旁）组成，本义是宽丝带，引申出结合等含义。

组 consists of 纟(silk) and 且(indicates pronunciation). Its original meaning is wide silk band and extended to mean to combine, etc.

纟 纟 纟 纠 纠 细 组 组

根 → 根 → 根
小篆　隶书　楷体

拼音：gēn　　**部件**：木、艮　　**部首**：木　　**结构**：左右
六书：形声　　**笔画**：10画　　**本义**：草木根部 the root of the plant
词语：①根本fundamental　②根据according to　③根源root
句子：①我们应该更注意他们之间的根本区别。We should pay more attention to their fundamental differences.
　　　　②参与者按性别分组。Participants were categorized according to their genders.
　　　　③不讲卫生是许多疾病的根源。Uncleanliness is the root of various diseases.

记忆贴士

"根"由"木"（草木）和"艮"（脚跟，"跟"的省写）组成，意思是草木的根部，引申出根基和根源等含义。

根 consists of 木(tree and grass) and 艮(omitted form of 跟, means heel). Its original meaning is the root of the plant and extended to mean basic and origin, etc.

根 十 オ 机 机 桓 根 根 根 根

階 → 階 → 階 → 阶
小篆　　隶书　　楷体（繁体）楷体（简体）

拼音：jiē　　**部件**：阝、介　　**部首**：阝　　**结构**：左右
六书：形声　　**笔画**：6画　　**本义**：台阶steps
词语：①阶段stage　②阶级class　③台阶step
句子：①这个计划包括三个阶段。There are three stages in this plan.
　　　　②他们都是中产阶级。They all belong to middle class.
　　　　③他从台阶上跳了下来。He jumped from the step.

记忆贴士

"阶"由"阝"（"阝"在字的左边，表示意思与地势高低有关）和"介"（声旁）组成，本义是台阶，引申出等级等含义。

阶 consists of 阝(阝 is on the left side of the character, indicating that it is related to the topography) and 介(indicates pronunciation). Its original meaning is steps and extended to mean rank, etc.

｜ 了 ｜ 阝 ｜ 阝 ｜ 阶 ｜ 阶 ｜ 阶 ｜

將 → 将 → 將 → 将
小篆　　隶书　　楷体（繁体）楷体（简体）

拼音：jiāng　　**部件**：丬、夕、寸　　**部首**：丬　　**结构**：左右
六书：会意　　**笔画**：9画　　**本义**：扶持support
词语：①将军general　②即将be about to　③将来future
句子：①这里是那位将军的家乡。Here is the hometown of that general.
　　　　②情况即将改变。The situation is about to change.
　　　　③在不久的将来，我们要去那里。In the near future, we will be there.

记忆贴士

"将"（小篆字形为將）由"丬"（桌子）、"夕"（肉）和"寸"（手）组成，表示把肉放在桌子上，本义是扶持，引申出带领和快要等含义。

将(xiaozhuan script is 將) consists of 丬(table), 夕(meat) and 寸(hand). It means to put meat on the table. The original meaning of 将 is to support and extended to mean to lead and be about to, etc.

｜ 丶 ｜ 冫 ｜ 丬 ｜ 丬 ｜ 扌 ｜ 圹 ｜ 将 ｜ 将 ｜ 将 ｜

改 → 改 → 改 → 改 → 改

甲骨文　金文大篆　小篆　　隶书　　楷体

拼音：gǎi　　　**部件**：己、攵　　　**部首**：己　　　**结构**：左右
六书：会意　　　**笔画**：7画　　　**本义**：改正 correct
词语：①改变 change　②改革 reform　③改进 improve
句子：①我们无法改变结果。We cannot change the result.
　　　　②最初他们抵制改革。At first, they resisted the reform.
　　　　③他改进了这项发明。He improved the invention.

记忆贴士

"改"（甲骨文字形为改）由"己"（像一个跪着的小孩儿）和"攵"（用手持棍）组成，表示教育孩子改正过错。"改"的本义是改正，引申出改变等含义。

改(oracle bone script is 改) consists of 己(looks like a kneeling child) and 攵(hold stick). It means to educate the child to correct the fault. The original meaning of 改 is to correct and extended to mean to change.

导 → 導 → 導 → 导

小篆　　隶书　楷体（繁体）　楷体（简体）

拼音：dǎo　　　**部件**：巳、寸　　　**部首**：巳　　　**结构**：上下
六书：形声　　　**笔画**：6画　　　**本义**：引导 lead
词语：①领导 leader　②导致 lead to　③指导 guidance
句子：①在他的陪同下，领导参观了工厂。Accompanied by him, the leader visited the factory.
　　　　②错误的政策导致了严重的后果。The wrong policy led to fatal results.
　　　　③我希望得到他的指导。I expect to seek guidance from him.

记忆贴士

"导"由"巳"（人）和"寸"（手）组成，本义是引导。

导 consists of 巳(person) and 寸(hand). Its original meaning is to lead.

眼 → 眼 → 眼
小篆　　隶书　　楷体

拼音：yǎn　　**部件**：目、艮　　**部首**：目　　**结构**：左右
六书：形声　　**笔画**：11画　　**本义**：眼睛eye
词语：①眼睛eyes　②眼镜glasses　③耀眼dazzling
句子：①她长着棕色的大眼睛。She has large brown eyes.
　　　②我的眼镜在哪里？Where are my glasses?
　　　③灯光很耀眼。The light is dazzling.

记忆贴士

"眼"（小篆字形为眼）由"目"（眼睛，小篆字形为目）和"艮"（看，小篆字形为艮）组成，本义是眼睛。

眼(xiaozhuan script is 眼) consists of 目(xiaozhuan script is 目, meaning eye) and 艮 (xiaozhuan script is 艮, meaning to look). It means eye.

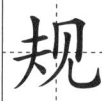

规 → 規 → 規 → 规
小篆　　隶书　　楷体（繁体）　楷体（简体）

拼音：guī　　**部件**：夫、见　　**部首**：见　　**结构**：左右
六书：会意　　**笔画**：8画　　**本义**：规则rule
词语：①规矩rule　②规律law　③规模scale
句子：①如果你守规矩，就不会有麻烦。If you follow the rules, you are not likely to get into trouble.
　　　②这个规律有许多例外。There are a lot of exceptions to that law.
　　　③它的规模仍然是惊人的。Its scale is still breathtaking.

记忆贴士

"规"由"夫"（男子）和"见"（见解）组成，合起来表示有智慧的男子的见解。"规"的本义为规则。

规 consists of 夫(man) and 见(opinion), meaning the opinion of a wise man's. Its original meaning is rule.

識 → 識 → 識 → 识
小篆　　隶书　　楷体（繁体）　楷体（简体）

拼音：shí　　**部件**：讠、只　　**部首**：讠　　**结构**：左右
六书：形声　　**笔画**：7画　　**本义**：认识 know
词语：①知识 knowledge　②意识 consciousness　③常识 common sense
句子：①通向知识的途径是学习。The way leading to knowledge is study.
　　　　②这些改变反映出了民族意识。These changes reflect their national consciousness.
　　　　③他缺乏常识。He lacks common sense.

记忆贴士

"识"的繁体字为"識"，由"言"（说）、"音"（说话的声音）和"戈"（兵器）组成，表示识别武器，本义是认识。简体字"识"由"讠"（说）和"只"（声旁）组成。

The traditional character of 识 is 識. It consists of 言(speak), 音(voice) and 戈(weapon). It indicates to identify the weapon and originally means to know. The simplified character 识 consists of 讠(speak) and 只(indicates pronunciation).

 → 革 → 革 → 革
金文大篆　　小篆　　隶书　　楷体

拼音：gé　　**部件**：革　　**部首**：革　　**结构**：独体
六书：象形　　**笔画**：9画　　**本义**：去毛的兽皮 animal skin without fur
词语：①革命 revolution　②变革 change　③革新 innovation
句子：①暴力革命摧毁了这个国家。The violent revolution ruined this country.
　　　　②重大的变革正在发生。Important changes are taking place.
　　　　③今天我们重点讨论技术革新。Today we will focus our discussion on technical innovation.

记忆贴士

"革"的金文字形  像拉平的兽皮，有动物的头、身、尾各部分。"革"的本义是去了毛的兽皮，引申出改变等含义。

革(bronze inscription is ) is like flattened animal skin, with head, body and tail. The original meaning of 革 is animal skin without fur and extended to mean to change.

第三十节

计 → 计 → 計 → 计
小篆　　隶书　　楷体（繁体）　楷体（简体）

拼音：jì　　　**部件**：讠、十　　　**部首**：讠　　　**结构**：左右

六书：会意　　**笔画**：4画　　　**本义**：计算 calculate

词语：①计划plan　②设计design　③会计accountant

句子：①我反对这项计划。I am against this plan.

②你的设计优点是什么？What's the advantage of your design?

③我哥哥是会计。My big brother is an accountant.

记忆贴士

"计"由"讠"（说话）和"十"（数字）组成，本义是计算，引申出谋划等含义。

计 consists of 讠(speak) and 十(number). Its original meaning is to calculate and extended to mean to plan, etc.

白 → 白 → 白 → 白 → 白
甲骨文　金文大篆　小篆　隶书　楷体

拼音：bái　　　**部件**：白　　　**部首**：白　　　**结构**：独体

六书：象形　　**笔画**：5画　　　**本义**：白色white

词语：①明白understand　②坦白confess　③洁白white

句子：①你最终会明白的。You will understand eventually.

②我要向你坦白。I'll confess to you.

③洁白的牙齿可以让你的外表更漂亮。White teeth can improve your appearance.

记忆贴士

"白"的甲骨文字形⊖像米粒，米粒是白色的，"白"的本义是白色，引申为清楚和空白等含义。

白(oracle bone script is ⊖) is like rice grain. The color of rice grain is white. The original meaning of 白 is white and extended to mean clear and blank, etc.

 甲骨文 → 金文大篆 → 小篆 → 隶书 → 楷体（繁体） → 楷体（简体）

拼音：mǎ　　**部件**：马　　**部首**：马　　**结构**：独体
六书：象形　　**笔画**：3画　　**本义**：马 horse
词语：①马上 at once　②马虎 careless　③马车 horse wagon
句子：①他马上就回来。He will be back at once.
②他做事相当马虎。He's rather careless.
③他备好了马车。He got his horse wagon ready.

记忆贴士

"马"的小篆字形像马的样子，本义是头小、脸长、颈上有鬃、尾有长毛，供人骑或拉东西的家畜。从繁体字"馬"中还能看出马头和马脚，简体字"马"保留了繁体字的轮廓。

马(xiaozhuan script is 馬) is like a horse. Its original meaning is horse. The simplified character retains the contour of the traditional character 馬.

 金文大篆 → 小篆 → 隶书 → 楷体

拼音：jīn　　**部件**：人、王、丷　　**部首**：金　　**结构**：上下
六书：会意　　**笔画**：8画　　**本义**：金属 metal
词语：①金色 golden　②定金 deposit　③金融 finance
句子：①田野看起来像金色的海洋。The field looks like a golden sea.
②你最好现在付定金。You'd better pay a deposit now.
③金融是个有意思的领域。Finance is an interesting field.

记忆贴士

"金"（金文字形）由"亼"（覆盖）、"土"（土地）和"丷"（矿物）组成，本义是金属，现在一般的意思是黄金和钱。

金(bronze inscription is 金) consists of 亼(cover), 土(soil) and 丷(mineral). Its original meaning is metal and it now commonly means gold and money.

 畍 → 界 → 界
小篆　　隶书　　楷体

拼音：jiè　　**部件**：田、介　　**部首**：田　　**结构**：上下
六书：形声　　**笔画**：9画　　**本义**：边界 boundary
词语：①边界 boundary　②世界 world　③政界 political circles
句子：①我们面临着边界地区敌人的威胁。We face the threat from the enemy at the boundary.
②它们只存在于客观实在的领域。They exist only in the physical realm.
③世界是在进步的。The world is progressing.

记忆贴士

"界"由"田"（疆域）和"介"（处于中间）组成，表示两个地方的分界线，本义是边界，引申出范围和领域等含义。

界 consists of 田(territory) and 介(in the middle). Its original meaning is boundary and extended to mean scope and circles, etc.

 取 → 取 → 取 → 取 → 取
甲骨文　金文大篆　小篆　隶书　楷体

拼音：qǔ　　**部件**：耳、又　　**部首**：耳　　**结构**：左右
六书：会意　　**笔画**：8画
本义：割下战俘耳朵 cut off war prisoner's ear
词语：①取得 get　②索取 demand　③取代 replace
句子：①我如何才能取得驾照？How can I get a driver's license?
②你必须索取赔偿。You must demand compensation.
③工人被机器取代了。Workers are replaced by machines.

记忆贴士

"取"（金文字形为 取 ）由"耳"（耳朵）和"又"（手）组成，本义是割下战俘的耳朵，引申为取得。

取(bronze inscription is 取) consists of 耳(ear) and 又(hand). Its original meaning is to cut off war prisoner's ear and extended to mean to acquire.

市

金文大篆 → 小篆 → 隶书 → 楷体

拼音：shì　　**部件**：亠、巾　　**部首**：亠　　**结构**：上下
六书：会意　　**笔画**：5画　　**本义**：集中做买卖的地方 market
词语：①市场 market　②城市 city　③市长 mayor
句子：①他比别人更了解市场。He knows the market better than others.
②这座城市有很多书店。There are many bookstores in this city.
③市长昨天辞职了。The mayor resigned yesterday.

记忆贴士

"市"的金文字形 上面的"止"（脚，金文字形为 ）表示"到……"，下面的"兮"（金文字形为 ）表示叫卖，合起来表示到集中做买卖的地方去。"市"的本义为集中做买卖的地方，引申出城市等含义。

The bronze inscription of 市 is . It consists of 止(bronze inscription is , meaning foot) and 兮(bronze inscription is , which means to shout to attract business), meaning to go to the market. The original meaning of 市 is market and extended to mean city, etc.

设

小篆 → 隶书 → 楷体（繁体） → 楷体（简体）

拼音：shè　　**部件**：讠、殳　　**部首**：讠　　**结构**：左右
六书：会意　　**笔画**：6画　　**本义**：安排 arrange
词语：①设计 design　②设置 set　③设备 equipment
句子：①谁设计的这栋房子？Who designed this house?
②我需要设置合适的字体大小。I need to set a right font size.
③雷电损坏了电器设备。The electrical equipment was damaged by the thunderstrike.

记忆贴士

"设"由"讠"（说话）和"殳"（指使，"殳"的甲骨文字形 表示手持大锤击杀）组成，表示用语言指使人，本义是安排，引申出设立和筹划等含义。

设 consists of 讠(speak) and 殳(oracle bone script of 殳 is , which indicates to hammer to kill). It means to ask people to do something. The original meaning is to arrange and extended to mean to set up and design, etc.

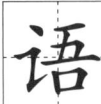 蛰 → 韶 → 語 → 語 → 语

金文大篆　　小篆　　隶书　楷体（繁体）楷体（简体）

拼音：yǔ　　　**部件**：讠、吾　　**部首**：讠　　**结构**：左右
六书：形声　　**笔画**：9画　　　**本义**：众人讨论many people discuss something
词语：①汉语Chinese　②标语slogan　③词语words and expressions
句子：①你会说汉语吗？Can you speak Chinese?
　　　　②墙上有条标语。There is a slogan on the wall.
　　　　③我们要学习一些新的词语。We will learn some new words and expressions.

记忆贴士

"语"由"讠"（说话）、"五"（交叉）和"口"（嘴巴）组成，本义是众人讨论，引申出说和说出来的话等含义。

语 consists of 讠(speak), 五(cross) and 口(mouth). Its original meaning is that many people discuss something and extended to mean to speak and words, etc.

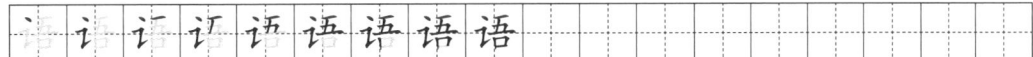

 宪 → 完 → 完

小篆　　隶书　　楷体

拼音：wán　　**部件**：宀、元　　**部首**：宀　　**结构**：上下
六书：形声　　**笔画**：7画　　　**本义**：保存完整keep intact
词语：①完美perfect　②完全completely　③完整complete
句子：①这是一个完美的解决办法。This is a perfect solution.
　　　　②我完全忘记了这件事。I completely forgot this.
　　　　③这个故事完整吗？Is this a complete story?

记忆贴士

"完"由"宀"（房子）和"元"（头）组成，表示房子可以保护人和财产不受侵害，本义是保存完整，引申出做成和消耗尽等含义。

完 consists of 宀(house) and 元(head), meaning that the house can preserve people and property. Its original meaning is to keep intact and extended to mean to finish and use up, etc.

第三十一节

宀 → 究 → 究
小篆　　隶书　　楷体

拼音：jiū　　**部件**：穴、九　　**部首**：穴　　**结构**：上下
六书：形声　　**笔画**：7画　　　　**本义**：穷尽 limit
词语：①究竟on earth　②终究at last　③研究research
句子：①他们究竟在想什么？What on earth were they thinking?
　　　②我们终究还是输了比赛。We lost the game at last.
　　　③这个研究被发表在一本学术期刊上。This research is published on an academic journal.

记忆贴士

"究"由"穴"（洞穴）和"九"（手，金文字形为 ）组成，表示用手在洞穴里摸索。"究"的本义是穷尽，引申出探究等含义。

究 consists of 穴(cave) and 九(bronze inscription is , meaning hand). It indicates to grope with hand in a cave. Its original meaning is limit and extended to mean to explore, etc.

黨 → 黨 → 黨 → 党
小篆　　隶书　　楷体（繁体）　楷体（简体）

拼音：dǎng　　**部件**：尚、儿　　**部首**：儿　　**结构**：上下
六书：形声　　**笔画**：10画　　　**本义**：不鲜明 not bright
词语：①政党political party　②死党best friend　③党员party member
句子：①这个政党被取缔了。This political party was banned.
　　　②她是玛丽的死党。She is one of the best friends of Mary's.
　　　③他们昨天接收了一名新党员。They took in a new party member yesterday.

记忆贴士

"党"的繁体字为"黨"，由"尚"（流行）和"黑"（不光明）组成，本义是不鲜明，引申出偏袒等含义。"党"现在常用的意思是政党。简体字"党"用"儿"取代"黑"。

The traditional character of 党 is 黨. It consists of 尚(popular) and 黑(dark). Its original meaning is not bright and extended to mean partical, etc. 党 now commonly means political party. 黑 is replaced by 儿 in the simplified character 党.

第二部分　500个常用汉字

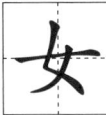
甲骨文 → 金文大篆 → 小篆 → 隶书 → 楷体

拼音：nǚ　　**部件**：女　　**部首**：女　　**结构**：独体
六书：象形　　**笔画**：3画　　**本义**：女人woman
词语：①妇女woman　②女孩girl　③子女children
句子：①妇女享有选举权。Women have the right to vote.
　　　②那个女孩有危险。The girl is in danger.
　　　③他有五个子女。He has five children.

记忆贴士

"女"的甲骨文字形 ᄼ 像一个交叉双臂、跪着的人，本义是女人。
女(oracle bone script is ᄼ) is like a kneeling person with the arms crossed. Its original meaning is woman.

金文大篆 → 小篆 → 隶书 → 楷体（繁体）→ 楷体（简体）

拼音：chuán；zhuàn　**部件**：亻、专　**部首**：亻　**结构**：左右
六书：形声　　**笔画**：6画　　**本义**：驿站courier station
词语：①传（chuán）统traditional　②传（chuán）奇legend　③传（zhuàn）记biography
句子：①我喜欢中国传统文化。I like traditional Chinese culture.
　　　②他是一个传奇人物。He is a legend.
　　　③这本书是一本关于乔布斯的传记。This book is a biography of Steve Jobs.

记忆贴士

"传"的繁体字为"傳"，由"亻"（人）和"專"（本义是纺锤，引申为旋转）组成，表示人转换车马的地方，本义是驿站，引申出传递和记载等含义。简体字"传"用"专"代替"專"。

The traditional character of 传 is 傳. It consists of 亻(person) and 專(original meaning is spindle and extended to mean to rotate), meaning the place to change carriages and horses. Its original meaning is courier station and extended to mean to pass and put down in writing, etc. 專 is replaced by 专 in simplified character 传.

风

風 → 風 → 風 → 风

小篆　隶书（繁体）　楷体（繁体）　楷体（简体）

拼音：fēng　　**部件**：几、乂　　**部首**：风　　**结构**：半包围

六书：形声　　**笔画**：4画　　**本义**：空气流动 wind

词语：①风暴 storm　②风格 style　③屏风 screen

句子：①这将引起一场政治风暴。This will cause a political storm.
②他的风格独树一帜。His style is unique.
③餐厅用屏风隔开了。The dining room is spaced by a screen.

记忆贴士

"风"的繁体字为"風"，由"凡"（声旁）和"虫"（飞虫扇动翅膀使空气流动）组成，本义是空气流动。简体字"风"用"乂"代替了"丿"和"虫"。

The traditional character of 风 is 風. It consists of 虫(flying insects flap their wings to make the air flow) and 凡(indicates pronunciation). The original meaning is air flow(wind).

丿 凡 风 风

信

信 → 信 → 信

小篆　隶书　楷体

拼音：xìn　　**部件**：亻、言　　**部首**：亻　　**结构**：左右

六书：会意　　**笔画**：9画　　**本义**：言语真诚 sincere

词语：①诚信 integrity　②信仰 believe in　③信心 confidence

句子：①他的诚信毋庸置疑。His integrity is unquestionable.
②我们信仰科学。We believe in science.
③你应该比他人更有信心。You should have more confidence than others.

记忆贴士

"信"由"亻"（人）和"言"（说话）组成，本义是言语真诚，引申出诚实和不怀疑等含义。

信 consists of 亻(person) and 言(speak). Its original meaning is sincere and extended to mean honest and no doubt, etc.

亻 亻 信 信 信 信 信 信 信

 凵 → 召 → 吕 → 名 → 名
甲骨文　金文大篆　小篆　　隶书　　楷体

拼音：míng　　**部件**：夕、口　　**部首**：夕　　**结构**：上下
六书：会意　　**笔画**：6画　　**本义**：说出自己的名字 introduce one's own name
词语：①名字 name　②名著 classic　③名片 business card
句子：①请告诉我您的名字和地址。Please tell me your name and address.
　　　　②《西游记》是一部中国文学名著。*Journey to the West* is a Chinese literary classic.
　　　　③这是我的名片。Here is my business card.

记忆贴士

"名"由"夕"（晚上）和"口"（说话）组成，表示天黑遇到人，报出自己的姓名。"名"的本义是说出自己的名字，引申出名字、著名等含义。

名 consists of 夕(night) and 口(speak), meaning that people meet at night and tell their own names. Its original meaning is to introduce one's name and extended to mean name and famous, etc.

丿 勹 夕 夕 名 名

 便 → 便 → 便
小篆　　隶书　　楷体

拼音：biàn；pián　　**部件**：亻、更　　**部首**：亻　　**结构**：左右
六书：会意　　**笔画**：9画　　**本义**：便利 convenient
词语：①方便（biàn）convenient　②方便（biàn）面 instant noodles　③便（pián）宜 cheap
句子：①您方便过来吗？Is it convenient for you to come?
　　　　②我中午吃方便面。I ate instant noodles for lunch.
　　　　③西红柿现在很便宜。Tomato is very cheap at the moment.

记忆贴士

"便"由"亻"（人）和"更"（更换）组成，表示更换人得到便利，本义是便利，引申出简单和物价较低等含义。

便 consists of 亻(person) and 更(change). It indicates to get convenience by substitution. The original meaning of 便 is convenient and extended to mean simple and cheap, etc.

丿 亻 仁 仨 伍 佰 佰 便 便

保

甲骨文 金文大篆 小篆 隶书 楷体

拼音：bǎo　　**部件**：亻、呆　　**部首**：亻　　**结构**：左右
六书：会意　　**笔画**：9画　　**本义**：背孩子 carry the baby on the back
词语：①保护 protect　②保险 insurance　③保留 keep
句子：①我们需要更好地保护地球。We need to protect our planet better.
　　　②他在保险公司工作。He works for an insurance company.
　　　③请保留所有的发票。Please keep all invoices.

记忆贴士

"保"由"亻"（人）和"呆"（小孩）组成，本义是背孩子，引申为保护和维持等含义。

保 consists of 亻(person) and 呆(child). Its original meaning is to carry the child on the back and extended to mean to protect and keep, etc.

育

甲骨文 小篆 隶书 楷体

拼音：yù　　**部件**：𠫓、月　　**部首**：月　　**结构**：上下
六书：会意　　**笔画**：8画　　**本义**：养孩子 raise the child
词语：①养育 bring up　②生育率 birth rate　③教育 education
句子：①感谢父母的养育之恩。Thank my parents for their raising.
　　　②生育率下降了。The birth rate has declined.
　　　③他们将要推进教育改革。They will advance education reform.

记忆贴士

"育"（小篆字形为𣫭）由"𠫓"（倒立的"子"，刚出生的婴儿）和"月"（肉）组成，表示让婴儿长肉，本义是养孩子。

育(xiaozhuan script is 𣫭) consists of 𠫓(inverted form of 子, means newborn baby) and 月 (flesh). It means to make baby increase flesh. Its original meaning is to raise the child.

第三十二节

队

𠂤 → 隊 → 隊 → 隊 → 队
金文大篆　小篆　　隶书　　楷体（繁体）楷体（简体）

拼音：duì　　　**部件**：阝、人　　**部首**：阝　　　**结构**：左右
六书：形声　　**笔画**：4画　　　**本义**：坠落drop
词语：①校队school team　②军队troops　③团队team
句子：①我们校队昨天获得了四分之一决赛的胜利。Our school team won the quarter final game yesteray.
②军队正在开往前线。The troops are moving to the front.
③我们需要团队精神。We need team spirit.

记忆贴士

"队"由"阝"（高处，"阝"出现在字的左边表示和地势高低有关）和"人"组成，表示人从高处掉下来，本义是坠落，引申出行列等含义。

队 consists of 阝(high place) and 人(person). It means that a person falls from a high place. Its original meaning is to drop and extended to mean a row, etc.

带

 → 帶 → 帶 → 带
小篆　　隶书　　楷体（繁体）楷体（简体）

拼音：dài　　　**部件**：艹、冖、巾　**部首**：巾　　　**结构**：上下
六书：象形　　**笔画**：9画　　　**本义**：腰带waistband
词语：①领带tie　②皮带belt　③宽带broadband
句子：①这个领带和你的衬衣很配。This tie goes with your shirt.
②你的领带下端要到皮带位置。Your tie should reach your belt.
③你家有宽带接口吗？Do you have broadband access in your home?

记忆贴士

"带"的小篆字形上面像腰间束的带子和结扣，下面像垂下的须子。"带"的本义是腰带，引申为随身拿着和引领等含义。

The xiaozhuan script of 带 is . It is like a tasseled waistband. Its original meaning is waistband and extended to mean to take and lead, etc.

叫

叫 → 叫 → 叫
小篆　隶书　楷体

拼音：jiào　　**部件**：口、丩　　**部首**：口　　**结构**：左右
六书：形声　　**笔画**：5画　　**本义**：呼喊 shout
词语：①喊叫 shout　②叫做 called　③尖叫 scream
句子：①他不得不喊叫以便别人能听到。He had to shout to make himself heard.
②这种工具叫做扳手。This tool is called a wrench.
③她大声尖叫。She screamed loudly.

记忆贴士

"叫"由"口"（嘴）和"丩"（声旁）组成，本义是呼喊，引申为称呼和让等含义。

叫 consists of 口(mouth) and 丩 (indicates pronunciation). Its original meaning is to shout and extended to mean to call and ask, etc.

丨 口 口 叫 叫

研

研 → 研 → 研
小篆　隶书　楷体

拼音：yán　　**部件**：石、开　　**部首**：石　　**结构**：左右
六书：形声　　**笔画**：9画　　**本义**：研磨 grind
词语：①研究 research　②调研 investigation　③研讨会 seminar
句子：①你的研究启发了我。Your research enlightened me.
②这个问题值得进一步调研。It deserves further investigation.
③我去北京参加了一个研讨会。I took part in a seminar in Beijing.

记忆贴士

"研"（小篆字形为 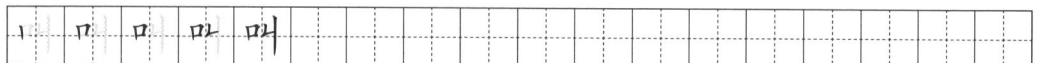）由"石"（石臼）和"开"（双杵，"开"的变形）组成，本义是研磨，引申为研究的意思。

研 consists of 石(stone mortar) and 开(deformation of 开, means double pestles). Its original meaning is to grind and extended to mean to research.

研 丁 丁 石 石 矴 矼 研 研

第二部分 500个常用汉字

领 → 领 → 领 → 领
小篆　隶书　楷体（繁体）　楷体（简体）

拼音：lǐng　　**部件**：令、页　　**部首**：页　　**结构**：左右
六书：形声　　**笔画**：11画　　**本义**：脖子neck
词语：①领悟understand　②领域field　③率领lead
句子：①我领悟了他的潜台词。I understood his unspoken words.
　　　　②他的研究已经涉及多个领域。His researches have extended into many fields.
　　　　③他率领人们抗击侵略者。He led people to fight against invaders.

记忆贴士

"领"由"令"（声旁）和"页"（头）组成，表示能令头转动的身体部位，本义是脖子，引申出指挥和理解等含义。

领 consists of 令(indicates pronunciation) and 页(head). It means the body part that can make the head rotate. Its original meaning is neck and extended to mean to command and understand, etc.

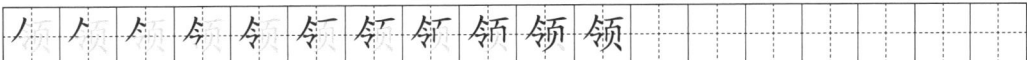

北 → 北 → 北 → 北 → 北
甲骨文　金文大篆　小篆　隶书　楷体

拼音：běi　　**部件**：丬、匕　　**部首**：匕　　**结构**：左右
六书：会意　　**笔画**：5画　　**本义**：相背opposite
词语：①北方north　②北极Arctic　③北风north wind
句子：①我出生在北方。I was born in the north.
　　　　②什么动物可以生活在北极？What animals can live in the Arctic?
　　　　③北风正在呼号。The north wind is whistling.

记忆贴士

"北"的甲骨文字形像两个人背对背，本义为相背。古代天子上朝时面向南方，所以背对的方向就是北。现在"北"的意思是北方。

北(oracle bone script is) is like two people back to back. The original meaning of 北 is opposite. The ancient emperors sat facing south in the palace, so their backs were to the north. Now 北 means north.

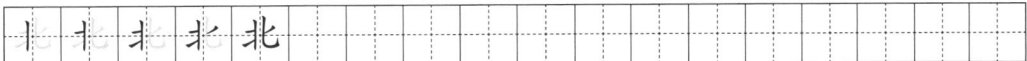

较

较 → 較 → 较
隶书　楷体（繁体）　楷体（简体）

拼音：jiào　　**部件**：车、交　　**部首**：车　　**结构**：左右
六书：形声　　**笔画**：10画
本义：古代车厢两旁木板上的横本 carriage's beam
词语：①比较compare　②计较care about　③较量measure one's strength with; try a fall with
句子：①我们仔细比较了这两家公司。We carefully compared the two companies.
　　　②我通常不会计较太多。I usually don't care about too much.
　　　③我们决定和他们较量一番。We have decided to try a fall with them.

记忆贴士

"较"由"车"（车辆）和"交"（声旁）组成，本义是古代车厢两旁木板上的横木，引申为较量等含义。

较 consists of 车(vehicle) and 交(indicates pronunciation). Its original meaning is the beam of wooden boards on both sides of the ancient carriage and extended to mean to compete.

张

張 → 張 → 张 → 张
小篆　隶书　楷体（繁体）　楷体（简体）

拼音：zhāng　　**部件**：弓、长　　**部首**：弓　　**结构**：左右
六书：形声　　**笔画**：7画　　**本义**：拉开弓 pull the bow
词语：①张开open　②紧张nervous　③主张assertion
句子：①请张开嘴。Please open your month.
　　　②他非常紧张。He is very nervous.
　　　③这是一个毫无道理的主张。This is an unreasonable assertion.

记忆贴士

"张"由"弓"（弓）和"长"（距离大）组成，本义是拉开弓，引申出紧张和张开等含义，还可以用作量词来修饰铺展形状的物体。

张 consists of 弓(bow) and 长(long distance). Its original meaning is to pull the bow and extended to mean nervous and to open, etc. It is also used as a measure word to modify the spreading objects.

即 → 即 → 即 → 即 → 即

甲骨文　金文大篆　小篆　隶书　楷体

拼音：jí　　**部件**：皀、卩　　**部首**：卩　　**结构**：左右

六书：会意　　**笔画**：7画　　**本义**：走近吃东西 come near to eat

词语：①即使 even if　②立即 at once　③即将 soon

句子：①即使这是真的，他也不能消除人们的怀疑。Even if this is true, he fails to dismiss other people's suspicion.

②我立即认出了她。I recognized her at once.

③更多的书即将出版。More books are soon to be published.

记忆贴士

"即"（甲骨文字形为 ）由"皀"（形状像食器）和"卩"（人）组成，本义是走近吃东西，引申出是和当时等含义。

即(oracle bone script is) consists of 皀(like a food utensil) and 卩(person). Its original meaning is to come near to eat and extended to mean to be and immediate, etc.

→ → → 至 → 至

甲骨文　金文大篆　小篆　隶书　楷体

拼音：zhì　　**部件**：一、厶、土　　**部首**：至　　**结构**：上下

六书：会意　　**笔画**：6画　　**本义**：到达 arrive

词语：①至于 as to　②甚至 even　③冬至 winter solstice

句子：①至于这个问题，我们还需要进一步研究。As to this question, we need a further research.

②他们甚至让人认为这很简单。They even convince others that it is easy for them.

③明天是冬至。Tomorrow is the winter solstice.

记忆贴士

"至"的甲骨文字形 上面是一个头冲下的箭，下面的"一"表示地面，表示箭落地。"至"的本义是到达，引申出最等含义。

The oracle bone script of 至 is . It is like an arrow falling onto the ground. Its original meaning is to arrive and extended to mean the most, etc.

第三十三节

計 → 訮 → 許 → 許 → 许

金文大篆　　小篆　　　隶书　　楷体（繁体）楷体（简体）

拼音：xǔ　　**部件**：讠、午　　**部首**：讠　　**结构**：左右
六书：形声　　**笔画**：6画　　**本义**：应允permit
词语：①允许allow　②许诺promise　③或许perhaps
句子：①宠物不允许带入博物馆。Pets are not allowed into the museum.
　　　　②不要相信轻率的许诺。Don't believe an hasty promise.
　　　　③或许你是对的。Perhaps you are right.

记忆贴士

"许"由"讠"（说话）和"午"（杵，"杵"的省写）组成，杵在使用时上下运动像点头，合起来表示说话时频频点头。"许"的本义是应允。

许 consists of 讠(speak) and 午(omitted form of 杵, means nod). When 杵 is used, its movement is like nodding. 许 means to nod frequently when one speaks. The original meaning of 许 is to permit.

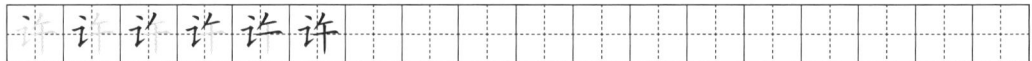

→ → → 步 → 步

甲骨文　金文大篆　　小篆　　　隶书　　楷体

拼音：bù　　**部件**：止、少　　**部首**：止　　**结构**：上下
六书：会意　　**笔画**：7画　　**本义**：行走walk
词语：①散步take a walk　②进步progress　③步骤step
句子：①你想散步吗？Would you like to take a walk?
　　　　②他在不断进步。He makes unceasing progress.
　　　　③最后一个步骤很关键。The last step is crucial.

记忆贴士

"步"的甲骨文字形像两只脚，表示两脚一前一后走路。"步"的本义是行走，引申出脚步等含义。

The oracle bone script of 步 is . It is like two feet and means to walk. The original meaning of 步 is to walk and extended to mean step, etc.

 甲骨文 → 金文大篆 → 小篆 → 隶书 → 楷体

拼音：wǎng　　**部件**：彳、主　　**部首**：彳　　**结构**：左右
六书：会意　　**笔画**：8画　　**本义**：去 go to
词语：①向往 look forward to　②交往 associate with　③以往 before
句子：①这就是我向往的生活。This is the life that I look forward to.
②他们交往很频繁。They associate with each other frequently.
③我们的生活比以往更方便了。Our life is more convenient than before.

记忆贴士

"往"的甲骨文字形像一个人在走路，脚迈向前方，后来加上表示和行走有关的偏旁"彳"。"往"的本义是去，引申出过去等含义。

The oracle bone script of 往 is . It is like a walking person with a foot ahead. 彳(walk) was added later. Its original meaning is to go to a place and extended to mean the past, etc.

 金文大篆 → 小篆 → 隶书 → 楷体（繁体）→ 楷体（简体）

拼音：tīng　　**部件**：口、斤　　**部首**：口　　**结构**：左右
六书：形声　　**笔画**：7画　　**本义**：用耳朵接收声音 listen
词语：①听见 hear　②听说 hear about　③听力 hearing
句子：①你能听见我说话吗？Can you hear me?
②你听说过这个名字吗？Have you heard about this name?
③他听力极好。His hearing is excellent.

记忆贴士

"听"的金文字形像耳朵和嘴。"听"由"口"（嘴）和"斤"（声旁）组成，本义是用耳朵接收声音，引申出顺从等含义。

The bronze inscription of 听 is . It is like an ear and mouths. 听 consists of 口(mouth) and 斤(indicates pronunciation). Its original meaning is to listen and extended to mean to obey, etc.

调

调 → 调 → 调 → 调
小篆　　隶书　　楷体（繁体）　楷体（简体）

拼音：tiáo；diào　　**部件**：讠、周　　**部首**：讠　　**结构**：左右
六书：形声　　**笔画**：10画
本义：和谐 harmonious
词语：①协调（tiáo）coordinate　②调（tiáo）节 adjust　③声调（diào）tone
句子：①各个部门之间协调得很好。Branches are well coordinated.
②你能帮我调节一下靠背吗？Could you help me adjust the back of my seat?
③汉语普通话有四个声调。There are four tones in Mandarin Chinese.

记忆贴士

"调"由"讠"（说话）和"周"（周全）组成，表示通过协商达成意见一致，本义是和谐，引申出协调和声调等含义。

调 consists of 讠(speak) and 周(considerate). It means that consensus is reached through consultations. Its original meaning is harmony and extended to mean to coordinate and tone, etc.

调 调 讠 讠 讠 讠 讠 调 调 调 调

务

務 → 務 → 務 → 务
小篆　　隶书　　楷体（繁体）　楷体（简体）

拼音：wù　　**部件**：夂、力　　**部首**：夂　　**结构**：上下
六书：形声　　**笔画**：5画　　**本义**：从事 be engaged in
词语：①服务 service　②务必 must　③义务 obligation
句子：①他们提供各种服务。They offer various kinds of services.
②你们务必准时到达。You must arrive on time.
③这是我们的义务。This is our obligation.

记忆贴士

"务"的繁体字为"務"，由"矛"（长矛）、"夂"（手持武器）和"力"（力量）组成，表示致力于做某事，本义是从事，引申出任务和必须等含义。

The traditional character of 务 is 務. It consists of 矛(spear), 夂(hold weapon) and 力(strength). It means to be committed to doing something. Its original meaning is to be engaged in and extended to mean tasks and must, etc.

花

𰻝 → 花
隶书　　楷体

拼音：huā　　**部件**：艹、化　　**部首**：艹　　**结构**：上下
六书：形声　　**笔画**：7画　　**本义**：种子植物的有性生殖器官 flower
词语：①花瓣 petal　②荷花 lotus　③花园 garden
句子：①白色花瓣漂浮在水面上。White petals are floating on the water.
　　　　②荷花盛开在池塘里。Lotuses are blooming in the pond.
　　　　③他在花园里种了棵苹果树。He grows an apple tree in the garden.

记忆贴士

"花"由"艹"（草木）和"化"（声旁）组成，本义是种子植物的有性生殖器官，引申为颜色和种类错杂以及用掉等含义。

花 consists of 艹(grass and tree) and 化(indicates pronunciation). Its original meaning is flower and extended to mean multicolored and to spend, etc.

争

 → 𤰔 → 争 → 争
甲骨文　　小篆　　隶书　　楷体

拼音：zhēng　　**部件**：⺈、彐　　**部首**：⺈　　**结构**：上下
六书：会意　　**笔画**：6画　　**本义**：争夺 contend
词语：①争夺 vie　②竞争 competition　③战争 war
句子：①两个选手正在争夺冠军。Two players are vying for the championship.
　　　　②这个公司面临激烈的竞争。This company faces intense competition.
　　　　③战争一触即发。War may break out at any moment.

记忆贴士

"争"的甲骨文字形像上面一只手和下面一只手争抢东西，本义是争夺。

The oracle bone script of 争 is . It is like two hands contending for something. The original meaning of 争 is to contend.

线

綫 → 線 → 线
隶书　楷体（繁体）　楷体（简体）

拼音：xiàn　　**部件**：纟、戋　　**部首**：纟　　**结构**：左右
六书：形声　　**笔画**：8画　　**本义**：线缕 twine
词语：①天线 antenna　②线索 clue　③路线 route
句子：①机器里装有天线。An antenna is assembled into the machine.
　　　　②没有任何关于他的线索。There is no clue about him.
　　　　③这是最短的路线。This is the shortest route.

记忆贴士

"线"的繁体字为"綫"，由"糹"（丝）和"戋"（细小）组成，本义是线缕，引申出用丝、金属、棉或麻等制成的细长东西以及像线的东西等含义。

The traditional character of 线 is 綫. It consists of 糹 (thread) and 戋(small). Its original meaning is twine and extended to mean a slender thing made of silk, metal, cotton or hemp and something like a thread, etc.

呢

呢 → 呢
隶书　楷体

拼音：ní；ne　　**部件**：口、尼　　**部首**：口　　**结构**：左右
六书：形声　　**笔画**：8画　　**本义**：悄声说话 whisper
词语：①呢（ní）子 woolen　②呢（ní）喃 twitter　③你呢（ne）how about you?
句子：①我有一件呢子大衣。I have a woolen clothes.
　　　　②燕语呢喃。The swallows are twittering.
　　　　③你呢？How about you?

记忆贴士

"呢"由"口"（说话）和"尼"（声旁）组成，本义是悄声说话。"呢"现在指一种毛织物，并普遍地用作疑问语气助词。

呢 consists of 口(speak) and 尼(indicates pronunciation). It originally means to whisper. Now 呢 refers to woolen cloth and it is commonly used as an interrogative modal particle.

第三十四节

甲骨文　金文大篆　小篆　隶书　楷体

拼音：měi　　**部件**：⺧、母　　**部首**：母　　**结构**：上下
六书：形声　　**笔画**：7画　　**本义**：草长得茂盛 flourish
词语：①每天every day　②每当whenever
句子：①孩子们每天步行上学。The children go to school by foot every day.
　　　②每当他看书的时候，总是放轻音乐。Whenever he was reading, light music was always played.

记忆贴士

"每"的甲骨文字形 上面是"屮"，"屮"的意思是草木初生，下面是"女"。"每"的本义是草长得茂盛，现在指全体中的任何一个或一组以及反复动作中的任何一次或一组。

The oracle bone script of 每 is . It consists of 屮(grass grow out) and 女(woman), meaning that grass flourish. Its original meaning is to flourish and now it commonly means every and often.

金文大篆　小篆　隶书　楷体（繁体）　楷体（简体）

拼音：biān　　**部件**：辶、力　　**部首**：辶　　**结构**：半包围
六书：形声　　**笔画**：5画　　**本义**：边疆borderland
词语：①边缘verge　②边疆borderland　③外边outside
句子：①他处在崩溃的边缘。He was on the verge of breaking down.
　　　②这支部队驻守边疆。This army is guarding the borderland.
　　　③他住在学校外边。He lives outside the campus.

记忆贴士

"边"的小篆字形 由"辶"（走路）、"自"（鼻子，代指脸）和"穴"（洞穴，艰苦的住宿条件）"方"（犯人戴着枷锁）组成，意思是将犯人脸上刺字，发配到边疆。"边"的本义是边疆，引申为事物的外缘。简体字"边"用"力"取代了复杂部件。

The xiaozhuan script of 边 is . It consists of 辶(walk), 自(nose, represents face), 穴(cave) and 方(prisoner), indicating that a prisoner is given a tattoo on the face and exiled to the borderland. The original meaning of 边 is borderland and extended to mean the outer edge of things. The simplified character 边 consists of 辶(walk) and 力(strength).

难 | 難 → 難 → 難 → 難 → 难
| 金文大篆 | 小篆 | 隶书 | 楷体（繁体） | 楷体（简体） |

拼音：nán；nàn　　**部件**：又、隹　　**部首**：又　　**结构**：左右
六书：形声　　**笔画**：10画　　**本义**：一种鸟 a kind of bird
词语：①困难（nán）difficulty　②难（nán）过 sad　③灾难（nàn）disaster
句子：①我们能战胜困难。We can overcome the difficulties.
　　　　②我很难过。I am so sad.
　　　　③灾难已经过去了。The disaster is gone.

记忆贴士

"难"的繁体字为"難"，"隹"表示短尾鸟，"難"的本义为一种鸟的名字，假借为灾难的意思，引申出困难等含义。简体字"难"用"又"取代了繁体字左边复杂的部件。

　　The traditional character of 难 is 難. Its original meaning is a kind of bird. It is used to mean disaster and extended to mean difficult. The complex radical is replaced by 又 in simplified character 难.

 太 → 太
| 隶书 | 楷体 |

拼音：tài　　**部件**：大、丶　　**部首**：大　　**结构**：独体
六书：指事　　**笔画**：4画　　**本义**：过于 excessively
词语：①太阳 sun　②太高 too high　③太大 too big
句子：①地球绕太阳公转。The earth rotates around the sun.
　　　　②银行贷款利率太高。The loan rate of the bank is too high.
　　　　③这个杯子太大。This cup is too big.

记忆贴士

"太"由"大"和"丶"（指事符号）组成，表示比大还大，本义是过于。

　　太 consists of 大(big) and 丶(indicative symbol), indicating bigger. Its original meaning is excessively.

共 → 共 → 共 → 共 → 共
甲骨文　金文大篆　小篆　　隶书　　楷体

拼音：gòng　　**部件**：廾、八　　**部首**：八　　**结构**：上下
六书：象形　　**笔画**：6画　　**本义**：手捧祭品祭拜 hold sacrifice for worship
词语：①公共 public　②共同 common　③共享 sharing
句子：①不要在公共区域抽烟。Don't smoke in the public area.
　　　　②我们有很多共同习惯。We have many common habits.
　　　　③这个技术将促进信息共享。This technology will boost information-sharing.

记忆贴士

"共"的金文字形 像双手捧东西的样子，本义是手捧祭品祭拜，引申出合起来的含义。

The bronze inscription of 共 is . It is like holding things in both hands. Its original meaning is to hold sacrifice for worship and extended to mean together.

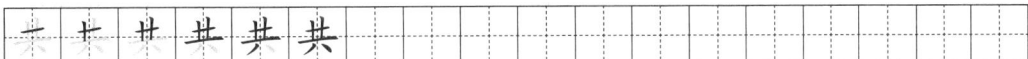

交 → 交 → 交 → 交 → 交
甲骨文　金文大篆　小篆　　隶书　　楷体

拼音：jiāo　　**部件**：亠、八、乂　　**部首**：亠　　**结构**：上下
六书：象形　　**笔画**：6画　　**本义**：交叉 cross
词语：①交通 transportation　②交流 communicate　③提交 submit
句子：①城市里公共交通很方便。It is very convenient to use public transportation in the city.
　　　　②我们使用互联网交流信息。We use the Internet to communicate information.
　　　　③请提交个人简历。Please submit a resume.

记忆贴士

"交"的小篆字形 像人两腿交叉，本义是交叉，引申出交流和给等含义。

The xiaozhuan script of 交 is . It is like a person with two legs crossed. Its original meaning is to cross and extended to mean to exchange and give, etc.

确

礭 → 确 → 确
小篆　隶书　楷体

拼音：què　　**部件**：石、角　　**部首**：石　　**结构**：左右
六书：形声　　**笔画**：12画　　**本义**：坚硬 firm
词语：①确实 indeed　②明确 expressly　③正确 correct
句子：①这台电脑确实便宜。This computer is indeed cheap.
②他已经明确指出了那个错误。He expressly pointed out the mistake.
③两个答案都正确。Both answers are correct.

记忆贴士

"确"由"石"（石头）和"角"（兽角）组成，本义是坚硬，引申出坚定和不可动摇等含义。

确 consists of 石(stone) and 角(horn). Its original meaning is firm, and extended to mean resolute and unshakable, etc.

劳

勞 → 勞 → 勞 → 劳
小篆　隶书　楷体（繁体）　楷体（简体）

拼音：láo　　**部件**：艹、冖、力　　**部首**：力　　**结构**：上下
六书：会意　　**笔画**：7画　　**本义**：努力劳动 work hard
词语：①劳动 labor　②勤劳 laborious　③劳累 weariness
句子：①我为他的劳动支付报酬。I paid him for his labor.
②蜜蜂是勤劳的昆虫。Bees are laborious insects.
③他因为劳累而晕倒。He fainted from weariness.

记忆贴士

"劳"的繁体字为"勞"，由"火"（心情焦虑）、"冖"（房子）和"力"（用力）组成，意思是在家里艰辛地劳动。"劳"的本义为努力劳动，引申出费力和辛苦等含义。简体字"劳"用"艹"代替"炏"。

The traditional character of 劳 is 勞. It consists of 火(anxious), 冖(house) and 力(strength). It means to work hard at home. Its original meaning is to work hard and extended to mean laborious. 炏 is replaced by 艹 in simplified character 劳.

据

据 → 据 → 据　據 → 據 → 據 → 据

金文大篆　隶书　楷体　小篆　隶书　楷体（繁体）楷体（简体）

拼音：jù；jū　　**部件**：扌、居　　**部首**：扌　　**结构**：左右
六书：形声　　**笔画**：11画　　**本义**：维持生活 maintain family life
词语：①占据（jù）occupy　②根据（jù）according to　③拮据（jū）short of money
句子：①读书占据了他的大部分业余时间。Reading occupies most of his spare time.
　　　　②我们会根据情况修改方案。We will modify the plan according to the situation.
　　　　③他生活很拮据。His life is very short of money.

记忆贴士

简体字"据"有两个来源，一个是"据"，另一个是"據"。

"据"由"扌"（手）和"居"（生活）组成，本义是维持家庭生活。

"據"由"扌"（手）和"豦"（老虎捕猪）组成，本义是强行占有，引申出凭借等含义。

现在"据"和"據"都写作"据"。

The simplified character 据 has two sources.

据 consists of 扌 (hand) and 居(live). Its original meaning is to maintain family life.

據 consists of 扌 (hand) and 豦(tiger catching pig). Its original meaning is to forcibly occupy and extended to mean to depend on, etc.

Now both 据 and 據 are written as 据.

一 扌 扌 扩 护 护 护 据 据 据 据

达

 達 → 薛 → 達 → 達 → 达

金文大篆　小篆　隶书　楷体（繁体）楷体（简体）

拼音：dá　　**部件**：辶、大　　**部首**：辶　　**结构**：半包围
六书：形声　　**笔画**：6画　　**本义**：道路通畅 road is unobstructed
词语：①到达 arrival　②发达 flourish　③表达 express
句子：①请告诉我准确的到达时间。Please tell me the specific time of arrival.
　　　　②这里的商业很发达。Commerce is flourishing here.
　　　　③语言无法表达我的感激之情。Words could not express my gratefulness.

记忆贴士

"达"由"辶"（行走）和"大"（人，也作声旁）组成，本义是道路通畅，引申为到达和告知等含义。

达 consists of 辶_(walk) and 大(person, also indicates pronunciation). Its original meaning is that the road is unobstructed and extended to mean to arrive and express, etc.

一 大 大 decided 达 达

第三十五节

住 → 住
隶书　楷体

拼音：zhù　　**部件**：亻、主　　**部首**：亻　　**结构**：左右
六书：形声　　**笔画**：7画　　**本义**：停止 stop
词语：①居住live　②记住remember　③住宿accommodation
句子：①他们居住在湖边。They live by the lake.
　　　②记住你的密码。Remember your password.
　　　③学校为我们提供住宿。School provides accommodation for us.

记忆贴士

"住"由"亻"（人）和"主"（声旁）组成，本义是停止，引申出停留等含义。

住 consists of 亻(person) and 主(indicates pronunciation). Its original meaning is to stop and extended to mean to stay, etc.

丿 亻 亻 仁 仁 住 住

 → 收 → 收
小篆　　隶书　　楷体

拼音：shōu　　**部件**：丩、攵　　**部首**：攵　　**结构**：左右
六书：形声　　**笔画**：6画　　**本义**：捕获capture
词语：①收获harvest　②收拾tidy up　③收集collect
句子：①秋天是收获的季节。Auntumn is the season for harvest.
　　　②他正在收拾房间。He is tidying up his room.
　　　③我正在为实验收集样本。I am collecting samples for the experiment.

记忆贴士

"收"由"丩"（绳索）和"攵"（手持棍棒）组成，表示用棍子和绳索捕获猎物。"收"的本义是捕获，引申出接收和结束等含义。

收 consists of 丩(rope) and 攵(hold stick). It means to capture prey with sticks and ropes. Its original meaning is to capture and extended to mean to receive and end, etc.

丩 丩 収 収 收 收

候 → 候 → 候
小篆　　隶书　　楷体

拼音：hòu　　**部件**：亻、丨、⊐、矢　　**部首**：亻　　**结构**：左右
六书：形声　　**笔画**：10画　　**本义**：侦查 reconnoitre
词语：①气候 clime　②问候 greet　③候鸟 migrant bird
句子：①这里气候寒冷。The climate here is cold.
　　　②他们彼此问候。They greeted each other.
　　　③候鸟飞往南方。Migrant birds fly to the south.

记忆贴士

"候"由"亻"（人）和"矦"（山崖和矢）组成，意思是猎人带着弓箭在山崖间埋伏等待猎物，本义是侦查，引申为等待和时节等含义。

候 consists of 亻(person) and 矦(cliff and arrow). It means that the hunter ambushes the prey with bow and arrow between the cliffs. Its original meaning is to reconnoitre and extended to mean to wait and season, etc.

需 → 需 → 需 → 需
金文大篆　　小篆　　隶书　　楷体

拼音：xū　　**部件**：雨、而　　**部首**：雨　　**结构**：上下
六书：会意　　**笔画**：14画　　**本义**：等待 wait
词语：①需要 need　②无需 no need　③需求 need
句子：①我们需要一位汉语导游。We need a Chinese-speaking guide.
　　　②在这方面无需多花费时间。There is no need to spend much time on it.
　　　③请告诉我你的需求。Please tell me your needs.

记忆贴士

"需"（小篆字形为𩂉）由"雨"（下雨）和"而"（人）组成，表示遇到雨天人停下来等待，本义是等待，由等待必有所求引申出需求等含义。

需(xiaozhuan script is 𩂉) consists of 雨(rain) and 而(person). It means that when it rains people stop walking and wait. Its original meaning is to wait and extended to mean to require, etc.

转

轉 → 轉 → 轉 → 转
小篆　　隶书　　楷体（繁体）楷体（简体）

拼音：zhuǎn；zhuàn　　**部件**：车、专　　**部首**：车　　**结构**：左右
六书：形声　　**笔画**：8画　　**本义**：迁徙 move
词语：①转（zhuǎn）让 transfer　②旋转（zhuǎn）spin　③转（zhuàn）动 turn
句子：①火车票不得转让。The train ticket cannot be transfered.
　　　②陀螺在桌子上不停旋转。The top is spinning incessantly on the table.
　　　③这个水龙头容易转动。This tap turns easily.

记忆贴士

"转"由"车"（车子）和"专"（声旁）组成，本义是迁徙，引申出改变方向、绕圈子等含义。

转 consists of 车(vehicle) and 专(indicates pronunciation). Its original meaning is to move and extended to mean to change the way and walk around, etc.

百

 → 百 → 百 → 百 → 百
甲骨文　金文大篆　小篆　　隶书　　楷体

拼音：bǎi　　**部件**：一、白　　**部首**：一　　**结构**：上下
六书：形声　　**笔画**：6画　　**本义**：十个十 a hundred
词语：①老百姓 common people　②百灵鸟 lark　③百合花 lily
句子：①经济改革给老百姓生活带来了巨大变化。The economic reform brought about great changes in the lives of common people.
　　　②他养了一只百灵鸟。He raises a lark.
　　　③我买了一些白色的百合花。I bought some white lilies.

记忆贴士

"百"在"白"（声旁）上面加一横，本义是十个十。

百 consists of 白(indicates pronunciation) and 一, meaning a hundred.

南

甲骨文　金文大篆　小篆　隶书　楷体

- **拼音**：nán
- **部件**：十、冂、丷、干
- **部首**：十
- **结构**：上下
- **六书**：象形
- **笔画**：9画
- **本义**：乐器名 name of a kind of musical instrument
- **词语**：①南方 south　②指南针 compass　③南极洲 Antarctic
- **句子**：①南方阳光充足。The south enjoys ample sunshine.
    ②指南针可以帮助我们找到正确的方向。The compass will help us find the right direction.
    ③南极洲终年被冰雪覆盖。The Antarctic is covered with ice all year round.

记忆贴士

"南"的甲骨文字形像一个悬挂的敲击乐器，本义是乐器名，假借为南方的南。

The oracle bone script of 南 is . It is like a hanging percussion instrument and its original meaning is the name of a kind of musical instrument. Now 南 refers to south.

清

小篆　隶书　楷体

- **拼音**：qīng
- **部件**：氵、青
- **部首**：氵
- **结构**：左右
- **六书**：形声
- **笔画**：11画
- **本义**：水清澈 limpid
- **词语**：①清澈 limpid　②清晰 clear　③清新 fresh
- **句子**：①湖水清澈见底。The lake water is limpid.
    ②图像很清晰。The image is very clear.
    ③我们喜欢清新的空气。We like fresh air.

记忆贴士

"清"由"氵"（水）和"青"（漂亮，"倩"的省写）组成，本义是水清澈，引申为明白和一点不留等含义。

清 consists of 氵(water) and 青(omitted form of 倩, means beautiful). Its original meaning is limpid and extended to mean clarified and nothing left, etc.

格

格 → 格 → 格 → 格
金文大篆　小篆　隶书　楷体

拼音：gé　　**部件**：木、各　　**部首**：木　　**结构**：左右
六书：形声　　**笔画**：10画　　**本义**：树木的长枝条 long branch of tree
词语：①格外extraordinary　②性格character　③风格style
句子：①他对老年人格外耐心。He has shown extraordinary patience towards the elder.
②他们的性格很相似。They are much alike in character.
③你喜欢哪种风格的衣服？What style of clothes do you like?

记忆贴士

"格"由"木"（树）和"各"（声旁）组成，本义是树木的长枝条，引申出标准和类型等含义。

格 consists of 木(tree) and 各(indicates pronunciation). Its original meaning is the long branch of tree and extended to mean norm and type, etc.

一 十 才 木 朾 柊 柊 格 格 格

影

影 → 影
隶书　楷体

拼音：yǐng　　**部件**：景、彡　　**部首**：彡　　**结构**：左右
六书：形声　　**笔画**：15画　　**本义**：影子shadow
词语：①影子shadow　②摄影photography　③倒影reflection
句子：①你看到的是你自己的影子。What you see is your own shadow.
②我喜欢摄影。I enjoy photography.
③我看到了湖中自己的倒影。I caught my reflection in the lake.

记忆贴士

"影"由"景"（太阳照在高大建筑上投射出的影子）和"彡"（光）组成，本义是影子，引申出影像等含义。

影 consists of 景(the shadow of tall buildings caused by the sun) and 彡(sunshine). Its original meaning is shadow and extended to mean image, etc.

丨 口 曰 旦 早 昙 景 景 景 景 景 影 影 影 影

第三十六节

書 → 書 → 書 → 書 → 书
金文大篆　小篆　　隶书　楷体（繁体）楷体（简体）

拼音：shū　　**部件**：书　　**部首**：一　　**结构**：独体
六书：形声　　**笔画**：4画　　**本义**：书写write
词语：①书籍books　②秘书secretary　③读书reading
句子：①阅读书籍可以拓宽你的知识面。Reading books can widen your horizon of knowledge.
　　　②他在这家公司做行政秘书。He works as an executive secretary in this company.
　　　③我花很多时间读书。I spent much time in reading.

记忆贴士

"书"的繁体字为"書"，由"聿"（手握笔）和"曰"（写的内容）组成，本义是书写，引申出著作、文件等含义。简体字"书"由"書"的草书字形楷化而成。

The traditional character of 书 is 書. It consists of 聿(hold pen) and 曰(character). Its original meaning is to write and extended to mean book and document, etc. The simplified character 书 is the deformation of the cursive script.

切 → 切 → 切
小篆　隶书　楷体

拼音：qiē；qiè　　**部件**：七、刀　　**部首**：刀　　**结构**：左右
六书：形声　　**笔画**：4画　　**本义**：用刀切割物体cut with knife
词语：①切（qiē）除cut off　②亲切（qiè）kind　③一切（qiè）everything
句子：①科学家切除了小鼠的脾脏。The scientist cut off the mouse's spleen.
　　　②他对学生很和善。He is kind to students.
　　　③我不相信你所说的一切。I don't believe everything that you said.

记忆贴士

"切"由"七"（切分）和"刀"组成，本义是用刀切割物体，引申出贴近和急迫等含义。

切 consists of 七(cut) and 刀(knife). Its original meaning is to cut with knife and extended to mean close and eager, etc.

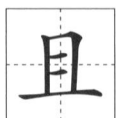

甲骨文　金文大篆　小篆　隶书　楷体

拼音：qiě　　**部件**：且　　**部首**：｜　　**结构**：独体
六书：象形　　**笔画**：5画　　**本义**：平均分割的肉 meat cut equally
词语：①而且 and　②暂且 for the moment　③并且 and
句子：①我们喜欢中国而且去过很多次。We like China and have been there many times.
　　　　②让我们暂且休息一下。Let us have a rest for the moment.
　　　　③他很年轻并且很有才华。He is young and gifted.

记忆贴士

"且"像平均分割的肉，本义是祭祀祖先时平分肉食。现在多用作连词，表示并列关系。

且 is like the meat that is equally cut. The meat is cut equally when ancestors are sacrificed. The original meaning of 且 is meat cut equally. Now it is used as a conjunction to indicate the parallel relationship.

隶书　楷体

拼音：què　　**部件**：去、卩　　**部首**：卩　　**结构**：左右
六书：形声　　**笔画**：7画　　**本义**：后退 move back
词语：①忘却 forget　②退却 quit　③冷却 cool down
句子：①我无法忘却她。I could not forget her.
　　　　②他绝不会退却。He will never quit.
　　　　③让发动机自行冷却。Let the engine cool down by itself.

记忆贴士

"却"由"去"（离开）和"卩"（人）组成，本义是后退，引申出拒绝等含义。现在主要用作副词表示转折关系。

却 consists of 去(leave) and 卩(person). Its original meaning is to move back and extended to mean to reject, etc. Now it is used as an adverb to indicate the adversative relationship.

金文大篆 → 小篆 → 隶书 → 楷体

拼音：zhì　　**部件**：士、心　　**部首**：士　　**结构**：上下
六书：形声　　**笔画**：7画　　**本义**：志向 ambition
词语：①志向 ambition　②意志 will　③标志 sign
句子：①我的志向是成为一名教师。It is my ambition to be a teacher.
②这支军队有钢铁般的意志。This army has an iron will.
③我没有看到那个标志。I didn't see the sign.

记忆贴士

"志"（小篆字形为 ）由"士"（前往，"止"的变形）和"心"组成，表示心之所向、内心追求的目标，本义是志向。

志 (xiaozhuan script is) consists of 士 (deformation of 止, means to go) and 心 (heart), meaning inner goal in the heart. Its original meaning is ambition.

一 十 士 志 志 志 志

小篆 → 隶书 → 楷体（繁体）→ 楷体（简体）

拼音：rè　　**部件**：扌、丸、灬　　**部首**：灬　　**结构**：上下
六书：形声　　**笔画**：10画　　**本义**：温度高 hot
词语：①闷热 stuffy　②热情 enthusiasm　③热烈 heated
句子：①这是个闷热的房间。This is a stuffy room.
②我有极大的工作热情。I have great enthusiasm about work.
③我们展开了热烈的讨论。We had a heated discussion.

记忆贴士

"热"的繁体字为"熱"，其小篆字形 像一个人手拿物品在火上加热，本义是温度高。简体字"热"用"扌"代替"埶"。

The traditional character of 热 is 熱. Its xiaozhuan script is , which is like a person holding something and heating it on the fire. Its original meaning is hot. 埶 is replaced by 扌 in simplified character 热.

一 十 扌 执 执 热 热 热 热 热

聯 → 聯 → 聯 → 联

小篆　　隶书　　楷体（繁体）楷体（简体）

拼音：lián　　　　**部件**：耳、关　　　　**部首**：耳　　　　**结构**：左右

六书：会意　　　　**笔画**：12画　　　　**本义**：连结 link

词语：①联系 connection　②对联 couplets　③联盟 union

句子：①这两个因素之间存在联系。There is a connection between the two factors.

②这些对联是他父亲写的。These couplets are written by his father.

③我们成立了一个新的联盟。We set up a new union.

记忆贴士

"联"的小篆字形为 聯，由"耳"和"丝"组成，本义为连结。简体字"联"用"关"代替繁体字中的复杂部件。

The xiaozhuan script of 联 is 聯. It consists of 耳(ear) and 丝(silk thread). The original meaning of 联 is to link. The complex radical of traditional character is replaced by 关 in simplified character.

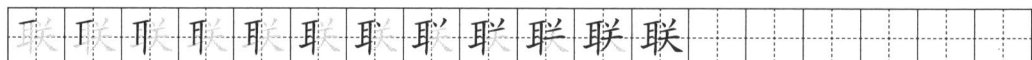

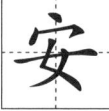

→ → → 安 → 安

甲骨文　金文大篆　小篆　　隶书　　楷体

拼音：ān　　　　**部件**：宀、女　　　　**部首**：宀　　　　**结构**：上下

六书：会意　　　　**笔画**：6画　　　　**本义**：稳定 stable

词语：①安全 safe　②安静 quiet　③安慰 console

句子：①现在安全了。It is safe now.

②保持安静。Keep quiet.

③我尝试着安慰她。I try to console her.

记忆贴士

"安"由"宀"（房子）和"女"（妻子）组成，意思是有房子和妻子，本义是生活稳定，引申出安全和安装等含义。

安 consists of 宀(house) and 女(wife). It means to have a house and a wife. Its original meaning is stable and extended to mean safe and to install, etc.

极

极 → 極 → 極 → 极
小篆　　隶书　　楷体（繁体）　楷体（简体）

拼音：jí　　**部件**：木、及　　**部首**：木　　**结构**：左右
六书：形声　　**笔画**：7画　　**本义**：房屋的正梁 ridgepole

词语：①积极positive　②消极negative　③极端extreme
句子：①他态度很积极。He has a positive attitude.
②我努力摆脱这件事的消极影响。I tried to get rid of the negative impact of this event.
③这是一个极端的例子。This is an extreme case.

记忆贴士

"极"的繁体字为"極"，由"木"和"亟"组成。"亟"的含义是在命令和鞭策下人所能达到的极限。"極"的本义是房屋的正梁，引申出极端等含义。简体字"极"用"及"代替"亟"。

The traditional character of 极 is 極. It consists of 木 and 亟. The original meaning of 亟 is the limits that people can reach under order and spur. The original meaning of 極 is ridgepole of the house and extended to mean extreme, etc. 亟 is replaced by 及 in the simplified character.

今

 → 今 → 今 → 今 → 今
甲骨文　金文大篆　小篆　　隶书　　楷体

拼音：jīn　　**部件**：人、丶、㇇　　**部首**：人　　**结构**：上下
六书：会意　　**笔画**：4画　　**本义**：自言自语 say to oneself

词语：①今天today　②今晚tonight　③今年this year
句子：①今天我们学习汉字。Today we will learn Chinese characters.
②今晚我给你打电话。I will call you tonight.
③他们今年必须削减开支。They have to reduce expenses this year.

记忆贴士

"今"的甲骨文字形像低头沉吟，本义是自言自语，引申为说话当时，即目前、现在的意思。

The oracle bone script of 今 is . It is like looking down and talking to oneself. The original meaning is to say to oneself and extended to mean present and now, etc.

第三十七节

 Y → ♀ → 単 → 單 → 單 → 单

甲骨文　金文大篆　小篆　隶书　楷体（繁体）楷体（简体）

拼音：dān　　**部件**：丷、田、十　　**部首**：丷　　**结构**：上下
六书：象形　　**笔画**：8画　　**本义**：一种狩猎工具 a kind of hunting tool
词语：①单调 monotony　②简单 simple　③孤单 lonely
句子：①旅游也许有助于改变你单调的生活。Having a tour may help break the monotony of your life.
②这是一个简单的游戏。This is a simple game.
③他在国外过着孤单的生活。He lives a lonely life abroad.

记忆贴士

"单"的金文字形♀像一种能发射弹丸的工具，本义是狩猎工具。因为每次只能发射一颗弹丸，引申出单独等含义。

The bronze inscription of 单 is ♀. It is like a tool that can launch projectiles. Its original meaning is hunting tool. Because each time only one projectile can be fired, it is extended to mean alone, etc.

 ⌘ → 禼 → 喬 → 商 → 商

甲骨文　金文大篆　小篆　隶书　楷体

拼音：shāng　　**部件**：亠、丷、冂、八、口　　**部首**：亠
结构：上下　　**六书**：会意　　**笔画**：11画　　**本义**：祭祀 sacrifice
词语：①商量 discuss　②商业 business　③商场 shopping mall
句子：①我们正在商量在哪见面。We are discussing where to meet.
②他是我的商业伙伴。He is a business partner of mine.
③这附近有个大商场。There's a big shopping mall near here.

记忆贴士

"商"的甲骨文字形⌘下面是祭祀用的台子，上面是焚烧柴薪，本义是焚薪祭天，引申为商量。

The oracle bone script of 商 is ⌘. It is like a sacrificial table on which the firewood lies. Its original meaning is to sacrifice and extended to mean to discuss.

粼 → 料 → 料
小篆　隶书　楷体

拼音：liào　　**部件**：米、斗　　**部首**：米　　**结构**：左右
六书：会意　　**笔画**：10画　　**本义**：称量粮食 weigh crops
词语：①材料 material　②资料 information　③塑料 plastic
句子：①这是一种特殊材料。This is a special material.
　　　　②电脑中存储了许多重要资料。There is a lot of important information on the computer.
　　　　③能给我一个塑料杯吗？Can I have a plastic cup?

记忆贴士

"料"由"米"（小米）和"斗"（称量粮食的器具）组成，本义是称量粮食，引申为猜想和材料等含义。

料 consists of 米(millet) and 斗(apparatus for weighing crops). Its original meaning is to weigh crops and extended to mean to speculate and material, etc.

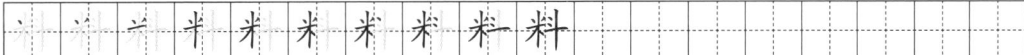

𢽾 → 技 → 技
小篆　隶书　楷体

拼音：jì　　**部件**：扌、支　　**部首**：扌　　**结构**：左右
六书：形声　　**笔画**：7画　　**本义**：技巧 skill
词语：①技巧 skill　②技术 technology　③竞技 competitive
句子：①你需要学习沟通技巧。You need to learn communication skills.
　　　　②我们想要这个领域的核心技术。We want the core technologies of this field.
　　　　③他喜欢竞技体育。He likes competitive sports.

记忆贴士

"技"由"扌"（手）和"支"（手拿木棍）组成，意思是利用工具巧妙地用力，本义是技巧。

技 consists of 扌(hand) and 支(hold stick). It means to use tools to work skillfully. Its original meaning is skill.

深 → 深 → 深 → 深

金文大篆　小篆　隶书　楷体

拼音: shēn　　**部件:** 氵、冖、八、木　　**部首:** 氵

结构: 左右　　**六书:** 形声　　**笔画:** 11画

本义: 水面到水底的距离大 deep

词语: ①深奥profound　②深刻deep　③深入in depth

句子: ①这是一本深奥的小说。This is a profound novel.
　　　　②他给我们留下深刻的印象。He made a deep impression on us.
　　　　③我们应该深入讨论这些问题。We should discuss the problems in depth.

记忆贴士

"深"由"氵"（水）和"罙"（用木棍探索洞穴）组成，表示用木棍试探河水的深浅，本义是水面到水底的距离大，引申出程度高等含义。

深 consists of 氵(water) and 罙(explore the cave with a stick). Its original meaning is deep and extended to mean high degree, etc.

验 → 驗 → 验

隶书　楷体（繁体）楷体（简体）

拼音: yàn　　**部件:** 马、佥　　**部首:** 马　　**结构:** 左右

六书: 形声　　**笔画:** 10画　　**本义:** 马名 horse's name

词语: ①实验experiment　②考验test　③经验experience

句子: ①这是一次伟大的实验。This is a great experiment.
　　　　②这是对我们关系的一次重大考验。This is a major test of our relationship.
　　　　③我有实际工作经验。I have actual work experiences.

记忆贴士

"验"由"马"和"佥"（检验，"检"的省写）组成，本义是马名，后被借用来表示检验等含义。

验 consists of 马(horse) and 佥(omitted form of 检, means test). Its original meaning is horse's name and borrowed to mean to test, etc.

增 → 增 → 增
小篆　　隶书　　楷体

拼音：zēng　　**部件**：土、曾　　**部首**：土　　**结构**：左右
六书：形声　　**笔画**：15画　　**本义**：添加 increase
词语：①增加increase　②增强enhance　③增添add
句子：①这是一个增加收入的好方法。This is a good way to increase income.
②我们需要增强互信。We need to enhance mutual trust.
③他为手稿增添了一章新内容。He added a new chapter to the manuscript.

记忆贴士

"增"由"土"（泥土）和"曾"（添加）组成，本义是添加，引申出扩大等含义。

增 consists of 土(soil) and 曾(increase). Its original meaning is to increase and extended to mean to expand, etc.

記 → 記 → 記 → 记
小篆　　隶书　　楷体（繁体）　楷体（简体）

拼音：jì　　**部件**：讠、己　　**部首**：讠　　**结构**：左右
六书：形声　　**笔画**：5画
本义：将信息用书面语记录下来 record the information in written language
词语：①记得remember　②记录record　③记忆力memory
句子：①我记得你说过的话。I remember what you used to say.
②他用相机记录下自己的生活。He recorded his life with a camera.
③你的记忆力很好。You have a good memory.

记忆贴士

"记"由"讠"（说话）和"己"（结绳记事）组成，本义是将信息用书面语记录下来，引申为将信息保留在大脑里。

记 consists of 讠(speak) and 己(keep records by making knots). Its original meaning is to record the information in written language and extended to mean to keep the information in brain.

近

篆 → 近 → 近
小篆　　隶书　　楷体

拼音：jìn　　**部件**：辶、斤　　**部首**：辶　　**结构**：半包围
六书：形声　　**笔画**：7画　　**本义**：距离短 near
词语：①走近approach　②亲近close　③附近near
句子：①他走近那尊雕像。He approached the statue.
②我和奶奶非常亲近。I am very close to my grandma.
③这附近有一个超市。There is a supermarket near here.

记忆贴士

"近"由"辶"（走路）和"斤"（声旁）组成，本义是距离短，引申为接近等含义。

近 consists of 辶(walk) and 斤(indicates pronunciation). Its original meaning is near and extended to mean close, etc.

言

→ → → 言
甲骨文　金文大篆　小篆　楷体

拼音：yán　　**部件**：言　　**部首**：言　　**结构**：独体
六书：指事　　**笔画**：7画　　**本义**：说话speak
词语：①语言language　②诺言promise　③格言aphorism
句子：①你应该掌握一门第二语言。You're expected to master a second language.
②我会信守诺言。I will keep promise.
③这是一句老格言。This is an old aphorism.

记忆贴士

"言"的甲骨文字形像张口动舌头讲话，上面一横表示说出来的话。"言"的本义是说话，引申出话语的意思。

言(oracle bone script is) is like using mouth and tongue to speak. Its original meaning is to speak and extended to mean word.

第三十八节

整

𢪬 → 整 → 整
小篆　　隶书　　楷体

拼音：zhěng　　**部件**：束、攵、正　　**部首**：攵　　**结构**：上下
六书：会意　　**笔画**：16画　　**本义**：强制管理 forcibly govern
词语：①整齐 neatly　②调整 adjust　③完整 complete
句子：①产品整齐地陈列在桌子上。The products are neatly laid out on the table.
　　　②调整你的安全带长度。Adjust the length of your seat belt.
　　　③这是篇完整的报告。This is a complete report.

记忆贴士

"整"由"束"（约束）、"攵"（敲打）和"正"（正确）组成，表示通过约束和敲打使改正，本义是强制管理，引申出收拾和有序等含义。

整 consists of 束(restrict), 攵(hit) and 正(correct). It indicates that correction is achieved by constraining and striking. Its original meaning is to forcibly govern and extended to mean to arrange and keep in order, etc.

精

精 → 精 → 精
小篆　　隶书　　楷体

拼音：jīng　　**部件**：米、青　　**部首**：米　　**结构**：左右
六书：形声　　**笔画**：14画　　**本义**：经过挑选的小米 selected millet
词语：①精神 spirit　②精致 delicate　③精英 elite
句子：①我们要弘扬科学精神。We want to promote the scientific spirit.
　　　②这件手工品看起来很精致。This handicraft looks so delicate.
　　　③他们是社会精英。They are social elites.

记忆贴士

"精"由"米"（小米）和"青"（漂亮，"倩"的省写）组成，本义是经过挑选的小米，引申出心神、准确和优秀等含义。

精 consists of 米(millet) and 青(omitted form of 倩, means beautiful). Its original meaning is selected millet and extended to mean mind, precise and excellent, etc.

集

甲骨文 → 金文大篆 → 小篆 → 隶书 → 楷体

拼音：jí　　**部件**：隹、木　　**部首**：隹　　**结构**：上下
六书：会意　　**笔画**：12画　　**本义**：群鸟在树上 birds perch in the tree
词语：①搜集 gather　②聚集 assemble　③召集 summon
句子：①我们正在忙于搜集资料。We are busy gathering information.
　　　　②工人们聚集在广场上。The workers assembled in the square.
　　　　③校长召集老师们开会。The principal summoned teachers to a meeting.

记忆贴士

"集"（金文字形为 ）由"隹"（短尾鸟）和"木"（树）组成，本义是群鸟落在树上，引申为集合等含义。

集(bronze inscription is) consists of 隹(bird) and 木(tree). Its original meaning is that birds perch in the tree and extended to mean to assemble, etc.

空

金文大篆 → 小篆 → 隶书 → 楷体

拼音：kōng　　**部件**：穴、工　　**部首**：穴　　**结构**：上下
六书：形声　　**笔画**：8画　　**本义**：洞穴 cave
词语：①空虚 empty　②天空 sky　③空间 space
句子：①我总感觉很空虚。I always feel empty.
　　　　②今天天空晴朗无云。The sky is cloudless today.
　　　　③车内有足够的空间。The car has enough inner space.

记忆贴士

"空"由"穴"（洞穴）和"工"（声旁）组成，本义是洞穴，引申出里面没有东西等含义。

空 consists of 穴(cave) and 工(indicates pronunciation). Its original meaning is cave and extended to mean empty, etc.

逵 → 槤 → 连 → 連 → 连
金文大篆　　小篆　　隶书　楷体（繁体）楷体（简体）

拼音：lián　　**部件**：辶、车　　**部首**：辶　　**结构**：半包围
六书：会意　　**笔画**：7画　　**本义**：人拉的车 man-drawn carriage
词语：①连接connect　②连累implicate　③连续consecutive
句子：①将打印机连接到电脑上。Connect the printer to the computer.
　　　②他连累到你怎么办？What if he implicates you?
　　　③我连续第二年获得冠军。I am the winner for the second consecutive year.

记忆贴士

"连"由"辶"（走路）和"车"组成，本义是人拉的车，引申出连接等含义。

连 consists of 辶(walk) and 车. Its original meaning is man-drawn carriage side and extended to mean to connect, etc.

斟 → 齃 → 報 → 報 → 报
金文大篆　　小篆　　隶书　楷体（繁体）楷体（简体）

拼音：bào　　**部件**：扌、艮　　**部首**：扌　　**结构**：左右
六书：会意　　**笔画**：7画　　**本义**：审判 judge
词语：①报道coverage　②报复revenge　③报告report
句子：①电视台对事件进行了现场报道。TV station gave live coverage for this event.
　　　②他们对敌人采取了报复行动。They took revenge on enemies.
　　　③我上交了我的报告。I turned in my report.

记忆贴士

"报"的金文字形 斟 像一只手抓住一个人给其戴上刑具，本义是审判，引申为告知。繁体字写作"報"，简体字用"扌"代替"幸"。

The bronze inscription of 报 is 斟. It is like arresting and interrogating a prisoner. Its original meaning is to judge and extended to mean to report, etc. The traditional character is 報. 幸 is replaced by 扌 in the simplified character.

覺 → 覺 → 覺 → 觉
小篆　　　隶书　　楷体（繁体）楷体（简体）

拼音：jué；jiào　　**部件**：⺍、冖、见　　**部首**：见　　**结构**：上下
六书：形声　　**笔画**：9画　　**本义**：睡醒 wake up
词语：①觉（jué）醒 awaken　②幻觉（jué）illusion　③睡觉（jiào）sleep
句子：①大众正在觉醒。The masses are awakening.
②那是幻觉。That's illusion.
③他在睡觉。He is sleeping.

记忆贴士

"觉"由"⺍"（声旁，"学"的省写）和"见"（看见）组成，本义是睡醒，引申出感知和睡眠等含义。

觉 consists of ⺍(omitted from of 学, indicates pronunciation) and 见(see). Its original meaning is to wake up and extended to mean to perceive and sleep, etc.

→ → 車 → 車 → 車 → 车
甲骨文　金文大篆　小篆　　隶书　　楷体（繁体）楷体（简体）

拼音：chē　　**部件**：车　　**部首**：车　　**结构**：独体
六书：象形　　**笔画**：4画　　**本义**：陆地上有轮子的交通工具 vehicle
词语：①汽车 auto　②火车 train　③晕车 carsick
句子：①汽车产业发展迅速。Auto industry developed quickly.
②我喜欢乘火车旅行。I like having a trip by train.
③他有点晕车。He felt a little carsick.

记忆贴士

"车"的甲骨文字形像马车，本义是陆地上有轮子的交通工具。繁体字为"車"，简体字"车"保留了"車"的轮廓。

The oracle bone script of 车 is . It is like a carriage and its original meaning is vehicle. The traditional character is 車 and the simplified character 车 retains the contour of 車.

 价 → 價 → 價 → 价
小篆　　隶书　　楷体（繁体）楷体（简体）

拼音：jià　　　**部件**：亻、介　　　**部首**：亻　　　**结构**：左右
六书：形声　　**笔画**：6画　　　　**本义**：价格 price
词语：①价格 price　②价值 value　③代价 cost
句子：①蔬菜价格稳定。The price of vegetable is steady.
　　　　②它的价值上涨了。Its value has risen.
　　　　③这样做的代价太大。Doing this will cost a lot.

记忆贴士

"价"的繁体字为"價"，由"亻"（人）和"賈"（做买卖）组成，本义是价格。简体字"价"用"介"代替"賈"。

The traditional character of 价 is 價. It consists of 亻(person) and 賈(do business). Its original meaning is price. 賈 is replaced by 介 in the simplified character.

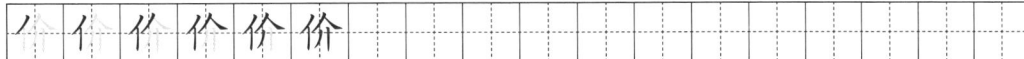

 音 → 音 → 音 → 音
金文大篆　　小篆　　隶书　　楷体

拼音：yīn　　　**部件**：立、日　　　**部首**：音　　　**结构**：上下
六书：指事　　**笔画**：9画　　　　**本义**：说话的声音 voice
词语：①声音 sound　②音乐 music　③发音 pronunciation
句子：①将声音调低。Turn down the sound volume.
　　　　②毕业后他继续学习音乐。He went on learning music after graduation.
　　　　③我的发音不准。My pronunciation is not accurate.

记忆贴士

"音"（小篆字形为 ）由"言"（说话）和"一"（指事符号）组成，本义是说话的声音，引申为一切声音。

The xiaozhuan script of 音 is . It consists of 言(speak) and 一(indicative symbol). Its original meaning is voice and extended to mean sound.

259

第三十九节

响　篆 → 響 → 響 → 响
　　小篆　　隶书　　楷体（繁体）　楷体（简体）

拼音：xiǎng　　**部件**：口、向　　**部首**：口　　**结构**：左右
六书：形声　　**笔画**：9画　　**本义**：回声 echo
词语：①响应 response　②影响 influence　③响亮 resounding
句子：①学生没有响应他的号召。There is no response to his appeal from students.
　　　　②他对这一事件有重大影响。He had a major influence on this event.
　　　　③那是一记响亮的耳光。That's a resounding slap on the face.

记忆贴士

"响"的繁体字为"響"，由"鄉"（声旁）和"音"（声音）组成，本义是回声，引申出发出声音和声音高等含义。简体字"响"由"口"（声音）和"向"（声旁）组成。

The traditional character of 响 is 響. It consists of 鄉(indicates pronunciation) and 音(sound). Its original meaning is echo and extended to mean to make a sound and loud, etc. The simplified character 响 consists of 口(sound) and 向(indicates pronunciation).

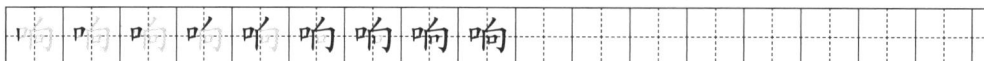

办　篆 → 辦 → 辦 → 办
　　小篆　　隶书　　楷体（繁体）　楷体（简体）

拼音：bàn　　**部件**：力、八　　**部首**：力　　**结构**：独体
六书：形声　　**笔画**：4画　　**本义**：治理 manage
词语：①办法 way　②举办 hold　③办公室 office
句子：①有什么解决办法吗？Is there any way to solve it?
　　　　②下周我们将召开一次会议。We will have a meeting next week.
　　　　③他的办公室在二楼。His office is on the second floor.

记忆贴士

"办"的繁体字为"辦"，由"辡"（声旁）和"力"（力量）组成，本义是治理，引申出处理和创设等含义。简体字"办"用"八"代替"辡"。

The traditional character of 办 is 辦. It consists of 辡(indicates pronunciation) and 力(strength). The original meaning of 辦 is to manage and extended to mean to handle and set up, etc. 辡 is replaced by 八 in the simplified character.

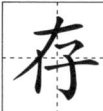 存 → 存 → 存
小篆　　隶书　　楷体

拼音：cún　　**部件**：子、𠂇　　**部首**：子　　**结构**：半包围
六书：形声　　**笔画**：6画　　**本义**：生存 live
词语：①存在 exist　②保存 save　③生存 live
句子：①这种现象广泛地存在于我们的社会。This phenomenon exists widely in our society.
②我将数据保存在电脑上。I saved the data on the computer.
③没有空气我们无法生存。We cannot live without air.

记忆贴士

"存"由"𠂇"（草木初生，"才"的变形）和"子"（孩子）组成，本义是生存，引申出存在和保留等含义。

存 consists of 𠂇(deformation of 才, means grass grow out) and 子(child). Its original meaning is to live and extended to mean to exit and save, etc.

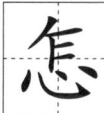 怎 → 怎
隶书　楷体

拼音：zěn　　**部件**：乍、心　　**部首**：心　　**结构**：上下
六书：形声　　**笔画**：9画　　**本义**：如何 how
词语：①怎么 how　②怎么样 how
句子：①我们怎么能得到奖学金？How can we get the scholarship?
②你的身体怎么样？How is your health?

记忆贴士

"怎"由"乍"（声旁）和"心"（关心）组成，本义是如何。

怎 consists of 乍(indicates pronunciation) and 心(care about). Its original meaning is how.

病

病 → 病 → 病
小篆　　隶书　　楷体

拼音：bìng　　**部件**：疒、丙　　**部首**：疒　　**结构**：半包围
六书：形声　　**笔画**：10画　　**本义**：重病 serious illness
词语：①疾病disease　②病房ward　③心脏病heart disease
句子：①这种疾病由病毒引起。This disease is caused by virus.
　　　　②他们把她转进了精神病病房。They transferred her to the psychiatric ward.
　　　　③他有严重的心脏病。He has severe heart disease.

记忆贴士

"病"由"疒"（疾病）和"丙"（声旁）组成，本义是重病，现在泛指所有的疾病。

病 consists of 疒(disease) and 丙(indicates pronunciation). It originally means serious illness and now refers to all diseases.

快

快 → 快 → 快
小篆　　隶书　　楷体

拼音：kuài　　**部件**：忄、夬　　**部首**：忄　　**结构**：左右
六书：形声　　**笔画**：7画　　**本义**：高兴 pleasant
词语：①快乐happy　②快速rapid　③尽快as soon as possible
句子：①新年快乐！Happy new year!
　　　　②我们的经济快速增长。We had a rapid economy growth.
　　　　③我尽快给您答复。I will reply to you as soon as possible.

记忆贴士

"快"由"忄"（心情）和"夬"（开口表达）组成，本义是高兴，引申出速度快等含义。

快 consists of 忄(mood) and 夬(express). Its original meaning is pleasant and extended to mean fast, etc.

 圖 → 圖 → 圖 → 圖 → 图
　　　　金文大篆　小篆　　隶书　楷体（繁体）楷体（简体）

拼音：tú　　**部件**：囗、冬　　**部首**：囗　　**结构**：全包围
六书：会意　　**笔画**：8画　　**本义**：地图map
词语：①企图attempt　②地图map　③意图intension
句子：①他企图逃跑。He attempted to escape.
　　　　②这是一幅中国地图。This is a map of China.
　　　　③我的意图是从左路进攻。My intension is to attack from the left wing.

记忆贴士

　　"图"的繁体字为"圖"（金文字形为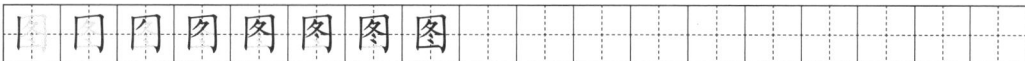），"圖"由"囗"（范围）和"啚"（像地形图）组成，本义是地图，引申出计划和图画等含义。简体字"图"用"冬"代替"啚"。

　　The traditional character of 图 is 圖(bronze inscription is). It consists of 囗(scope) and 啚(like a map). Its original meaning is map and extended to mean plan and drawing, etc. 啚 is replaced by 冬 in the simplified character.

丨 冂 冂 冈 肉 肉 图 图

 況 → 況 → 況 → 况
　　　　　小篆　　隶书　楷体（繁体）楷体（简体）

拼音：kuàng　　**部件**：冫、兄　　**部首**：冫　　**结构**：左右
六书：形声　　**笔画**：7画　　**本义**：寒冷的水cold water
词语：①情况situation　②状况condition　③概况general situation
句子：①我们想了解那里的情况。We want to know the situation there.
　　　　②经济状况得到了改善。Economic conditions have been improved.
　　　　③这本书介绍中国概况。The general situation of China is introduced in this book.

记忆贴士

　　"况"由"冫"（水）和"兄"（声旁）组成，本义是寒冷的水，引申为情形。

　　况 consists of 冫(water) and 兄(indicates pronunciation). Its original meaning is cold water and extended to mean situation.

丶 冫 冫 冴 况 况 况

例

例 → 例 → 例
小篆　隶书　楷体

拼音：lì　　**部件：**亻、歹、刂　　**部首：**亻　　**结构：**左右
六书：形声　**笔画：**8画　　**本义：**对比 compare
词语：①例外exception　②比例proportion　③惯例convention
句子：①这是一个例外。This is one of the exceptions.
②从事这个职业的女性比例已经达到10%。The proportion of women in this profession had risen to 10%.
③按照惯例，领导是男性。By convention, the leader is a man.

记忆贴士

"例"由"亻"（人）和"列"（列队）组成，本义是对比，引申出共同点和有代表性的事物等含义。

例 consists of 亻(person) and 列(line up). Its original meaning is to compare and extended to mean commonality and representative things, etc.

丿 亻 仁 仃 佤 伤 例 例

消

消 → 消 → 消
小篆　隶书　楷体

拼音：xiāo　**部件：**氵、肖　　**部首：**氵　　**结构：**左右
六书：形声　**笔画：**10画　　**本义：**减少 decreases
词语：①消失disappear　②消除eliminate　③消息news
句子：①汽车消失在雨中。The car disappeared in the rain.
②他试图消除不良影响。He tried to eliminate the bad effects.
③我有好消息。I have good news.

记忆贴士

"消"由"氵"（河水）和"肖"（变小）组成，本义是减少，引申出除掉和使用等含义。

消 consists of 氵(river water) and 肖(become small). The original meaning is to decreases and extended to mean to eliminate and use, etc.

消 消 消 消 消 消 消 消 消 消

第四十节

小篆 → 隶书 → 楷体

拼音：róng　　**部件**：宀、谷　　**部首**：宀　　**结构**：上下
六书：会意　　**笔画**：10画　　**本义**：容纳contain
词语：①容纳accommodate　②宽容tolerant　③容易easy
句子：①新礼堂能容纳5000人。The new auditorium can accommodate 5,000 people.
　　　　②你应该再宽容点。You should be more tolerant.
　　　　③这件事很容易处理。It is easy to handle.

记忆贴士

"容"由"宀"（房子）和"谷"（山洼）组成，本义是容纳，引申出外表等含义。

容 consists of 宀(house) and 谷(valley). Its original meaning is to contain and extended to mean appearance, etc.

甲骨文 → 金文大篆 → 小篆 → 隶书 → 楷体

拼音：shǐ　　**部件**：史　　**部首**：丨　　**结构**：独体
六书：会意　　**笔画**：5画　　**本义**：史官official historian
词语：①历史history　②史料historical material　③史上in history
句子：①中国是一个历史悠久的国家。China is a nation with a long history.
　　　　②掌握足够丰富的史料很重要。It's important to have enough historical materials.
　　　　③她是史上最有名的歌手之一。She's one of the best known singers in history.

记忆贴士

"史"的小篆字形为 ，上面像放简册的容器，下面是手，合起来表示掌管文书，本义是史官，现在的意思是历史。

The xiaozhuan script of 史 is . The upper part is like a container for bamboo slips and the lower part is like a hand. Its original meaning is official historian and now it refers to history.

非	非 → 非 → 非 → 非 → 非
	甲骨文　金文大篆　小篆　　隶书　　楷体

拼音：fēi　　**部件**：彐、丨　　**部首**：非　　**结构**：左右

六书：指事　　**笔画**：8画　　**本义**：违背 violate

词语：①非常very　②除非unless　③非洲Africa

句子：①我非常高兴。I am very happy.

②除非他坚持，否则不要同意。Don't agree unless he insists.

③尼罗河在非洲。Nile lies in Africa.

记忆贴士

"非"的甲骨文字形 非 像两个背对背站着的人。人头顶的一横表示观点不一致，互相矛盾。"非"的本义是违背，现在一般表示错误、不是等含义。

非(oracle bone script is 非) is like two people standing back to back. The short 一 above the head indicates that the views are contradictive with each other. The original meaning of 非 is to violate. Now it commonly means wrong and not, etc.

丨	丨	丨	丰	丰	非	非	非							

离	 → 離 → 離 → 离
	小篆　　隶书　　楷体（繁体）　楷体（简体）

拼音：lí　　**部件**：亠、凶、厶、冂　　**部首**：亠

结构：上下　　**六书**：形声　　**笔画**：10画

本义：黄鹂鸟Chinese oriole

词语：①离开leave　②距离distance　③离奇bizarre

句子：①离开前把灯关掉。Turn off the light before you leave.

②我在很远的距离就能看到那栋大楼。I can see the tall building from a great distance.

③他做了一个离奇的梦。He had a bizarre dream.

记忆贴士

"离"的繁体字为"離"，由"离"（声旁）和"隹"（短尾鸟）组成，本义是黄鹂鸟，现在表示分开和相距等含义。简体字"离"去掉了繁体字"離"中的"隹"。

The traditional character of 离 is 離. It consists of 离(indicates pronunciation) and 隹 (short-tailed bird). The original meaning of 离 is Chinese oriole and now it means separation and distance, etc. The simplified character only retains 离.

亠	亠	亣	离	离	离	离	离	离						

266

节

箾 → 筇 → 節 → 節 → 节

金文大篆　小篆　隶书　楷体（繁体）　楷体（简体）

拼音：jié　　**部件**：艹、卩　　**部首**：艹　　**结构**：上下
六书：形声　　**笔画**：5画　　**本义**：竹节 bamboo joint

词语：①礼节 etiquette　②节约 save　③节日 festival
句子：①你需要遵守礼节。You need to follow the etiquette.
②我们要节约用水。We should save water.
③今天是足球迷的节日。Today is a festival for football fans.

记忆贴士

"节"的繁体字为"節"，由"⺮"（竹子）和"即"（声旁）组成，本义是竹节，引申出克制和节点等含义。简体字"节"用"艹"代替"⺮"，"卩"代替"即"。

The traditional character of 节 is 節. It consists of ⺮(bamboo) and 即(indicates pronunciation). Its original meaning is bamboo joint and extended to mean to restrain and node, etc. ⺮ is replaced by 艹 and 即 is replaced by 卩 in the simplified character.

亲

親 → 親 → 親 → 亲

小篆　隶书　楷体（繁体）　楷体（简体）

拼音：qīn　　**部件**：立、木　　**部首**：立　　**结构**：上下
六书：形声　　**笔画**：9画　　**本义**：亲近 close

词语：①亲情 familial affection　②亲戚 relative　③母亲 mother
句子：①亲情是必不可少的。Familial affection is necessary.
②你在北京有亲戚吗？Do you have relatives in Beijing?
③她是两个男孩的母亲。She is the mother of two boys.

记忆贴士

"亲"的繁体字为"親"，由"亲"（声旁）和"見"（看到，引申为近）组成。"親"的本义是亲近，引申为家人等含义。简体字"亲"去掉了"親"中的"見"。

The traditional character of 亲 is 親. It consists of 亲(indicates pronunciation) and 見(see, extended to mean near). Its original meaning is close and extended to mean kinfolk, etc. 見 is removed in the simplified character.

 → 丂 → 萬 → 萬 → 萬 → 万

甲骨文　金文大篆　　小篆　　　隶书　　楷体（繁体）楷体（简体）

拼音：wàn　　　　**部件**：万　　　　**部首**：一　　　　**结构**：独体
六书：象形　　　 **笔画**：3画　　　 **本义**：蝎子 scorpion
词语：①万物 all things　②千万不要 never　③万幸 lucky
句子：①万物在春天复苏。All living things on earth revive in spring.
　　　　②千万不要忽视细节。Never ignore the details.
　　　　③你平安回来真是万幸。It is very lucky for you to return safely.

记忆贴士

"万"的繁体字为"萬"，甲骨文字形像蝎子，本义是蝎子。现在"万"表示十个一千，也表示极多的意思。

The traditional character of 万 is 萬(oracle bone script is). It is like a scorpion and its original meaning is scorpion. Now it means ten thousand and also means a large number, etc.

 → 八 → 八 → 八 → 八

甲骨文　金文大篆　小篆　　隶书　　楷体

拼音：bā　　　　**部件**：八　　　　**部首**：八　　　　**结构**：独体
六书：象形　　　**笔画**：2画　　　**本义**：分开 part
词语：①八卦 gossip　②八仙过海 the Eight Immortals soaring over the ocean　③八角 anise
句子：①他们很八卦。They love to gossip.
　　　　②你们得八仙过海，各显神通。Like the Eight Immortals soaring over the ocean, each of you should show your true gift.
　　　　③八角是中国的一种调料。Anise is a kind of Chinese condiment.

记忆贴士

"八"的甲骨文字形)(像相背分开的样子，本义是分开，现在的意思是七与九之间的整数。

八(oracle bone script is)() is like that two objects are separated and its original meaning is to part. Now it means eight.

构

構 → 構 → 構 → 构
小篆　隶书　楷体（繁体）　楷体（简体）

拼音：gòu　　**部件**：木、勾　　**部首**：木　　**结构**：左右
六书：形声　　**笔画**：8画　　**本义**：用木头建造房屋 build wooden house
词语：①结构 structure　②机构 organization　③构思 conception
句子：①这个房屋结构很复杂。The structure of this house is complex.
　　　　②他供职于一家研究机构。He works for a research organization.
　　　　③这是一个绝妙的构思。This is a brilliant conception.

记忆贴士

"构"的繁体字为"構"，由"木"（木头）和"冓"（连接）组成，本义是用木头建造房屋，引申出构造的意思。简体字"构"用"勾"代替"冓"。

The traditional character of 构 is 構. It consists of 木(wood) and 冓(connect). Its original meaning is to build wooden house and extended to mean construction and so on. 冓 is replaced by 勾 in the simplified character.

一 十 才 木 朳 构 构 构

族

甲骨文　金文大篆　小篆　隶书　楷体

拼音：zú　　**部件**：方、人、矢　　**部首**：方　　**结构**：左右
六书：会意　　**笔画**：11画　　**本义**：箭头聚集 arrowheads assemble
词语：①民族 national　②家族 family　③汉族 Han nationality
句子：①他们都穿着民族服装。They are all dressed in national costume.
　　　　②这个公司是家族企业。This company is a family business.
　　　　③道教是土生土长的汉族宗教。Taoism is the indigenous religion of Han nationality.

记忆贴士

"族"的甲骨文字形  像箭头汇聚在旗帜下方，本义是箭头聚集，古代打仗前要集合武器和众人，引申出聚合和民族等含义。

The oracle bone script of 族 is . It is like arrowheads assembling under a flag. Its original meaning is that arrowheads assemble and extended to mean to gather and nationality, etc.

族 亠 方 方 方 方 扩 族 族 族

第四十一节

ᄀ → 石 → 石 → 石 → 石
甲骨文　金文大篆　小篆　隶书　楷体

拼音：shí　　**部件**：石　　**部首**：石　　**结构**：独体
六书：象形　　**笔画**：5画　　**本义**：石头stone
词语：①石头stone　②陨石meteorite　③化石fossil
句子：①一块石头击中了他的身体。A stone hit him on the body.
②他们在河边发现了陨石。They found a meteorite by the river.
③许多鸟类化石在那里展览。Many bird fossils are exhibited there.

记忆贴士

"石"的甲骨文字形ᄀ像岩石的角，本义是石头。
The oracle bone script of 石 is ᄀ. It is like a tip of a rock and originally means stone.

一ア不石石

满　滿 → 滿 → 滿 → 满
　　小篆　隶书　楷体(繁体)　楷体(简体)

拼音：mǎn　　**部件**：氵、艹、两　　**部首**：氵　　**结构**：左右
六书：形声　　**笔画**：13画　　**本义**：充满filled
词语：①满足satisfy　②美满happy　③满意satisfied
句子：①我们总是以优质的服务来满足顾客需求。We always satisfy our customers with good service.
②祝你婚姻美满！May you have a happy married life!
③他们一定对我的作品很满意。They must be satisfied with my works.

记忆贴士

"满"的繁体字为"滿"，由"氵"（水）和"㒼"（声旁）组成，表示充满水，本义是充满，引申出饱满和满足等含义。
The traditional character of 满 is 滿. It consists of 氵(water) and 㒼(indicates pronunciation). It means filled with water. Its original meaning is filled and extended to mean full and satisfied, etc.

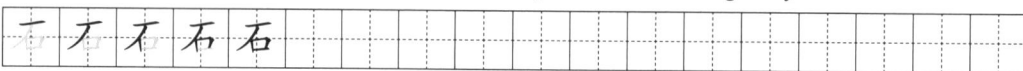

| 甲骨文 | 金文大篆 | 小篆 | 隶书 | 楷体 |

拼音: hé　　**部件:** 亻、可　　**部首:** 亻　　**结构:** 左右
六书: 象形　　**笔画:** 7画　　**本义:** 担carry something with a shoulder pole
词语: ①如何how　②任何any　③几何学geometry
句子: ①如何实现目标？How to achieve the goal?
　　　　②我不需要任何帮助。I don't need any help.
　　　　③我喜欢几何学。I like geometry.

记忆贴士

"何"的甲骨文字形 像一个人担着担子，本义是担，后假借为表示疑问的代词。

The oracle bone script of 何 is . It is like a person carrying a burden with a shoulder pole. Its original meaning is to carry something with a shoulder pole. Now it is used as an interrogative pronoun.

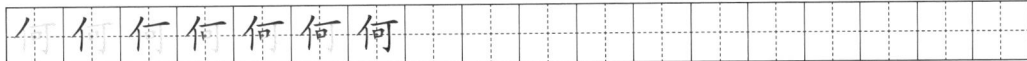

| 金文大篆 | 小篆 | 隶书 | 楷体（繁体） | 楷体（简体） |

拼音: guǎng　　**部件:** 广　　**部首:** 广　　**结构:** 独体
六书: 形声　　**笔画:** 3画
本义: 宽大的房屋 spacious house
词语: ①广泛widely　②广告advertisement　③广场square
句子: ①塑料袋被广泛使用。Plastic bags are widely used.
　　　　②这是一个著名的广告。This is a famous advertisement.
　　　　③这是世界上最大的广场。This is the biggest square in the world.

记忆贴士

"廣"的本义是宽大的房屋，引申出宽阔和广泛等含义。简体字"广"只保留了繁体字的轮廓。

廣 originally means spacious house. It is extended to mean spacious and widely, etc. 黄 is removed in the simplified character.

律

𦘒 → 律 → 律
小篆　　隶书　　楷体

拼音：lǜ　　**部件**：彳、聿　　**部首**：彳　　**结构**：左右
六书：形声　　**笔画**：9画　　**本义**：法律 law
词语：①法律 law　②规律 regular　③纪律 discipline
句子：①我们要遵守法律。We should abide by the law.
②我生活很有规律。I live a quite regular life.
③他已经强调了纪律。He has stressed the discipline.

记忆贴士

"律"的小篆字形 𦘒 像手拿篙划船，持篙一举一送，反复而有规律。"律"的本义是法律，引申出规律和约束等含义。

The xiaozhuan script of 律 is 𦘒. It is like rowing a boat with pole. The action of rowing is repeated and regular. The original meaning of 律 is law and extended to mean regular and to restrain, etc.

青

𤯞 → 靑 → 青 → 青
金文大篆　　小篆　　隶书　　楷体

拼音：qīng　　**部件**：龶、月　　**部首**：青　　**结构**：上下
六书：会意　　**笔画**：8画　　**本义**：绿色 green
词语：①青春 youth　②青年 young people　③垂青 favor
句子：①我又找回了逝去的青春。I have found my lost youth again.
②青年是创新的主力。Young people are the main force for the innovation.
③机会只垂青有准备的人。Chance only favors those who are prepared.

记忆贴士

"青"的金文字形 𤯞 上面是初生的草木，下面是土地，合起来表示一片草木呈绿色。"青"的本义是绿色，引申出年轻等含义。

The bronze inscription of 青 is 𤯞. The upper part is young grass and the lower part is field. Its original meaning is green and extended to mean young, etc.

 甲骨文 → 金文大篆 → 小篆 → 隶书 → 楷体

拼音：lín　　**部件**：木、木　　**部首**：木　　**结构**：左右

六书：会意　　**笔画**：8画　　**本义**：树林woods

词语：①森林woods　②林场forest farm　③竹林bamboo grove

句子：①他们在森林里打猎。They hunted in the woods.

②他在林场里过着孤单的生活。He lives a lonely life on the forest farm.

③我家房后有片竹林。Behind our house is a bamboo grove.

记忆贴士

"木"（金文字形为 ✻）表示树，"林"（金文字形为 ✻✻）的本义是树林。

木(bronze inscription is ✻) means tree, and the original meaning of 林(bronze inscription is ✻✻) is woods.

 甲骨文 → 金文大篆 → 小篆 → 隶书 → 楷体

拼音：kè　　**部件**：十、口、儿　　**部首**：十　　**结构**：上下

六书：象形　　**笔画**：7画　　**本义**：用肩膀来扛物 use the shoulders to carry things

词语：①克服overcome　②攻克conquer　③克制restrain

句子：①我们克服了许多困难。We overcame many difficulties.

②一支部队攻克了这个城镇。An army unit conquered the town.

③你得克制你自己。You should restrain yourself.

记忆贴士

"克"的甲骨文字形像人的肩膀，本义是用肩膀来扛物，引申为战胜和约束等含义。

The oracle bone script of 克 is. It is like a person's shoulder. Its original meaning is to use the shoulders to carry things and extended to mean to overcome and restrain, etc.

王

甲骨文 → 金文大篆 → 小篆 → 隶书 → 楷体

拼音：wáng　　**部件**：王　　**部首**：王　　**结构**：独体
六书：会意　　**笔画**：4画　　**本义**：君主monarch
词语：①国王king　②王子prince　③王冠crown
句子：①大家欢呼拥戴他为国王。People hailed him as King.
②王子继承了国家元首的职位。The prince acceded to the position of head of state.
③他从头上取下王冠。He took the crown from his head.

记忆贴士

"王"的甲骨文字形  像斧钺，象征王权。"王"的本义是君主。

The oracle bone script of 王 is . It is like an axe which symbolizes the kingship. The original meaning of 王 is monarch.

历

甲骨文 → 小篆 → 隶书 → 楷体(繁体) → 楷体(简体)　　金文大篆 → 隶书 → 楷体(繁体) → 楷体(简体)

拼音：lì　　**部件**：厂、力　　**部首**：厂　　**结构**：半包围
六书：形声　　**笔画**：4画　　**本义**：1. 经过go through　2. 日历 calendar
词语：①历史history　②经历experience　③农历lunar calendar
句子：①我们从历史课本里知道第二次世界大战。We learned the Second World War from history textbook.
②他给我讲述了他在中国的经历。He told us his experiences in China.
③中国传统节日依据农历设置。Chinese traditional festivals are based on the lunar calendar.

记忆贴士

简体字"历"有两个来源，一个是"歷"，另一个是"曆"。
"歷"中的"止"表示脚。"歷"的本义是经过，引申出经历等含义。
"曆"中的"日"表示日期。"曆"的本义是历法。
现在"歷"和"曆"都写作"历"。

The simplified character 历 has two sources.
歷 is related to the meaning of 止(walk). Its original meaning is to go through and extended to mean experience, etc.
曆 is related to the meaning of 日(sun). Its original meaning is calendar.
Now both 歷 and 曆 are written as 历.

第四十二节

權 → 權 → 權 → 权
小篆　　隶书　　楷体(繁体)　楷体(简体)

拼音：quán　　**部件**：木、又　　**部首**：木　　**结构**：左右
六书：形声　　**笔画**：6画　　**本义**：一种质地坚硬的木材 a kind of hardwood
词语：①权力 power　②权益 rights and interests　③权威 authority
句子：①他的权力受到了限制。His power is circumscribed.
　　　②儿童的权益要受到保护。Children's rights and interests should be protected.
　　　③他是语言学界的权威。He is an authority on linguistics.

记忆贴士

"权"的繁体字为"權"，由"木"（树木）和"雚"（声旁）组成，本义是一种质地坚硬的木材。因为这种木材质地硬可做秤杆，引申出称重量和支配等含义。简体字"权"用"又"代替"雚"。

The traditional character of 权 is 權. It consists of 木(wood) and 雚(indicates pronunciation). Its original meaning is a kind of hardwood. Because this kind of wood is very hard, it can be used to make scale beams. It is extended to mean to weigh and dominate, etc. 雚 is replaced by 又 in the simplified character.

素 → 素 → 素
小篆　　隶书　　楷体

拼音：sù　　**部件**：龶、糸　　**部首**：糸　　**结构**：上下
六书：会意　　**笔画**：10画　　**本义**：未染色的编织物 undyed braided fabric
词语：①素质 quality　②朴素 simple　③元素 element
句子：①我们有一支高素质科研队伍。We have a high quality research team.
　　　②她衣着朴素。She wears a simple dress.
　　　③他们给晚会增加了中国元素。They added Chinese element to the party.

记忆贴士

"素"的小篆字形像编织物，本义是未染色的编织物，引申出颜色单纯、不加修饰等含义。

The xiaozhuan script of 素 is . Its original meaning is undyed braided fabric and extended to mean plain, etc.

始

𦣝 → 𱉢 → 始 → 始
金文大篆　　小篆　　隶书　　楷体

拼音：shǐ　　**部件**：女、厶、口　　**部首**：女　　**结构**：左右
六书：形声　　**笔画**：8画　　**本义**：生命的开始 the beginning of life
词语：①开始 begin　②原始 primeval　③始终 from beginning to end
句子：①他开始在屋里走来走去。He began to move around in the room.
　　　②铁路穿过一片原始森林。The railway cuts through a primeval forest.
　　　③她始终面带微笑。She smiled from beginning to end.

记忆贴士

"始"的金文字形𦣝由"女"（女性）和"台"（胎儿，"胎"的省写）组成，本义是生命的开始，引申出源头和进入发展状态等含义。

The bronze inscription of 始 is 𦣝. It consists of 女(female) and 台(omitted form of 胎, means fetus). Its original meaning is the beginning of life and extended to mean source and to begin to develop, etc.

断

𣂢 → 斷 → 斷 → 断
小篆　　隶书　　楷体（繁体）　　楷体（简体）

拼音：duàn　　**部件**：⺅、斤　　**部首**：斤　　**结构**：左右
六书：会意　　**笔画**：11画
本义：将物体截成两段 cut the object into two segments
词语：①果断 decisive　②判断 judgment　③切断 cut off
句子：①你应该再果断一些。You should be more decisive.
　　　②这会影响我们的判断。This will affect our judgment.
　　　③紧急情况下需要切断电源。Cut off the power when there is an emergency.

记忆贴士

"断"的繁体字为"斷"，表示用斧子（斤）将绳子（幺幺）砍断，本义是将物体截成两段，引申出终止和下结论等含义。简体字"断"用"米"代替左边四个"幺"和"一"。

The traditional character of 断 is 斷. It means to cut the rope(幺幺) with axe(斤). The original meaning is to cut the object into two segments and extended to mean to stop and make conclusion, etc. The left complex radical of 斷 is replaced by ⺅ in the simplified character.

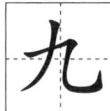

ζ → ζ → 九 → 九 → 九
甲骨文　金文大篆　小篆　隶书　楷体

拼音：jiǔ　　**部件**：九　　**部首**：丿　　**结构**：独体
六书：象形　　**笔画**：2画　　**本义**：手臂 arm
词语：①九龙壁 Nine-Dragon Screen　②九牛一毛 a hair off a bull's back　③九个月 nine months
句子：①我在九龙壁前拍了一张照片。I took a photo before the Nine-Dragon Screen.
　　　　②这对他们来说，不过是九牛一毛。It's only a hair off a bull's back to them.
　　　　③他们用了九个月拍摄这部电影。They spent nine months shooting this movie.

记忆贴士

"九"的金文字形 ζ 像一只手臂，本义是手臂，后被借用为数词。

The bronze inscription of 九 is ζ. It is like an arm. Its original meaning is arm and now it means number 9.

丿 九

隙 → 際 → 際 → 际
小篆　隶书　楷体（繁体）楷体（简体）

拼音：jì　　**部件**：阝、示　　**部首**：阝　　**结构**：左右
六书：形声　　**笔画**：7画　　**本义**：墙壁连接处的缝隙 gap at the wall joint
词语：①实际 actual　②交际 communication　③国际 international
句子：①你有实际的工作经验吗？Do you have any actual work experience?
　　　　②他汉语口语交际能力很强。He is quite competent in oral communication in Chinese.
　　　　③这是一个国际化都市。This is an international city.

记忆贴士

"际"的繁体字为"際"，由"阝"（墙壁）和"祭"（声旁）组成，本义是墙壁连接处的缝隙，引申出会合和两者之间等含义。简体字"际"用"示"代替"祭"。

The traditional character of 际 is 際. It consists of 阝(wall) and 祭(indicates pronunciation). Its original meaning is gap at the wall joint and extended to mean to meet and between, etc. 祭 is replaced by 示 in the simplified character.

了 阝 阝 际 际 际 际

秫 → 積 → 積 → 积
小篆　　隶书　　楷体（繁体）楷体（简体）

拼音：jī　　**部件**：禾、口、八　　**部首**：禾　　**结构**：左右
六书：形声　　**笔画**：10画　　**本义**：堆积谷物 pile up the grain
词语：①积极active　②积累gather　③积蓄saving
句子：①作为学习者我们必须积极主动。We must be active as learners.
　　　②我需要积累经验。Gathering experience is what I need.
　　　③这些钱是他所有的积蓄。This amount of money is all his saving.

记忆贴士

"积"的繁体字为"積"，由"禾"（谷物，粮食）和"責"（要求）组成，"積"的本义为堆积谷物，引申出聚集和保存等含义。简体字"积"用"只"代替"責"。
The traditional character of 积 is 積. It consists of 禾(grain, crop) and 責(demand). Its original meaning is to pile up the grain and extended to mean to collect and save, etc. 責 is replaced by 只 in the simplified character.

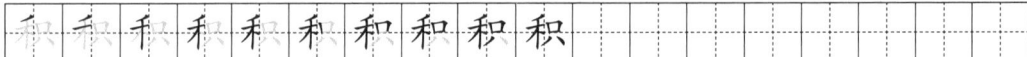

吩 → 吃 → 吃
小篆　　隶书　　楷体

拼音：chī　　**部件**：口、乞　　**部首**：口　　**结构**：左右
六书：形声　　**笔画**：6画　　**本义**：口吃stutter
词语：①口吃stutter　②吃惊startled　③吃饭have meal
句子：①他说话有点口吃。He speaks with a little stutter.
　　　②结果令他感到吃惊。The result made him startled.
　　　③该吃饭了。It is time to eat.

记忆贴士

"吃"由"口"（嘴）和"乞"（气息不畅，气短）组成，本义是口吃。
吃 consists of 口(mouth) and 乞(breath is not smooth). Its original meaning is stutter.

篆 → 態 → 態 → 态
小篆　　隶书　　楷体（繁体）楷体（简体）

拼音：tài　　**部件**：太、心　　**部首**：心　　**结构**：上下
六书：会意　　**笔画**：8画
本义：有心理倾向性的表现 psychologically inclined performance
词语：①态度 attitude　②生态 ecology　③状态 state
句子：①他那漠不关心的态度使我恼怒。His nonchalant attitude irritated me.
　　　　②他是湿地生态学方面的专家。He's an expert on the ecology of wetlands.
　　　　③这是火山的正常状态。This is the normal state of a volcano.

记忆贴士

"态"的繁体字为"態"，由"能"（可行）和"心"（心理）组成，本义是有心理倾向性的表现，引申出存在方式等含义。简体字"态"用"太"代替"能"。

The traditional character of 态 is 態. It consists of 能(feasible) and 心(mentality). Its original meaning is psychologically inclined performance and extended to mean way of existence, etc. The simplified character 态 consists of 太(indicates pronunciation) and 心(mentality).

藝 → 藝 → 艺
隶书　　楷体（繁体）楷体（简体）

拼音：yì　　**部件**：艹、乙　　**部首**：艹　　**结构**：上下
六书：会意　　**笔画**：4画　　**本义**：种植 plant
词语：①艺术 art　②才艺 talent　③文艺复兴 Renaissance
句子：①这是现代艺术。This is modern art.
　　　　②他的才艺表演大获成功。His talent show was a great success.
　　　　③这是文艺复兴时期的绘画。This is a painting of the Renaissance.

记忆贴士

"艺"的繁体字为"藝"，由"艹"（草）、"埶"（手拿土块）和"云"（除草，"耘"的省写）组成，本义是种植，引申出富有创造力的才能等含义。简体字"艺"由"艹"（草）和"乙"（声旁）组成。

The traditional character of 艺 is 藝. It consists of 艹(grass), 埶(hold the clod) and 云(omitted form of 耘, means to weed). Its original meaning is to plant and extended to mean creative talent, etc. The simplified character 艺 consists of 艹 (grass) and 乙(indicates pronunciation).

第四十三节

证　證 → 證 → 證 → 证
小篆　　隶书　　楷体（繁体）　楷体（简体）

拼音：zhèng　　**部件**：讠、正　　**部首**：讠　　**结构**：左右
六书：形声　　**笔画**：7画　　**本义**：报告上级 report to superior
词语：①证明 prove　②保证 assure　③见证 witness
句子：①结果证明他是错的。The result proved that he was wrong.
　　　　②我可以向你保证，你是安全的。I can assure you that you are safe.
　　　　③我见证了这所大学的许多变化。I witnessed many changes in this university.

记忆贴士

"证"的繁体字为"證"，由"言"（说话）和"登"（步入大堂）组成，本义是报告上级。

The traditional character of 证 is 證. It consists of 言(speak) and 登(mount). It originally means to report to superior.

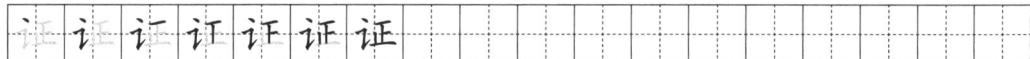

众　𠱾 → 眾 → 衆 → 众
小篆　　隶书　　楷体（繁体）　楷体（简体）

拼音：zhòng　　**部件**：人、人、人　　**部首**：人　　**结构**：上下
六书：会意　　**笔画**：6画　　**本义**：众人 the masses
词语：①群众 crowds　②众多 numerous　③受众 audience
句子：①他煽动群众闹事。He fermented crowds to riot.
　　　　②他拥有众多拥趸。He has numerous fans.
　　　　③年轻人是他的目标受众。Young people are his target audience.

记忆贴士

"众"由三个"人"组成，本义是众人。

众 consists of three 人. Its original meaning is the masses.

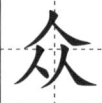

创

創 → 創 → 創 → 创
小篆　　隶书　　楷体（繁体）　楷体（简体）

拼音：chuàng；chuāng　　**部件**：人、㠯、刂　　**部首**：刂　　**结构**：左右
六书：形声　　**笔画**：6画　　**本义**：伤口 wound
词语：①创（chuàng）新 innovate　②创（chuàng）造 create　③创（chuāng）伤 wound
句子：①我们必须学会创新。We must learn to innovate.
　　　　②劳动者为社会创造价值。Workers create wealth for the society.
　　　　③时间可以治愈所有的创伤。Time cures all wounds.

记忆贴士

"创"的繁体字为"創"，由"倉"（声旁）和"刂"（刀）组成，本义是伤口，引申出伤害和开始做等含义。简体字"创"用"仓"代替"倉"。

The traditional character of 创 is 創. It consists of 倉(indicates pronunciation) and 刂(knife). Its original meaning is wound and extended to mean to harm and start doing something, etc. 倉 is replaced by 仓 in the simplified character.

丿　个　今　仓　仓　创

红

 → 紅 → 紅 → 红
小篆　　隶书　　楷体（繁体）　楷体（简体）

拼音：hóng　　**部件**：纟、工　　**部首**：纟　　**结构**：左右
六书：形声　　**笔画**：6画　　**本义**：浅红色的丝 light red silk
词语：①红色 red　②粉红 pink　③红茶 black tea
句子：①这本书封面是红色的。The book has a red cover.
　　　　②她有一支粉红色的口红。She has a pink lipstick.
　　　　③我喜欢红茶。I like black tea.

记忆贴士

"红"由"纟"（丝）和"工"（声旁）组成，本义是浅红色的丝，现在指红色。

红 consists of 纟(silk) and 工(indicates pronunciation). Its original meaning is light red silk. Now it means red.

纟　纟　纟　红　红　红

望

甲骨文 → 金文大篆 → 小篆 → 隶书 → 楷体

拼音：wàng　　**部件**：亡、月、王　　**部首**：王　　**结构**：上下
六书：会意　　**笔画**：11画　　**本义**：远望 look far into the distance
词语：①希望 hope　②绝望 despair　③失望 disappointed
句子：①我希望你能来。I hope you could come.
　　　　②他们看起来近乎绝望。They seem close to despair.
　　　　③他很失望。He is very disappointed.

记忆贴士

"望"的甲骨文字形  像一个人在远望。"望"的小篆字形为 望，由"臣"（眼睛）、"月"（月亮）和"王"（人）组成，本义为远望，引申出期待和拜访等含义。如今"望"用"亡"代替"臣"。

The oracle bone script of 望 is 望. It is like a person looking far into the distance. The xiaozhuan script of 望 is 望. It consists of 臣(eye), 月(moon) and 王(person). Its original meaning is to look far into the distance and extended to mean to hope and visit, etc. Now 臣 is replaced by 亡.

须

甲骨文 → 小篆 → 隶书 → 楷体（繁体）→ 楷体（简体）

拼音：xū　　**部件**：彡、页　　**部首**：彡　　**结构**：左右
六书：象形　　**笔画**：9画　　**本义**：胡须 beard
词语：①必须 must　②胡须 beard　③须后水 aftershave
句子：①我们必须现在开始。We must begin now.
　　　　②他留着胡须。He wears a beard.
　　　　③我的须后水用完了。I have run out of aftershave.

记忆贴士

"须"（甲骨文字形为 须）由"页"（头）和"彡"（毛发）组成，本义是胡须，引申出必要和须状物等含义。

须(oracle bone script is 须) consists of 页(head) and 彡(hair). Its original meaning is beard and extended to mean necessary and something like a beard, etc.

金文大篆 → 小篆 → 隶书 → 楷体

拼音：qún　　**部件**：君、羊　　**部首**：羊　　**结构**：左右
六书：形声　　**笔画**：13画　　**本义**：羊群 flock of sheep
词语：①群众masses　②群居gregarious　③群岛archipelago
句子：①群众有无穷的创造力。The masses have boundless creative power.
　　　②人是一种群居动物。Human beings are gregarious.
　　　③群岛由一系列小岛组成。An archipelago is a group of small islands.

记忆贴士

"君"的甲骨文字形为♪，由"攴"（手拿棍子）和"口"（发号施令）组成，意为统治。"群"由"君"（手拿鞭子，发号施令）和"羊"组成，表示用鞭子抽打和吆喝着把羊赶到一起，本义是羊群，引申出聚集、会合等含义。

The oracle bone script of 君 is ♪. It consists of 攴(hand holding a stick) and 口(order). It means to govern. 群 consists of 君(govern) and 羊(sheep). Its original meaning is flock of sheep and extended to mean to gather and assemble, etc.

金文大篆 → 小篆 → 隶书 → 楷体（繁体）→ 楷体（简体）

拼音：shī　　**部件**：丿、帀　　**部首**：丨　　**结构**：左右
六书：会意　　**笔画**：6画　　**本义**：军队 troops
词语：①老师teacher　②师傅master　③师团division
句子：①他们给老师献花。They presented flowers to teacher.
　　　②他在工厂里当师傅。He is a master worker in the factory.
　　　③几个师团正从英国调来。Several divisions are being moved from the UK.

记忆贴士

"师"的繁体字为"師"，由"𠂤"（土山）和"帀"（包围）组成，表示四周围都是土山，本义是军队，引申出在某一领域有一定积累的人。简体字"师"用"丿"代替"𠂤"。

The traditional character of 师 is 師. It consists of 𠂤(dirt hill) and 帀(surround). It indicates to be surrounded by dirt hills and originally means troops. It is extended to mean a person who has a certain accumulation in a certain field, etc. 𠂤 is replaced by 丿 in the simplified character.

283

该

籀 → 该 → 該 → 该
小篆　　隶书　　楷体（繁体）　楷体（简体）

拼音：gāi　　**部件**：讠、亥　　**部首**：讠　　**结构**：左右
六书：形声　　**笔画**：8画　　**本义**：军中口令 army password
词语：①应该 should　②活该 serve right　③不该 should not
句子：①他应该受到重视。He should be appreciated.
②你完全活该。It serves you perfectly right.
③你不该在公共场合大声说话。You should not speak loudly in public.

记忆贴士

"该"由"讠"（说话）和"亥"（声旁）组成，本义为军中口令，引申出应当和理应如此等含义。

该 consists of 讠(speak) and 亥(indicates pronunciation). Its original meaning is army password and extended to mean should and deserve, etc.

复

 → 獲 → 復 → 復 → 复
金文大篆　　小篆　　隶书　　楷体（繁体）　楷体（简体）

拼音：fù　　**部件**：宀、日、夂　　**部首**：夂　　**结构**：上中下
六书：形声　　**笔画**：9画　　**本义**：回来 return
词语：①恢复 recover　②复杂 complex　③重复 repeat
句子：①她的肩伤正在恢复。She's recovering from a shoulder injury.
②这些问题很复杂。These problems are complex.
③你能重复一遍吗？Can you repeat that?

记忆贴士

"复"的繁体字为"復"，由"彳"（行走）和"复"（回到城里，"夂"表示脚）组成，本义是回来，引申出重新开始、做同样的事和回应等含义。

简体字"复"去掉了繁体字中的"彳"。

The traditional character of 复 is 復. It consists of 彳(walk) and 复(means to go back to town and 夂 means foot). Its original meaning is to return and extended to mean to start again, do the same thing and respond, etc. 彳 is removed in the simplified character.

第四十四节

细 → 细 → 细 → 细
小篆　隶书　楷体（繁体）楷体（简体）

拼音：xì　　**部件**：纟、田　　**部首**：纟　　**结构**：左右
六书：形声　　**笔画**：8画　　**本义**：微小 small
词语：①细节 detail　②细致 minutely　③详细 in detail
句子：①我们很留心细节。We are attentive to details.
②他细致地考察了贸易情况。He examined the trade situation minutely.
③他详细地描述了制作过程。He described the working process in detail.

记忆贴士

"细"的小篆字形为 ，由"糸"（丝）和"囟"（声旁）组成，意为像丝一样微小，本义是微小。

The xiaozhuan script of 细 is . It consists of 糸(silk) and 囟(indicates pronunciation). Its original meaning is tiny(as fine thread).

包 → 包 → 包
小篆　隶书　楷体

拼音：bāo　　**部件**：勹、巳　　**部首**：勹　　**结构**：半包围
六书：会意　　**笔画**：5画　　**本义**：包裹 wrap
词语：①包含 cover　②包括 include　③包扎 bind up
句子：①这些文件包含所有的细节。These documents cover all the details.
②文学包括小说、诗歌、散文等。Literature includes novels, poems and essays, etc.
③她用纱布包扎了我的手指。She bound up my finger with gauze.

记忆贴士

"包"的小篆字形  像胎儿包裹在胎衣中，本义为包裹。

包(xiaozhuan script is ) is like a fetus wrapped in the afterbirth. Its original meaning is to wrap.

土

甲骨文 → 金文大篆 → 小篆 → 隶书 → 楷体

拼音：tǔ　　**部件**：土　　**部首**：土　　**结构**：独体
六书：象形　　**笔画**：3画　　**本义**：泥土 soil
词语：①土地 land　②土豆 potato　③土著 aboriginal
句子：①这块土地永久归他们所有。This land belongs to them forever.
②我喜欢吃炸土豆。I like fried potatoes.
③土著居民为他们的土地而战。The aboriginal men fight for their lands.

记忆贴士

"土"的甲骨文字形上面像土块，下面像地面。"土"的本义是泥土，引申出本地等含义。

The oracle bone script of 土 is . It is like a clod on the ground. Its original meaning is soil and extended to mean local, etc.

持

小篆 → 隶书 → 楷体

拼音：chí　　**部件**：扌、土、寸　　**部首**：扌　　**结构**：左右
六书：形声　　**笔画**：9画　　**本义**：拿着 hold
词语：①坚持 persist　②持续 continue　③支持 support
句子：①如果你能坚持，就一定能胜利。If you can persist, you are sure to win.
②经济持续增长。Economy continues to grow.
③我们仍然需要他们的支持。We still need their support.

记忆贴士

"持"由"扌"（手）和"寺"（拿着不动，小篆字形为 ）组成，本义是拿着，引申出保持和主管等含义。

寺(xiaozhuan script is) consists of 止(still) and 寸(hand). 持 consists of 扌(hand) and 寺(hold still). Its original meaning is to hold and extended to mean to keep and manage, etc.

第二部分　500个常用汉字

服 → 服 → 服 → 服 → 服
甲骨文　金文大篆　小篆　隶书　楷体

拼音：fú　　**部件**：月、卩、又　　**部首**：月　　**结构**：左右
六书：会意　　**笔画**：8画　　**本义**：使犯人屈服 make the prisoner yield
词语：①服务 service　②佩服 admire　③征服 conquer
句子：①这家餐厅提供二十四小时服务。This restaurant offers round-the-clock service.
　　　②我佩服你的深谋远虑。I admire your forethought.
　　　③国王征服了这块土地。King conquered this land.

记忆贴士

"服"的金文字形 服 由"舟"（枷锁，误写为"舟"）、"人"（犯人）和"又"（手）组成，表示使犯人屈服，引申出衣服和信服等含义。隶书和楷体字"服"用"月"代替"舟"，用"卩"代替"人"。

The bronze inscription of 服 is 服. It consists of 舟(miswritten as 舟, means shackle), 人(prisoner) and 又(hand). Its original meaning is to make the prisoner yield and extended to mean clothes and convinced, etc. 舟 is replaced by 月 and 人 is replaced by 卩 in clerical script and regular script 服.

笑 → 笑 → 笑
小篆　隶书　楷体

拼音：xiào　　**部件**：⺮、夭　　**部首**：⺮　　**结构**：上下
六书：形声　　**笔画**：10画　　**本义**：因高兴而出声 laugh
词语：①笑话 joke　②微笑 smile　③大笑 laugh
句子：①他有时给我们讲笑话。He sometimes tells us jokes.
　　　②她微笑着讲话。She is speaking with a smile.
　　　③它能令你大笑。It will make you laugh.

记忆贴士

"笑"（小篆字形为 笑）由"⺮"（弯弯的竹叶像人笑时候的眼睛）和"夭"（人手舞足蹈的样子）组成，表示高兴得手舞足蹈。"笑"的本义是因高兴而出声。

笑(xiaozhuan script is 笑) consists of ⺮ (a person's eyes are like bamboo leaves when he or she is laughing) and 夭(dance). It means to laugh and dance. Its original meaning is to laugh.

德

德(金文大篆) → 德(小篆) → 德(隶书) → 德(楷体)

拼音：dé　　**部件**：彳、十、罒、一、心　　**部首**：彳

结构：左右　　**六书**：会意　　**笔画**：15画　　**本义**：德行 moral integrity

词语：①道德 ethic　②德国 Germany　③公德 social morality

句子：①他很有职业道德。He has work ethic.
　　　　②他刚从德国回来。He has just returned from Germany.
　　　　③这种行为有违公德。This behavior violated social morality.

记忆贴士

"德"的金文字形 由"彳"（行走）、"直"（正直）和"心"组成，表示随正直的心而行的状态，本义是德行，引申出道德等含义。

The bronze inscription of 德 is . It consists of 彳(walk), 直(upright) and 心(heart), meaning a state of walking with an upright heart. The original meaning of 德 is moral integrity and extended to mean morality, etc.

般

般(甲骨文) → 般(金文大篆) → 般(小篆) → 般(隶书) → 般(楷体)

拼音：bān　　**部件**：舟、殳　　**部首**：舟　　**结构**：左右

六书：会意　　**笔画**：10画　　**本义**：搬运 move

词语：①一般 usually　②般配 match each other　③百般 all sorts of

句子：①这一般指成人。This usually refers to adult.
　　　　②他们很般配。They match each other.
　　　　③他们对我们百般刁难。They created all sorts of obstacles for us.

记忆贴士

"般"由"舟"（船）和"殳"（手拿船桨）组成，表示撑船运送人和货物，本义是搬运，引申出种类和类型等含义。

般 consists of 舟(boat) and 殳(hold a paddle). It means to transport people and goods by boat. Its original meaning is to move and extended to mean type, etc.

第二部分　500个常用汉字

金文大篆　小篆　隶书　楷体（繁体）楷体（简体）

拼音： yuǎn　　**部件：** 辶、元　　**部首：** 辶　　**结构：** 半包围
六书： 形声　　**笔画：** 7画　　**本义：** 走很长的路walk for a long distance
词语： ①远方in the distance　②遥远far　③偏远remote
句子： ①远方我什么也看不到。I see nothing in the distance.
　　　②我在离家很遥远的地方。I am far from home.
　　　③他生活在偏远地区。He lives in a remote area.

记忆贴士

"远"的繁体字为"遠"（金文字形为 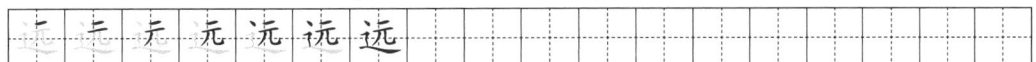），由"辶"（走路）和"袁"（衣物）组成，表示带着衣物出发。"远"的本义是走很长的路，引申出距离大等含义。简体字"远"由"辶"（走路）和"元"（声旁）组成。

The traditional character of 远 is 遠(bronze inscription is). It consists of 辶(walk) and 袁(clothes). It means to set off with clothes. The original meaning of 远 is to walk for a long distance and extended to mean far. 袁 is replaced by 元 in the simplified character.

小篆　隶书　楷体（繁体）楷体（简体）

拼音： ài　　**部件：** 爫、冖、友　　**部首：** 爫　　**结构：** 上下
六书： 会意　　**笔画：** 10画　　**本义：** 对人或物的深挚感情love
词语： ①爱情love　②可爱cute　③酷爱ardently love
句子： ①她正在读一本爱情小说。She is reading a love novel.
　　　②多可爱的一只小猫！What a cute cat!
　　　③他酷爱音乐。He ardently loves music.

记忆贴士

简体字"爱"由"爫"（接受，"受"的省写）和"友"（相互扶持，金文字形为 ）组成，本义是对人或物的深挚感情，引申出喜好和容易等含义。

The simplified character 爱 consists of 爫(omitted form of 受, means accept) and 友(bronze inscription is , meaning to support each other with hand). It means to love and is extended to mean to like and be apt to, etc.

289

第四十五节

准

澅 → 準 → 準 → 准

小篆　　隶书　　楷体（繁体）　楷体（简体）

拼音：zhǔn　　**部件**：氵、隹　　**部首**：冫　　**结构**：左右
六书：形声　　**笔画**：10画　　**本义**：平的 horizontal
词语：①标准 standard　②准备 prepare　③准确 accurate
句子：①这个产品需要新的技术标准。This product needs a new technical standard.
②我们正在准备晚饭。We are preparing dinner.
③这些数字是准确的。These figures are accurate.

记忆贴士

"准"的繁体字为"準"，由"氵"（水）和"隼"（用像隼一样锐利的眼睛看）组成，表示工匠看物体表面是否水平。"準"的本义是水平，引申出与目标一致、允许等含义。简体字"准"用"冫"代替"氵"，用"隹"代替"隼"。

The traditional character of 准 is 準. It consists of 氵(water) and 隼(look with sharp eyes like a falcon). It means that craftsman sees whether the surface of an object is horizontal. The original meaning of 準 is horizontal and extended to mean consistent with the goal and to allow, etc. 氵 is replaced by 冫 and 隼 is replaced by 隹 in the simplified character.

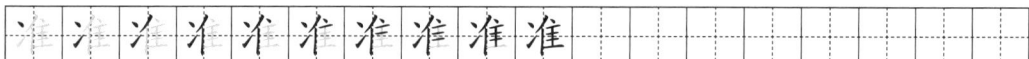

写

寫 → 寫 → 寫 → 写

小篆　　隶书　　楷体（繁体）　楷体（简体）

拼音：xiě　　**部件**：冖、与　　**部首**：冖　　**结构**：上下
六书：形声　　**笔画**：5画　　**本义**：移置 replace
词语：①撰写 write　②写真集 photo album　③描写 describe
句子：①他为一家报纸撰写专栏文章。He writes a column for a newspaper.
②这是她的写真集。This is her photo album.
③小说描写了很多和战争有关的事。The novel describes a great many things related to the war.

记忆贴士

简体字"写"由"冖"（鸟巢）和"与"（鸟的形状）组成，一笔一画写字就像鸟儿筑巢。

The simplified character 写 consists of 冖(bird nest) and 与(bird). Writing character stroke by stroke is like bird nesting.

 算 → 算 → 算
小篆　　隶书　　楷体

拼音：suàn　　　　**部件**：⺮、目、廾　　**部首**：⺮　　　　**结构**：上下
六书：会意　　　　**笔画**：14画　　　　　**本义**：计算calculate
词语：①打算intend　②计算calculate　③预算budget
句子：①他们打算明年去中国。They intend to go to China next year.
　　　　②我们可以计算出货物的重量。We can calculate the weight of the goods.
　　　　③我们部门已经开始削减预算。Budget cuts are starting in our department.

记忆贴士

"算"由"⺮"（竹子）、"目"（算筹）和"廾"（双手）组成，表示用手使用竹质的算筹进行计算。"算"的本义是计算，引申出计划和当作等含义。

算 consists of ⺮(bamboo), 目(counting rods) and 廾(two hands). It means to calculate using bamboo counting rods. The original meaning of 算 is to calculate and extended to mean to plan and regard as, etc.

 → → 火 → 火
甲骨文　小篆　隶书　楷体

拼音：huǒ　　　　**部件**：火　　　　**部首**：火　　　　**结构**：独体
六书：象形　　　　**笔画**：4画　　　**本义**：物体燃烧的自然现象fire
词语：①火焰flame　②烟火firework　③火柴match
句子：①火焰蹿到了二楼。Flames sprang up to the second floor.
　　　　②他在那里放烟火。He is there letting off fireworks.
　　　　③他点燃一根火柴。He struck a match.

记忆贴士

"火"的甲骨文字形像火焰，"火"的本义是物体燃烧的自然现象。

火(oracle bone script is) is like fire and its original meaning is fire.

死

死 → 死 → 死 → 死 → 死
甲骨文　金文大篆　小篆　　隶书　　楷体

拼音：sǐ　　　　　**部件**：歹、匕　　**部首**：歹　　　**结构**：半包围
六书：会意　　　　**笔画**：6画　　　**本义**：生命终止die
词语：①死亡die　②死板inflexible　③杀死kill
句子：①事故造成两人死亡。Two people died in the accident.
②他这个人很死板。He is inflexible.
③新的杀菌法也可以杀死微生物。New sterilization method can also kill microorganisms.

记忆贴士

"死"的金文字形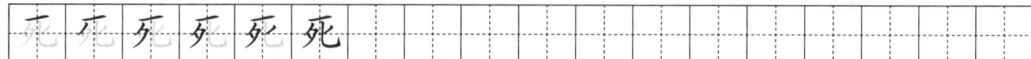左边是"歹"（尸骨），右边是"匕"（人的灵魂），表示人的形体和魂魄分离，本义是生命终止，引申出不灵活等含义。

The bronze inscription of 死 is 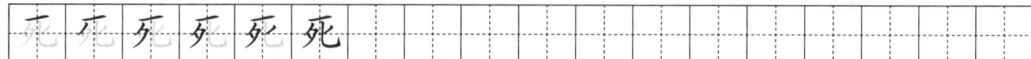. The left radical is 歹(dead body) and the right radical is 人 (a person's soul). It means that the human body and the soul are separated. The original meaning of 死 is to die and extended to mean not flexible, etc.

半

半 → 半 → 半 → 半
金文大篆　小篆　　隶书　　楷体

拼音：bàn　　　　 **部件**：丷、一、十　**部首**：丶　　　**结构**：独体
六书：会意　　　　**笔画**：5画　　　**本义**：二分之一half
词语：①半天a long while　②半夜midnight　③半岛peninsula
句子：①他半天没说话。He remained speechless for a long while.
②他昨天工作到半夜。He didn't finish work until midnight yesterday.
③朝鲜半岛的紧张局势可能持续。The tension on the Korean Peninsula is likely to remain.

记忆贴士

"半"由"丷"（分解）和"半"（牛）组成，表示把牛分成两半，本义是二分之一，引申出部分等含义。

半 consists of 丷(divide) and 半(cow). It means to divide a cow into two halves. The original meaning of 半 is half and extended to mean part, etc.

第二部分 500个常用汉字

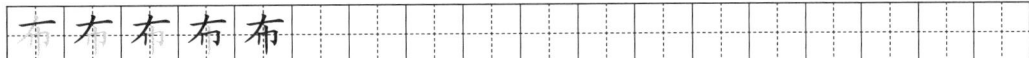

金文大篆　　小篆　　隶书　　楷体

拼音：bù　　**部件**：𠂆、巾　　**部首**：巾　　**结构**：半包围
六书：形声　　**笔画**：5画　　**本义**：麻布 sackcloth
词语：①布置 assign　②桌布 tablecloth　③瀑布 waterfall
句子：①教师给学生布置了家庭作业。The teacher assigned homework to students.
　　　　②别把桌布弄脏。Don't make the tablecloth dirty.
　　　　③他们意外地发现一处壮观的瀑布。They stumbled on a magnificent waterfall.

记忆贴士

"布"的金文字形由"攴"（手拿棍子捶打）和"巾"（麻）组成，表示捶打麻类植物得到做麻布的材料。"布"的本义是麻布，引申出安排和散布等含义。

The bronze inscription of 布 is . It consists of 攴(beat with a club) and 巾(hemp). It means to beat the hemp to get the material of the sackcloth and its original meaning is sackcloth. It is extended to mean to arrange and spread, etc.

小篆　　隶书　　楷体（繁体）　　楷体（简体）

拼音：suí　　**部件**：阝、辶、冇　　**部首**：阝　　**结构**：左右
六书：形声　　**笔画**：11画　　**本义**：跟随 follow
词语：①随意 at random　②随笔 essay　③随和 easygoing
句子：①他随意拿了一本书。He took a book at random.
　　　　②他有空时写些随笔。He writes essays when he is free.
　　　　③她非常随和。She is very easygoing.

记忆贴士

"随"由"阝"（土山）、"辶"（行走）和"冇"（猎物）组成，表示打猎时跟踪猎物，本义是跟随，引申出任凭和顺便等含义。

随 consists of 阝(dirt hill), 辶(walk) and 冇(prey). It means to track the prey during the hunting. The original meaning of 随 is to follow and extended to mean to let somebody do as he or she likes and along with, etc.

| 甲骨文 | 金文大篆 | 小篆 | 隶书 | 楷体 |

拼音：liù　　**部件**：亠、八　　**部首**：亠　　**结构**：独体
六书：象形　　**笔画**：4画　　**本义**：房子house
词语：①六边形hexagon　②六岁six years old　③六月June
句子：①这个建筑像个巨大的六边形。This building looks like a huge hexagon.
　　　②他六岁了。He is six years old.
　　　③假期从六月开始。The vacation begins from June.

记忆贴士

"六"的甲骨文字形 像一座房子，本义是房子。可以通过联想一座房子内部空间有六个面，帮助记忆"六"表示数字6。

六(oracle bone script is) is like a house and its original meaning is house. Now 六 means six.

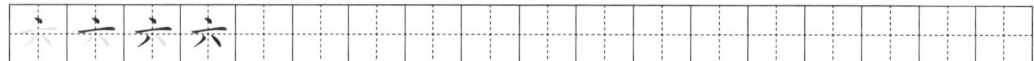

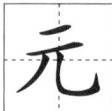

| 甲骨文 | 金文大篆 | 小篆 | 隶书 | 楷体 |

拼音：yuán　　**部件**：二、儿　　**部首**：一　　**结构**：上下
六书：指事　　**笔画**：4画　　**本义**：头head
词语：①元首head of state　②元素element　③元宵节Lantern Festival
句子：①他担任国家元首已满六年。He's been head of state for six years.
　　　②钻石只含有一种元素。Diamond consists of only one element.
　　　③什么时候是元宵节？Which date is Lantern Festival?

记忆贴士

"元"的甲骨文字形 像人形，由"二"（上）和"人"组成，合起来指明头的位置。"元"的本义是头，引申出初始和基本等含义。

The oracle bone script of 元 is . It consists of 二(upper) and 人(person). It indicates the position of head and the original meaning of 元 is head. It is extended to mean initial and basic, etc.

第四十六节

𝙸 → 低 → 低

小篆　　隶书　　楷体

拼音：dī　　**部件**：亻、氐　　**部首**：亻　　**结构**：左右
六书：形声　　**笔画**：7画　　**本义**：低头 bow one's head
词语：①低调 low profile　②低沉 low and deep　③贬低 depreciate
句子：①他为人低调。He keeps a low profile.
　　　②大提琴发出低沉的声音。The cello makes low and deep sounds.
　　　③你不应该贬低自己的价值。You should not depreciate your own value.

记忆贴士

"低"由"亻"（人）和"氐"（低头的样子，金文字形为 𝑞 ）组成，本义是低头，引申出不高和差等含义。

低 consists of 亻(person) and 氐(bow one's head). Its original meaning is to bow one's head and extended to mean low and inferior, etc.

亻	亻	仁	仟	伝	低	低								

稱 → 稱 → 稱 → 称

小篆　　隶书　　楷体（繁体）　楷体（简体）

拼音：chèng；chèn；chēng　　**部件**：禾、尔　　**部首**：禾
结构：左右　　**六书**：形声　　**笔画**：10画
本义：称量重量的器具 weight-measuring tool
词语：①匀称（chèn）shapely　②称（chèn）心如意 satisfactory　③称（chēng）赞 praise
句子：①她的身材很匀称。She has a shapely figure.
　　　②他有一个称心如意的工作。He has a satisfactory job.
　　　③我渴望得到称赞。I am avid for praise.

记忆贴士

"称"的繁体字为"稱"，由"禾"（粮食）和"爯"（手抓鱼称重）组成，本义是称重量的器具，引申出称重量、称呼和符合标准等含义。简体字"称"用"尔"代替"爯"。

The traditional character of 称 is 稱. It consists of 禾(crop) and 爯(grip fish to weigh). Its original meaning is weight-measuring tool and extended to mean to weigh, call and meet a criterion, etc. 爯 is replaced by 尔 in the simplified character.

千	千	千	禾	禾	利	称	称	称	称					

引

引 → 引 → 引 → 引
金文大篆　小篆　隶书　楷体

拼音：yǐn　　**部件**：弓、丨　　**部首**：弓　　**结构**：左右
六书：会意　　**笔画**：4画　　**本义**：拉开弓pull the bowstring
词语：①引用quote　②引导guide　③吸引attract
句子：①报纸引用了总统的话。The President was quoted in the newspaper.
　　　　②你的职责是引导他人。Your role is to guide others.
　　　　③汉语课吸引了很多学生。Chinese class attracts many students.

记忆贴士

"引"（小篆字形为引）由"弓"和"丨"（箭）组成，本义是拉开弓准备射箭，引申出带领和引起等含义。

引(xiaozhuan script is 引) consists of 弓(bow) and 丨(arrow). Its original meaning is to pull the bowstring to prepare for shooting and extended to mean to lead and cause, etc.

照

照 → 照 → 照
小篆　隶书　楷体

拼音：zhào　　**部件**：日、刀、口、灬　　**部首**：灬
结构：上下　　**六书**：形声　　**笔画**：13画
本义：明亮bright
词语：①照顾look after　②照常as usual　③照相take a picture
句子：①他可以照顾自己。He can look after himself.
　　　　②一切照常进行。Everything proceeds as usual.
　　　　③你能帮我们照相吗？Can you take a picture of us?

记忆贴士

"照"由"日"（太阳）、"灬"（火）和"召"（声旁）组成，本义是明亮，引申出照射和拍摄等含义。

照 consists of 日(sun), 灬(fire) and 召(indicates pronunciation). Its original meaning is bright and extended to mean to illuminate and take a picture, etc.

第二部分 500个常用汉字

失 → 失 → 失
小篆　隶书　楷体

拼音：shī　　**部件**：失　　**部首**：丿　　**结构**：独体
六书：会意　　**笔画**：5画　　**本义**：掉落 drop
词语：①失望 disappointing　②消失 disappear　③失去 lose
句子：①结果令人失望。The result is disappointing.
②如果不加以保护，这片森林就会消失。The forest will disappear without protection.
③他失去了所有的财产。He lost all his wealth.

记忆贴士

"失"的小篆字形由"手"（小篆字形为）和"丶"（物品）组成，表示物品从手中掉落，本义为掉落，引申为不见、未把握好和过错等含义。

The xiaozhuan script of 失 is. It consists of 手(xiaozhuan script is) and 丶(thing). It indicates that something has fallen from the hand. Its original meaning is to drop and extended to mean to disappear, out of control and fault, etc.

养 → 養 → 養 → 养
小篆　隶书　楷体（繁体）楷体（简体）

拼音：yǎng　　**部件**：羊、介　　**部首**：丷　　**结构**：上下
六书：形声　　**笔画**：9画　　**本义**：饲养 raise
词语：①营养 nutritive　②饲养 raise　③培养 cultivate
句子：①这种食物很有营养。This food is nutritive.
②饲养宠物需要花很多时间。It takes a lot of time to raise pets.
③培养发散性思维能力很重要。To cultivate divergent thinking is important.

记忆贴士

"养"的繁体字为"養"，由"羊"和"食"（喂食）组成，本义是饲养，引申为精心照看使成长。简体字"养"用"丌"代替"良"。

The traditional character of 养 is 養. It consists of 羊(sheep) and 食(feed). Its original meaning is to raise and extended to mean to care to grow. 良 is replaced by 丌 in the simplified character.

视

视 → 视 → 视 → 视
小篆　　隶书　　楷体（繁体）　楷体（简体）

拼音： shì　　　　**部件：** 礻、见　　　**部首：** 礻　　　　**结构：** 左右
六书： 会意　　　**笔画：** 8画
本义： 看 look at
词语： ①歧视 discriminate　②视野 horizon　③电视 television
句子： ①他们感觉到被歧视。They felt discriminated.
②学习一门新语言将拓宽你的视野。Learning a new language will expand your horizons.
③这是最新款的智能电视。This is the latest type of smart television.

记忆贴士

"视"由"礻"（启示）和"见"（看）组成，表示祭祀时仔细察看征兆，本义是看，引申出看待等含义。

视 consists of 礻 (revelation) and 见(look). It means to look at the sign carefully during the sacrifice. Its original meaning is to look at and extended to mean to regard, etc.

习

 → 習 → 習 → 習 → 習 → 习
甲骨文　　金文大篆　　小篆　　隶书　　楷体（繁体）　楷体（简体）

拼音： xí　　　　**部件：** 习　　　　**部首：** 乛　　　　**结构：** 独体
六书： 会意　　　**笔画：** 3画　　　　**本义：** 幼鸟练习飞翔 young bird practices to fly
词语： ①学习 study　②习惯 habit　③习俗 custom
句子： ①我在北京大学学习。I study at Peking University.
②人们的消费习惯正在发生变化。Consumption habits are changing.
③我们需要尊重他人的习俗。We need to respect other people's customs.

记忆贴士

"习"的繁体字为"習"（甲骨文字形为），由"羽"（羽毛）和"白"（鸟巢）组成。"習"的本义是幼鸟练习飞翔，引申出学习和习惯等含义。简体字"习"用"羽"的一半表示"习"。

The traditional character of 习 is 習(oracle bone script is ). It consists of 羽(feather) and 白(bird nest). Its original meaning is that a bird practices to fly and extended to mean to learn and habit, etc. The simplified character 习 only retains half of 羽.

金文大篆　　小篆　　隶书　　楷体

拼音：duàn　　**部件**：𠂉、殳　　**部首**：殳　　**结构**：左右
六书：形声　　**笔画**：9画　　**本义**：用锤击打 hit with hammer
词语：①手段 means　②片段 clip　③阶段 stage
句子：①手机短信提供了一种沟通手段。Short message provided a means of communication.
　　　②他们提供了一个视频片段。They provided a video clip.
　　　③这是我们工作的第二阶段。This is the second stage of our work.

记忆贴士

"段"的金文字形为 𠬝，表示手持锤子在山崖上开采石头，本义是用锤击打，引申出片段等含义。

The bronze inscription of 段 is 𠬝. It is like mining stones on the cliff with a hammer. Its original meaning is to hit with hammer and extended to mean segment and so on.

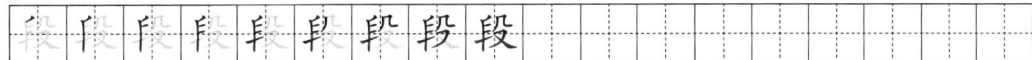

金文大篆　　小篆　　隶书　　楷体

拼音：zì　　**部件**：宀、子　　**部首**：宀　　**结构**：上下
六书：形声　　**笔画**：6画　　**本义**：生孩子 give birth to a child
词语：①字典 dictionary　②汉字 Chinese character　③名字 name
句子：①他们正在编纂一部字典。They are compiling a dictionary.
　　　②汉字的历史很悠久。Chinese characters have a long history.
　　　③警察弄清了他的名字和职业。Police figured out his name and occupation.

记忆贴士

"字"（金文字形为 𪧂）由"宀"（房屋）和"子"（孩子）组成，表示在屋里生孩子，本义是生孩子，引申出古代成年人的字和文字符号等含义。

字(bronze inscription is 𪧂) consists of 宀(house) and 子(baby). It means to give birth to a child. The original meaning is to give birth and extended to mean style name and character, etc.

第四十七节

纖 → 織 → 織 → 织
小篆　　隶书　　楷体(繁体)　楷体(简体)

拼音：zhī　　**部件**：纟、口、八　　**部首**：纟　　**结构**：左右
六书：形声　　**笔画**：8画　　**本义**：织布 weave
词语：①组织 organize　②纺织业 textile industry　③编织 braid
句子：①我们将组织一次演讲比赛。We will organize a speech contest.
②纺织业是劳动密集型产业。Textile industry is a labor-intensive industry.
③工人们正忙着编织地毯。Workers are busy braiding rugs.

记忆贴士

"织"的繁体字为"織",由"糹"(丝)和"戠"(声旁)组成,本义是织布。简体字"织"用"纟"(丝)和"只"(声旁)分别代替"糹"和"戠"。

The traditional character of 织 is 織. It consists of 糹 (silk) and 戠(indicates pronunciation). Its original meaning is to weave. The simplified character consists of 纟(silk) and 只(indicates pronunciation).

子 → 毛 → 斗 → 斗　　鬥 → 鬥 → 鬥 → 鬥 → 斗
甲骨文　小篆　隶书　楷体　　甲骨文　小篆　隶书(繁体)　楷体(繁体)　楷体(简体)

拼音：1. dǒu；2. dòu　　**部件**：斗　　**部首**：斗　　**结构**：独体
六书：象形　　**笔画**：4画　　**本义**：勺子 spoon
词语：①泰斗(dǒu)leading authority　②战斗(dòu)battle　③奋斗(dòu)strive for
句子：①他是这个领域的泰斗。He is a leading authority in this field.
②战斗正在进行中。The battle is on.
③我会为成功而奋斗。I will strive for success.

记忆贴士

简体字"斗"有两个来源,一个是"斗",另一个是"鬥"。

"斗"的甲骨文字形子像勺子,本义是勺子,引申出称量单位以及形状像斗的东西等含义。

"鬥"的甲骨文字形像两个人打斗的样子,本义是相搏,引申出较量等含义。

现在"斗"和"鬥"都写作"斗"。

The simplified character 斗 has two sources.

斗(oracle bone script is 子) is like a spoon. Its original mening is spoon and extended to mean a measure unit and object like a cup or a dipper, etc.

鬥(oracle bone script is 鬥) is like two people fighting. Its original meaning is to fight and extended to mean to contest and so on.

Now both 斗 and 鬥 are written as 斗。

团

小篆　　隶书　　楷体（繁体）楷体（简体）

拼音：tuán　　**部件**：囗、才　　**部首**：囗　　**结构**：全包围
六书：形声　　**笔画**：6画　　**本义**：圆形 round

词语：①团圆reunion　②团体team　③集团group
句子：①春节意味着团圆。Spring Festival means reunion.
　　　　②这是一个团体比赛。This is a team match.
　　　　③他在一家大型传媒集团工作。He works in a big media group.

记忆贴士

"团"的繁体字为"團"（小篆字形为 ），由"囗"（缠绕）和"專"（手拿纺纱轮的样子，小篆字形为 ）组成，本义为圆形，引申出球状物和集体组织等含义。简体字"团"用"才"代替"專"。

The traditional character of 团 is 團(xiaozhuan script is). It consists of 囗(wrap) and 專 (xiaozhuan script is , meaning to hold a spindle). Its original meaning is round and extended to mean ball-like object and collective organization, etc. 專 is replaced by 才 in the simplified character.

丨 冂 冃 用 团 团

器

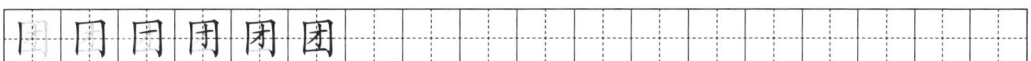

金文大篆　　小篆　　隶书　　楷体

拼音：qì　　**部件**：口、口、口、口、犬　　**部首**：口
结构：上中下　　**六书**：会意　　**笔画**：16画
本义：器皿 utensil

词语：①机器machine　②瓷器chinaware　③电器electrical appliance
句子：①这个机器是自动控制的。This machine is automatically controlled.
　　　　②这是一个瓷器博物馆。This is a chinaware museum.
　　　　③冰箱是常见的家用电器。Refrigerator is a common household electrical appliance.

记忆贴士

"器"由"犬"（狗）和四个"口"（物品）组成，表示用狗看管物品，本义是器皿，引申出用具的总称等含义。

器 consists of 犬(dog) and four 口(goods). It means to guard goods with dog. Its original meaning is utensil and extended to mean appliance, etc.

丨 口 口 吅 吅 吅 哭 哭 哭 哭 哭 哭 器 器 器 器

301

金文大篆 → 小篆 → 隶书 → 楷体（繁体）→ 楷体（简体）

拼音：xìng；xīng　　**部件**：⺍、一、八　　**部首**：八　　**结构**：上下

六书：会意　　**笔画**：6画　　**本义**：起来 rise

词语：①高兴（xìng）pleased　②兴趣（xìng）interest　③振兴（xīng）revitalize

句子：①很高兴见到你。I'm pleased to see you.
　　　　②我对汉语很感兴趣。I have great interest in Chinese.
　　　　③我们要振兴实体经济。We need to revitalize the real economy.

记忆贴士

"兴"的繁体字为"興"（小篆字形为 𦥯），由"舁"（举起，小篆字形 𦥑 像四只手）和"同"（共同）组成，本义是起来，引申出情绪高、发起和振兴等含义。简体字"兴"简化了上半部分，保留下半部分。

The traditional character of 兴 is 興. It consists of 舁(xiaozhuan script is 𦥑, indicating four hands and meaning to lift) and 同(together). Its original meaning is to rise and extended to mean high mood, to initiate and to promote, etc. The upper complex radical is replaced by ⺍ in the simplified character.

兴 兴 兴 兴 兴 兴

甲骨文 → 金文大篆 → 小篆 → 隶书 → 楷体（繁体）→ 楷体（简体）

拼音：yuè；lè　　**部件**：乐　　**部首**：丿　　**结构**：独体

六书：象形　　**笔画**：5画　　**本义**：音乐 music

词语：①乐（yuè）曲 music　②快乐（lè）happy　③乐（lè）观 optimistic

句子：①这是一首伤感的乐曲。This is a piece of melancholy music.
　　　　②他是一个快乐的年轻人。He is a happy young man.
　　　　③我对此并不乐观。I am not optimistic about this.

记忆贴士

"乐"的繁体字为"樂"（金文字形为 ），由两个"幺"（弦）、"白"（说唱）和"木"（木头）组成，表示用带弦的木质乐器为说唱伴奏，本义为音乐，引申出快乐等含义。

The traditional character of 乐 is 樂(bronze inscription is). It consists of two 幺(string), 白(speak and sing) and 木(wood), indicating to sing with wooden string instrument. Its original meaning is music and extended to mean happy and so on.

乐 乐 乐 乐 乐

302

 甲骨文 金文大篆 小篆 隶书 楷体

拼音：xiào　　**部件**：交、攵　　**部首**：攵　　**结构**：左右
六书：形声　　**笔画**：10画　　**本义**：制作箭 make arrow

词语：①效益benefit　②效率efficiency　③效果effect

句子：①这项技术产生了很大的经济效益。This technology has produced great economic benefits.　②他的学习效率非常高。His study efficiency is very high.
③这种药对于那种病没有效果。This medicine has no effect on that disease.

记忆贴士

"效"（金文字形为 ）由"交"（箭，"矢"的误写）和"攵"（手拿工具）组成，本义是手拿工具制作箭，引申出模仿和奋力等含义。

效(bronze inscription is) consists of 交(miswritten form of 矢, means arrow) and 攵(hold the tool). Its original meaning is to make arrow and extended to mean to imitate and devote, etc.

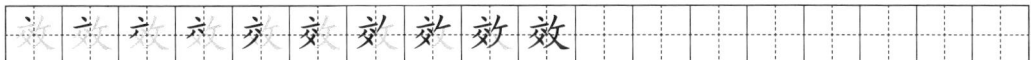

 金文大篆 小篆 隶书 楷体（繁体） 楷体（简体）

拼音：xiǎn　　**部件**：日、业　　**部首**：日　　**结构**：上下
六书：会意　　**笔画**：9画　　**本义**：看得清楚 see clearly

词语：①显著salient　②显示show　③明显obvious

句子：①这种方法显著的特征是方便。The salient feature of this method is convenience.
②数据显示情况不正常。The data showed that the situation was abnormal.
③这是一个明显的失误。This is an obvious mistake.

记忆贴士

"显"的繁体字为"顯"（金文字形为 ），由"日""丝"和"页"（看见，"见"的误写）组成，表示丝在阳光下丝丝可见，本义为看得清楚，引申出表现和有权势等含义。

The traditional character of 显 is 顯(bronze inscription is). It consists of 日(sun), 丝(silk) and 页(miswritten form of 见, means see), indicating to see the silk clearly in the sun. Its original meaning is to see clearly and extended to mean to show and influential, etc.

斯 → 斯 → 斯 → 斯
金文大篆　小篆　隶书　楷体

拼音：sī　　**部件**：其、斤　　**部首**：斤　　**结构**：左右
六书：形声　　**笔画**：12画　　**本义**：劈开 split
词语：①歇斯底里 hysterical　②俄罗斯 Russia
句子：①他歇斯底里地大喊。He shouted hysterically.
②俄罗斯大部分领土位于亚洲。Most of Russia's territory is located in Asia.

记忆贴士

"斯"由"其"（簸箕）和"斤"（斧子）组成，表示用斧子劈竹篾做簸箕，本义是劈开，在文言文中借为指示代词。

斯 consists of 其(winnowing basket) and 斤(axe), indicating to use axe to make bamboo winnowing basket. Its original meaning is to split. It is used as a demonstrative pronoun in ancient Chinese.

↑ → ↑ → 千 → 千 → 千　　韆 → 韆 → 千
甲骨文　金文大篆　小篆　隶书　楷体　　隶书　楷体（繁体）楷体（简体）

拼音：qiān　　**部件**：千　　**部首**：丿　　**结构**：独体
六书：形声　　**笔画**：3画　　**本义**：十个一百 thousand
词语：①千万 must　②千克 kilogram　③秋千 swing
句子：①你千万别迟到。You must not be late.
②一吨是一千千克。A ton is 1,000 kilograms.
③他想玩秋千。He wanted to play on the swing.

记忆贴士

简体字"千"有两个来源，一个是"千"，另一个是"韆"。

"千"的甲骨文字形↑由"人"和"十"组成，本义是十个百。

"韆"由"革"（皮）和"遷"（移动）组成，本义是一种供人在空中荡来荡去的游乐设施。

现在"千"和"韆"都写作"千"。

The simplified character 千 has two sources.

The oracle bone script of 千 is ↑. It consists of 人(person) and 十(ten). Its original meaning is one thousand.

韆 consists of 革(leather) and 遷(move). Its original meaning is a recreation facility for people to swing in the air.

Now both 千 and 韆 are written as 千.

第四十八节

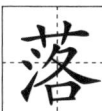

篆 → 落 → 落
小篆　隶书　楷体

拼音：luò　　**部件**：艹、氵、各　　**部首**：艹　　**结构**：上下
六书：形声　　**笔画**：12画　　**本义**：叶落 leaf falls
词语：①坐落located　②堕落decadence　③降落land
句子：①这个城堡坐落在山顶。This castle is located on the hilltop.
　　　②道德的堕落对于国家是不利的。The moral decadence is bad for the nation.
　　　③飞机降落在机场。Plane landed at the airport.

记忆贴士

"落"由"艹"（草木）和"洛"（声旁）组成，本义是树叶落下，引申出物体从高处掉下来等含义。

落 consists of 艹(grass and tree) and 洛(indicates pronunciation). Its original meaning is that a leaf falls and extended to mean to fall and so on.

甲 → 示 → 示 → 示 → 示
甲骨文　金文大篆　小篆　隶书　楷体

拼音：shì　　**部件**：二、小　　**部首**：示　　**结构**：上下
六书：会意　　**笔画**：5画　　**本义**：上天的启示 heaven's revelation
词语：①展示demonstrate　②表示mean　③指示instruction
句子：①这是一个他展示技能的机会。This is an opportunity to demonstrate his skills.
　　　②点头表示同意。Nodding means agreement.
　　　③我遵照他的指示来做。I followed his instructions。

记忆贴士

"示"的甲骨文字形为甲，"示"上面的"二"表示上，"小"表示上天显示的迹象。"示"的本义是上天的启示，引申为显示等含义。

示(oracle bone script is 甲) consists of 二(up) and 小(sign). Its original meaning is heaven's revelation and extended to mean to show and so on.

僅 → 僅 → 僅 → 仅
小篆　　隶书　　楷体（繁体）楷体（简体）

拼音：jǐn　　**部件**：亻、又　　**部首**：亻　　**结构**：左右

六书：形声　　**笔画**：4画　　**本义**：只能 only

词语：①不仅 not just　②仅仅 only　③绝无仅有 one and only

句子：①教育的对象不仅是孩子。Education is not just for the children.
②这些仅仅是猜测。These are only speculations.
③她是一位绝无仅有的演员。As an actress, she is one and only.

记忆贴士

"仅"的繁体字为"僅"，由"亻"和"堇"（声旁）组成，本义是只能。简体字"仅"用"又"代替"堇"。

The traditional character of 仅 is 僅. It consists of 亻 and 堇(indicates pronunciation). Its original meaning is only. 堇 is replaced by 又 in the simplified character.

⺉ → 🈁 → 🈁 → 企 → 企
甲骨文　　金文大篆　　小篆　　隶书　　楷体

拼音：qǐ　　**部件**：人、止　　**部首**：人　　**结构**：上下

六书：会意　　**笔画**：6画　　**本义**：踮起脚 stand on tiptoe

词语：①企业 enterprise　②企图 try to　③企鹅 penguin

句子：①他在一家私营企业工作。He works in a private enterprise.
②他们企图逃走。They tried to escape.
③我最喜欢的动物是企鹅。My favorite animal is penguin.

记忆贴士

"企"的甲骨文字形⺉由"人"（甲骨文字形为⺉）和"止"（脚，甲骨文字形为⻀）组成，表示人踮起脚，本义为踮起脚，引申出盼望等含义。

The oracle bone script of 企 is ⺉. It consists of 人(oracle bone script is ⺉) and 止(oracle bone script is ⻀, meaning foot). Its original meaning is to stand on tiptoe and extended to mean to look forward, etc.

 甹 → 𠜱 → 似 → 似

金文大篆　　小篆　　隶书　　楷体

拼音：sì　　　　**部件**：亻、以　　　**部首**：亻　　　**结构**：左右
六书：形声　　　**笔画**：6画　　　　**本义**：相像 look like

词语：①似乎 seem　②相似性 similarity　③类似 similar

句子：①他似乎不同意你的意见。He seemed to disagree with your opinion.
②它们之间有相似性。There is similarity between them.
③这是一种类似于羚羊的动物。This is a kind of animal that is similar to antelope.

记忆贴士

"似"由"亻"和"以"（声旁）组成，本义是相像，引申出好像等含义。

似 consists of 亻 and 以 (indicates pronunciation). Its original meaning is to look like and extended to mean to seem, etc.

| 亻 | 亻 | 化 | 似 | 似 | 似 | | | | | | | | | |

 𤰈 → 𤰈 → 備 → 備 → 备

金文大篆　　小篆　　隶书　　楷体（繁体）　楷体（简体）

拼音：bèi　　　　**部件**：夂、田　　　**部首**：夂　　　**结构**：上下
六书：形声　　　**笔画**：8画　　　　**本义**：盛放箭的容器 arrow container

词语：①责备 blame　②准备 prepare　③储备 reserve

句子：①不负责任的人应该受到责备。An irresponsible person deserves to be blamed.
②你最好准备一张电子地图。You'd better prepare an electronic map.
③我们必须储备些食物和饮用水以应对紧急情况。We must reserve food and drinking water for emergencies.

记忆贴士

"备"的繁体字为"備"（金文字形为 𤰈），由"亻"（人）和"𦰏"（箭筒）组成，本义是盛放箭的容器，引申出拥有、筹划和全面等含义。

The traditional character of 备 is 備 (bronze inscription is 𤰈). It consists of 亻(person) and 𦰏 (arrow container). Its original meaning is arrow container and extended to mean to have, prepare and fully, etc.

| 亻 | 夂 | 冬 | 冬 | 备 | 备 | 备 | 备 | | | | | | | |

 隊 → 除 → 除
小篆　　隶书　　楷体

拼音：chú　　**部件**：阝、余　　**部首**：阝　　**结构**：左右
六书：形声　　**笔画**：9画　　**本义**：宫殿的台阶 steps of palace
词语：①删除delete　②除了except　③废除abolition
句子：①文件被删除了。The file was deleted.
②除了这个其他的我都要了。I will buy all except this one.
③他们宣布废除奴隶制度。They announced the abolition of slavery.

记忆贴士

"除"（小篆字形为隊）由"阝"（台阶）和"余"（房屋）组成，本义是宫殿的台阶，由一级一级地走过去，引申出去掉之意。

除(xiaozhuan script is 隊) consists of 阝(steps) and 余(house). Its original meaning is steps of palace and extended to mean to remove and so on.

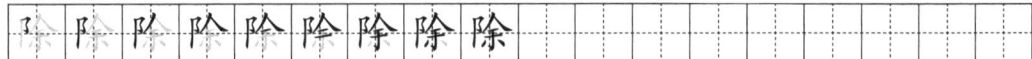

 𢻳 → 支 → 支
小篆　　隶书　　楷体

拼音：zhī　　**部件**：十、又　　**部首**：支　　**结构**：上下
六书：会意　　**笔画**：4画
本义：去除枝叶的竹子 branchless bamboo
词语：①支持support　②支配dominating　③透支overdraw
句子：①我需要你的支持。I need your support.
②这个品牌过去在市场上占支配地位。This brand was dominating over the market.
③我的账户已经透支了。My account is already overdrawn.

记忆贴士

"支"（小篆字形为𢻳）由"十"（"竹"的一半）和"又"（手）组成，本义是去除枝叶的竹子，引申出支持和分支等含义。

支(xiaozhuan script is 𢻳) consists of 十(half of 竹, means bamboo) and 又(hand). Its original meaning is branchless bamboo and extended to mean to support and branch, etc.

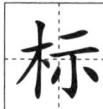

檦 → 標 → 標 → 标
小篆　　隶书　　楷体（繁体）楷体（简体）

拼音：biāo　　**部件**：木、示　　**部首**：木　　**结构**：左右
六书：形声　　**笔画**：9画　　**本义**：树梢 tip of a tree
词语：①标点符号 punctuation　②目标 target　③标准 standard
句子：①这几句话没有标点符号。These sentences have no punctuation.
　　　②他们达到了这个月的销售目标。They have reached this month's sales target.
　　　③这是最低的工资标准。This is the minimum wage standard.

记忆贴士

"标"的繁体字为"標"，由"木"（树）和"票"（飘摇）组成，表示树木随风飘摇最明显的部分，本义是树梢。因为树梢很显眼，所以引申出标准和记号等含义。简体字"标"用"示"代替"票"。

The traditional character of 标 is 標. It consists of 木(tree) and 票(sway), indicating the part of a tree that sways the most obviously with the wind. The original meaning of 標 is the tip of a tree. Because the tip of a tree is obvious, it is extended to mean standard and mark, etc. 票 is replaced by 示 in the simplified character.

㫃 → 早 → 早
小篆　　隶书　　楷体

拼音：zǎo　　**部件**：日、十　　**部首**：日　　**结构**：上下
六书：会意　　**笔画**：6画　　**本义**：早晨 morning
词语：①早晨 morning　②早餐 breakfast　③早出晚归 go out early and come back late
句子：①他喜欢早晨跑步。He likes jogging in the morning.
　　　②我到达时他们正在吃早饭。They were having breakfast when I arrived.
　　　③他每天早出晚归。He goes out early and comes back late every day.

记忆贴士

"早"由"日"（太阳）和"十"（草）组成，表示太阳在草之上，本义是早晨，引申出一个时段靠前的部分。

早 consists of 日(sun) and 十(grass). It means that the sun is above the grass. Its original meaning is morning and extended to mean the early part of a time period.

第四十九节

吧 → 吧

隶书　　楷体

拼音：bā；ba　　**部件**：口、巴　　**部首**：口　　**结构**：左右
六书：形声　　**笔画**：7画
本义：象声词，东西爆裂或撞击的声音 onomatopoeia, the sound of something breaking
词语：①酒吧bar　②网吧Internet bar　③吧台bar counter
句子：①这是全城最受欢迎的酒吧。This is the city's most popular bar.
　　　②你经常去网吧吗？Do you often go to Internet bars?
　　　③有人在吧台等你。Someone is waiting for you at the bar counter.

记忆贴士

"吧"由"口"（用口模仿）和"巴"（声旁）组成，本义是象声词，表示东西爆裂或撞击的声音。现在主要是作为句末语气词以及用来音译外来词。

吧 consists of 口(imitate sounds with mouth) and 巴(indicates pronunciation). It is an onomatopoeia—the sound of something breaking. It is now mainly used as a modal particle at the end of a sentence and used to transliterate foreign words.

用 → 𠰠 → 周 → 周 → 周

甲骨文　金文大篆　小篆　隶书　楷体

拼音：zhōu　　**部件**：冂、土、口　　**部首**：冂　　**结构**：半包围
六书：象形　　**笔画**：8画　　**本义**：稠密 dense
词语：①周到considerate　②周游travel around　③周末weekend
句子：①你考虑得如此周到。You are so considerate.
　　　②我想周游世界。I want to travel around the world.
　　　③这个周末我们有个聚会。We are having a party this weekend.

记忆贴士

"周"的金文字形𠰠由"田"（农田）和"口"（划分地界）组成，表示在划定的范围内种植庄稼，本义是稠密，引申出周围和全面等含义。

The bronze inscription of 周 is 𠰠. It consists of 田(farm) and 口(delimit boundary), indicating to plant crops within the delimited range. The original meaning of 周 is dense and extended to mean surrounding and thorough, etc.

 籆 → 速 → 速
小篆　　隶书　　楷体

拼音：sù　　**部件**：辶、束　　**部首**：辶　　**结构**：半包围
六书：形声　　**笔画**：10画
本义：速度快 fast
词语：①迅速prompt　②速度speed　③光速speed of light
句子：①我们非常迅速地执行了这些任务。We have been so prompt in carrying out all these missions.
②技术变革的速度加快了。The speed of technological change quickened.
③光速是一个不变常数。The speed of light is an invariant constant.

记忆贴士

"速"由"辶"（走路）和"束"（声旁）组成，本义是速度快，引申出速度等含义。

速 consists of 辶(walk) and 束(indicates pronunciation). Its original meaning is fast and extended to mean speed, etc.

 垠 → 跟 → 跟
小篆　　隶书　　楷体

拼音：gēn　　**部件**：𧾷、艮　　**部首**：𧾷　　**结构**：左右
六书：形声　　**笔画**：13画　　**本义**：脚后跟heel
词语：①跟踪tail　②跟随follow　③跟上keep up with
句子：①警察正在跟踪嫌疑犯。The police are tailing the suspect.
②我们跟随他上了台阶。We followed him up the steps.
③每个人都想跟上时代的步伐。Everyone wants to keep up with the times.

记忆贴士

"跟"由"𧾷"（脚）和"艮"（回头看）组成，本义为脚后跟，引申出跟随等含义。

跟 consists of 𧾷 (foot) and 艮(look back). Its original meaning is heel and extended to mean to follow and so on.

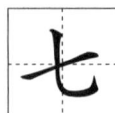

| 甲骨文 | 金文大篆 | 小篆 | 隶书 | 楷体 |

拼音：qī　　**部件**：七　　**部首**：一　　**结构**：独体
六书：会意　　**笔画**：2画　　**本义**：切 cut
词语：①七夕节Chinese Valentine's Day　②七上八下agitated　③七七事变the July 7th Incident
句子：①农历七月初七是七夕节。The seventh day of the seventh lunar month is Chinese Valentine's Day.
②我心里七上八下。I had got so agitated.
③这是一本关于七七事变的书。The book is about the July 7th Incident.

记忆贴士

"七"的甲骨文字形为十，本义是切，现在表示数字7。
The oracle bone script of 七 is 十. Its original meaning is to cut and now it means seven.

| 甲骨文 | 金文大篆 | 小篆 | 隶书 | 楷体 |

拼音：cǎi　　**部件**：爫、木　　**部首**：爫　　**结构**：上下
六书：会意　　**笔画**：8画　　**本义**：采摘collect
词语：①采购purchase　②采集gather　③采取adopt
句子：①两家公司正在讨论设备采购。Two companies are discussing the purchase of equipment.
②蜜蜂从花上采集花蜜。Bees gather nectar from flowers.
③政府已经采取了紧急措施。The government has adopted an urgent action.

记忆贴士

"采"（金文字形为 ）由"爫"（手，金文字形为 ）和"木"（树，金文字形为 ）组成，表示用手采树上的果实或叶子，本义是采摘，引申为收集和利用等含义。

采(bronze inscription is) consists of 爫(bronze inscription is , meaning hand) and 木(bronze inscription is , meaning tree), indicating to collect fruit or leaf from the tree. Its original meaning is to collect and extended to mean to select and adopt, etc.

 狀 → 狀 → 狀 → 状
小篆　　隶书　　楷体（繁体）　楷体（简体）

拼音：zhuàng　　**部件**：丬、犬　　**部首**：丬　　**结构**：左右
六书：形声　　**笔画**：7画　　**本义**：狗的形状 the shape of a dog
词语：①状态 state　②形状 shape　③状语 adverbial
句子：①这支球队状态不佳。This football team is not in good state.
②我们有各种形状的贺卡。We have greeting cards in various shapes.
③状语也叫修饰语。Adverbials are also called adjuncts.

记忆贴士

"状"的繁体字为"狀"，由"爿"（强壮，"壮"的省写）和"犬"（狗）组成，本义为狗的形状，引申为形状和状态等含义。简体字"状"用"丬"代替"爿"。

The traditional character of 状 is 狀. It consists of 爿(omitted form of 壮, means strong) and 犬(dog). Its original meaning is the shape of a dog and extended to mean shape and condition, etc. 爿 is replaced by 丬 in the simplified character.

 吗 → 吗
隶书　　楷体

拼音：ma　　**部件**：口、马　　**部首**：口　　**结构**：左右
六书：形声　　**笔画**：6画　　**本义**：语气词 modal particle
句子：①我们一起去好吗？Shall we go together?
②你去吗？Are you going?
③我坐这里可以吗？Can I take this seat?

记忆贴士

"吗"由"口"和"马"（声旁）组成，"吗"在现代汉语中一般放在句子末尾表示疑问或反问的语气。

吗 consists of 口 and 马(indicates pronunciation). In modern Chinese, 吗 is generally used at the end of the sentence to indicate the tone of question or rhetorical question.

𦁋 → 約 → 約 → 约

小篆　　隶书　　楷体（繁体）　楷体（简体）

拼音：yuē　　**部件**：纟、勺　　**部首**：纟　　**结构**：左右
六书：形声　　**笔画**：6画　　**本义**：缠束 bundle
词语：①约束 bind　②制约 limit　③约会 date
句子：①我们受到合同条款的约束。We are bound by the terms of the contract.
②高等教育规模受到经济发展的制约。The scale of higher education is limited by economic development.
③我和他有个约会。I have a date with him.

记忆贴士

"约"由"纟"（丝线）和"勺"（声旁）组成，本义是缠束，引申出限制和邀请等含义。

约 consists of 纟(silk thread) and 勺(indicates pronunciation). Its original meaning is to bundle and extended to mean to restrain and invite, etc.

戓 → 城 → 城 → 城

金文大篆　　小篆　　隶书　　楷体

拼音：chéng　　**部件**：土、成　　**部首**：土　　**结构**：左右
六书：形声　　**笔画**：9画　　**本义**：有兵把守的城墙 city wall guarded by soldiers
词语：①城市 city　②城堡 castle　③长城 great wall
句子：①上海是沿海城市。Shanghai is a coastal city.
②城堡四周有一条护城河。A moat runs about the castle.
③长城是世界奇观之一。The Great Wall is one of the wonders of the world.

记忆贴士

"城"（金文字形为戓）由"土"（城墙，金文字形为土）和"成"（武力守城，金文字形为戓）组成，本义是有兵把守的城墙，引申为城市。

The bronze inscription of 城 is 戓. It consists of 土(bronze inscription is 土, meaning city wall) and 成(bronze inscription is 戓, meaning armed forces protect the city). Its original meaning is city wall guarded by soldiers and extended to mean city.

第五十节

層 → 層 → 層 → 层
小篆　隶书　楷体（繁体）楷体（简体）

拼音：céng　　**部件**：尸、云　　**部首**：尸　　**结构**：半包围
六书：形声　　**笔画**：7画　　**本义**：楼房 storied building
词语：①层次 level　②阶层 stratum　③层出不穷 emerge in an endless stream
句子：①这是我们最高层次的合作。This is our highest level of cooperation.
　　　②他们代表社会各个阶层。They represent each society stratum.
　　　③怪事层出不穷。Strange things emerged in an endless stream.

记忆贴士

"层"的繁体字为"層"，由"尸"（屋子，"屋"的省写）和"曾"（楼层隔板）组成，本义是楼房。简体字"层"用"云"代替"曾"。

The traditional character of 层 is 層. It consists of 尸(omitted form of 屋, means house) and 曾(two-layer). Its original meaning is storied building and extended to mean level and layer, etc. 曾 is replaced by 云 in the simplified character.

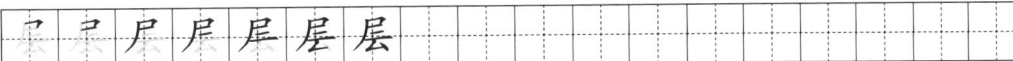

→ → → 專 → 專 → 专
甲骨文　金文大篆　小篆　隶书　楷体（繁体）楷体（简体）

拼音：zhuān　　**部件**：专　　**部首**：一　　**结构**：独体
六书：会意　　**笔画**：4画　　**本义**：纺锤 spindle
词语：①专业 major　②专家 specialist　③专心 absorbed
句子：①我的专业是中国语言文学。My major is Chinese Language and Literature.
　　　②他是计算机方面的专家。He is a specialist on computer.
　　　③他在专心地读小说。He is absorbed in reading a novel.

记忆贴士

"专"的繁体字为"專"（金文字形为 ），由"叀"（纺锤）和"寸"（手）组成，本义是纺锤，引申出注意力集中和不包容等含义。简体字"专"由繁体字"專"的草书楷化而成。

The traditional character of 专 is 專(bronze inscription is). It consists of 叀(spindle) and 寸(hand). Its original meaning is spindle and extended to mean concentrated and exclusive, etc. The simplified character 专 is transformed from cursive script.

315

劃 → 劃 → 劃 → 划　　划 → 划
小篆　　隶书　楷体（繁体）楷体（简体）　隶书　　楷体

拼音：huà；huá　　**部件**：戈、刂　　**部首**：戈　　**结构**：左右
六书：会意　　**笔画**：6画　　**本义**：以桨拨水使船前进 paddle
词语：①计划（huà）plan　②策划（huà）plot　③划（huá）船 row
句子：①我在考虑我的旅行计划。I am thinking over my travel plan.
　　　　②他策划了那场袭击。He plotted that attack.
　　　　③我带她去划船。I took her for a row.

记忆贴士

简体字"划"有两个来源，一个是"劃"，另一个是"划"。
"劃"（huà）由"畫"（画）和"刂"（刀）组成，本义是有意图地把东西分开。
"划"（huá）由"戈"（武器）和"刂"（刀）组成，本义是以桨拨水使船前进，引申为将另一物体分开或者在表面划过。
"劃"和"划"现在都写作"划"。

The simplified character 划 has two sources.

劃(huà) consists of 畫(draw) and 刂(knife). Its original meaning is to intentionally divide things.

划(huá) consists of 戈(weapon) and 刂(knife). Its original meaning is to paddle and extended to mean to separate other things or slide through the surface of something.

Now both 劃 and 划 are written as 划.

輕 → 輕 → 輕 → 轻
小篆　隶书　楷体（繁体）楷体（简体）

拼音：qīng　　**部件**：车、巠　　**部首**：车　　**结构**：左右
六书：形声　　**笔画**：9画　　**本义**：轻车 light carriage
词语：①轻蔑 contemptuous　②轻视 look down upon　③轻松 relaxed
句子：①他用轻蔑的眼光看着我。He was looking at me with a contemptuous glance.
　　　　②不要轻视你的对手。Don't look down upon your rival.
　　　　③午餐时的气氛是轻松的。The atmosphere at lunch was relaxed.

记忆贴士

"轻"的繁体字为"輕",由"車"(车辆)和"巠"(小路,"徑"的省写)组成,表示能在小路上行驶的车辆,本义是轻车,引申为不重要和容易等含义。简体字"轻"分别用"车"和"圣"代替"車"和"巠"。

The traditional character of 轻 is 輕. It consists of 車(vehicle) and 巠(omitted form of 徑, means footpath). It means a light carriage that can drive on a footpath. Its original meaning is light carriage and extended to mean not important and easy, etc. 車 and 巠 are replaced by 车 and 圣 separately in the simplified character.

轻 轻 轻 轻 轻 轻 轻 轻

小篆　　隶书　　楷体

拼音: lā　　**部件:** 扌、立　　**部首:** 扌　　**结构:** 左右
六书: 形声　　**笔画:** 8画
本义: 折断 break
词语: ①拉手 handle　②拖拉机 tractor　③拉拢 draw somebody over to one's side
句子: ①箱子的拉手坏了。The handle of this case is broken.
　　　②拖拉机方便了耕种。Tractors facilitate farming.
　　　③他极力拉拢我们。He made an utmost effort to draw us over to his side.

记忆贴士

"拉"由"扌"(手)和"立"(声旁)组成,本义是折断,引申出牵引和运输等含义。

拉 consists of 扌(hand) 和 立(indicates pronunciation). Its original meaning is to break and extended to mean to drag and transport, etc.

拉 扌 扌 扣 扣 拉 拉 拉

适

小篆 → 隶书 → 楷体（繁体）→ 楷体（简体）

拼音：shì　　**部件**：辶、舌　　**部首**：辶　　**结构**：半包围
六书：形声　　**笔画**：9画　　**本义**：往 go
词语：①舒适 comfortable　②合适 suitable　③适当 appropriate
句子：①我的房间很舒适。My room is comfortable.
　　　②他是这个工作的合适人选。He is a suitable man for this job.
　　　③我们会提供适当的补偿。We will offer an appropriate recompense.

记忆贴士

"适"的小篆字形为 𧗟，由"辵"（行走）和"啻"（声旁）组成，本义是前往，引申出符合标准和舒服等含义。"适"的繁体字为"適"，简体字"适"用"舌"代替"啻"。

The xiaozhuan script of 适 is 𧗟. It consists of 辵(walk) and 啻(indicates pronunciation). The original meaning is to go and extended to mean to meet the standard and comfortable, etc. The traditional character of 适 is 適. 啻 is replaced by 舌 in the simplified character.

英

小篆 → 隶书 → 楷体

拼音：yīng　　**部件**：艹、央　　**部首**：艹　　**结构**：上下
六书：形声　　**笔画**：8画　　**本义**：花 flower
词语：①英雄 hero　②英语 English　③英俊 handsome
句子：①英雄激励了千百万人。Hero inspired millions of people.
　　　②他的母语是英语。His native language is English.
　　　③他是个英俊的小伙子。He is a handsome guy.

记忆贴士

"英"由"艹"（花草）和"央"（声旁）组成，本义是花，引申出精华和杰出等含义。

英 consists of 艹(grass and flower) and 央(indicates pronunciation). Its original meaning is flower and extended to mean elite and outstanding, etc.

告

甲骨文 → 金文大篆 → 小篆 → 隶书 → 楷体

拼音：gào　　**部件**：牛、口　　**部首**：口　　**结构**：上下
六书：会意　　**笔画**：7画　　**本义**：祷告 pray
词语：①报告 report　②告诫 warn　③告别 farewell
句子：①我明天上交报告。I will turn in my report tomorrow.
②我们告诫过他不要出门。We warned him not to go out.
③他们在车站相互告别。They bid farewell to each other at the station.

记忆贴士

"告"的甲骨文字形由"牛"（"牛"的省写）和"口"（说话）组成。古人用牛作为牺牲进行祭祀，"口"表示向上天表达崇敬之意。"告"的本义是祭祀中祷告，引申为对人诉说和揭发等含义。

The oracle bone script of 告 is. It consists of 牛(omitted form of 牛, means cow) and 口 (speak). Ancient people used the cow as sacrifices, and 口 means to pray. The original meaning of 告 is to pray and extended to mean to tell and accuse, etc.

讲

講 → 講 → 講 → 讲
小篆　隶书（繁体）　楷体（繁体）　楷体（简体）

拼音：jiǎng　　**部件**：讠、井　　**部首**：讠　　**结构**：左右
六书：形声　　**笔画**：6画　　**本义**：和解 become reconciled
词语：①讲究 be paticular about　②讲述 tell　③讲座 lecture
句子：①他很讲究卫生。He is very paticular about hygiene.
②他给我们讲述了他的故事。He told us his story.
③成百上千的人参加了讲座。Hundreds of people attended the lecture.

记忆贴士

"讲"的繁体字为"講"，由"言"（说话）和"冓"（沟通）组成，本义是和解，引申出说话和注重等含义。简体字"讲"用"井"代替"冓"。

The traditional character of 讲 is 講. It consists of 言(speak) and 冓(communicate). Its original meaning is to become reconciled and extended to mean to speak and stress, etc. 冓 is replaced by 井 in the simplified character.

值 → 值 → 值 → 值
小篆　隶书　楷体　宋体

拼音：zhí　　**部件**：亻、直　　**部首**：亻　　**结构**：左右
六书：形声　　**笔画**：10画　　**本义**：放置 place
词语：①值班 on duty　②值得 worth　③价值 value
句子：①我们有门卫值班。We have guards on duty.
②这本书值得买。This book is worth buying.
③他的工作没有价值。His work has no value.

记忆贴士

"值"由"亻"（人）和"直"（声旁）组成，本义是放置，引申出遇到和值得等含义。

值 consists of 亻 (person) and 直 (indicates pronunciation). Its original meaning is to place and extended to mean to happen to and worthy, etc.